The Da

MY FAIRY-TALE LIFE

Hans Christian Andersen

MY
FAIRY-TALE
LIFE

Translated by W. Glyn Jones

Dedalus

Dedalus would like to thank The Danish Arts Council's Committee for Literature and Arts Council England, London for their assistance in producing this book.

Published in the UK by Dedalus Limited,
24-26, St Judith's Lane, Sawtry, Cambs, PE28 5XE
email: info@dedalusbooks.com
www.dedalusbooks.com

ISBN printed book 978 1 907650 57 4
ISBN ebook 978 1 909232 97 6

Dedalus is distributed in the USA by SCB Distributors,
15608 South New Century Drive, Gardena, CA 90248
email: info@scbdistributors.com   web: www.scbdistributors.com

Dedalus is distributed in Australia by Peribo Pty Ltd.
58, Beaumont Road, Mount Kuring-gai, N.S.W. 2080
email: info@peribo.com.au

First published by Dedalus in 2013
My Fairy-Tale Life translation copyright © W. Glyn Jones 2013

The right of W. Glyn Jones to be identified as the editor & translator of this work has been asserted by him in accordance with the Copyright, Designs and Patents Act, 1988.

Printed in Finland by Bookwell
Typeset by Marie Lane

This book is sold subject to the condition that it shall not, by way of trade or otherwise, be lent, resold, hired out or otherwise circulated without the publisher's prior consent in any form of binding or cover other than that in which it is published and without a similar condition including this condition being imposed on the subsequent purchaser.

The Translator

W. Glyn Jones read Modern Languages at Pembroke College Cambridge, with Danish as his principal language, before doing his doctoral thesis at Cambridge. He taught at various universities in England and Scandinavia before becoming Professor of Scandinavian Studies at Newcastle and then at the University of East Anglia. He also spent two years as Professor of Scandinavian Literature in the Faeroese Academy. On his retirement from teaching he was created a Knight of the Royal Danish Order of the Dannebrog.

He has written widely on Danish, Faeroese and Finland-Swedish literature including studies of Johannes Jørgensen, Tove Jansson and William Heinesen.

He is the author of *Denmark: A Modern History* and co-author with his wife, Kirsten Gade, of *Colloquial Danish* and the *Blue Guide* to Denmark.

His translations from Danish include *My Fairy-Tale Life* by Hans Christian Andersen, *Seneca* by Villy Sørensen and for Dedalus *The Black Cauldron*, *The Lost Musicians*, *Windswept Dawn*, *The Good Hope* and *Mother Pleiades* by William Heinesen, *Ida Brandt* by Herman Bang and *Barbara* by Jørgen-Frantz Jacobsen.

He is currently translating *As the Trains Pass By (Katinka)* by Herman Bang.

Introduction

"Fiction and faction", this contemporary adaptation of the title of Johann Wolfgang von Goethe's famous autobiography *Dichtung und Wahrheit* (1811–33) can also be applied to the autobiography of the Danish fairy tale writer and story teller Hans Christian Andersen entitled *My Fairy-Tale Life* from 1855. This title, in fact, encompasses precisely the same two elements, "fiction" ("The Fairy Tale") and "faction" ("Life"). Thus, we do, of course, find in Andersen's autobiography basic information about his life. This information, however, must be read with a grain of salt as Andersen tended to arrange and re-arrange, even to fictionalize events to fit his concept of life as a fairy tale composed by God. Furthermore, in 1855 he had reached the apex of his career, which had made the son of a poor shoemaker a famous European celebrity dining with kings and queens all over Europe. So, naturally, he wished to present his life in the most advantageous light according to his well-known statement: "First, you have a terrible amount of adversity to go through, and then you become famous." The fictitious element of *My Fairy-Tale Life*, however, can also apply to the fact that Andersen not only presents the biographical facts but time and again intersperses his prose with beautiful passages of descriptive and, occasionally, poetic prose.

There are numerous sources of information about Andersen, not only of general biographical nature, but also about the author as a visitor and explorer in foreign places and about what they could offer him as a traveller and an artist. Furthermore, one must keep in mind that Andersen was the greatest traveller of his time, going abroad 30 times in all to countries as far away as Turkey and Morocco in an age when travelling could be not only a demanding experience but outright dangerous. He left behind several autobiographies, extensive diaries, pocket calendars and a vast array of letters. Taken together they contain innumerable facts and details which provide us with an almost day-by-day account of what he saw, read and did, his

7

opinions and innermost thoughts.

At the core of this material we have, of course, his autobiography from 1855, which, however, is not his only autobiography. Andersen's first attempt, entitled *Levnedsbogen* (The Book of my Life), was written in 1832 and ends with a detailed, psychologically penetrating account of his relationship with his first love, Riborg Voigt. It was intended for publication in the case of his premature death, and her family name was deliberately omitted by Andersen. For many years the manuscript was thought to have been lost. It was found in the Royal Library in Copenhagen and published in 1926. For a planned German edition of his collected works Andersen wrote another autobiography, published in 1847 as *Das Märchen meines Lebens ohne Dichtung*. Already the same year an English edition, *The True Story of My Life*, was published in London and immediately afterwards reprinted in the United States. The Danish edition, *Mit eget Eventyr uden Digtning* (My Own Fairy Tale without Poetizing) did not appear until 1942! The German autobiography was finally expanded by Andersen and published in Danish in 1855 as *Mit Livs Eventyr* (*My Fairy-Tale Life*). It is this text which is presented here in English in a new translation by the Andersen scholar W. Glyn Jones.

My Fairy-Tale Life opens with the well-known statement, which clearly reveals Andersen's worldview as well as his writing strategy: "My life has been a beautiful fairy tale, so abundant and so marvellously happy. The story of my life will tell the world what it tells me: that there is a loving God who directs all things for the best", from the outset a clear indication of an intended idealization of his life and career as likewise presented in the famous autobiographical tale about "The Ugly Duckling" that – after having suffered so much adversity and cruelty – finally emerges as the beautiful white swan admired by the whole world.

Thus already the initial description of his childhood in the provincial town of Odense, where Andersen was born on April 2, 1855, contains disinformation about his family background, hiding the fact that it was marked by promiscuity and alcoholism. In a confidential letter to a friend in 1833 he, more precisely, calls himself "a swamp plant".

In *My Fairy-Tale Life* we read about Andersen's first attempts – when he was only 14 years of age and without money and education

– at gaining a foothold in the Danish capital Copenhagen, his first attempts as a writer and his reactions to any negative criticism, which hurt him beyond rhyme and reason. We can admire his persistency in not giving up and returning to Odense, instead securing personal and financial support for his endeavours. Andersen would never give up because, in the final account, he felt that a "loving God" would help him. We follow him in his way towards recognition, through his many affairs of the heart. Riborg Voigt was only the first in a series of unhappy love stories. Andersen was a typical romantic in as much as one gets the impression that he was more in love with his love than with the woman in question. On the other hand, he is immensely discreet when it comes to the many carnal temptations he suffered, when travelling abroad in particular in southern Europe. There is, however, no doubt about his sincerity when he expresses his affection for the famous Swedish soprano Jenny Lind, whom he met for the first time in 1840. She undoubtedly served as a role model as well as the artistic inspiration for the magnificent tale about true art, "The Nightingale". Undoubtedly, Jenny Lind was Andersen's greatest love, even though in *My Fairy-Tale Life* he is rather discreet about his feelings for her. However, nothing came of this relationship either, but Andersen established friendships with numerous other women and men who cared for him and admired him as a writer and a human being.

Andersen's journeys abroad frequently served as a remedy for unrequited love, and as a traveller he was in his natural element. But to travel was for him not just an escape from home, neither was it the urge felt by a young man from the provinces to see the big world, but a scrupulously planned educational trip which took him to the art treasures of Europe – in Berlin, Paris, Dresden, Vienna, Florence and Rome. Over the years Andersen developed an impressively unerring but also critical taste with regard to painting, sculpture, theatre and music.

Like the ugly duckling he was driven by an elementary curiosity, but to travel was for Andersen even more discovering a new world beyond the duck yard. It became just as important to him to use his travel experiences and impressions as sources of inspiration for his writing. In his diaries, which above all were travel diaries, he painstakingly wrote down all his observations, which later, either directly or artistically reworked, were utilized in his works including *My Fairy-Tale Life*. But not only did he record his longing to go abroad and his exuberance while en route, but he also expressed his misgivings and depression when realizing that he also had to return home to the duck yard, where according to his perception, petty and unprofessional criticism was all that awaited him.

For *My Fairy-Tale Life* is also a unique documentation of Andersen's extreme vulnerability, his vanity and his insatiable craving for recognition, features of his personality which remained present until his death on August 4, 1875. They were, of course, rooted in his social background and ensuing insecurity, which made him a permanent outsider in the upper-class and aristocratic milieus in which he moved. On almost every page of his autobiography we sense his restlessness, his vanity, his urge to make acquaintances and to be accepted by others in order to overcome his social trauma. A hectic social life, successful recitals, friendships with internationally known artists and writers, and visits to royal courts all over Europe alternate with expressions of loneliness and dejection that hardly bear evidence of the direction of divine guidance that Andersen calls upon time and again and clearly did not want to be without. His memory was quite literally fabulous and his style exquisite. In his autobiography he combines these two qualities into a piece of literary art which is truly unique (in world literature), and which makes the reading of Hans Christian Andersen's *My Fairy-Tale Life* such a delightful and captivating experience.

Sven Hakon Rossel
University of Vienna

I

My life has been a wonderful fairy tale, so abundant and so marvellously happy. Even if I had met a good fairy when I went out into the world poor and friendless as a boy, and she had said, "Choose your own way in life and the goal you want to achieve, and then, according to how your mind develops and as things will probably go in the world, I will guide and defend you," my fate could not have been more wisely and happily and better directed. The story of my life will tell the world what it tells me: that there is a loving God who directs all things for the best.

In the year 1805 there lived in a tiny, mean room in Odense a newly married couple who were terribly fond of each other; he was a young shoemaker, scarcely twenty-two years old, a remarkably gifted man of a truly poetic bent, while his wife, a few years older than himself, knew nothing of life or the world, but was kind to the bottom of her heart. Shortly before this, the young man had become an independent master cobbler and had built his own workshop as well as the bridal bed. This bed was made from the wooden frame which only a short time previously had supported the coffin of the late Count Trampe as he lay in state, and the remnants of the crape that had adorned the woodwork were a reminder of this. Instead of a noble corpse, surrounded by crape and candelabras, there lay here on the second of April, 1805 a living, crying child. It was I, Hans Christian Andersen.

During the first days of my life my father is said to have sat by my mother's bed reading passages from Holberg to her while I continued to squall out at the top of my voice. "Will you go to sleep or else be quiet and listen?" I have been told my father joked; but I still went on crying; and especially in church, when I was taken to be baptised, I cried so loudly that the parson, who my mother always said was an irritable man, exclaimed, "That child sounds like a cat yowling!" Words my mother never forgave him for. However, a poor French immigrant by the name of Gomard, who acted as godfather to me, consoled her by saying that the louder I cried as a child, the more beautifully I would sing as I grew older.

The home where I spent my childhood was one single little room where almost all the space was taken up by the workshop, the bed and the settle on which I slept. The walls, however, were covered with pictures; on the chest of drawers there were some pretty cups, glasses and bric-a-brac, and above my father's bench there was a shelf containing books and songs. There was a plate-rack full of tin plates over the cupboard in the little kitchen which always seemed lovely and spacious. The door itself had a panel decorated with a landscape painting, and it meant as much to me then as a whole picture gallery now.

By means of a ladder it was possible to go from the kitchen on to the loft, and there, in the gutters between it and the neighbour's house, stood a box of soil with chives and parsley growing in it; this was all the garden my mother possessed, and in my story *The Snow Queen* that garden still blooms.

I was an only child and was extremely spoiled, but my mother constantly told me how very much happier I was than she had been, and that I was being brought up like the son of a count. As a small child, she had been sent out by her parents to beg, and as she was not able to do it she had sat weeping a whole day long under a bridge over the river at Odense. I could see this so clearly in my childish imagination, and I wept over it. In old Domenica in *The Improvisatore* and in Christian's mother in *Only a Fiddler* I have given two different versions of her character.

My father, Hans Andersen, let me have my own way in everything. I possessed his whole heart; he just lived for me. So on Sundays, the only free day he had, he spent all his time making toys and pictures for me. In the evening he would often read aloud to us from Lafontaine's *Odd Enough, To Be Sure*, from Holberg and from *The Arabian Nights*. It is only in such moments as these I remember having seen him smile, for he was never really happy in his life as an artisan.

His parents had been wealthy country people, but misfortunes had showered down upon them: their cattle died, their farmhouse was burned down, and finally the husband lost his reason. After this,

his wife moved to Odense with him, and there she apprenticed her intelligent son to a shoemaker. There was no other way, although it was his ardent desire to go to the grammar school. A few well-to-do citizens had at one time spoken of joining to ensure free board for him and so to give him a start in life, but nothing came of it. My poor father never saw his dearest wish fulfilled, but he never forgot what it had been. I remember that once, as a child, I saw tears in his eyes when a scholar from the grammar school came to our house to order a pair of new boots and showed us his books and told us what he was learning. "That's the way I ought to have gone, too," said my father. He kissed me affectionately, and then he was silent for the rest of the evening.

He rarely associated with his peers, but his relatives and friends came to visit us. As I have already said, he read aloud or made toys for me in the evenings in winter; in the summer he would go for a walk in the woods almost every Sunday and take me with him. He did not talk much out there, but sat in silent thought while I ran about gathering strawberries on a straw or tying garlands. Only once a year, in May when the woods had just come into leaf, did my mother go with us. It was the only occasion each year when she went for a walk for pleasure, and then she wore a flowered dress of brown calico which she only donned on these occasions and when she went to Holy Communion; so it is the only dress I remember in all those years as her best frock. Then when we went home after our walk in the woods she always took with her an armful of birch branches, which were then put behind our polished stove. We always put sprigs of St. John's wort into the chinks of the beams and from the way in which they grew we could see whether our lives would be long or short. We decorated our little room with green branches and pictures, and my mother kept it neat and clean; she always took great pride in making sure that the bed linen and curtains were snow-white.

One of the first things I remember, of little importance in itself, but of great significance for me because of the way my childish fancy impressed it on my mind, was a family party, and where do you think it was? It was in the one place in Odense, in the one building which I always looked on with fear and trembling, just as children in Paris must have looked on the Bastille. It was in Odense Prison.

My parents knew the gaoler there, and he invited them to a family dinner; I was to go, too. I was still so little at that time that I had to be carried home, as will be seen shortly. Odense Prison was for me the centre of stories about thieves and robbers; I often stood, although of course always at a safe distance, listening to the men and women inside singing as they sat at their spinning wheels.

I went to the gaoler's party together with my parents; the great, iron-barred gate was opened and locked again with the key from the clanging bunch; we went up a steep staircase. We ate and drank and were waited on by two of the prisoners. I could not be brought to taste anything, and I pushed even the sweetest things away from me. My mother said I was ill and I was laid on a bed. But I could hear the spinning wheels humming nearby and merry singing, whether it was in my imagination or in reality I cannot tell, but I do know that I was afraid and on edge all the time; and yet it was pleasant to lie there and imagine I had entered the robbers' castle. When my mother and father went home late that evening they carried me; it was a rough night, and the rain dashed against my face.

In my earliest childhood, Odense itself was quite a different town from what it is now that it has beaten Copenhagen with its street lighting and running water and I don't know what else. In those days I think it was a hundred years behind the times; a whole lot of customs and traditions were still observed there, which had long since disappeared from the capital. When the guilds "removed their signs" they went in procession with flying banners and with lemons and ribbons on their swords. A harlequin with bells and a wooden sword ran merrily ahead of them; one of them, an old fellow called Hans Struh, made a great impression with his merry chatter and a face that was painted black, except for his nose which was allowed to keep its natural, bright red colour. My mother was so delighted with him that she tried to convince us that he was a distant relative of ours, admittedly very distant, but I still clearly remember that, with all the pride of an aristocrat, I protested against any relationship with the "fool".

On Carnival Day the butchers used to lead a fat ox through the streets; it was decorated with garlands of flowers; a boy in a white shirt and wearing wings rode on it. The seamen also paraded through the streets at carnival time with a band and all their flags flying, and finally the two most spirited of them had a wrestling-match on a plank placed between two boats. The one who did not fall into the water was the winner.

But what was particularly fixed in my memory and was often revived by repeatedly being talked of, was the time when the Spaniards were in Funen in 1808. Denmark had entered into an alliance with Napoleon on whom Sweden had declared war, and before we knew where we were a French army with Spanish auxiliaries (under the command of Marshal Bernadotte, Prince of Pontecorvo) was stationed in the middle of Funen in order to cross to Sweden. I was not more than three years old at the time, but I can still clearly remember the row those dark brown men made in the streets, and the cannon that were fired on the market-place and in front of the bishop's residence. I saw the foreign soldiers stretching out on the footpaths and on bales of straw in the half-ruined Greyfriars Church. Kolding Castle was burned down, and Pontecorvo came to Odense, where his wife and son Oscar were staying. In the surrounding countryside schools had been turned into guardrooms, and Mass was celebrated under the great trees in the fields and by the roadside. The French troops were said to be haughty and arrogant, the Spanish good-natured and friendly, and a fierce hatred existed between them; the poor Spaniards gained the most sympathy. One day a Spanish soldier took me up in his arms and pressed against my lips a silver image which he wore on his naked breast. I remember that my mother was angry about this, for it was something Catholic, she said, but I liked the image and the foreign soldier who danced around with me, kissed me and wept. He must have had children of his own at home in Spain. I saw one of his comrades led off to execution for having killed a Frenchman. Many years afterwards, at the memory of this, I wrote my little poem, *The Soldier*, which has been translated into German by Chamisso and become popular there and has been included in the German *Soldiers' Songs* as an original German song.

Just as vivid as the impression made on me by the Spaniards when I was three years old was that of a later event in my sixth year, that is to say the great comet of 1811. My mother had told me that it

15

would destroy the earth, or that other dreadful things threatened us which we could read about in *The Sybilla's Prophecies*. I listened to everything foretold by superstitious tongues in the neighbourhood and held it in reverence just like some profound religious truth. With my mother and some of the neighbours I stood in the square in front of St. Canute's Church and saw what we were all dreading so much, the mighty ball of fire with its great shining tail. Everyone was talking about the evil omen and the Day of Judgement. My father joined us, but he was by no means of the same opinion as the others and gave what must have been a correct and sound explanation; but my mother sighed, and the neighbours shook their heads; my father laughed and went away. I was terribly frightened because he did not believe the same as we did. In the evening my mother and my old grandmother talked about it; I do not know how she explained it, but I sat on her lap, looked up into her mild eyes and every moment expected the comet to strike and the Day of Judgement to arrive.

My grandmother came to my parents' house every day even if only for a few moments; it was especially to see her little grandson, Hans Christian, for I was her pride and joy. She was a quiet and most lovable old lady with gentle blue eyes and a fine figure. Life had been a severe trial for her; from having been the wife of a wealthy countryman she had now fallen into great poverty, and lived together with her feeble-minded husband in a small house they had bought with the last, poor remains of their fortune. I never saw her shed a tear; but all the more profound was the impression she made on me when she quietly sighed and told me of her mother's mother, that she had been a noble lady in a big German town called *Cassel* and married what she called a "comedy-player" and run away from her parents and her home, for all of which the generation following her had to suffer. I cannot recollect ever hearing her mention her maternal grandmother's family name, but her own maiden name was Nommesen. She was employed to look after the garden belonging to the hospital, and every Saturday evening she brought us some flowers which they allowed her to take home with her. These flowers adorned my mother's chest of drawers, but they were my flowers, and I was allowed to put them in the vase. What pleasure this gave me. She brought everything to me; she loved me from the bottom of her heart; I knew this and I understood it.

Twice a year she burned the green rubbish from the garden. It was burned to ashes in a big furnace in the hospital, and on those days I spent most of my time with her and lay on the great heaps of green leaves and pea-plants. I had flowers to play with, and – something which I specially appreciated – was given better food than I could expect at home. All the harmless mental patients were allowed to walk about in the hospital courtyard, and they often came to look at us. I listened to their singing and chatter with a mixture of curiosity and fear. I would often even go a little way with them to the pleasance, under the trees; indeed when the attendants were present I even dared to go into the building where the dangerous lunatics were kept. There was a long corridor between the cells; one day I crouched down and peeped through the crack in the door, and inside I could see a naked woman sitting on a pile of straw and singing in a most beautiful voice; her hair hung right down over her shoulders. Suddenly she sprang up and with a cry threw herself against the door where I was lying; the attendant had gone away, and I was all alone; she struck the door so violently that the little grating through which food was passed in to her flew open; she saw me through it and stretched one of her arms out after me. I screamed in terror and pressed myself flat against the floor. Even as a grown man I cannot rid myself of this sight and this impression. I felt the tips of her fingers touching my clothes and was half dead when the attendant came back.

Close beside the place where the leaves were burned there was a spinning room for poor old women. I often went there and was soon a favourite of theirs, for when I was with these people I spoke with an eloquence which, they said, indicated that "such a clever child could not live long", a suggestion which greatly flattered me. I happened to have heard of doctors' knowledge of the inner structure of the human body, of the heart, lungs and intestines, and that was sufficient for me to give an impromptu talk to the old women. I boldly drew a large number of flourishes on the door to represent the intestines; I talked about the heart and the kidneys, and everything I said made a deep impression on the assembly. I was considered a remarkably clever child, and they rewarded my chatter by telling me fairy tales;

a world as rich as that in the *Arabian Nights* was revealed to me. The stories these old women told me and the figures of the mental patients I saw around me in the hospital all made such an impression on me, superstitious as I was, that when it grew dark I scarcely dared go out of my parents' house. So I was usually allowed to go to bed at sunset – not on my own settle, for it was too early to get it ready as it took up too much room in our little parlour – but I was put in my parents' big bed, where the flowered calico curtains hung close around me. I could see the light burning and hear everything going on in the room, and yet I was so much alone in my thoughts and my dreams that it almost seemed as though the real world did not exist. "He's lying there so nice and quiet, the dear little thing," my mother would say. "He's well out of the way and can't come to any harm."

I was very much afraid of my weak-minded grandfather. He had only ever spoken to me once, and then he had called me "Sir", a form of address to which I was not accustomed. He used to cut curious figures in wood, men with the heads of animals, and animals with wings, and strange birds; he would pack them all in a basket and go out into the countryside with them and was everywhere well received by the peasant women; indeed they even gave him oatmeal and ham to take home because he gave them and their children these curious playthings. One day when he returned to Odense I heard the boys in the street shouting after him. Horrified, I hid behind a flight of steps while they rushed by, for I knew I was of the same flesh and blood as he.

I only very rarely played with the other boys; even in school I took no part in their games but remained sitting indoors. At home I had plenty of toys which my father had made for me; I had pictures which could be changed by pulling a string and a treadmill that made the miller dance around when it was set in motion; I had magic lanterns and a lot of amusing knick-knacks. In addition, I took great delight in sewing doll's clothes or in sitting in the yard by our solitary gooseberry bush and stretching my mother's apron from the wall with the help of a broom-handle. That was my tent both in sunshine and pouring rain. There I sat and gazed at the leaves on the gooseberry bush and followed their progress from day to day, from their being tiny, green buds until they fell off as big, yellow leaves.

I was a singularly dreamy child and usually walked about with my eyes shut, so that at last I gave the impression of not being able to see well, although my sight was, and still is, unusually good.

An old teacher who ran a dame school taught me the alphabet and how to spell and read properly. She used to sit in a high-backed armchair near the clock where some small, moving figures appeared when it struck the hour. She always had a big rod with her, and she made use of it in the class which consisted mostly of girls. It was the custom in the school for us all to spell out aloud, as noisily as possible. The teacher didn't dare to strike me, as my mother had made it a condition of my going there that I should not be hit; so one day when I was given a tap with the rod together with the others I immediately got up and without further ado went home to my mother, demanding to be sent to another school. And I had my way. My mother put me in Mr. Carstens' school for boys. There was also one girl there. She was quite small and although she was a little older than I, we became good friends; she used to talk about useful and practical things and of going into service with a good family. And she said that she was going to school especially to learn to be good at sums, because then, her mother said, she would be able to become a dairy-maid in some big manor. "Then you must come to my castle when I am a nobleman," I said, and she laughed at me and told me I was only a poor boy. One day I had drawn something which I called my castle and I assured her on that occasion that I was a child of high birth who had been taken from his parents, and that God's angels came and spoke to me. I wanted to impress her like the old women over in the hospital, but she did not take it in the same way as they did; she gave me a strange look and said to one of the other boys standing nearby, "He's mad like his grandfather!", words that made me shudder. I had said that in order to make myself look important, but the only effect of what I said was that they thought I was as insane as my grandfather. I never again spoke to her of such things, but we were no longer the same playmates as before. I was the smallest in the school, so when the other boys were playing Mr. Carstens always held my hand in case I should be knocked over. He was fond of me and gave me cakes and flowers and patted me on my cheek, and one day when one of the bigger boys hadn't learnt his lesson and so as a punishment was placed, book in hand, on the table around which we were seated I was quite inconsolable, and so the sinner was pardoned. Later in life this dear old teacher became the manager of the telegraph station at Thorseng; he was still alive there a few years ago, and I have been told that, when showing visitors around, the old man told them with a delighted smile, "Do you know, you will probably not believe me when I tell you that such a poor, old man as I was the first teacher for one of our most famous poets. Hans Christian Andersen used to go to my school."

During the harvest season my mother sometimes went out into the fields to glean. I went with her and felt like Ruth in the Bible, gleaning in Boaz's fertile fields. One day we had gone to a place where there was known to be an ill-natured bailiff. We saw him coming with a dreadful big whip in his hand, and my mother and all the others ran away. I had wooden clogs on my bare feet, and in my haste I lost them. The stubble pricked my feet and so I could not run away quickly enough, and was left behind alone. He caught up with me and had already raised his whip; I stared him in the face and without thinking said, "How dare you strike me when God can see it!" And immediately the stern man became quite gentle; he patted my cheek, asked me my name and gave me some money. When I showed this to my mother she looked at the others and said,

"My Hans Christian's a strange child. Everyone's kind to him, and even this bad fellow has given him money."

I grew up pious and superstitious. I had not the faintest idea what it was to lack anything. I know my parents lived from hand to mouth, as the saying goes, but for me they had everything in abundance. As far as my dress was concerned I could even be said to be smart. An old woman altered my father's clothes to fit me; three or four big pieces of silk which my mother owned were pinned in turn on my breast and served as waistcoats; a large kerchief was tied round my neck with a huge bow, my head was washed with soap and my hair combed over to the sides, and then I was in all my finery. Thus dressed I went to the theatre for the first time with my parents. Even at that time Odense had a well-built theatre which, I believe, had been started for either Count Trampe's or Count Hahn's troupe; the first performances I attended were in German. The director was called Franck, and he put on operas and comedies. *Das Donauweibchen* was the town's favourite; but the first performance I saw was Holberg's *The Political Tinker* arranged as an opera. I have not since been able to discover who wrote the music, but it is quite certain that this text had been arranged in German as an opera. The first impression otherwise that the theatre and the assembled crowd made on me was not, as might be expected, to make me believe I was a future poet. As my parents later told me, my first exclamation on seeing the theatre and so many people was, "Now if we only had as many casks of butter as there are people here, what a lot of butter I would eat!" It was, however, not long before the theatre became the place I liked best, though I could only go there very occasionally each winter. I made friends with Peter Junker, the man who took the posters out, and every day he gave me a poster, while I, in return, dutifully distributed a few others in my part of town. Even if I could not go to the theatre I could sit in a corner at home with the poster, and according to the name of the play and the characters in it I could make up a whole comedy for myself. That was my first, unconscious literary work.

It was not only plays and stories my father liked reading, but historical works and the Bible as well. He pondered in silence on what he had read, but my mother did not understand him when he talked to her about it, and so he became more and more taciturn. One day he closed the Bible with the words, "Christ was a man like us, but he was an unusual man." My mother was horrified by these words and burst into tears, and in my fright I prayed to God that He would forgive my father for this dreadful blasphemy.

"There is no other Devil than the one we have in our own hearts," I heard my father say once, and I was filled with concern for him and his soul. So one morning when my father found three scratches on his arm, which had probably been caused by a nail in the bed, I was completely of my mother's and the neighbours' opinion that it was the Devil who had been there during the night to prove his existence. My father had but few friends, and he liked best to spend his leisure hours alone or out in the woods with me. It was his dearest wish to live out in the country, and now it happened that one of the manor houses on Funen urgently required a shoemaker who would settle down in the village nearby, where he would have a house free of rent, a small garden and grazing for a cow; with all this and regular work from the manor he would be able to manage nicely. My mother and father could talk of little other than how happy they would be if they could get this place, and my father was given a piece of work as a test. He was sent a piece of silk from the manor house and was to sew a pair of dancing shoes, providing the leather himself. We talked and thought of nothing else for a couple of days; I so looked forward to the little garden we were to have with flowers and shrubs where I would be able to sit in the sunshine and listen to the cuckoo. I prayed to God so fervently that He would fulfil our wishes; He could bestow no greater happiness upon us. At last the shoes were ready; at home we looked solemnly at them, for they were to decide our future. Father wrapped them in his handkerchief and went off. We sat and waited for him to come home radiant with joy, but when he came he was pale and angry. Her ladyship, he said, had not even tried the shoes on, but had merely given them a sour look and said that the silk was ruined and that she could not engage him. "If you have wasted your silk," my father said, "then I will be content to waste my leather!" at which he had taken out his knife and cut the soles off. So our hopes of living in the country came to nothing. We wept, all three of us, and I thought that God could easily have granted our prayers. Had he done so, I would have been a peasant and all my future very different from what it has been; since that time I have often wondered whether it was for the sake of my future that our Lord denied my parents their happiness.

My father's rambles in the woods became more frequent and he knew no rest. The events of the war in Germany, which he eagerly followed in the newspapers, completely occupied his thoughts. Napoleon was his hero, and he thought his rise from obscurity was the finest example to follow. Denmark made an alliance with France. People talked of nothing but war, and my father volunteered as a soldier in the hope of coming home as a lieutenant. My mother wept and the neighbours shrugged their shoulders and said it was madness for him to go out and get himself shot when there was no need for it. At that time soldiers were considered pariahs, and only in more recent times, during the war against the rebels in the Duchies have we given them the honour they deserve; they are the right arm which wields the sword.

The morning on which the company my father was in was due to march off I heard him singing and talking merrily, but at heart he was deeply agitated. I could see this from the passionate way in which he kissed me good-bye. I lay in bed with measles and was alone in the room when the drums beat and my mother, in tears, accompanied him as far as the city gate. When they had gone my old grandmother came in and looked at me with her mild eyes and said it would be a good thing if I could die now, but that God's will was always best. That was one of the first really sad mornings I can remember.

However, the regiment to which my father belonged came no further than Holstein. Peace was concluded and the volunteer soldier was soon sitting in his workshop again, and everything seemed to be as usual once more.

I played with my puppets and acted comedies, always in German, for it was only in this language I had seen them acted. But my German was a sort of gibberish which I made up as I went along and in which there only occurred one single real German word, *Besen,* a word I had picked up from the various expressions my father had come home with from Holstein. "You've certainly had some benefit from my travels," he said in fun. "Goodness knows whether you will ever travel so far afield. But you must. Remember that, Hans Christian." But my mother said that as long as she had any say in this matter I should remain at home and not ruin my health as he had done.

His good health had been ruined; it had suffered from the marching and the soldier's life, to which he was not accustomed. One morning he awoke in a state of delirium, talking of campaigns and Napoleon. He fancied he was taking orders from him and that he was in command himself. My mother immediately sent me to fetch help, but not from the doctor; oh no, I was to go to a so-called "wise woman" who lived a couple of miles from Odense. I arrived at her house, and the woman asked me several questions. Then she took a woollen thread and measured my arm, made strange signs over me and finally laid a green twig on my breast; she said it was the same sort of tree as that on which Christ had been crucified, adding, "Now go home along the river bank. And if your father is going to die, you'll meet his ghost."

My terror can well be imagined, full of superstition and dominated entirely by my imagination as I was. "But you've not met anything, have you?" inquired my mother when I came home. "No," I assured her with beating heart. On the third evening my father died. His body was left on the bed, and I slept on the floor with my mother; and a cricket chirped throughout the night. "He *is* dead already," my mother called to it. "You needn't call him; the Ice Maiden has taken him," and I understood what she meant. I remembered the previous winter when our windows were frozen over; my father had shown us a figure on one of the panes like that of a maiden stretching out both her arms. "She must have come to fetch me," he said in fun. And now, as he lay dead on the bed, my mother remembered this, and his words occupied my thoughts.

He was buried in St. Knud's churchyard, outside the door on the left as you come from the altar. My grandmother planted roses on his grave. In later years other bodies have been buried in the same place, and now the grass grows high over these too.

After my father's death I was as good as left to my own devices; my mother went out washing and I would sit alone at home with the little theatre my father had made for me. I would make clothes for my puppets and read plays. I am told that I was tall and lanky at that time; my hair was fair and very thick and I always went bareheaded and wore wooden clogs on my feet.

Not far from my home a parson's widow, Mrs. Bunkeflod, lived together with her late husband's sister. They let me go and visit them when I wanted, and as they took a liking to me I spent most of my days there. This was the first house belonging to the educated classes where I found a home. The late clergyman had written poems and had at that time something of a name in Danish literature; everyone knew his spinning songs, and in my *Vignettes to Danish Poets* I wrote the following words of a man whom my contemporaries had forgotten:

> Breaks the thread, the wheel stands still,
> Spinning-songs are silent last.
> Songs of youth soon vanish will
> In the distant, far-off past.

This was where I first heard the word "poet", and it was spoken with such reverence as though it were something sacred. My father had read Holberg's comedies for me, but it was not of these they spoke, but of verse, of poetry. "My brother, the poet," said Bunkeflod's elderly sister with sparkling eyes. From her I learned that a poet's calling is a glorious thing, a happy thing. Here, too, I read Shakespeare for the first time, admittedly in a bad translation, but the bold descriptions, violent incidents, witches and ghosts were just to my taste. I immediately began to perform the Shakespearean tragedies in my puppet theatre, and to my imagination the ghost in *Hamlet* and the mad King Lear on the heath were living figures. The more deaths there were in a play, the more interesting I thought it. It was about now I wrote my first play; it was nothing less than a tragedy in which, of course, everyone died. I had borrowed the story from an old song about Pyramus and Thisbe, but had extended the action by adding a hermit and his son, who both loved Thisbe and took their own lives when she died. Most of the hermit's speeches were quotations from the Bible and passages from Bishop Balle's Short Catechism, especially the ones about our duty towards our neighbours. I called the play *Abor and Elvira*. You mean it should be called 'A Bore and a Pain', said our neighbour wittily when I visited her with it after reading it with great pleasure and satisfaction to everyone else I could think of. This put a complete damper on my spirits because I felt that she was making fun both of me and my play, while everyone else had praised it. Much upset, I told my mother what had happened. "She only says that because it's not her son who's written it," she said. And I was consoled and began on a new play which was to be in a more pompous style; a king and a princess were to appear in it. Of course I could see that such people in Shakespeare's plays talked like other men and women, but it did not seem to me to be quite right that they should do so. I asked my mother and several people in the neighbourhood how a king really spoke, but no one knew for sure. They said it was many years since a king had visited Odense, but that he probably spoke a foreign language. So I found myself a sort of dictionary in which there were German, French and English words with Danish translations, and

25

this helped me. I took a few words from each language and fitted them into each sentence spoken by my king or my princess. "Guten Morgen, mon père; har De godt sleeping" was one of the lines; it was really and truly the language of Babel, and that, I considered, was the only suitable way for such elevated personages to speak. Everyone had to listen to my play, and it gave me a profound joy to read it aloud. It never occurred to me that it could be anything but a pleasure for everyone else to listen to it.

Our neighbour's son had been set to work in a cloth-mill, whereby he earned a small sum every week. On the other hand, according to what people said, I just hung around doing nothing at all, so my mother decided that I, too, should go and work in the mill. "It's not for the sake of the money," she said, "but so I know where he is."

My old grandmother took me there and was deeply distressed, for, she said, she had never thought to see the day when I should mix with all those wretched boys.

Many of the journeymen working there were German; they sang and talked merrily together, and many a coarse joke of theirs caused great amusement. I listened to it and have learned from that that a child can listen to such things with an innocent ear, for it did not reach my heart. In those days I had a remarkably beautiful and high-pitched soprano voice which I retained until my fifteenth year; I knew people liked to hear me sing, and when I was asked in the mill whether I knew any songs I immediately began to sing, and did so with great success; it was left to the other boys to do my work. When I had finished my song I told them that I could also perform plays; I knew whole scenes of Holberg and Shakespeare off by heart, and I recited them. Both men and women nodded amicably to me and laughed and clapped their hands. In this way I found the first days in the mill extremely cheerful. But one day, just as I was singing to them and everyone was talking about the clarity and remarkable pitch of my voice, one of the journeymen exclaimed, "That can't be a boy; it's a little girl!" He took hold of me. I cried out and screamed, but the other journeymen found the coarse joke amusing and held my arms and legs fast. I screamed at the top of my voice, and, as bashful as a girl, I rushed out of the mill and home to my mother, who immediately promised me that I should never go there again.

I started visiting Mrs. Bunkeflod again. I listened to her reading aloud, did a lot of reading myself and even learnt to sew, a skill I found necessary for my puppet theatre. And I sewed a white pin cushion as a birthday present for Mrs. Bunkeflod. As a grown man I have noticed that this pincushion has been preserved. I also made the acquaintance of another clergyman's widow in the neighbourhood, and she allowed me to read aloud to her from books she borrowed from the lending library. One of them began roughly as follows: "It was a tempestuous night, and the rain was beating against the window panes." "That's going to be a lovely book," she said, and I innocently asked how she knew. "I can tell from the beginning," she said. "It's going to be excellent." I looked up to this very clever woman with a kind of reverence.

Once during the harvest my mother took me with her from Odense to a mansion near her native town of Bogense. The lady of the house, for whose parents my mother had once worked, had said that we must come and visit her some time. I had been looking forward to this for years, and it was going to happen. It took us a whole two days to get there, for we had to go on foot. It was a lovely house, and we were given delicious food to eat, but apart from this the countryside itself made such an impression on me that all I wanted was to remain there for ever. It was in the hop-picking season, and over in the barn I sat together with my mother and a whole lot of peasant folk and helped to pick the hops. They told stories and talked about all the wonderful things they had experienced and seen. They knew all sorts about such things as the Devil with his cloven hoof, ghosts and signs. There was an old peasant among them who said that God knew everything, both what had happened and what was going to happen. These words made a deep impression on me; they constantly occupied my thoughts, and towards evening, as I was walking alone some distance from the house, I came to a deep pond. I crawled out on to one of the big stones in the water, and in some strange way the thought entered my mind as to whether God really knew everything that was to happen. "Well, He's decided now that I'm going to live to be a very old man," I thought, "but if I jump out into the water and drown myself things won't turn out quite as He wants them to." And all at once I was firmly and resolutely determined to drown myself.

I turned towards the spot where the water was deepest – and then a new thought went through my head: "It's the Devil who wants me in his power!" And I cried out, ran home as quickly as I could and, weeping bitterly, flung myself, into my mother's arms. But neither she nor anyone else could persuade me to say what was the matter. "He must have seen a ghost of some kind," said one of the women, and I almost thought so myself.

My mother married again, and her second husband was also a young shoemaker. His family, too, were artisans, but they thought he had married below himself, and neither my mother nor I was permitted to visit them. My stepfather was a quiet young man with lively, brown eyes and was reasonably good-tempered. He said he wouldn't interfere in my education, and he did indeed allow me to follow my own interests. So I lived entirely for my pictures and my puppet theatre. And it was my greatest delight that I had collected a considerable number of pieces of coloured cloth which I cut out myself and made into costumes. My mother regarded this as good practice for me if I were to become a tailor, and that, she believed, was what I was born to be. I, on the other hand, said I wanted to go on the stage, something my mother firmly opposed, for the only actors she knew of were tight-rope walkers and strolling players, and these she classed as one and the same thing. "Then you can be sure you will get some good beatings," she said. "And you'll be starved to make you light, and you'll be given oil to drink to make your limbs supple." No, I was to be a tailor. "Just see what a fine position Mr. Stegmann has." He was the best tailor in town. "He lives in Korsgade, and look what big windows there are in his shop, and there are assistants sitting on the table. Oh, if only you could become one of them."

The only consolation I could find in the prospect of becoming a tailor was that then I should really be able to get a lot of odd bits of cloth for my theatre wardrobe.

My parents had moved further up the street to a house just by the Monkmill Gate, and there we had a garden; it was very small and narrow, and was actually no more than a long bed with red currant and gooseberry bushes in it, and then the path which led down to the river behind the Monkmill. Three great waterwheels turned beneath the fast flowing water and stopped suddenly when the sluice-gates were closed. Then all the water ran from the river; the bed dried up and the fish splashed about in the pools that were left, so that I could catch them with my hands; and under the great waterwheels fat water-rats came out from the mill to drink. Suddenly the sluice-gates were raised again; the water rushed down again, foaming and roaring, the rats were no longer to be seen, the river bed filled up, and I, who had been standing out there, splashed back through the water to the bank as fast as I could. I was just as frightened as amber-gatherers on the North Sea coast when they are a long way out and the tide turns. I used to stand on one of the big stones my mother used as a scrubbing board and sing all the songs I knew at the top of my voice. There was often neither sense nor tune in them, just what I made up as I went along. The garden next to ours belonged to a Mr. Falbe, whose wife Oehlenschläger mentions in his autobiography. She had been an actress and had looked beautiful as Ida Münster in the drama *Herman von Unna*; she was known as Miss Beck in those days. I knew that when they had company in the garden they always listened to my singing. Everyone told me that I had a beautiful voice and that I should be able to make a name for myself with it. I often wondered how this name would come, and as I saw the sort of thing that happens in fairy tales as the truth, I expected all kinds of wonderful things to happen. I had been told by an old woman who washed her clothes in the river that the Empire of China was right under Odense River, and I didn't think it was by any means impossible that a Chinese prince, one moonlit night as I was sitting there, might dig his way up through the earth to us, hear me singing and take me down to his kingdom with him and there make me rich and give me a high position. But then, of course, he would allow me to go and visit Odense, where I would live and build a castle. I could sit for evening after evening drawing and planning it. I was simply a child, and so I was, long afterwards, when I appeared in Copenhagen and read my poems. I still believed and expected to find some prince in my audience, and that he would understand me and help me. But it was not to happen in this way – though it was to happen.

My passion for reading, the many dramatic scenes I knew by heart and my extremely fine voice all attracted the attention of several distinguished families in Odense. I was invited to their houses, and all my remarkable characteristics awoke their interest. Of the many people I visited, Colonel Høegh-Guldberg was the one who, together with his family, showed me the most genuine interest. Indeed he even spoke of me to Prince Christian, subsequently King Christian the Eighth, who at that time was residing in Odense Castle, and one day Guldberg took me there with him.

"If the Prince should ask you what you want to do," he said, "you must answer that you would most of all like to go to the grammar school." And indeed I said this immediately when the prince actually asked me this question, but he replied that my being able to sing and recite poetry in a lively manner was fine but not necessarily a sign of genius. And I must remember that studying would take a long time and require a lot of money. He would, however, give me his support if I agreed to learn some interesting craft, for example that of a turner. But I did not at all want to become a turner and I was not entirely happy when I left although what the noble prince had said was both natural and right. Later, when the passage of time revealed my abilities, he was, as we shall see, good and kind to me until his death; and I remember him with profound feelings of gratitude.

I stayed at home, shot up and became a tall lad, and my mother said she could no longer let me go and waste my time in that way. I attended the charity school in the workhouse, but learned only religion, writing and arithmetic, and the latter only badly; I could scarcely spell a single word correctly. I never did my homework at home but managed it more or less on the way to school, and my mother used to boast of my aptitude at the expense of our neighbour's son. "He uses his brains from morning to evening," she said, "but our Hans Christian never looks at his schoolbooks, and yet he knows it all."

On our teacher's birthday I always wove him a garland and wrote him a poem; he usually accepted it with a smile, but once or twice he chided me for it. He came from Norway and was called Velhaven. He was doubtless a splendid person, but of a violent disposition and by no means happy. He talked to us very seriously about religion, and when he told us stories from the Bible he did it so vividly that, as I listened to him, all the paintings on the walls seemed to come to life and acquire the same beauty, truth and freshness as did the magnificent paintings of Raphael and Titian later in life. I often sat daydreaming and staring at the colourful wall, and then I would be gently scolded for being "miles away again". Then I used to tell the other boys strange stories in which, of course, I never failed to make myself the central figure, though I was sometimes laughed at for this. The street lads had also heard about my peculiar personality from their parents and knew I was in the habit of mixing with the gentry, and so one day a whole wild crowd of them chased me down the street, mocking me and shouting, "There goes the playwright." I hid in a corner at home, weeping and praying to God.

I was in my fourteenth year, and my mother started to think of having me confirmed so that I could be apprenticed to a tailor and do something useful. She loved me with all her heart, but she didn't understand my aspirations and endeavours; and neither did I myself understand them. The people she mixed with always criticised my odd ways, and this upset and worried her.

We belonged to the parish of St. Knud, and the candidates for confirmation could submit their names either to the dean or the curate. The children of the so-called distinguished families together with the pupils from the grammar school went to the former, while the poorer children went to the latter. I gave in my name to the dean, and he was forced to accept me, although he could only have seen vanity in my wish to be in his class. They were placed at the front in the church and the curate's class had to follow them. However, I do not believe it was vanity which made me do this: I was always frightened of the poor boys who had made fun of me, and I always felt a profound urge to approach the scholars from the grammar school whom I then regarded as being much better than the others. When I saw them playing in the churchyard I used to stand outside the wooden railings and peep in and wish I was one of the fortunate ones, not for the sake of the games they played, but because of all the books they had and all the things they could become in the world. In the dean's confirmation class, then, I could mix with them and be as one of them – but I cannot remember a single one of them from that time, so little would they have to do with me. Every day I had the feeling of having thrust myself in where people thought I did not belong.

Even the dean let me feel this, and once when I had declaimed some scenes from a comedy in the presence of some friends of his, he sent for me and declared it was not fitting that I should do such things at a time when I was preparing for my confirmation, and if anything of the kind came to his ears again I would be turned out of his class. This frightened and upset me, and I felt even more like a bird that had gone astray when I was in those unaccustomed surroundings. There was, however, one of the confirmation candidates who was always good and kind to me, a young lady by the name of Tønder-Lund, who was considered to be the most distinguished of them all – I shall have more to tell about her later. She always looked kindly at me and greeted me in a friendly manner, and she once even gave me a rose, and I went home full of happiness because, after all, there was one among them who did not overlook and reject me.

An old seamstress cut down my late father's overcoat to make a confirmation suit for me. I thought I had never before worn such a fine coat, and for the first time in my life I was given a pair of boots. I was ever so pleased to have these, and the only thing I was afraid of was that not everybody would be able to see that they were boots, and so I pulled them up outside my trousers and thus dressed walked up the aisle in the church. The boots squeaked, and this gave me great delight, for the congregation would now be able to hear that they were new. But my devotions were spoiled. I was aware of this and at the same time had a dreadful conscience because my thoughts were just as much on my boots as on God. I prayed to Him from the bottom of my heart to forgive me, and then I thought of my new boots again.

During the last few years I had saved up all the coppers I had been given on various occasions, and when I counted them I found I had thirteen *Rigsdaler*. I was quite overwhelmed to know I possessed such wealth, and when my mother now most definitely insisted I should be apprenticed to a tailor I begged and pestered her instead to let me go and seek my fortune in Copenhagen, which at that time was the greatest city in the world to me.

"What will become of you there?" asked my mother.

"I will become famous," I answered and told her what I had read about remarkable men who had come from poor homes. "First, you have a terrible amount of adversity to go through," I said, "and *then* you become famous." I was driven by some completely inexplicable impulse. I wept, I begged, and finally my mother gave in. But first she sent for an old "wise woman" from the hospital and had her read my future in a pack of cards and in coffee dregs.

"Your son will be a great man," said the old woman, "and all Odense will one day be illuminated in his honour." My mother wept when she heard this and no longer had any objection to my leaving home. Everyone who heard of the decision spoke to my mother and said what a dreadful thing it was to let me, a mere child of fourteen, go off to Copenhagen, such a big city and so far away, a place with which I was unfamiliar, and where I knew not a soul.

"Oh, he won't leave me alone," replied my mother, "so I've had to let him go. But it's all right, I'm sure he'll go no further than Nyborg. When he sees the rough sea there I guarantee he'll be frightened and come home again. And then he shall be a tailor's apprentice."

"If only we could find him a job as a clerk somewhere here," said my grandmother. "That would be a fine position, and Hans Christian is clever enough for that."

"If he can be a tailor like Mr. Stegmann, then I shall be quite satisfied," said my mother. "Just let him get as far as Nyborg."

The summer before my confirmation, some of the singers and actors from the Royal Theatre had been in Odense to perform a number of operas and tragedies. The whole town still talked of little else. Since I was good friends with the man who distributed the posters, I had not only been able to see all the performances from the wings, but I had appeared on the stage as both a page and a shepherd, and indeed I had even had a couple of lines to say in *Cinderella* I was so keen that when the actors came to the dressing-rooms before the performance I was already in my costume. This attracted their attention to me. My childlike manner and my enthusiasm amused them, and they spoke kindly to me, especially Haack and Enholm, and I looked up to them as to earthly divinities. Everything I had heard about my singing and the way I recited verse and monologues now made me realise that it was the theatre for which I was born, and that it was there I should become a famous man; and so the theatre in Copenhagen was the goal of my endeavours. The actors' visit to Odense had been the event of a lifetime for many people, and especially for me. Everyone spoke of it with great enthusiasm and always finished by saying, "How lovely it would be if we were in Copenhagen and could go to the theatre there." Now there were a few who had been there, and they talked about something they called a ballet, which was supposed to be even finer than either opera or drama. Madame Schall, the ballet dancer, was said to be the best and most influential of them all. So it seemed to me she must be queen of it all, and in my imagination she figured as the one person who, if I could gain her interest and support, could help me on my way to honour and fortune.

Filled with these thoughts I went to see the old printer, Iversen, one of the foremost citizens in Odense, whom I knew to have been visited every day by the actors while they were in Odense. He knew them all and presumably also knew the ballet dancer. I would ask him for a letter of introduction to her, and then God would presumably do the rest.

It was the first time the old man had seen me and he listened very kindly to what I had to say, but strongly advised me not to venture on such a journey. He said I ought to learn a trade. "That would really be a great shame," I answered, and he was quite taken aback by the way I said it. It was this that influenced him in my favour, as his family have since told me. He said that he did not know the dancer personally, but all the same he would see about giving me a letter to her. I received it, and now it seemed the door to good fortune already stood open for me.

My mother packed a small bundle of clothes for me and asked the driver of the coach if I could go as a stowaway; yes, I could, and the whole journey would only cost three *Rigsdaler*. The afternoon of my departure arrived at last. My mother, who was very upset, accompanied me to the city gate, where my old grandmother was waiting for me. Over the last few months her beautiful hair had turned grey; she fell on my neck and wept, but could not say a word. As for me, I was profoundly upset – and thus we parted. I never saw her again. She died the following year. I do not even know her grave. She is buried in the paupers' cemetery.

The postilion blew his horn. It was a lovely sunny afternoon and soon the sun was shining in my light-hearted, innocent mind. I delighted in all the new things I saw, and I was travelling towards the goal of all my longings. But when we sailed out into the Great Belt at Nyborg and the ship carried me away from the island of my birth I really felt how alone and friendless I was, with no one to put my trust in but God in heaven. As soon as I came ashore in Zealand I went behind a hut standing on the beach, fell on my knees and prayed that God would help and guide me. I felt comforted after that and relied firmly on God and my good fortune – and then I drove through towns and villages all that day and the following night. I stood all alone to eat my piece of bread while the coach was repacked. Everything was so strange to me, and I felt I was far away in the wide world.

II

On the morning of Monday, the sixth of September, 1819, I caught my first glimpse of Copenhagen from Frederiksberg Hill. There I got out with my little bundle and walked into the city through the park, the long avenue and the suburb. The evening before my arrival Copenhagen had seen a start of the Jew baiting that had spread through several European countries at the time. The whole city was in turmoil, and crowds of people thronged the streets; yet all that noise and tumult did not surprise me. It coincided exactly with all the bustle I had always imagined there must be in Copenhagen, the centre of the world. With scarcely ten *Rigsdaler* in my pocket, I put up in one of the smaller hostelries called The Guards Inn near the West Gate, Vesterport, through which I had entered the city.

The first place I sought when I went out was the theatre. I walked round it several times, looked up at its walls and regarded the whole building as a home that was not yet open to me. One of the ticket touts on the corner stopped me and asked if I would like a ticket. I said, "Yes, please," and thanked him profusely; but he thought I was making fun of him and became angry, so I took fright and ran away from the place which to me was the dearest in the city. Little did I imagine then that ten years later my first drama would be produced there, and that I would thus after all make my bow to the Danish public in this theatre. The following day I put on my confirmation suit, not, of course, forgetting the boots, which were pulled right up over my trousers. So in my best attire and with a hat that slipped right down over my eyes I went to visit Madame Schall, the ballet dancer, and give her my letter of introduction. Before I rang the bell I fell on my knees in front of the door and prayed to God that I might find help and protection here. Just at that moment a maidservant came up the staircase; she smiled kindly to me and put a copper into my hand and tripped off. I looked at her and at the coin. But I had my confirmation suit on, and thought I must look well dressed, so how could she believe I was begging? I called out after her. "Oh, keep it, keep it," she called down to me and was gone.

At length I was shown in to the dancer who looked at me in astonishment and then listened to what I had to say. She had never heard of old Iversen who had written the letter; and my whole personality and behaviour seemed most peculiar to her. In my own way I explained to her my heartfelt desire to go on the stage, and when she asked which parts I thought I could perform I answered, "Cinderella; I like that so much." The royal players had performed this in Odense, and the chief role had so captivated me that I could act it by heart from beginning to end. I wanted to show her what I could do, and as she was a dancer I thought it would probably be of most interest to her if I performed the scene where Cinderella dances. Meanwhile I asked permission to take off my boots as I was not otherwise light enough for this part. And then I took my big hat and used it as a tambourine, beat on it and began to dance and sing:

> What do riches mean to me,
> What is pomp and pageantry?

My strange gestures and curious agility caused her to think me out of my mind, as she has often told me, and she got rid of me as quickly as possible.

Now I went to Mr. Holstein, the manager of the theatre and asked to be engaged. He looked at me and said that I was too thin for the theatre. "Oh," I said, "if you will only give me a salary of a hundred *Rigsdaler* I shall soon put on weight." The manager looked serious and sent me away, adding that they only employed people with some education. There I was, deeply distressed and without a soul to advise and comfort me. I thought of death as being the only thing left for me, and my thoughts flew towards God. I clung to Him with all the confidence of a child in its father. I wept and then said to myself, "Only when everything is going utterly wrong does He send help; that is what I have read. You have to suffer a lot and only then can you really become something worthwhile." Now I went and bought a gallery ticket for the opera *Paul and Virginia*. The separation of the lovers made such an impression on me that I burst into a loud wailing. A couple of women sitting at the side of me consoled me as best they could by saying that it was only a play and nothing to upset myself over, and one of them gave me a big sausage sandwich. After this we all sat there together like the best of friends, and it seemed to me we were all good and kind folk. I had great confidence in all people and so I quite openly told all those sitting in the gallery with me that I was not really weeping for Paul and Virginia, but because I regarded the theatre as my Virginia, and if I were to be separated from it I should be just as unhappy as Paul. They looked at me and seemed not to understand me, and so I told them why I had come to Copenhagen and how lonely I was – and the woman gave me another sandwich and some fruit and cake.

The following morning I paid my bill at the inn, and saw that a single *Rigsdaler* was all the fortune I possessed. So I should either have to see about finding some skipper or other who would take me home, or apprentice myself to some craftsman in Copenhagen. The latter idea seemed the wiser of the two, because if I returned to Odense I would also have to become an apprentice, and I could foresee that people would laugh at me and make fun of me if I went back again in this manner because everything had gone wrong for me. So the best thing to do was to become an apprentice in Copenhagen. It was a matter of the greatest indifference to me what sort of trade I learned and I only chose to do this in order to keep myself alive there.

A woman who had travelled to Copenhagen as an unofficial passenger along with me gave me food and lodging; indeed she even went with me to buy a newspaper. We looked through it and found that a carpenter living in Borgergade was willing to take on an apprentice, so it was to him I went. The man received me kindly but said that before taking me on permanently he must have confirmation from Odense that I was a respectable boy, and then he would want to know more about me and my parents. A baptismal certificate was also required, but until all this arrived, and if I had nowhere else to live, I could move into his house and try the job immediately to see how it suited me.

I went to the workshop as early as six o'clock the next morning. There I met several journeymen and apprentices – and what a merry way of talking they had. The master had not yet arrived, and they passed the time in trivial and coarse chatter which made me as bashful as a girl. When they discovered this they started to tease me, and indeed later in the day the rude jokes of these young men went so far that in remembrance of the scene in the mill I became so scared, burst into tears and decided to abandon life as an artisan. I went down to the master and said that I could not put up with that language and those jokes, that I didn't fancy the trade and that I wanted to say goodbye and thank him for his kindness. He listened to me in amazement and tried to comfort me and cheer me up; but it was no use, for I was so overwhelmed and upset, and I hurried away.

There I went through the streets; no one knew me, and I was quite forlorn. Then I remembered that while I was in Odense I had read in the newspapers about an Italian called Siboni who had been given the post of the Director of the Royal Academy of Music in Copenhagen. Now everyone had spoken highly of my voice, so perhaps this man would take an interest in me, and if he did not, then I would that very evening find a skipper who would take me back to Funen. The thought of going home made me even more upset, and in this emotional frame of mind I hurried off to Siboni's house. It appeared that he was giving a dinner party for our famous composer, Professor Weyse, the poet, Baggesen and several other guests. To the housekeeper who opened the door to me I not only explained why I had come – because I wished to be engaged as a singer – but I recited the whole story of my life. She listened very sympathetically to me and must have repeated a good deal of it to the guests, for I had to wait a long time; and when she returned they all came with her. They all looked at me, and Siboni took me into the drawing room where there was a piano. I was asked to sing, and he listened to me attentively. Then I recited a couple of scenes from Holberg's plays as well as several poems in which the sense of my own unhappy position so overwhelmed me that I burst into tears, and all the guests applauded.

"I prophesy," said Baggesen, "that you'll make a name for yourself one day. But don't be vain when everyone applauds you." And then he said something about a pure and true product of nature and how it was destroyed with the passage of time and contact with people. I did not understand it all; but I must have been a peculiar child of nature, quite an antique revelation, not to say a phenomenon.

I believed implicitly in everything people said and was convinced that everyone wished me well, and I did not keep a thought to myself, but always spoke quite openly. Siboni promised to train my voice and was of the opinion that I would be able to appear in the Royal Theatre as a singer. I was wonderfully happy, and laughed and wept, and when the housekeeper showed me out and saw the state of excitement I was in, she patted my cheek and advised me to go and visit Professor Weyse the next day. He meant to do something for me, she said, and I could depend on him.

I went to call on Weyse who had been a poor boy himself and had worked his way up. He had truly understood my unhappy position, and having taken advantage of everybody's feelings at that moment he had collected seventy *Rigsdaler* for me. It was nothing less than a fortune, and for the time being, he said, he would let me have ten *Rigsdaler* each month. I immediately wrote my first letter home, a letter full of rejoicing, for all the good fortune in the world had been heaped upon me, I said. So great was my mother's delight that she showed the letter to everyone. Some listened in amazement, while others merely smiled at it, for what was going to come of it all?

Siboni could not speak Danish; and so that I could understand him and make myself understood it was necessary for me to learn some German. The lady with whom I had travelled from Odense was willing to help me as far as her means allowed, and she persuaded a language teacher by the name of Bruun to give me some German lessons free of charge. I learned a few words, and then Siboni threw open his house to me, gave me food and several times sang scales with me. He had an Italian cook and two bright servant girls, one of whom had worked for Casorti and spoke Italian. It was with them I spent my days. I gladly ran errands for them and listened to what they had to say, but one day, when they sent me into the dinner-table with one of the dishes, Siboni got up, went into the kitchen and told the servants that I was not a "*cameriere*". From that day I spent more time in the drawing room where Siboni's niece Marietta, a talented girl, spent much of her time drawing a picture of Siboni as Achilles in Paër's opera. I acted as model, dressed in the large tunic and toga that had been made for the broad and strong Siboni and not for a lean and overgrown boy like me. However, this contrast amused the cheerful Italian lady who laughed heartily and continued her sketching.

The opera singers came every day for practice, and sometimes I was told I might listen to them. While they were singing, il maestro sometimes became so angry that his Italian blood ran to his cheeks and in his temper he burst out sometimes in German and sometimes in a curious form of Danish, so that although it had nothing to do with me I trembled all over and became more and more afraid of this man on whom I thought all my future depended. And when I was to sing scales for him his stern gaze could make my voice tremble and bring tears to my eyes. "You no fright," he would say, and when he had finished with me and I reached the door, he called me back and put some coppers into my hand; "*wenig amüsiren*", he said with a kind smile.

According to what I have since been told, Siboni was an excellent singing master and he created a good school of dramatic singing; but he was not appreciated as he deserved by the public at large. Without realising that there was no Dane as clever and capable as he, people merely saw him as a foreigner who was using up a wage a Dane would have been glad of. The Italian operas which at that time were being performed throughout Europe and were introduced to the Danish stage by Siboni, were given a hostile reception merely because they came from Italy and Siboni was an Italian. *La Gazza Ladra* was hissed off the stage, as was *La Straniera*, and when Siboni, who, according to his contract was to have a benefit, chose to play the leading role in a performance in German of Paër's *Die Rache des Achilles* – a part that had once been his most famous in Italy – the Copenhagen audience hissed him. The injustice of this and Siboni's great merits have since his death been acknowledged by many who at that time overlooked and despised compositions by Rossini and Bellini but years later were forced to surrender to Verdi and Ricci. And then it went so far that no music or singing was of any value unless it was Italian. But Siboni did not live to see this revolution. He tried with all his heart and soul not only to teach his pupils to sing, but to understand and feel the character they were representing. He lacked words to express himself in German, and Danish he mastered even less. Most of his singers only understood him in one of the two, and so if he happened to express himself in some amusing manner it was quickly picked up and mocked.

I was at Siboni's house from early in the morning until the evening. On the other hand, my ignorance of the world had led me to spend my nights in a house which was respectable enough but in a street which was anything but. It was impossible for me to live at an inn for the ten *Rigsdaler* I received from Weyse each month, and I had to find some cheaper lodgings. So I went to live in a house in Holmensgade, which at that time was called Ulkegaden. It sounds strange, but that is how it was. I really had no idea of the world surrounding me, and I was so completely the innocent child that not a single tainted shadow was cast upon my soul.

So I went in and out of Siboni's home for about nine months. Then I lost my voice. It was breaking, and throughout the winter and spring I was compelled to wear bad shoes, and got my feet wet every day. My voice disappeared and there was no longer any prospect of my becoming the fine singer people had promised. Siboni told me so quite openly and advised me, now summer had arrived, to go to Odense and learn a trade.

Having in glowing, ardent words described to my mother the happiness I really felt had befallen me, I was now to return home and become a figure of fun. I knew this would happen. I felt it and stood there bowed down with grief. Yet precisely in this apparent misfortune lay the stepping stones to something better.

Once more I was deserted and forlorn. I considered what I should do now and to whom I should turn, and then it occurred to me that of course the poet Guldberg lived here in Copenhagen. He was the brother of the Odense colonel who had shown me so much kindness. I soon discovered that he lived close to the Assistens Cemetery, of which he has written so beautifully in his poems. I wrote to him, for I was too embarrassed to talk about my position and my poverty face to face as I had done on previous occasions. After he had received the letter I went out to visit him and found him surrounded by books and tobacco pipes. He was still a robust man; he received me kindly, and since he had seen from my letter how bad my spelling was he promised to give me lessons in the Danish language. When he went on to test my knowledge of German, which I told him I had spoken at Siboni's, he rightly decided that I needed considerable help in that, too, and this he was prepared to give me. In addition, he made me a present of the profits from a little work he had just published – I believe it was a speech to honour the birthday of Frederik the Sixth. People knew to what use the money was going to be put, and I think it brought in more than a hundred *Rigsdaler*. Weyse, too, continued to show an interest in me, and he and several others subscribed a small sum for me. And here I must in particular mention that the two servant girls from Siboni's also were kind enough each to subscribe a small sum quarterly from their wages. Admittedly they only paid the first quarter, but the thought was there all the same. I have since lost touch with both of them. The composer Kuhlau, to whom I never once spoke, was also among the subscribers. He, too, knew what it was to be a poor child. He had been brought up in poverty, and I have been told that he had to run errands in the bitter cold of the winter. One evening when he had been to fetch a bottle of beer, he fell and broke it; and the broken glass from it robbed him of the sight of one eye.

When the lady in whose house I lived in the street I have mentioned above, heard of the money I was assured of receiving through Guldberg and Weyse, she agreed to provide me with board and lodgings. When she went on to explain how well she would be able to look after me, and how dreadful most people were all over the city, it seemed to me that her home was the only place in which I could be safe. The room she gave me was in fact no more than a windowless empty larder with no more daylight than what came in through the open door from the kitchen. But she promised me that I might sit in her parlour as much as I liked. She said I should try it for two days and see what good food and drink I was given before finally deciding. But she must tell me that she would not be able to take me for less than twenty *Rigsdaler* a month. This placed a hard demand on me, especially as all my sources of income together amounted to no more than sixteen *Rigsdaler* a month, for which money I had not only to live but also to dress and buy everything I needed. "Yes, I must have twenty *Rigsdaler*," said my landlady, and she repeated it after dinner the following day, telling me about all the dreadful people I might encounter. She then said that when she came home a couple of hours later she must have a definite answer as to whether I would pay the twenty *Rigsdaler*. Otherwise I must leave without further ado.

I became attached to people so easily, and in the two days I had been there I had become fond of her and regarded her almost as a mother. I felt so much at home. It was heartbreaking to have to leave her, and where and to whom should I turn? But I was unable to produce more than the sixteen *Rigsdaler*. I would willingly have given them all to her, but too little it was and too little it remained. And there I stood, deeply distressed. My landlady had gone out, and the tears ran down my cheeks. I noticed the portrait of her late husband hanging over the sofa, and I was such a child that I went across to it and rubbed the portrait's eyes with my tears in order, I thought, for the dead man to be able to feel how upset I was and perhaps persuade his wife to take me in for the sixteen *Rigsdaler*. She must have realised that no more was to be squeezed out of me, for when she came home she said I could stay there for the sixteen *Rigsdaler* a month. I was so happy and thanked God and the dead man. The following day I gave her all the money, indescribably happy that I had a home now. However, I did not myself possess even a single copper with which to buy shoes, clothes or any other such necessities.

I was in the midst of the mysteries of Copenhagen, but did not understand enough to interpret them. My landlady had another lodger as well as me, a friendly young lady who had a room overlooking the yard. She lived alone and sometimes I saw her weeping. She had no visitors except her old father, and he only came in the evening after dark. I let him in through the kitchen door. He wore a plain coat, buttoned up at the neck and had his hat pulled well down over his eyes. He was said to have a cup of tea in his daughter's room each evening, and no one was to disturb them as he was very shy. As the time for his arrival drew near she always looked very serious and did not seem at all happy.

Many years later, when I was at a different stage in my life and accustomed to fine society, I once found myself in a brightly lit room and saw a distinguished looking elderly gentleman wearing decorations enter. It was the shy old father, the man I had let in

44

through the back door when he used to come in the shabby old overcoat. We did not know each other. At least it never dawned on him that I was the poor boy in that house that had opened the door for him when he made his guest appearances. In those days I had seen him only as a dignified father and thought of nothing but my *own* play-acting. Why, even at the age of sixteen I was still so much a child that I played with puppets and a puppet theatre which I had made myself, just as I had done at home in Odense. Every day I sat sewing clothes for the puppets, and in order to get the coloured pieces of cloth I needed for this I would go into the shops in Østergade and Købmagergade and ask for samples of different kinds of cloth and ribbons. My imagination was so completely occupied with this finery for my puppets that I often stood still in the streets and gazed at the rich ladies in their silks and velvets and pictured to myself how many royal cloaks, trains and knightly garments I could have made out of their clothes. In my imagination I saw all their finery at the mercy of my scissors, and this was enough to exercise my thoughts for hours on end.

As I have already said, I hadn't a penny I could call my own. My landlady took everything, but when, as occasionally happened, I went an errand for her to some place far away in town, she would always give me the odd coin. I'd deserved it, she said, and she didn't want to put on anyone. I used the money either to buy writing paper or copies of old plays. I soon gained access to quite a lot of books to read for my own amusement, and that was in no lesser place than the University Library. I had heard of the Provost of Regensen, old Rasmus Nyerup, at Bunkeflod's, and knew he was a farmer's son who had attended the grammar school in Odense. So one day I paid him a visit and told him that I came from Odense, too. My odd personality appealed to the old man, and he took a liking to me. He let me go and look at the books in the library above the Round Church on condition that I put them back in their right places. I was extremely conscientious in this, as I was also with the many illustrated books he allowed me to take home. I was very happy! And the other thing that made me happy was that Guldberg persuaded Lindgreen, the actor, to train me as a future actor. I had to learn several of the parts for Holberg's servant Henrich and also how to play foolish lads like Jacquinot in *The Two Grenadiers,* and I am said to have shown talent for that type of part. However, I wanted to play Correggio, and I was indeed allowed to learn that part off by heart. Lindgreen made me recite the monologue in the art gallery for him, and before I started he had laughed and asked me whether I really thought I could play the great master Correggio. He listened to me more and more seriously, and when I had finished he patted my cheek and said, "You certainly have feeling. But you are not made to be an actor. Heaven knows what it is you are made for, but have a talk to Guldberg and see if he can't teach you some Latin. That will always help you to go on to study."

Go on to study! It was a long time since that thought had struck me. I felt more closely and fondly tied to the theatre. But of course I had nothing against learning Latin, and besides, it sounded so fine to be able to say I was learning Latin. First of all I talked about it to the lady who had obtained free lessons in German for me, but she told me that Latin was the most expensive language in the world and that it could not be learnt free of charge! However, Guldberg persuaded one of his friends, the late Dean Bentzien, to be kind enough to give me a few hours' tuition in it each week.

The solo dancer, Dahlén, and his wife – she especially an artist of repute at the time whom Rahbek and several other poets praised in their works – opened their comfortable home to me, and at that time it was the only place I could think of as home. I spent most of my evenings there, and the gentle, warm-hearted Mrs Dahlén was a kind mother to me. Her husband took me with him to his school of dancing, which was at least a step nearer the theatre. There I stood throughout the morning by the long bar stretching my legs and learning to do a battement, but despite my eagerness and good intentions I did not show great promise as a dancer. Mr Dahlén declared that I would hardly get any further than the corps de ballet. One thing, however, I had achieved, and that was to be allowed to go into the wings in the evenings. The orderliness we know today did not exist there at that time, and the place was full of all sorts of people, while the actual loft provided accommodation for members of the audience. They paid the stagehands a few coppers, and this part of the theatre was always full, often with the "best society".

People were so keen to see the mysteries of the theatre, and I know of very distinguished ladies who were content to sit side by side with women from Nyboder just in order to discover what things were like up there. So I was allowed in the wings and was even permitted to sit in the box up in the top balcony that was reserved for the ladies of the corps de ballet. There I could sit in the back row, and in spite of being so tall I was simply regarded as a child. But how happy I was! It seemed to me that I already had one foot on the stage and belonged to the staff. But so far I had not had an evening on stage, although even this long awaited moment arrived. One evening they were performing the light opera *The Children from Savoy*. Ida Wulff, now Lady Holstein, was a pupil there at the time. I knew her from Siboni's where she had always had a quiet and kindly word for me. Shortly before the operetta was due to begin we met each other in the wings, and she told me that in the market scene everyone, even the stagehands, could go on to fill the stage. The only thing was that they had to put some make up on their cheeks first. I soon had that, and blissfully happy I went on stage together with the others. I saw the footlights, the prompter and the darkened auditorium. I was wearing my ordinary clothes, my confirmation suit, I think. It could still be worn; but however much I brushed and stitched it, it was not a very good cut; and it was badly made, too. My hat was far too big for me and almost covered my eyes. I was aware of all these shortcomings, and in order to hide them I performed all sorts of curious antics. I dared not stand straight, for then people would be able to see that my waistcoat was too short for me. The heels of my shoes were fairly worn, and that did not help my posture. I was tall and thin, and I knew from experience that it was not difficult to make fun of me. Yet at that moment I was only filled with the joy of appearing for the first time on a lighted stage. My heart was beating wildly when I went on – and then one of the singers who enjoyed quite a reputation at that time but is quite forgotten today, took me by the hand and mockingly congratulated me on my début. "May I present you to the Danish public," he said and drew me over towards the footlights. He wanted people to laugh at my curious mannerisms. I sensed it, and tears came to my eyes. I tore myself away and left the stage.

At about that time Dahlén was composing a ballet called *Armida*.

I was to take part in it as a troll with my own face hidden in a hideous mask. As a little girl Johanne Louise Heiberg also took part in this ballet. This is the first time I remember meeting her, and in the programme for *Armida* her name appeared in print for the first time, just as did mine. It was a great moment in my life to see my name in print, and I thought it meant a halo of immortality for me. I gazed at those printed letters all day long. I took the programme to bed with me in the evening and stared at my name by the light of a candle, and then I put it down, only to take it up again. It was sheer bliss.

I was already in my second year in Copenhagen. The money I had received from Guldberg and Weyse was all gone. In the course of one year I had grown older, at least as far as shyness was concerned, and I suffered greatly if I had to talk to anyone about all the things I lacked or needed. I had moved to the home of a seaman's widow, where apart from my lodgings I had nothing but a cup of coffee in the mornings. Those were dark, depressing days. My landlady thought that I went out in the afternoons to have dinner with various different people I knew, but I used to sit in the King's Garden and eat a small white loaf. Just occasionally I gathered courage and went to one of the cheapest cafés, where I sat at the most unobtrusive table I could find. There were holes in my boots and in rainy weather my feet were always wet. I had no warm clothes to wear in the cold weather. I was really generally forlorn, but this was no great burden to me. I thought everyone who spoke kindly to me was a true friend. God was with me in my little room, and many an evening when I had said my prayers I could turn to Him with all the simplicity of a child and say, "It will soon be all right." I believed with all my heart that it would be and must be, for God could not fail me.

Ever since my earliest childhood I had had the idea that New Year's Day would give a hint of what sort of a year was to follow. What I wished for most of all was to be given a part in a play in the new year and to appear on the stage. Then, surely, a salary would follow. On New Year's Day itself the theatre was shut, although the stage entrance was open. There was an old, half-blind porter on duty there, and with a beating heart I dodged past him and went in between the wings and curtains, straight across the stage towards the orchestra pit and there fell on my knees. But not a line could I remember, and I had to recite something aloud if I was to speak from the stage that year. So I said the Our Father in a loud voice and left in the confident expectation that I would be given a part during the course of the year.

Months passed; but I was not given any part in a play. Spring came, and it was already more than two years since I had arrived in Copenhagen. During all that long time I had only once been out in the woods. I had gone out to the Deer Park and had been completely fascinated to watch people enjoying themselves there in the same spirit as in Oehlenschläger's *Midsummer Eve Comedy*. There were crowds of people in the pleasure gardens, circus riders, wild animals, swings and side-shows, waffle shops with pretty Dutch waitresses and the Jew beneath the Tree – all these things were there along with screeching violins, singing and shouting. All this captivated me much more than all the natural beauty of the woods. Everything was so much alive, so colourful, so new.

One day in spring I had gone out to Frederiksberg, and in the park there I suddenly found myself standing under the first big beech trees to have come into leaf. The leaves were transparent in the sun and the air was fresh and sweet smelling. The grass was so tall and the birds were singing, and I was quite overwhelmed by it all and began to rejoice along with them; I flung my arms round one of the trees and kissed its bark, and at that moment I was completely a child of nature. "Are you mad?" said a man nearby. It was one of the park-keepers; I ran away in terror and then walked calmly and sedately back to town.

My singing voice had meanwhile begun to improve and become more resonant. Mr. Krossing, a brother of the poet, was the Royal Theatre chorus master at that time. When he heard me sing he offered me a place in the school, for he believed that by singing in the chorus I could develop my voice and thus gain an opportunity to appear on stage; and perhaps in time I might be given one or two small parts. A possible new way of making progress where I most wanted to seemed to open up before me. From the school of dancing I now went over to the school of singing and appeared in the chorus, sometimes as a shepherd for instance in *The Robbers' Castle* and *Johanne Montfaucon* and sometimes as a warrior, a sailor and the

49

like. I was now allowed to go into the pit when all the seats had not been sold, and I never missed an opportunity. The theatre was all the world to me; there I lived and there I dreamed, and so it was quite natural that I should forget to learn my Latin grammar. Besides I heard several people say that you didn't need to know Latin to sing in the chorus, and it was also quite possible to become a great actor without it. I thought this was extremely reasonable, and as I was tired of Latin I excused myself from my lessons on several occasions – with or without reason – and went to the theatre instead. Guldberg heard of this and he was angry, and rightly so, and for the first time in my life I was sternly and severely rebuked. I was completely overcome with shame; I do not believe that any criminal can be more shocked on hearing his death sentence pronounced than I was on hearing Guldberg's words. My face must have expressed this clearly, for he told me to stop putting it on. But I was not putting it on. I was now no longer to learn Latin.

More than ever before, I felt my dependence on other people's kindness. I lacked even the basic necessities. At various times I was overcome by dark and serious thoughts about my future, but at others I was again just as carefree as a child.

The first two representatives of the upper classes who were kind to the poor child that I was were the widow of the famous Danish statesman Christian Colbjørnsen and her daughter, Mrs. van der Maase, who at that time was a lady-in-waiting to Crown Princess Caroline. They listened sympathetically to me and regularly had me out in their home. Mrs. Colbjørnsen spent the summer in Bakkehuset, a house that was then owned by the poet Rahbek and his wife, "Philemon and Baucis" as they have been called in a poem. Now I visited their house, and was soon invited into their drawing room. Rahbek himself never spoke to me, and the nearest he ever came to doing so was once in the garden when he came towards me as if he were going to say something. However, as soon as he got near to me and looked at me, he turned round again and went away. Mrs. Rahbek, however, lively and kindly person as she was, would often chat to me. I had begun to write a sort of comedy and I read it to her. As soon as she heard the first few scenes she exclaimed, "Why, there are whole passages in it that you have taken from Oehlenschläger and Ingemann!" "Yes, but they are so beautiful!" I replied quite innocently and went on reading. One day when I was going to go up to Mrs. Colbjørnsen's from her house, she gave me a bunch of roses and said, "Will you take these up with you. Mrs. Colbjørnsen will be so pleased to receive them from the hand of a poet." These words were spoken half in jest, but it was the first time the word poet had ever been uttered in connection with me. I felt it throughout my body and my soul. Tears came to my eyes, and I know that from that moment all I thought of was writing and composing poetry. It had so far only been a sort of game as a change from playing with my puppet theatre, but now it was something far more – now it was the objective of my whole life.

I went there one day, very well dressed as I thought. Edward Colbjørnsen had given me a fine, blue coat, such a one as I had never possessed before. But it was too big for me, especially across the chest. I couldn't afford to have it altered, so I buttoned it right up to the neck. It looked new and the buttons shone brightly, although it was rather baggy across the chest. In order to improve it a little I filled it out with a bundle of the old theatre posters I still possessed. They hung loosely one on top of the other between my chest and my coat, which they now filled out. That is to say I had a hump on my chest, and in this state I presented myself to Mrs. Colbjørnsen and Mrs. Rahbek. They asked me straight away what all that was that I had on my chest. I ought to undo my coat, they said, for the weather was so hot. But I made sure that no one should persuade me to unbutton my coat, for then all the posters would have fallen out.

Apart from the Rahbeks and Colbjørnsens, a man by the name of Thiele – now a titular councillor of state – used to live out there in the summer. At that time he was only a young student, but had already quite a reputation as the man who had solved Baggesen's riddle, written some beautiful sonnets and published a book of *Danish Myths*. I had seen a performance of his tragedy *The Pilgrim* in the Royal Theatre. I was happy to be able to talk to him. He was a man of sensitivity, enthusiasm and understanding; he has always followed my career quietly and attentively until we now consider each other to be friends. He was in those days one of the few people to tell me the truth when everyone else made jokes at my expense and could see nothing but the comical sides of my natural simplicity. Rahbek's favourite, the actress Madame Andersen, who also lived in Bakkehuset, had for fun given me the name of "der kleine Declamator", and the name stuck. I was a curiosity. People laughed at me, while I only read approval in their smiles. Someone who has since become a friend of mine has told me that it was about that time he first met me. It was in a rich merchant's salon, and so that people could amuse themselves at my expense I was asked to recite one of my own poems. I am said to have recited it with such feeling and to have expressed myself with such unconscious depth in the poem that their mockery was transformed into sympathy.

One place of refuge, if I can call it such, I did find and I must not omit to mention it. It was a place where voices from the past seemed to echo in my receptive heart, the home of a dignified old lady, the mother of one of our famous men, the late Urban Jürgensen. She was a brilliant, cultured lady, but she belonged entirely to a vanished age and lived by the memory of those who had vanished with it. Her father had been bailiff of Antvorskov Castle, and she told me that Holberg often used to go there of a Sunday. He and her father used to walk up and down the room discussing politics. One day her mother, who was sitting at the spinning-wheel, wanted to take part in the conversation. "I think the distaff's speaking," said Holberg. "Mother could never forgive the witty old gentleman for those rude words." She had been a little child at that time, and now she was sitting there as a very old woman, telling me all this. The poet Wessel had often come to her home and had once played a dreadful trick on Reiser, the pernickety old man whose dreadful tales of the great fire we all know so well. He had made the poor man walk home through the muddy streets in his shoes and silk stockings. She read the classics, Corneille and Racine, every day and talked to me about them, about their lofty thoughts and the characters they portrayed. So it was not easy for the more modern Romantic poetry to fill her with enthusiasm. With all the warmth of a mother she talked about her exiled son, who during the war had put in such an incredible appearance in Iceland as the king of that island, and explained why he could never more return to Denmark. She could point to features in his character and resolve which had already been revealed in his childhood. You will understand how attractive the old lady's company was to me on account of all her experiences and thoughts. And for her part, she thought me a nice child and liked to have me there. She listened to my first verses and my tragedy *The Chapel in the Forest*, and one day, in a voice so serious that I was moved by it, she said, "You are a poet; perhaps as great as Oehlenschläger! In ten years – ah, by then I shall be long gone – but do think of me." I remember that tears suddenly welled up in my eyes, and I felt so solemn, so strangely moved and exalted by what she had said, while at the same time I know I could not conceive it was possible for me to become a poet who could be recognised as such, least of all one who could be named in the same breath as Oehlenschläger.

"Actually you ought to go on to study," she said, "but there are many roads that lead to Rome, so you will probably find your own road there."

"You ought to go on to study." That was what everyone kept on saying. Every day I used to hear what a good thing it would be, and how important, even how necessary it would be for me. I was encouraged to take an interest in learning. Indeed, there were even people who grumbled at me for not doing so, saying that it was my duty to study as I would never get anywhere otherwise – but of course, they said, I probably preferred simply to waste my time. This was meant quite seriously, but no one made any effort to help me. I was fundamentally leading a pitiful existence, and I was finding it difficult to keep myself alive. Then I had the idea of writing a tragedy and submitting it to the Royal Theatre. Then, when it was performed, I would start studying with the money I earned from it. While Guldberg was still reading Danish with me I had written a tragedy in blank verse based on a German short story entitled *The Chapel in the Forest* that was to be found in Rosenkilde's *The Carrier Pigeon*. Guldberg saw it as a Danish essay and an exercise in the language, and he had strictly forbidden me to submit this work to the theatre. So I wrote a new play, again a tragedy. The name of the author was to remain unknown. I made up the story myself. It was a "patriotic tragedy" called *The Robbers of Vissenberg*. I had completed it and written a fair copy within a fortnight, but there was scarcely a word in it that was spelt correctly, for no one had helped me with it. The play was to be submitted anonymously, but one person was let into the secret. That was Miss Tønder-Lund, the young lady who had been confirmed along with me in Odense, the only one there who had been good and kind to me and had given me a rose. I had visited her in Copenhagen and she had spoken sympathetically about me to the Colbjørnsen family, where one acquaintance had led to another. She paid someone to produce a more readable copy than mine because, we thought, my handwriting must not be recognised; and so the tragedy was sent off.

After a space of six weeks, during which I lived in great, bold expectations, the play was rejected and returned, and the letter with it said that plays betraying such a lack of the most elementary education should not be submitted to the theatre in future.

It was just at the end of the theatre season in May 1822 that I received another letter from the theatre management saying that I was to be "dismissed" from the Chorus and Ballet School, as my further attendance there would lead nowhere. However, they expressed the hope that my many friends would take care of me and ensure for me the education and learning necessary to obtain a position in the world, without which it was of no avail to be endowed with talent of any kind.

Once more I felt as though I had been thrown out into the open sea without help or refuge. I *must* write a play for the theatre, and it *must* be accepted; that was my only hope and the only means of salvation left to me, and so I wrote a tragedy called *Alfsol* based on a story by Samsøe. I was personally enraptured by the first acts, and with these in my hand I made myself known to the man who had translated Shakespeare, the late Admiral Peter Wulff, in whose house and family circle I later found a true home. Years later, he told me in fun and with a little exaggeration of the way in which we got to know each other. He said that as I came in through the door I blurted out: "You have translated Shakespeare, and I like him so much; but I have written a tragedy, as well; just listen." Wulff invited me to have lunch with him first. But I would have nothing to eat and simply read at full speed. When I had finished I said, "Do you not think I can be a success, because I would so much like to be." Then I stuffed the papers into my pocket and, according to his account, when he invited me to visit him again, I replied, "Yes, I will when I have written a new tragedy."

"Yes, but that will take rather a long time," he replied. "Oh, no," I said. "I think I can have another ready in a fortnight." And with these words I was off.

This account is probably a little exaggerated, but it gives a glimpse of my personality as it then was. I had also introduced myself to H. C. Ørsted. It was just as though some divine guidance made me approach the very noblest and best people, whose significance I had no idea of or any means of appreciating. From the very first moment and until his death Ørsted followed my progress with an ever-increasing interest which turned into true friendship during the last years of his life. He had a great influence on my intellectual progress, and it was he more than anyone else who kept me going all the time I was developing my poetic talent. It was he who gave me courage and prophesied that one day in the future I would be recognised even in my native land. His home soon became a home for me; I played with his children while they were small and have seen them grow up and retain their affection for me. It was in his home I found my oldest and most faithful friends. In Dean Gutfeld, too, who was still alive at that time and enjoyed a great reputation as a preacher, I found a friend and supporter. He was the man who spoke most warmly of me and had the greatest hopes of me, and when he had read my youthful tragedy *Alfsol* he submitted it for me along with a letter of recommendation to the management of the theatre. I lived in a mixture of hope and fear. If this play, too, were rejected, I didn't know what I should turn to! During that summer I had experienced bitter poverty, although I never spoke of it, otherwise all those people who knew me now would certainly have helped me. False modesty prevented me from saying how difficult life was for me. My face was radiant with joy when people spoke kindly to me, and there was one thing that gave me infinite pleasure: I read Walter Scott for the first time. His novels were a spiritual life for me, and a new world was revealed to me. Here, I forgot the pressure of the reality surrounding me, and the money I ought to spend on my dinner went to the lending library instead.

It is from that very time I can date my first acquaintance with the man who over all the succeeding years has become a dear father to me, and in whose children I have found my siblings, the family I so to speak have grown into. I need only mention the name of this man, and then all the older generation will know how much he did in the service of the state for the benefit both of individuals and the country as a whole. He was one of the most gifted figures in commercial life, and he had the noblest and kindest heart combined with a strong and decisive will. This man was the titular Privy Councillor, Jonas Collin. Among his many and extremely varied spheres of activity was that of the director of the Royal Theatre. Everyone told me that if I were fortunate enough to gain this man's interest, then something would really be done for me. It was Dean Gutfeld who first mentioned me to him, and now, for the first time, I went into that house which was to become for me the home of homes.

In his novel *Chronicles from the Age of Christian the Second*, Carl Bernhard has written about the Collins' residence from its early days to the present. When the East Gate of Copenhagen was at the end of Østergade, and what is now Kongens Nytorv consisted of open fields, there was a country house near St. Anne's Chapel where the Spanish ambassador lived during the summer. This lopsided and angular half-timbered house had stood in this impressive street ever since those early times and until a few years ago. An old-fashioned wooden balcony gave access to the entrance on the first floor. The narrow, enclosed courtyard was surrounded by a clumsy, wooden gallery under the overhanging roof, but facing the actual road there was an old lime tree that spread its branches across the courtyard and up towards the pointed gable. This house was to become a parental home for me, and who does not delight in lingering over the description of his home? Now a splendid new residence adorns the spot, and while they were building it the workmen sang:

> In the new as in the old,
> May fortune find its home.

But the old one, yes, that very one:

> 'Tis now but memories of the past.

I went out there, and Collin had a talk with me. I saw in him nothing but a businessman. He said little, and what he did say seemed to me to be serious and almost stern. I went away again without expecting any interest on the part of this person. But Collin was the very man who with all his heart considered what was best for me and quietly helped me to achieve it, just as he has done throughout his life for many of the leading figures in the country. At that time I could not understand the calm way in which he apparently listened to people in need, while his heart could bleed at the supplicant's story. And when he was alone again tears would come to Collin's eyes and he would eagerly and successfully find a way of acting and helping. As for the play I had sent to the theatre, and for which so many people had heaped praise on me, he dealt with it nonchalantly and haphazardly, so that I felt him to be an enemy rather than a protector. But a few days later the management of the theatre sent for me. Rahbek spoke on their behalf. He returned the manuscript of *Alfsol* to me and said that the play was unsuited for the stage, but that, on the other hand, they had found so many "nuggets" in it, that they cherished a hope that through serious study and by going to school and learning everything necessary from the start I might perhaps one day be able to produce plays for the Danish theatre which were worthy of being performed. In order that I might be able to live and acquire the necessary education, Collin had spoken on my behalf to King Frederik the Sixth who had graciously granted me a sum from the state finances that was sufficient to live on for some years. In addition, he said that the Grammar School Board had agreed I should have free tuition at Slagelse Grammar School, to which, they said, an energetic new headmaster had recently been appointed. I could scarcely speak for surprise. I had never for a moment thought that my life would take this turn. I was strangely fascinated and had actually no real idea of the course on which I was now to embark. I was to leave for Slagelse with the first coach. Every three months Collin would send me sufficient money to live on. I was to keep in touch with him, and he was to be informed of my diligence and progress.

I went to visit him a second time in order to thank him. This time he was a little more forthcoming. He spoke gently and kindly and said, "Write openly to me and tell me what you need and how you are progressing". And from that moment he opened his heart to me. No father could have been more to me than he was and remains. No one has been more profoundly delighted with my later progress and recognition. No one else has given me more heartfelt comfort in my troubles and felt for me as though I were one of his own children. He gave me this help without a word or a glance to make it a burden to me. This was not the case with everyone to whom I had to address my thanks for this change in my fate. Many people told me to remember how inconceivably fortunate I was and how poor I had been, and sternly admonished me to work hard.

The time for my departure was soon decided, and I myself had still one matter to attend to. At the same time as I had sent *Alfsol* to the theatre I had had a talk to an acquaintance from Odense, a young man who ran a printing press on behalf of a widow he knew. He had promised me that *Alfsol* and a little story called *The Ghost at Palnatoke's Grave* should be printed. I gave the manuscript to him, but it was to remain untouched in the press until I found an adequate number of subscribers. So far, I had not found these. Before leaving I ran across to the press, but it was closed, and so I let the matter rest, presumably quite content with the possibility that it might be printed and read after all. Unfortunately this is just what happened, though not until many years later when the man who had taken the manuscript from me had died and I thought the whole thing had been put aside and forgotten. The book was published without my knowledge and without my wishing it. It was published in its original form and under a pseudonym. I had chosen one that at first glance seems to suggest enormous vanity on my part, and yet it was not that but rather the love that a child can possess and so call a doll after the person it loves most. I loved William Shakespeare and Walter Scott, and then of course I loved myself as well, and so I took my own name Christian, producing the pseudonym of William Christian Walter. The book is still in existence and contains the tragedy *Alfsol* and the story *The Ghost at Palnatoke's Grave* in which neither a ghost nor Palnatoke play any part at all. It is a very rough imitation of what had captivated me in Walter Scott. Dana, who speaks the prologue, says that I am "but seventeen" and that I here present:

a garland made of roots of beech and Danish flowers.

The whole thing is an extremely immature work. It could be little else.

One lovely day in autumn I left Copenhagen by coach. I was on my way to start school in Slagelse, the place where Baggesen and Ingemann had gone to school before me. By my side, radiant with joy at the prospect of the new life before him, sat a young student who had left school only a month before. He was now travelling home to Jutland to show himself as a graduate from school and to visit his parents and friends. He assured me he would be the unhappiest man on earth if he were in my place and had to start grammar school again. It was a dreadful place, he said. But my spirits were high as I travelled towards the old town. My mother received a blissfully happy letter from me, and I wished with all my heart that my father and my old grandmother had been alive to hear that now I was going to a grammar school.

III

When I reached Slagelse late that evening I alighted at the inn and asked the innkeeper's wife what there was of interest in the town.

"There is the new English fire-engine and Pastor Bastholm's library," she replied, and that was about all there was worth seeing. A couple of officers from the Lancers constituted the fine society of the town. Every home knew whether such and such a pupil had been put up or down a class last month, for the school was a main subject of conversation in the town, varied only by discussion of the private theatre. The pupils from the school and the maidservants from the town were given free tickets to the dress rehearsals with the result that the actors were used to performing for a full house. I have given a sketch of this in the fourth evening in *A Picture Book without Pictures*.

I found board and lodging in the house of a respectable widow from the educated classes. My little room overlooked the garden and the fields beyond, and there were vine leaves hanging down over the green, sundrenched windows. In the school I was put among the small children in the next-to-the-bottom class, for I knew absolutely nothing at all.

I was really like a wild bird that has been put into a cage. I had the best will in the world to learn, but I was immediately out of my depth. I behaved like one who has been thrown out into the sea unable to swim: it was a matter of life and death to make progress, but I was confronted by wave after wave, one called mathematics, another geography, grammar, and so on. I felt overwhelmed and feared that I would never be able to swim through it all. Sometimes I would pronounce a name quite wrongly, sometimes I would get things completely mixed up, or perhaps I would ask some ridiculous question that no well brought up schoolboy would dare to ask. The headmaster, who had his own way of mocking us, naturally found ample opportunity for doing so in me, so I became fearful and disheartened. I had very sensibly given up all thought of writing verse for the present, and yet I was immediately asked to exercise my powers. The headmaster was to be installed when the bishop came on a tour of inspection, and the singing master gave me the task of writing a song to mark the event. I wrote it and the school sang it. But although at one time I would have been glad to have been one of those to make a contribution to such an occasion, I here for the first time felt the unhealthy melancholy that was to be mine for several years to come. During the celebrations I went out of the church and walked around in the little churchyard, stopping by a neglected grave. I knew the name on it, for here lay the doctor and poet Frankenau, the man who had sung of *The Ruins of Christiansborg Palace* and *Held Far from Thee by Mountains, Waves and Valleys*. I was strangely sad at heart and prayed to God that either in spite of everything I might become a poet like Frankenau or soon like him lie beneath the ground. The headmaster said not a word to me about my celebratory song; indeed I even thought he looked at me more sternly than usual. I looked up to him in every way as to a superior being, so without hesitation I believed everything he said, even when he was mocking me. So on one of the first days, when I gave a wrong answer to his question and he immediately said I was stupid, I conscientiously reported this to Collin, telling him I was afraid I did not deserve all he was doing for me. Collin wrote a few consolatory words to me, and it was not long before I really did receive quite good marks in some subjects. Yet despite making regular progress I increasingly lost confidence in myself. However, in one of the first examinations I was praised by the headmaster, and he even wrote it down in my report; and, delighted at this, I was able to spend a couple of days' holiday in Copenhagen. Guldberg, who could see the progress I had made and recognised my earnest desire to do well, gave me a kind welcome and praised me for my efforts. "But just don't write any poetry," he said. That was what everyone else said, and so I wrote no poetry, but sternly fixed my attention on my duty and the distant and uncertain hope of passing my school-leaving examination.

The editor of the West Zealand newspaper, a learned man by the name of Bastholm, lived completely cut off from social life, devoting himself entirely to his studies. I had called on him and given him a few odd things that I had written previously, and as a result he took an interest in me. His advice, reasonably enough, was also that I should keep my attention fixed entirely on my schoolbooks. By virtue of its sincere and good advice, a letter he wrote to me on this subject speaks with such true authority that many people will probably always be able to take it to heart. He wrote:

I have read your prologue, my young friend, and I must admit that God has endowed you with a lively imagination and a warm heart. The only thing you still lack is a certain development of the mind. But that can still come, for you have now been given an opportunity to acquire it. So you must undertake to work as hard as you can to finish your studies and put everything else aside. I wish your youthful efforts had not been published, for why must the public be burdened with things that are not perfect? We have plenty of those. And yet it is a good thing, since it can help to justify the public support that has been given to you. A young poet has simply to be on guard against the snares of vanity and to watch over the purity and strength of his feelings. I repeat my advice: only rarely write poetry during this time while you are studying, and do so only to give expression to your feelings. Write nothing in which you have to seek for words or thoughts, but do so only when your soul has been fired with an idea and your heart warmed with feelings. Look at nature, mankind and yourself with an attentive eye in order to find original material for your works. Choose small subjects from the things around you. Contemplate everything you see from all points of view before you grasp your pen. Become a poet as though no poet had ever lived in this world before you, and as though you were to learn from no one, and always preserve that nobility of mind and that exalted purity of the soul without which the poet's crown can never be accorded to a mortal man.

Slagelse, 1st February, 1823

Colonel, now General, Guldberg from Odense, whom I have mentioned before, followed my progress with no less interest. His joy on hearing of the great step forward I had taken and learning that I was going to a grammar school was great and profound. He wrote to me regularly, and his letters were full of encouragement and confidence. When my first summer holidays were approaching he invited me to go and visit him, and indeed even sent me the money for the journey.

I had not been in my native town since setting out on my adventures. My grandmother had died in the meantime, and then my grandfather as well. My mother had often said to me while I was still a child that I certainly had good prospects, for I was heir to my grandfather, and he owned his own house. That was only a poor little half-timbered building which was sold on his death and immediately pulled down, while most of the money went towards paying the tax he still owed. The bailiff's men had taken belongings representing this amount; and the big brass-covered stove, a piece of furniture that was said to be worth inheriting, now stood in the town hall. And there was enough money to make an entire seat in a coach, but it was the old currency, which was no longer valid and could no longer be changed. In 1813, when it had to be changed, the weak-minded old man was told that the money was no longer of any use. "But no one can say the King's money is not valid," he said, "and the King certainly will not." That was all the answer he made. Now I was given the great inheritance; as far as I remember it was twenty-odd Rigsdaler. But I must admit that the inheritance was of no great concern to me. Both the past and the future seemed so bright at the thought of visiting Odense; I felt so rich and so happy, and my mind was elated by joy and longing.

I crossed the Great Belt and then went on foot from Nyborg to Odense, carrying my clothes in a small bundle. As I approached the town and saw the tall old tower of St. Knud's Church my heart grew softer and softer, and I sincerely felt how God had looked after me, and I burst into tears. My mother was blissfully happy to see me again, and she told me that there were ever so many of her acquaintances and "fine folk" I simply must visit, both the grocer's and the clerk's. Iversens and Guldbergs gave me a hearty welcome; in all the narrow streets I could see people opening their windows to have a look at me, for they all knew how remarkably fortunate I

63

had been and even that I was studying for money given to me by the King. "Marie Shoemaker's Hans Christian had not done so badly after all," my mother told me they were saying. Indeed, when Søren Hempel, the owner of the bookshop, took me up into a high tower that he had built above his house in order to amuse himself with a little astronomy, I looked down on the town and the meadows, and below me in Greyfriars Square I saw some poor women from the hospital pointing up at me and showing that I, whom they had known as a little boy, was right up there now. I really felt that I was standing on the highest pinnacle of fortune. One afternoon I went out with the Guldbergs and the bishop's family for a sail on the river among the gardens, and my mother wept with joy at seeing me "honoured like the son of a count." But all that splendour, all the halo was gone when I was back in Slagelse once more.

I think I may say that I worked very hard, as a consequence of which I was moved into the next class as soon as possible. However, as I was scarcely mature enough for this, it was a continual strain on me and almost too big an intellectual burden. Many an evening as I sat in my little room reading but almost overpowered by sleep, I would bathe my head in cold water or run around in the quiet, little garden until I was wide awake again and could start afresh. Despite being a learned and gifted man who has enriched our literature with excellent translations of the ancient classical poets, the headmaster was completely unsuited to educating young children, as time has also shown. Teaching seems to have been a torment to him, and under his supervision it was no less a torment to us. Most of the pupils, and I especially, were afraid of him, not because he was strict, but because of the way in which he mocked us and gave us all nicknames. If a herd of cattle chanced to be driven past while he was teaching us and a single pupil noticed it, the headmaster could quite easily tell us all to stand up and go over to the window to see "our brethren walking past". If we failed to answer quickly and correctly enough during an examination, he would sometimes interrupt us, get up from his desk and go across and put the questions to the stove. To be laughed at was the worst torment of all for me. Consequently, when the headmaster came in at the beginning of the lesson, I was often completely paralysed with fear, and my answers were the opposite of what they should have been. So the man was right when he said that he was unable to get a word of sense out of me. I despaired at my own lack of ability, and one evening when I was in a sombre, depressed state of mind I wrote to Mr. Quistgaard, the first master, and asked for his advice and support, saying that I considered myself to be so dull that it was impossible for me to go on studying. I was convinced that people in Copenhagen had made a complete mistake with me, and that the money spent on me was simply being wasted. And I thought, too, that I ought to report all this to Collin. Then I asked Quistgaard what I should turn to. This wonderful, kindly man wrote a long, affectionate letter to me, encouraging me with gentle words and telling me not to lose heart. He said the headmaster meant well by me, that this was simply his way of behaving, and that I was really and truly making all the progress that could be expected of me and must not doubt my ability. He told me how he had started going to school as a twenty-three-year-old farmer's son that is to say when he was considerably older than I. He knew what it was like, and said the real trouble as far as I was concerned was that I needed treating and educating in quite a different way from the rest of the pupils, but that was not easy to do in a school. Meanwhile I did make progress, and in some subjects did very well indeed. In religion, scripture and Danish I always had excellent marks; indeed pupils from all the school, even the top class, would come up to my room if they wanted help in writing a Danish essay. "But don't make it so good that they'll find out," they said. And in return they helped me with my Latin. For conduct marks all the teachers regularly gave me "Excellent" on my monthly report. However, it happened once that I was only given "Fairly Good", and I was so profoundly upset over this poor report that I immediately wrote a tragic-comical letter to Collin assuring him that it was not my fault at all that I had only been classed as "Fairly Good".

That the headmaster had a different opinion of me from the one he normally expressed and indicated, was something we will see later. An occasional spark of good will revealed itself, and I was usually among the pupils he invited to his home on Sundays, when he was quite a different man from the one he was in school. He was full of fun, told us amusing stories, arranged toy soldiers and played with us and his own children. Moreover, one of the classes in the school, together with a teacher, always went to church on a Sunday, and as I was so tall and lanky the headmaster always let me go with the top class. All the pupils in that class used to do their history or mathematics homework while in church, and none of them listened to the old parson. This example was catching, but as I considered it least sinful to do my scripture homework, that is what I did. That was what Sunday service was like for me.

One of the bright spots in school life was the fact that we pupils were allowed to go to the dress rehearsals of the Dramatic Society. The theatre had formerly been a stable, and was situated in a back yard, where we could hear the cows lowing in the meadows. As their street scene they had painted the town's market-place, which meant that there was always something homely about the plays: the scene was always set in Slagelse, and it amused people to see their own and their friends' houses. On Saturday evenings I would normally make my way out to Antvorskov Castle, which even then was half ruined; Frankenau has said of it:

> A castle stands instead of cloister
> Beneath the hill the aged monks repose.

With great curiosity I followed the progress as they excavated the ancient vaults; it was a whole Pompeii to me. A young married couple from distinguished families lived out there in a small house. I believe they had married against the wishes of their families. I think they were poor, but they seemed to be so happy, and there was a kind of comfort and beauty about their white-washed, low-ceilinged parlour. There were always fresh flowers on the table and they had some beautifully bound books. There was also a musical instrument – a harp – in the house. I had chanced to make the acquaintance of this young couple and they were always pleased to see me and gave me a kind welcome. There was a lovely feeling of idyll about this little home situated below the lonely wing of the castle on the hill.

From Antvorskov I went on to St Anders' Cross, one of the few wooden crosses from Catholic times which are still to be found in Denmark; it stands on the left-hand side of the main road to Korsør, not far from Slagelse. Tradition has it that St. Anders was a priest in Slagelse and journeyed to the Holy Land. On his last day there he spent so much time praying by the side of the Holy Sepulchre that his ship sailed without him. He was walking despondently along the shore when a man riding on an ass came towards him and invited the priest from Slagelse to climb up behind him. He did so and fell asleep, and when he awoke he heard the bells of Slagelse ringing and found he was lying on the "Hill of Rest" as the rise is now called. And in memory of him the cross now stands there with an image of the crucified Christ. He had come home long before the ship that had sailed without him, for an angel of the Lord had carried him home to Denmark. I liked the legend and the spot; here on the rise I sat many an evening and gazed across the meadows and cornfields, right across to Korsør where Baggesen was born. He, too, as a pupil at Slagelse Grammar School must often have sat there gazing across the Belt to Funen. I let my imagination roam on St. Anders' Mount, and later, when from the coach I saw the hill with the cross on it I thought of the chapter in my fairytale life that was linked to this spot.

I was happiest if I could occasionally go off to Sorø on a Sunday to visit the poet Ingemann, who was a teacher at the Academy and had recently married a Miss Mandix. He had been so kind as to receive me in Copenhagen, and in Sorø his welcome was even heartier, if that were possible, for his interest in me had increased. His wife, a brilliant and extremely kind lady, approached me as though she were a fond, elder sister. It was so good to be in their home, and I was filled with a sense of bliss, for it all seemed to be so truly poetical. The house was situated in a delightful, quiet spot close to the lake and the woods. There were vines around the windows, the sitting rooms were decorated with paintings and sketches; and in the little garden room there hung portraits of almost all the famous European poets as well as the well-known Danish ones. The garden itself was resplendent with beautiful flowers, and wild plants from the woods and meadows were allowed to grow there as they liked. We sailed on the lake with an Æolian harp fixed to the mast. Ingemann had a vivid way of relating things, which made everything come to life. I discovered such a natural charm in him and his wife, and I became very fond of them; our friendship has grown over the years. Many a summer since then I have been a welcome guest in their home for weeks on end and have felt there are people in whose company it is as though one becomes a better person. Bitter memories are dispersed and all the world is bathed in a sunshine that in fact radiates from the delightful home.

Among the pupils in the "Noble Academy" of Sorø there were two who wrote verse; they knew that I did the same and made friends with me. One of them was called Petit, and has since published a couple of my books in Germany. I think I can say he did so with the best will in the world, but they are not very accurate translations. And then he wrote a remarkably imaginative biography of me, one feature of which is that the description of my parents' house seems to be based on that of the hut in *The Ugly Duckling*. My mother is portrayed as something of a Madonna, and I am seen running around on pink feet in the evening sunshine, along with many other things of that ilk. Petit was actually not without talent and he possessed a warm and noble heart. Life inflicted heavy burdens on him. He is dead now and his lively spirit knows greater serenity and repose.

The other poet from Sorø was Carl Bagger, one of the soundest and most gifted poets to have appeared in Danish literature in my time, though he has been judged harshly and unfairly. His poems are full of freshness and originality, and his story *My Brother's Life* is a brilliant book of which the periodical *Maanedsskrift for Litteratur* published a much too severe and one-sided assessment. I know what a bitter and painful impression this criticism made on the author. These two Academy pupils were very different from me. Their blood flowed with life; they were both spirited and had a future to look forward to, whereas I was weak and nothing but a child despite my being the tallest and lankiest of the three of us. Thus quiet Sorø with its woodland solitude became the home of poetry and friendship to me.

An event that created a stir in our little town was the execution of three people down at Skælskør. The daughter of a rich farmer had persuaded her lover to murder her father, who was opposed to the match. The farm servant had helped them and was hoping to marry the widow. Everybody wanted to go to this execution, and that day was like a holiday. The headmaster gave the top class the day off. We were to go and watch it, for he thought it would do us good to see something like that.

We drove in open coaches through the night, and by sunrise we were just outside Skælskør. It made a terrible and unforgettable impression on me to see the condemned being driven up, the deathly pale girl leaning her head on her powerfully built lover's breast. Behind them sat the farm servant, pale and with wispy black hair; he had a squint and nodded to the few acquaintances who shouted goodbye to him. On the scaffold, where they stood at the side of their coffins, they sang a hymn together with the minister, the girl's voice sounding high above the others. My legs could scarcely bear me, and these few minutes were more dreadful to me than the actual moment of death. Then I saw a poor, sick creature, whose superstitious parents, in order to cure him from a stroke, made him drink a bowl of the blood of the executed criminals, and then dashed off with him in wild flight until he sank to the ground. A jobbing poet went round selling his "mourning song" in which the text was supposed to be spoken by the criminals; and it sounded rather odd that it was set to the tune of *A stranger I came to this place*.

The whole event had such an effect on my imagination that for a long time I was continually haunted by the memory of it. It forced its way into my dreams, and even now, after many years have passed, I can see it all as vividly as though it had happened yesterday.

However, there were no other events as powerful as that or indeed any happenings of any importance at all; one day passed like another. But the less you experience, the more monotonously your life slips by, the sooner it occurs to you to write down and preserve what does happen, to keep what they call a diary. I bought one about that time; a few pages of it still exist in which the strangely childish nature I possessed in those days is admirably reflected. I will include a few sentences from that time, written down word for word. I was then in the next to the top class, and all my happiness and my entire existence depended on my being put up into the top class after the approaching term examination. I wrote:

"Wednesday – Out of spirits. I took my Bible, which lay in front of me. I wanted to see if it would not be an oracle for me. I opened it and without looking put my finger on a page and read, "O Israel, thou hast destroyed thyself; but in me is thine help." (Hosea) "Yes, Father,

69

I am weak, but Thou seest my innermost thoughts and will be a help to me to be put up into the fourth form. Did quite well in Hebrew."

"Thursday: Happened to pull the leg off a spider. Did well in Mathematics. Oh, God, God, thank you from the bottom of my heart."

"Friday: Oh, God, help me! The evening out there is so wintry and clear. Now the examinations are over; the result comes tomorrow. Oh, Moon, tomorrow you will behold either a pale and miserable wretch or the happiest creature on earth! Read Schiller's *Kabale und Liebe*.

"Saturday: Oh, God, now my fate is sealed but still hidden from me. What awaits me? Oh, God, my God, do not forsake me; my blood is pulsing so rapidly through my veins and my nerves are on edge. Oh God, almighty God, help me, I do not deserve it, but have mercy on me, oh God, God – (later) – I did it. Strange, my joy at this is not as great as I expected. Wrote to Guldberg and my mother at eleven o'clock."

It was at that time, too, that in silent thought I promised Our Lord that if He let me go up into the fourth class, then the first Sunday after that I would take Holy Communion; and so I did, too. You will be able to see from this what vague ideas I had in my really pious heart, and what stage I had reached in my development, and I was already twenty years old at this time. All other young people of that age are far more advanced in writing such diaries!

The headmaster didn't like being in Slagelse. He applied for the vacant headship at Elsinore Grammar School and was appointed to it. He told me of this and to my surprise suggested I should go with him. He said that he wanted to give me private lessons so that I could take my final examination within eighteen months, something of which there was no prospect if I remained in the school in Slagelse. He added that I could immediately move into his house for the same rent as I gave elsewhere, and that I should write to Collin and tell him about it and obtain his permission. This I did, and moved to the headmaster's house.

So I was to leave Slagelse! It was difficult for me to take leave of my school friends and the few families I had come to know; of course on this occasion I bought myself an autograph book in which my old teacher, Mr. Snitker, was among those who wrote a few lines. He had also been a teacher at the school when Ingemann and Poul Møller were pupils there. Carl Bagger wrote a poem to me in which it sounded more as though I was now leaving to lead the life of a poet, and not to sit at a school desk, though that is where my path was taking me, to distressing and difficult days:

To the Poet H.C. Andersen
From his friend Carl Bagger

A dangerous way you are to tread,
Which second best no homes afford
A patch of roses here you seek. Instead
A withered flower is oft reward.
To be a poet is fine, they say,
And many a golden dream he dreams;
But seldom does his hidden way
Pursue the pathways of the world, it seems.

He lacks a friend to give him solace
When sorrow comes on stealthy foot
The tempest rough in all its rage
Breaks off his hope, a tender shoot.
Then let no tear from tired eye start;
Recall he draws a poet's breath.
But let him in his beating heart
Find comfort, hope and laurel wreath.

Fight like a man life's bitter game;
A child's simplicity preserve.
The lamp of fortune burns with fame,
Will give you all that you deserve.
To share your joy will ever me delight
When, youth, raised up on high, I view
You splendid with a poet's might,
Desired by all, achieved by few.

Sorø, May 1826

I went to Elsinore together with the headmaster. I was enchanted on first catching sight of the Sound with all its ships, the mountains of Kullen and the entire beautiful landscape. I said this in a letter to Rasmus Nyerup, and of course, as I considered it was well written, I dispatched the very same letter to several other people. Unfortunately, Nyerup was so impressed with the letter that he had it published in *Pictures of Copenhagen*, so that everyone who had received that letter, or rather copies of it, thought it was theirs that had been published.

The range of new experiences, the new surroundings and the duties raised the headmaster's spirits, though only for a short time, and before long I felt lonely, apprehensive and oppressed by mental suffering. Yet at the same time the headmaster had sent Collin a report on me, which I still have, in which he expresses a completely different view of me and my abilities from the one I and those around me heard from his lips or could imagine him saying. If I had been able to believe he could say such things of me it would have given me strength. It would have made me mentally strong and my whole being would have benefited. I had every day to hear him deny that I possessed any mental ability whatever and to be addressed as an idiot, a child with no more intelligence than a dumb animal, while yet at the same time he wrote earnest letters about me to my patron Collin, who, on constantly hearing from me how dissatisfied the headmaster was with me and my limited capacity for learning, had demanded an explanation:

"H. C. Andersen was sent to Slagelse Grammar School at the end of 1822, and, despite his rather advanced age, he was placed in the school's second lowest class because of his lack of even the most elementary education. As he is naturally gifted and possessed of a lively imagination and warm sensitivity, he understood and mastered the various subjects with a degree of success dependent on his liking for them. However, he made such progress in every subject that it was right to allow him gradually to be promoted from the lower classes to the top class where he is now, the only difference

72

being that he moved from Slagelse to Elsinore together with the undersigned.

He has hitherto been enabled to study by virtue of people's charity, and I cannot deny that he has shown himself in every respect worthy of this. His is endowed with excellent abilities, and in certain subjects can even be said to be outstanding. He has consistently worked diligently, and his conduct has been based on a delightful good nature such as can serve as a model for the pupils in a school. Moreover I can add that if he continues his praiseworthy efforts he will be ready for the Academy in October 1828.

As the three qualities of ability, diligence and excellent conduct, which a school teacher so often seeks but so rarely finds combined in one pupil, are unmistakably to be seen in Hans Christian Andersen, I can only recommend him for any support that might be made available to him to enable him to continue on the course on which he has now embarked, and from which, indeed, his advanced age scarcely permits him to withdraw. Not merely his honest disposition, but his faithful perseverance and unmistakable talent are a guarantee that whatever is expended on his progress will in no way be wasted."

Elsinore, the 18th of July, 1826
S. Meisling,

Doctor of Philosophy and Headmaster
Elsinore Grammar School

As I say, I had no knowledge of this report, which reveals so much kindness towards me that it ought to be made known. I was completely cowed and had neither belief nor confidence in myself. I received a few affectionate lines from Collin:

Do not lose courage, my dear Andersen, take a grip on yourself. Be calm and steady, and then you will see that everything will be all right. Your headmaster means you well. His behaviour is perhaps a little different from that of others, but it nevertheless achieves its purpose. Perhaps more next time, for I have much to do at the moment.

May God give you strength!

Yours, Collin.

The beautiful landscape surrounding us must have made a lively impression on me, but I only dared look at it from a distance. I hardly ever went out. As soon as school was over, the gate was shut and I had to remain in the stuffy classroom. It was still warm there, I was told, so I could do my homework there. Afterwards I would play with the headmaster's children or sit in my own small room. For a long time the school library was my living room and bedroom, and there I breathed amid the old folios and school programmes. No one came to visit me, for my playmates didn't dare. They didn't want to meet the headmaster. My life in Elsinore still comes back to me sometimes in bad dreams. I once more sit trembling on my bench; I cannot and dare not answer and angry looks are directed at me; I am surrounded by the echoes of mockery and laughter. These were difficult, cheerless times. I lived in the headmaster's house in Elsinore for a year and a quarter, and sometimes I was on the point of succumbing to a treatment which gradually became harsher and harsher, much too harsh. Every evening my prayer to God was that He would take this cup from me or that I might not live to see the next day. In school the headmaster took a delight in mocking me, turning me into a laughing-stock and talking of my lack of intelligence. And when school was over I was left in his house.

Charles Dickens has given us several portrayals of poor children in their distress, and had he known the life I was experiencing, what I felt and how much I suffered, he would not have thought it less cruel or more amusing than what he has described. There are certain things in one's life which are so intimately bound up with the lives of others that one can scarcely regard them as one's own private experiences. For this reason I have nothing to say of that time, just as even then I never mentioned it to anyone and never complained to any of those around me. I complained only of myself, for I was convinced that I had chosen the wrong course as I seemed to be nothing but either a figure of fun or one to be pitied. The letters I wrote to Collin at the time are evidence of a sombre mood of despair. That they moved him deeply he told me himself, but there was nothing to be done about it. He assumed and could not but take for granted that the real trouble lay in my own mind, a sort of nervous strain, and not that it came from an outside source as was actually the case. My mind was flexible, open to every ray of sunshine, but that was something I only experienced during the few days, once a year during the holidays, when I was allowed to go to Copenhagen.

To be moved from my home in the school to the family life awaiting me in Copenhagen, to the home in the capital that was the direct opposite of the other, was a remarkable contrast, almost the stuff of fairy tale. I stayed at the home of Admiral Wulff, whose wife had developed a maternal affection for me and whose children received me warmly and like a dear friend. This family was the first to adopt me as though I were their own child and I found a happy home with them. The Naval Academy, of which Wulff became the Principal, was then situated in one of the Royal Palaces of Amalienborg. I was given a room overlooking the square, and I remember that on my first evening there I stood at my window and looked out, and suddenly I remembered Aladdin's words as he gazes down from his sumptuous palace on the square below: "Down there I once did walk, a pauper boy". I felt that God had guided me mercifully and lovingly; my very soul was filled with gratitude.

During all the time I had been in Slagelse I had scarcely written more than three or four short poems; two of these, *The Soul* and *To My Mother* are to be found in my *Collected Poems* and are among the oldest I still have. In Elsinore I only wrote two poems while I was at school, *New Year's Night* and *The Dying Child*, the latter being the first of all my poems to attract attention and meet with people's approval; it was the first to be widely known and translated into other languages. I took it with me to Copenhagen and read it aloud to the people I knew. Some listened to it for the sake of the poem, while others listened in order to enjoy themselves at my expense and that of my Funen accent. I received a great deal of praise and from most people a lecture on modesty and the need not to gain too big an opinion of myself. Indeed one of my well-intentioned patrons said to me, later repeating it in a letter: "For Heaven's sake, do not imagine you are a poet just because you can write a few lines of poetry. It can turn into an obsession with you. What would you say if I went around believing I was going to be the Empress of Brazil! You would think it was madness; and so is your believing you are a poet." But that was not what I believed. Had it been, it would have been a life-giving spark and a comfort to me. Otherwise my clumsy behaviour was what I was most told about during my stay in Copenhagen. And then the fact that without further ado I was in the habit of saying what I thought. Yet the days in Copenhagen were the time when I lived. There I saw and met the man whom I revered and looked up to more than anyone else, the poet Adam Oehlenschläger. His praises were sung by all around me, and he meant more to me than anyone else. How great was my delight one evening in a brightly lit room where I was deeply conscious that my suit was the poorest of them all and, mindful of this, had retired to a place under the long curtains hanging there, when he came up to me and shook me by the hand. I could have fallen on my knees before him. We often saw each other in Wulff's home. Weyse, too, was a guest there, who also spoke kindly to me; I listened to him improvising on the piano. Brøndsted, who had returned to Denmark, livened up the evenings with his eloquence and Wulff himself read passages from his translation of Byron. The elegant, cultured man of the world, Adler, the friend of Christian the Eighth, completed the circle in which Oehlenschläger's young daughter, Charlotte, surprised me with her joie de vivre and gaiety. How lovely they were, those days and evenings I spent in Copenhagen.

After the holidays I returned from such a home to the headmaster's residence. Even under less severe conditions it would have meant a great change, but now it was as though I were being sent to a mental torture chamber. One day the headmaster came in to see me: he had heard from Copenhagen, from Oehlenschläger I think, that I had read a poem I had written called *The Dying Child*. I could see on the man's face what was going to happen; he fixed his penetrating eyes on me and demanded to see the poem, adding that if he found a single spark of poetry in it he would forgive me. Trembling all over I gave him the poem; he read it, laughed and said it was nothing but a lot of sentimental nonsense, and then gave vent to his anger in a stream of cruel words. Had he done this in the belief that I was wasting all my time writing poetry or that I was a child who needed dealing with in that way – all of which his report on me contradicts – the intention might have been good enough, but here it was surely merely his mood, a passing whim, that was the cause of my suffering. Day after day my situation became increasingly unhappy; I suffered such mental anguish that I was in danger of completely breaking down unless a change soon took place. It was not merely during school hours that I felt like a hunted bird, but in my room and in the family's sitting room as well. This was the darkest and most cheerless time in all my life. My other teachers saw it and understood. One of them was called Werliin. He is now a clergyman, and in those days he taught us Hebrew. He went to Copenhagen and visited Collin and told him how I was being treated both in school and in the headmaster's home. Collin decided on the spot that I should immediately be moved to Copenhagen and given private tuition. The headmaster was absolutely furious when he discovered this. When I went to take leave of him and thank him for all he had done for me, his last words to me were that I would never be able to pass my final examination, and that, even if they were printed, my poems would rot as waste paper in the bookshop storerooms, while I myself would end my days in the lunatic asylum. Profoundly shocked, I left him.

Several years later, when my works were being read and *The Improvisatore* had been published, I encountered him in Copenhagen. He offered me his hand in reconciliation, and said graciously and kindly that he had mistaken me and treated me wrongly, but now I was lucky enough to have firm ground under my feet and need no longer concern myself about him.

These were the gentle words of reconciliation; the dark and heavy days through which I had passed had also brought blessings to my life.

The late Reverend Ludvig Müller, who was then a student but subsequently became known for the zeal with which he studied Scandinavian languages and history, became my tutor. I rented a tiny garret over in Vingaardsstræde. This is the room I describe in *Only a Fiddler*, with its sloping walls up under the roof. And in *A Picture*

Book without Pictures that is the room the moon visits, just as in those days I saw it move across the tower of St. Nicholas' Church, which at that time was not hidden by tall houses, for there was no St. Nicholas' Street in those days. I still had a small fixed sum from the King to live on, but my tuition had to be paid for, so I had to save on everything else. A few families invited me to take my dinner in their homes, and I managed to find somewhere to go to almost every day. I lived by having my dinner with different people in turn, just as many a poor student in Copenhagen still does. I found plenty of variety in this and gained an insight into the family life of different sorts of people, something from which I have also derived considerable benefit. I studied diligently, and as I had done very well in certain subjects at Elsinore, for instance arithmetic and geography, these were more or less left to me to deal with alone. Most of our time had to be devoted to Greek and Latin. Something for which I had always received excellent marks in Slagelse and Elsinore, but which my new tutor thought me weakest in, was religion, and Müller, who in every other way was an excellent tutor, believed that it must be improved. My knowledge of religion, which even when I went to the charity school had been said to be very good indeed, and in which I was always thought to be an excellent pupil while at the grammar school, was something that Müller decided was weak, far too weak. He kept strictly to the words of the Bible, and these I knew, for from my very first days at school I had clearly understood everything I heard or was taught in connection with them. The Bible spoke to me through my feelings, and I felt that God was infinite love; I refused to acknowledge anything contradicting this such as a fiery Hell, in which the flames are *eternal*, and I said so with the full force of my conviction. After having been a timorous child on a school bench I now freely and confidently put forward these beliefs and opinions of mine; I expressed myself like a child of nature, and my teacher, who was one of the noblest and kindest of men, but who adhered to the literal sense of the Scriptures, often felt rather anxious for me. We argued the matter, while the same sacred flame burned equally brightly in both our hearts. But it did me a world of good to talk to this unspoiled and gifted young man who had just as many peculiar features as I had. On the other hand something that was not part of my nature, but which was characteristic of me at the time, was the desire, not to mock, but to play with my own noblest feelings and to regard the intellect as the most important thing in the world. This new manner of behaving was a phase I had to pass through. At school the headmaster had so completely misunderstood my extremely sensitive nature, mocking and suppressing my exuberant feelings that once I felt myself freed from this pressure I moved in a direction that was only an adopted affectation. My timorousness was transformed, not into ebullience but into an unsuccessful attempt to seem different from what I really was. I mocked feelings and tried to convince myself that I had done away with them, and yet at the same time I could quite well go around depressed for a whole day and be quite unhappy because I had encountered an unfriendly face where I expected to find kindness. I now parodied the titles of the poems I had earlier written amid tears and from the bottom of my saddened soul and furnished them with ridiculous refrains. The whole of such a poem, with a few alterations, entitled *The Cat's Complaint* is to be found in *The Journey on Foot*. Another poem that I wrote with deep feeling was *The Sick Poet*. Throughout this period I only wrote a few poems, but they were all humorous, for instance *The Evening*, *The Dreadful Hour*, *Complaint to the Moon* and *The Pigs*. A complete change had taken place within me; the tender plant had been transplanted and was beginning to send up fresh shoots.

Wulff's eldest daughter Henriette, a clever and lively girl who throughout her life remained a faithful sister and friend to me through all the changes brought by the years, was the only person who could understand me at that time. She encouraged me in the humour that was to be seen in my poems. She won all my confidence and valiantly defended me against all the petty attacks to which, especially on account of my personality, I was exposed in her circle. She was a kind sister to me and had a great deal of influence on my moods.

About that time, too, a lively new trend was making its appearance in Danish literature and catching people's attention. Politics played only a small part in their interests, and literature and the theatre were the subjects that everyone talked about. Thanks to Collin having taken his part against the other directors, who were not in favour of producing his *King Salomon*, Johan Ludvig Heiberg, who enjoyed a high standing among Danish writers on account of his excellent works *Psyche* and *Walter the Potter*, had recently introduced the vaudeville to the Danish stage. The vaudeville was a Danish product, people said, our own flesh and blood, and so it was received with delight and quite took the place of everything else. Thalia gave a carnival performance in the Royal Theatre, and Heiberg was her choice. It was at a dinner party at H. C. Ørsted's that I first made the acquaintance of Heiberg. He was elegant, spoke well and was the favourite of the moment, and I liked him. He spoke kindly to me, and I later visited him at his home. When he heard my humorous poems he thought them worth publishing in his excellent weekly journal, *Den flyvende Post*. *The Evening* and *The Dreadful Hour* were the first to appear, though without any name attached, only with the letter H – –, which was meant to represent H. C. A. However, everyone thought it stood for Heiberg, and this belief was doubtless to the great advantage of the poems, which were a great success. I can clearly remember the evening the newspaper appeared with the two poems in it. I was together with a family who were very kind to me but considered all I wrote to be no more than a bit of versifying, as they often informed me – with the best of intentions of course. The husband came into the parlour with *Den flyvende Post* in his hand. He was smiling all over his face and said, "There are two wonderful poems in *Den flyvende Post* this evening. He is a clever chap, this Heiberg." And then he read both my poems for the rest of us. My heart was beating wildly, but I did not say a word. However, a young lady who was present and knew I had written the poems could not hide her delight at the pleasure they gave, so she said, "It was Andersen who wrote those poems!" There was a long pause; everyone was silent; the husband said not another word, but looked at me and left the room. No one mentioned the poems any more, and I was very upset. The only poem which had previously been published in any other paper in Copenhagen was *The Dying Child*. I had written this while at school, and it was only with the help of one of the theatre managers called Olsen that I managed to get it published, for no one was otherwise prepared to accept a poem written by a schoolboy. While I was still at school I sent it to Mr. Søeborg, the writer of the song *In a Hundred*

Years All Will Be Gone, and he promised to get it published in the Jutlandic magazine *Læsefrugter*. However, the editor there would have nothing to do with a poem by someone still at school. Finally it was published in *Kjøbenhavnsposten*, and soon afterwards J. L. Heiberg printed it in *Den flyvende Post* with the comment that he was pleased to publish it even though it had already appeared elsewhere. This was the first gratifying sign of recognition that I had received, but the general opinion among those around me was that my poetic talent was negligible. One of our less important authors, but one who enjoyed a distinguished position in the city, invited me to dinner at his home. He told me that there was to be a New Year publication and that he had been asked for a contribution. I told him that so had I, and that I had promised them a short poem.

"Oh, so they are going to take all kinds in that book!" exclaimed the man angrily. "Well then, he doesn't need anything from me! I don't think I'll bother letting him have anything now."

Words of that sort might perhaps be of little importance in themselves and scarcely seem worth mentioning, but at the time they were of profound and painful significance for me and sufficient to upset me for several days.

My tutor lived in Christianshavn. I went out there twice a day, and on the way my thoughts were filled with nothing but my homework. On the way home I breathed freely and thought of neither homework nor learning. All sorts of colourful, poetical images passed through my mind, but not one was ever put on paper; four or five humorous poems were all I wrote during the whole of that year. They were, as Bastholm says in the letter I have quoted above, "only to give expression to my feelings". They disturbed me less once they had been brought to rest on paper than they would have if they had gone on living in my mind.

I took my examination in September 1828. Oehlenschläger happened to be Dean that year and he kindly held out his hand to welcome me as a member of the University. It filled my thoughts and moved me as though it were a great and momentous occasion. I was already 23 years old but still very much a child, both in the way in which I behaved and the way in which I spoke; a little story from that time will perhaps give some idea of this. Shortly before the day of my examination I met a young man at dinner at H. C. Ørsted's; he was very quiet and shy, and as I had not seen him before I thought he must just have come from the country. I blithely asked him, "Do you have an examination too this year?"

"Yes," he said with a little smile, "I have."

"Yes, so have I," I said, and then I embarked on a lively discussion of this event which was of such importance to me. I talked to him as to a school friend and then he turned out to be the professor who was to examine me in mathematics. He was that excellent, brilliant Professor von Schmidten, famous for looking so much like Napoleon that people in Paris are said to have confused the two. When we met at the examination table we were both embarrassed. He was just as kind-hearted as intelligent. He so much wanted to give me courage and did not quite know how to do it. So he leaned over to me and whispered, "What is your first poem going to be about after the examination?" I looked at him in amazement and nervously replied, "I don't know. But are you not going to ask me some questions in mathematics? Please don't make them too difficult!"

"Do you know any?" he asked in the same tone of voice. "Yes, I'm quite good at mathematics. At Elsinore School I was even sometimes allowed to go through the exercises for the others, and I was given 'Excellent' in my report; but now I am nervous." Thus the professor and the candidate chatted to each other, and when, during the examination, I broke all his pens in my eagerness, he said nothing but quietly put one of them aside so as to be able to write my report.

After I had taken my examination, all the colourful fancies and ideas I seemed to be pursued by on my walks home from my tutor's flew out into the world like a swarm of bees in the form of my first work, *A Journey on Foot from Holmens Canal to the Eastern Tip of Amager*; it was a strange, humorous book, a sort of fantastic arabesque, which, however, gives quite a good indication of my personality and my point of view at that time, especially in the desire to play with everything, and to make tearful fun of my own feelings. This poetical improvisation was varied and colourful, quite a tapestry, but no publisher had the courage to print this youthful work of mine and so I risked doing it myself. A few days after the book appeared, Reitzel the publisher bought the rights for a second edition, and indeed later for a third edition, too. Up in Fahlun a copy was made of the Danish version, something which otherwise has only happened in the case of Oehlenschläger's most important works. A German translation has appeared in Hamburg within the last few years. All Copenhagen read my book. I heard only that people were delighted with it. Admittedly, I was given a sound scolding by a distinguished admirer, but that verged on the comical: the person concerned had noticed that I had satirised the Royal Theatre in the *Journey on Foot*. He considered this not merely inappropriate but even ungrateful; inappropriate because it was a Royal Theatre, and therefore, he said, the King's property, and ungrateful because I had free access to it. This reprimand, comical in itself although deriving from a sensible person, was completely drowned in the delight and praise which, as I say, was all I heard. I was on the crest of a wave, I had passed my final school examination, I was a poet, and my dearest wish had been fulfilled.

Heiberg gave the book a friendly and charming review in *Maanedsskrift for Litteratur*. Several fragments had already been published in his *Flyvende Post*, and, as is to be seen from Poul Møller's writings, these were read, indeed devoured, by readers up in Norway, all of which annoyed Poul Møller, who was merciless in his criticism of the book. But I knew nothing of this at the time, and it never occurred to me that there was anyone who did not like my *Journey on Foot to Amager*.

About two hundred young men and women took their final school examination that year, and among them were several who wrote poems and had even had them published. It was said for fun that four great and twelve lesser poets finished school that year, and indeed you could make up this number if you were not too fussy. The four major ones were Arnesen, whose first vaudeville, *The Intrigue in the Comedy Playhouse,* was performed by the Royal Theatre within a year of his taking his examination, F. J. Hansen, who at just that time published *Reading for the World of Culture*, Hollard Nielsen, and finally, as the fourth of them, Hans Christian Andersen. Among the twelve lesser writers, there was one, however, who has undoubtedly since become one of the great poets in Danish literature, that is to say Paludan-Müller, the author of *Adam Homo*. At that time, nothing by him had yet been published or was known; it was merely whispered among his friends that he wrote poetry. One day I received a letter from him in which he suggested to me that the two of us together should begin to publish a weekly magazine.

"You will perhaps be surprised that this letter should come from me," he says, "by whom you have not yet seen any work that could indicate that I have sufficient talent to carry out such a proposal. Yet I think I can quite confidently assure you that I am by no means the stepson of the Muses, as I believe is proven by the collection of poems which I have composed for my own amusement and which is at home in my drawer." And now followed the plan and the conditions: the review was not to consist of translations or fragments from other papers, the whole of it should consist of original work, and so forth. As a short sample of his work he enclosed a little poem called *The Smile*. However, I had no desire to be tied to a magazine, so nothing came of it all. Before the publication of the *Journey on Foot*, Carl Bagger and I had arranged that we should publish a joint collection of our poems in one volume. However, when my book attracted attention and found so many readers Bagger declared firmly and proudly that our poems could no longer be published together, as it would be as though he was being held aloft by my work. So the plan, but not our friendship, was abandoned. On the other hand no friendship developed between me and Paludan-Müller, who subseqently made a brilliant name for himself. Among my fellow students and friends I enjoyed a great reputation and I went about in a youthful poetical intoxication, laughing and seeking the amusing side of everything. During those early days, in the midst of all this merriment, I wrote my first dramatic work, the heroic vaudeville in rhymed verse, *Love on St. Nicholas' Tower or What the Rear Stalls Say*, which, as the *Maanedsskrift for Litteratur* also remarked, suffered from the serious fault that it was a satire on fate tragedies, something we had already left far behind. Yet when the play was produced it was given an enthusiastic reception by my friends, who shouted out, "Long live the author!" I neither looked to the future nor thought of it. I was overwhelmed with joy and attached so much importance to it, an importance which the play did not justify. I could not contain my happiness but rushed out of the theatre, into the street straight to Collin's house, where I found Mrs Collin alone at home. Almost in a state of collapse, I sank into a chair and sobbed and wept violently. Mrs. Collin was extremely sympathetic but had no idea what it was all about and so she began to comfort me by saying, "Don't be so upset about it, you know Oehlenschläger and many other great poets have been hissed off stage before now."

"Yes, but they have not hissed at me," I sobbed. "They have clapped and cheered me."

Oh, what a blissfully happy creature I was then! I thought everyone was so kind; I had the courage of a poet and the vivacity of youth. All homes began to be thrown open to me and I flew from one circle to another in blissful satisfaction at my own achievement. But in the midst of all these moving days I studied very diligently, and, without the help of a tutor, I prepared for what was called the second examination, the philologicum and philosophicum, which I passed with distinction. A quite curious incident took place while H. C. Ørsted was examining me. I had answered all his questions correctly; he was pleased at this, and as I was finishing and about to go he stopped me and said, "There is just one more little question!" His face was beaming with kindness. "Tell me what you know about electro-magnetism."

"I have never heard that word," I replied.

"Think hard; you have answered everything so well up to now, and you must know something about electro-magnetism."

"There is nothing about it in your chemistry book," I said firmly.

"That is true," he replied, "but I have spoken about it in my lectures."

"I have been to them all except one, so it must just have been on that day you talked about it, for I do not know the least thing about it; I do not even know the word." Ørsted smiled at this unusual admission, nodded and said, "It's a pity you didn't know it, as I would otherwise have given you a distinction, but now you will receive a credit, for you have answered very well."

Later when I went to visit Ørsted I asked him to tell me a little about electro-magnetism, and now I heard about it for the first time and how he was concerned with it. Ten years later when an electro-magnetic wire was demonstrated to us in the College of Technology it was I who, after a written request from Ørsted himself, made the electro-magnetic telegraph known. I wrote under the pseudonym Y–, and I believe it was in the newspaper *Kjøbenhavnsposten*. I explained how the telegraph stretched from the front to the back of the College of Technology, and I tried to persuade the people of Copenhagen to go and see this "invention which science owes to a Dane".

Now I had passed my examination and had achieved the best possible result. My first collection of poems was published towards Christmas, and to the best of my knowledge and understanding, it was heartily approved by public and critics alike. I liked best to listen only to the tinkling bells of praise. I was infinitely young and infinitely happy; and life lay before me bathed in sunshine.

IV

I had as yet only seen a small part of my native country; I had been to a few places in Funen and Zealand as well as to the cliffs of Møn, which in no way corresponded to my expectations. These were exaggerated in themselves and had been made even more so by Molbech's descriptions of the cliffs. Now, in the summer of 1830, I was to go on a longer journey; I wanted to see Jutland and travel right over to the North Sea coast and after that get to know the whole of my native island of Funen. I had no idea how many serious problems this summer expedition was to bring into my life or what change was to take place in my innermost being. I was especially looking forward to seeing the Jutland heath and to the possibility of meeting a family of gypsies there. My interest had been awakened by tales I had heard as well as by the stories of Steen Blicher. That part of the country was not visited so regularly then as it is now. A steamship service had only recently been started. A bad, slow ship called the Dania took something like twenty-four hours to do the journey, although this was an unbelievable speed in comparison with what was normal at that time. Steamships had not as yet gained people's confidence. The previous year, I had done the journey on such a vessel, the Caledonia, the first steamship to be seen in Danish waters. The crews of all the small sailing vessels poured scorn on it and nick-named it "Splashy Molly". Ørsted was of course delighted with this wonderful invention and was quite full of the topic, and one day at a dinner at which I was present it was quite amusing to hear an old sailor, a relative of Ørsted, complaining bitterly about "these confounded smoke-ships". "Ever since the creation of the world," he said, "we've been content with sensible ships propelled by the wind, but then people had to go and change everything; there's never one of these chimney pots goes past but that I take out my megaphone and berate them as long as they are within earshot." It was quite an event in those days to travel by steamship. This sounds almost unbelievable today. As far as we are concerned, steamships are so much part of the age in which we live that their invention seems to be something from the distant past. And we forget that it is such a short time ago that legend has it, although we are not sure about this, that on seeking refuge with the English Napoleon saw the arrival of the first steamship.

To spend a whole night sailing through the Kattegat on this new sort of vessel was a great event which thrilled my imagination, and I was looking forward to it. However, we struck bad weather and I was seasick, and we didn't arrive in Århus until the following evening. Both there and in all the other towns in Jutland people knew my *Journey on Foot* and my humorous poems and I was well received. I drove across the heath, and all the strange things I saw here made a deep impression on me. However, the weather was not good. I had not taken a great many clothes in which to travel, and the wet, biting sea mist affected me badly. So from Viborg, where I stayed for a few days, I had to turn back and go down towards the south east, giving up the west coast completely. However, that did not prevent me from my writing my *North Sea Fantasy* and *A Picture of the West Coast of Jutland*, neither of which I had ever seen, but only knew from what others had told me about them. Now I saw the countryside around Skanderborg, Vejle and Kolding, going on then to Funen where I was entertained in several large manor houses. I spent several weeks just outside Odense as the welcome guest of Iversen the printer's widow at her country residence of Mariehøj near where the canal runs past the castle hill at Næsbyhoved. From my earliest childhood I had seen this as the ideal country residence. All over the little garden there were inscriptions and verses saying what you ought to think and feel in each spot. A little battery of wooden cannons had been constructed pointing towards the canal and all the passing ships. There was a guard-room and a sentry-box with a wooden soldier in it, all beautiful and child-like. Here I stayed at the home of this delightful, gifted old lady who was surrounded by a host of charming and intelligent grandchildren, girls, all of them. The eldest of them, Henriette, later made her public appearance with the two short novels, *Aunty Anna* and *An Authoress' Daughter*, of which I shall have more to say later. The weeks passed here in merriment and delight. I wrote a few humorous poems including *The*

Thief of my Heart, and apart from this I spent some time working on a novel called *Christian the Second's Dwarf*, for which I was given a good deal of historical notes and information about that period by the learned old antiquarian, Vedel-Simonsen from Elvedgaard near Bogense. About sixteen pages of manuscript were completed, and these I read aloud to Ingemann, who found them extremely attractive. It was on these that he based the favourable remarks he wrote on my behalf when soon after this I applied for a bursary on which to travel abroad. But I had done with humorous poems, for the time being at least, and the novel, too, was laid aside. For a new chord had been struck in me: one of the profoundest feelings, one of those of which I had so often made fun, was going to take its revenge.

During my summer excursion I had stayed in the home of a wealthy family in one of our smaller market towns. There, suddenly and with overwhelming power, a new world was revealed to me, a world of vast proportions which nevertheless is contained in the four lines I wrote then:

> Two eyes of brown I here have seen,
> There lies my home, my world serene.
> So bright they are, with child-like peace,
> For me, that sight will never cease.

We met again later that autumn in Copenhagen. I was full of new plans for my life. I would give up writing verse, for what could that lead to? I would study for the Church. She was my only thought, but there was a disappointment in store for me: she loved someone else, and she married him. Not until many years later did I feel and admit that this, too, was the best thing that could happen, both for me and for her. Perhaps she didn't even have any idea how profound my feelings were and what an effect they had on me. She married a good man and is an excellent wife and a happy mother. May God give them His blessing.

Parody was the most noticeable element both in my *Journey on Foot* and most of the other things I had written, and quite a lot of people disapproved of this and thought that such a tendency would not lead to any good results. The critics said so and repeated it at the very time when the quality they were attacking had been quite replaced by a deeper sensitivity. A new collection of poems, *Fantasies and Sketches*, which appeared about New Year, were evidence of what I had at heart. A version of the story of my own heart was the subject of a serious vaudeville, *To Meet and to Part*, which I wrote and in which the only difference was that love in this case was mutual. The play was performed five years later in the Royal Theatre.

Among the young friends I had in Copenhagen at that time was Orla Lehmann. His sparkling vitality and eloquence appealed greatly to me and bound me close to him, and as he at the same time revealed his sensitivity and profound feelings I was fond of his company. His father hailed from Holstein, so a great deal of German was both spoken and read in his home. Heine had recently made his appearance, and his poems enraptured and elevated the minds of young folk. One day I went out to visit Lehmann who lived with his family in Valby, and he jubilantly declaimed a verse by Heine as he came to greet me:

Thalatta, Thalatta, du ewiges Meer!

Thalatta, thalatta, thou eternal sea!

And now we read Heine together; the afternoon and the evening passed and the night wore on. I had to stay there until the next morning, but I had got to know a poet who sang as though from my very soul, plucking the most vibrant strings in it. He took the place of Hoffmann, who had had a considerable influence on me at that time, as can be seen from the *Journey on Foot*. So there were only three writers who so to speak became absorbed in the blood of my youth, authors in whose works I was completely lost for a time. They were Walter Scott, Hoffmann and Heine.

Day by day I increasingly fell under the spell of a sickly sort of humour and felt an urge to seek the melancholy things in life and to linger over its more sombre aspects. I became irritable and was more inclined to remember the criticism than the praise that came my way. This tendency was rooted in my starting school at such a late age, the fact that I was continually pushed, and the compulsion I felt both from within and without to produce and publish works which were not yet ready for publication. My education had resembled a hothouse, and I had been forced on from one class to another until I could take my final examination, all of which had resulted in my being left far behind in some respects, as was most noticeable in my grammar, that is to say my ability to spell consistently according to the accepted spelling rules of the day. So, in the *Journey on Foot* there were a few mistakes, not printing errors but spelling mistakes that conflicted with the normal way of writing the words. I could have avoided any unpleasantness by paying some student or other to read the proofs for me, a task at which I was not proficient. But I omitted to do so. So now people dwelt on these mistakes that any first-year student could have dealt with better than I. They lingered over them, pointed them out, laughed at them and censured me for them, while, on the other hand, they took little notice of the better, poetical qualities in the work. I know of people who read my poems only to find faults in the language or to see how often I used one and the same expression, for instance the word "beautiful", which, people said, did not make my work "beautiful". One person, who is now a parson in Jutland but had then just finished his university training and who wrote vaudevilles and criticism, could not even refrain from going through some of my poems when visiting friends one day when I was present. He did it in such a way that a little girl of six, who had listened in amazement to everything he said about my work being terrible, went and took the book when he put it down and a slight pause ensued. Then in all innocence she pointed to the word "and" on one page and said, "There is still one little word you have not complained about." He felt how telling the child's words were, blushed and kissed her. I suffered under all this, and moreover the oppression under which I had suffered while at school still made itself felt and indeed seemed to regain more and more of its old strength, so that I quietly bowed my head and suffered what people said with inconceivable patience. And they all made the most of any opportunity that presented itself. I was too sensitive and unforgivably patient. Everyone knew this, and so a small number of people became almost cruel. The bonds of dependence and gratitude were often thoughtlessly or unconsciously put to a hard test. Everyone lectured me, and almost everyone said that I was being spoiled by praise so that *they* at least would tell me the truth. Thus I constantly heard of nothing but my faults, of weaknesses both imagined and real. On some occasions, however, I suppose my feelings did reveal themselves, and this often occurred when people who were perhaps materially rich but of limited intelligence and artistic judgement, made some empty but completely crushing comment on my work, that I forgot to be calm and tearfully but vehemently exclaimed that I would be a poet whose name was highly honoured. People pounced on such words and scattered them like evil seeds, which immediately sprang up and blossomed as the plants of vanity and foolishness. Everyone knew these things. "He is the vainest creature in existence," people said everywhere, though they added, "But he is such a good child." And at this time I was often so lonely as to be in danger of giving up and perishing because of a lack of confidence in myself and my abilities. I remembered every word of criticism and, just as in the darkest days at school, I had a feeling that all my talents were only going to lead to disappointment. I was not far from believing this, but I could not always tolerate hearing other people say it to me in harsh and provocative language. If I then made some proud but ill-considered reply they used it as a whip to scourge me, and when those who whip us are those we love most, then the lashes are changed into scorpions.

Collin believed that it would be a good thing for me to go away on a short trip abroad, even if only for a few weeks, so that I could move among strangers, tear myself away from my usual surroundings and receive some new impressions. By virtue of hard work and careful living I had managed to save up a small sum of money, and with this I would be able to spend a couple of weeks visiting northern Germany.

It was in the spring of 1831 I left Denmark for the first time. I visited Lübeck and Hamburg. Everything surprised me and filled my thoughts. There were still no railways here. A broad, sandy road led across the Lüneburg Heath, which looked just as I imagined after reading about it in Baggesen's much admired *The Labyrinth*. I arrived in Brunswick and saw mountains for the first time in my life. They were the Harz Mountains, and there I went on foot from Goslar across the Brocken to Halle. The world expanded wonderfully before me. My good spirits returned like birds of passage, but sorrow is like a flock of sparrows which stay behind and build in the nests left by the migratory birds.

In the book at the top of the Brocken, where all the hosts of travellers write their names, feelings and impressions, I, too, had written of mine in a little verse:

> Above the clouds I stand up here,
> Yet must my heart confess
> That heaven seemed to be more near
> When I her hand could press.

The following year a friend told me that he had visited the Brocken and found my verse, under which some fellow countryman of mine had written, "Dear little Andersen, save your verses for Elmquist's *Fruits for Reading* and don't trouble us with them when we are abroad, for they will never find their way there unless you go and write them there yourself."

In Dresden I made the acquaintance of Ludwig Tieck, to whom Ingemann had given me a letter of introduction; I heard him read from Shakespeare's *Henry IV* one evening, and when I took leave of him he wrote a few words in my album, wished me success as a poet, embraced me and kissed me; it all made a profound impression on me. He fixed his big, kind, blue eyes on me in a way I have not forgotten. I wept as I left him and I prayed most fervently to God for strength to follow the course for which I longed with all my heart and all my thoughts, for strength to express what I felt within my breast, so that when I saw Tieck again I might be recognised and appreciated by him.

We did not see each other again until several years later, by which time my later works had been translated into German and well received. I felt his true handshake, the handshake of the man who, it has always seemed to me, gave me the kiss of consecration outside my own native country and among foreign peoples.

In Berlin a letter from Ørsted was intended to introduce me to Chamisso. The tall, serious man with honest eyes and long curls hanging down to his shoulders opened the door himself when I rang the bell. He read the letter, and in some way I do not comprehend we understood each other from the very beginning. I felt confidence in him and expressed myself freely and naturally in his presence, even if it was in bad German. I gave him a copy of my *Poems*, and he was the first person to translate me and introduce me into Germany. He then wrote these words of me in *Morgenblatt für gebildete Stände* The Morning Paper for the Educated Classes:

"Mit Witz, Laune, Humor und folksthümlicher Naivetät begabt, hat Andersen auch tieferen Nachhall erweckende Töne in seiner Gewalt. Er versteht besonders, mit Behaglichkeit aus wenigen, leicht hingeworfenen treffenden Zügen kleine Bilder and *Landschaften ins Leben zu rufen, die aber oft zu örtlich-eigentümlich sind, um den anzusprechen, der in der Heimath des Dichters nicht selbst heimisch ist. Vielleicht ist, was von ihm übersetzt werden konnte, oder übersetzt worden ist, am wenigsten geeignet, ein Bild von ihm zu geben."*

"Possessed of wit, fancy, humour and the simplicity of the common people, Andersen also can produce notes that awaken deeper echoes. In particular by means of a few fleeting but vivid strokes he can easily bring to life small pictures and landscapes, which, however, are often too local in their inspiration to appeal to anyone who is not himself a native of the writer's homeland. Perhaps those works of his which could be translated or which have been translated are those least suited to give an impression of him."

After that Chamisso was always a faithful and understanding friend to me; his delight in what I wrote is to be seen in his letters to me, which are printed in the *Gesammt-Ausgabe* (complete edition) of his works.

My Copenhagen friends recognised that this short visit to Germany had been of great importance to me. I immediately wrote down my impressions from the journey and published them under the title of *Rambles in the Romantic Regions of the Harz Mountains and Saxon Switzerland*, a book that has since appeared in various German translations as well as in English. It was generally thought at home in Denmark that there were obvious signs of progress and development in this book, but the way in which people continued to behave to me did not lead me to feel that this was generally recognised. I could still see the same petty desire to pick on my faults and weaknesses and only pay attention to them, the same everlasting attempts to educate me, which I was weak enough to tolerate even from people who had nothing whatever to do with me. One day, after my *Rambles* had appeared, I found one of those who were constantly attempting to teach me with a copy in his hand. At the bottom of one page he had found the letters "fi" and at the top of the next page "do"; it was intended to be the name "Fido", but because it went on from one page to the next the mistake with the capital letter had been overlooked; now this man addressed me in a stern voice, asking, "What is this? Are you starting to write Fido with a small letter?" I was in a bad mood and also irritated to think that he really could believe this mistake was due to ignorance, and so I jestingly replied, "It was only a little puppy, so I didn't think it necessary to give him a capital F." But my joke was called arrogance, vanity and unwillingness to listen to reason.

Perhaps people will say that these were only small troubles, but it is the drops that hollow out the stone. I mention it in order to protest against the incessant accusations of vanity which, because people could point to no other fault in my private life, were kept in circulation and for many, many years were occasionally flung at me.

I liked to read my latest things to anyone I visited, for it was in what I had written that I lived and was happy, and I didn't have sufficient experience to know how rarely an author ought to do that, at least here in Denmark. Any and every lady or gentleman who can tinkle on a piano or sing a few songs may perfectly well take their music with them wherever they go, and settle down at the piano. No one ever comments on that. In addition, an author can read passages from works by others but not from his own, for that is vanity. People have had enough to say about Oehlenschläger on that account, for he liked to read his works aloud, and beautifully, for the various circles in which he moved. Many is the remark I have heard about myself because of the same thing, hearing it from people who thought they were making themselves sound interesting or superior to the writer. If they dared talk of Oehlenschläger in this way, and to such an extent as they did, how much further did they dare go when it was someone of no more importance than little Andersen?

My mood was occasionally sufficient to raise me above the bitterness by which I was surrounded. I discovered other people's weaknesses as well as my own, and it was at such a moment that I wrote my little poem *Tittle-Tattle*, which was understood as a lampoon and so in a host of periodicals and newspapers I was berated by the verse and prose of other fine folk. Indeed one gracious lady, whose home I frequently visited, sent for me and asked me with an inquisitorial look whether I visited any homes to which this poem might apply. It could certainly not, she said, apply to the circle in which she moved, but because I was a guest there, it might occur to people to maintain that they were the ones I had in mind! And what a dressing down I was given! One evening in the foyer of the theatre a well-dressed lady, a complete stranger to me, came towards me and with an indignant look stared me straight in the face and said, "Tittle-tattle merchant". I raised my hat to her. Courtesy is also an answer.

From the end of 1828 until 1839 I had to maintain myself entirely on what I could earn by writing. My earnings were not great, and it was difficult for me to cope, especially as I had to ensure that I was dressed more or less in keeping with the circles in which I moved. No fee was paid for contributions to periodicals and newspapers. To produce and produce and produce was wearying, in fact impossible. During that time I translated a couple of plays for the Royal Theatre, *La Quarantaine* and *La reine des seize ans*, and I wrote the librettos for a couple of operas. Through Hoffmann's works my attention had been drawn to Gozzi's comedies, and I had realised that one of these, *Il Corvo*, was an excellent subject for an opera libretto. I read it in Meisling's translation and was fascinated by it, and a few weeks later I had completed the libretto for an opera called *The Raven* which I gave to a young composer who was completely unknown but came from a musical family and had talent. He was the grandson of the man who composed the Danish National Anthem. My young composer was the present Professor J. P. E. Hartmann, who is now rightly known and honoured. There will be many people who will smile now on learning that in the letter I wrote to the management of the Royal Theatre on this occasion, I had, as it were, to accept responsibility for Hartmann's music. I had to recommend the man who is now the most important composer Denmark possesses and indeed is sufficiently important for us to be proud of him. I had so to speak to write a reference for him, stating that he was a man of talent and that he would produce a good and sound piece of work. My libretto for *The Raven* is lacking in freshness and poetry and I have already shown that I realise this by not including it in my *Collected Works*, with the exception of a chorus and a song which I later revised so that they could be performed at concerts. These are included in my *Poems*. As everyone knows, the subject is an old fairy tale, and I made great use of Gozzi's version as he has treated it so elegantly. Hartmann, however, has created from it a brilliant and beautiful composition which in time will probably regain its rightful place in the Danish opera repertoire from which it has long been excluded. All that is known of it are excerpts heard at concerts given by the Music Society, which has published the whole score along with the text belonging to it.

For another young composer, the conductor I. Bredal, I arranged Walter Scott's novel *The Bride of Lammermoor*. Both operas were produced but, although especially in the case of the latter the lyrical element cannot to my mind be considered unfortunate, I was subjected to absolutely merciless criticism. I was reproached for having maltreated the works of other poets, something that was said to me scornfully and mockingly and always in the strongest of terms. I remember a little thing about Oehlenschläger from that time that certainly reveals his irritability but equally his kind heart and the intensity of his feelings. *The Bride of Lammermoor* had been produced and had been acclaimed in the theatre. I took the printed text to Oehlenschläger who smilingly congratulated me on all this approval, a share of which belonged to me. He said I had come to it easily by taking the theme from Walter Scott and relying on the composer's support. It upset me to hear him speak in this way and tears came to my eyes. However, the moment he saw this he fell on my neck and kissed me, saying, "It is the others who make me so

97

cruel!" After this he was cordiality itself, making me a present of one of his books and writing both his and my name in it.

Weyse, the first man to take an active interest in me and a man whom I regularly met at Admiral Wulff's home, saw the first performance of *The Bride of Lammermoor* and was delighted with the way I had dealt with the subject. He came to me and told me that for a long time he had wanted to compose an opera based on the story in Walter Scott's *Kenilworth*. He had long ago asked Heiberg to write the libretto for him, but a promise was all he had received. Now, of course, I could do it, he said. This was something the two of us could work on together. – Little did I realise then what a storm would gather over my head if I did as the composer wished. – I needed money on which to live, but I can truly say it was not the fee I would earn that decided me to do it. No, I was both pleased and flattered to be able to work together with Weyse, our greatest and finest composer. I was filled with joy to think that I, the poor boy on whom he had been the first to take pity in Siboni's house, was now to embark on a kind of superior relationship with him, and I immediately began work. However, I had not finished half the libretto before it was known all over town, and cruel, harsh words were spoken of me. A couple of newspapers said that I was "tearing one work after another limb from limb". I was discouraged and decided to give up all thought of completing the task. However, Weyse both joked about it and talked seriously in order to dissuade me from this and to encourage me to continue, and he expressed great satisfaction with everything I had shown him. He asked me to go on, whatever I did, and his wishes meant more to me than all the harshness and censure of the crowd. He immediately started work on the composition and wrote the little aria in the second act, *The Shepherd with His Sheep*. It was not long before he had the whole of the opera libretto from me, and as it was written for him in every sense of the word, I left him to do with it whatever he wanted when I left to go abroad shortly afterwards. He added or changed whole verses in what I had written for him. So my text went:

> Through these murky passages
> Death's serpent winds its way.

But Weyse altered it to:

> From out this murky corner
> The snake of death unwinds.

And when I later made some critical comment on this he answered in his usual humorous manner, "In murky passages there is always a murky corner, and a snake is a little serpent, so you see that I have not altered your image at all, but have merely made it fit the music better." This excellent man had the peculiar characteristic that he could not read to the end of a book if he realised the ending was going to be tragic. So Emmy Robsart in *Kenilworth* had to marry Leicester. "Why make them unhappy when a few strokes of the pen can make things so good for them?" he said. "But it is not historically correct," I answered. "And in that case, what are we going to do about Queen Elizabeth?"

"She can say, 'Proud England, I am thine'," he replied and so I did indeed let the opera end with her uttering these words. *The Feast at Kenilworth* was performed, but I have only published the songs from it. Two of them have become very popular at home because of the melodies to them. These are: *Brothers, far away from here* and *The Shepherd with His Sheep*.

Anonymous attacks, offensive letters through the post in which unknown individuals scorned and mocked me in the most uncouth and puerile manner were part of my life during this period. However, that same year I nevertheless ventured to publish a new collection of poems, *The Twelve Months of the Year*, which the critics have subsequently recognised as a volume containing several of my best poems, though in those days it was rejected and trampled on by everybody.

The periodical *Maanedsskrift for Litteratur* was at its peak at that time. I believe it was H. C. Ørsted who started it. Among its contributors it counted several of the country's most highly respected scientists. It was an intellectual judgement seat of importance, although, as Ørsted did in fact admit, it lacked experts on aesthetic subjects. In that field they had often to take anyone they could find.

Unfortunately most people believe that their opinions are as good as anyone else's when it comes to aesthetic subjects. No one makes such a claim when it comes to sewing a pair of boots or preparing a meal. However, it has been and remains the case that even if a man can write a good Latin grammar or is a diligent collector of expressions for a dictionary, that same man can still be an incompetent judge in the realm of beauty. *Maanedsskrift for Litteratur* has provided ample evidence of this; and while it wrote its name according to a new and unaccustomed orthography, it was still strict in its condemnation of minor errors on my part.

It gradually became increasingly difficult for the directors to find a critic for works of literature. However, a man whose curious eagerness to write and talk about anything at all meant that he was always prepared to help them out was the historian Molbech, who at that time was manager of the theatre. He has expressed his opinion of me so often that I must now for once be allowed to state my opinion of him: I recognise in him a man who has been diligent in collecting his material, and accept that with his dictionary he has especially contributed to filling what has been referred to as a gap in literature. This is despite the fact that this work, which is his most important, is somewhat incomplete and extremely biased. He fails to show in it how the best writers of Danish actually write, but demonstrates how his own whims demand that people should spell. As a judge of aesthetic works he has often shown himself to be biased and full of prejudice, while his own creative genius only produced works during his youth such as *A Ramble Through Denmark*, written in the flowery language of the time, and *A Journey Through Germany, France and Italy* which seems to draw on books more than on experience. He used to sit in his study and in the Royal Library, and it was generally said that he had not been in a theatre for years when he was suddenly made manager of the Royal Theatre and censor of all plays submitted to it. He was an obsessive individual, one-sided and crabby; the result can easily be imagined.

In my very earliest days as an author he was particularly favourably disposed to me, but my star soon sank and gave way to another which was in the ascendant. This was Paludan-Müller who appeared with *The Ballerina* and later with *Cupid and Psyche*. And when Molbech no longer loved me, then he was against me, that is the whole story. And now I have said what I had to say.

There is a proverb which runs, "When the carriage is about to overturn, then everyone will push it," and this I experienced at that time: people everywhere could talk of nothing but my faults. It is only human to wince on being asked to bear too much, and this – as was my nature – was my complaint to those who called themselves my friends. And they spread it all over the great city, which often seems to be a very small city indeed. I even met well dressed people who sniggered at me as they passed by and made some scornful remark to me. There is a notable element of mockery in the Danish character, or to put it more pleasantly, we have a great sense of the comical, and that is why we have so many writers of comedies.

Then it happened that a new star emerged in Danish literature: Henrik Hertz made an anonymous appearance with his *Letters from the Dead*. People said they were intended to expel all impurity from the temple. The late Jens Baggesen was supposed to be sending polemical letters from Paradise and these were such skilful copies of Baggesen's style, both in spirit and form, that people could do no more than say, "It really is Baggesen who has written them". Heiberg was here in all his glory; Oehlenschläger and Hauch were attacked and the old story of my spelling mistakes in the *Journey on Foot* was brought up again. My name and my schooldays in Slagelse were mentioned in connection with "St. Anders", and so the joke was established about "St. Andersen" riding on the "Muse's night-old foal". Holberg would surely have found a better way of saying it! I was thoroughly punished now. The anonymous *Letters from the Dead* occupied everyone's thoughts and interest; a wave of enthusiasm swept across the entire country and all else was forgotten. I have never since known any other work fascinate people as this did, except perhaps *Clara Raphael* on account of Heiberg's introduction. The fact that no one could discover who had written this book made it all the more intriguing; people were delighted, and rightly so. Books like this are not published every year. In his periodical *Den Flyvende Post* Heiberg made excuses for, or perhaps rather took the side of, some of his friends who had been criticised. He made not a single reference to me.

101

To be publicly exposed to mockery in an article had a much greater effect in those days than it has now. The predecessor of the periodical *Corsaren*, Mathias Winther's *Raketten*, was a real pillory which gave a touch of importance to its victims as far as the public was concerned, for people thought in those days that there must be a grain of truth in anything that was printed. No one except a man who wrote under the pseudonym *Davieno* took my side. He was a student by the name of Drejer, the brother of the botanist (they are both dead now) and a gifted young man whose posthumous works have been published together with a biography of him, but not including the fairly long poem *A Letter in Rhyme to Knud Sjællandsfar* – the work he wrote in defence of me.

There was nothing I could do about it all, and I had to let the great wave pass over me. Everyone was of the opinion that it would completely wash me away. Deep down, I felt the wound caused by the sharp knife, and I was on the verge of giving up, just as almost everyone else gave me up. There was no Allah apart from the author of *Letters from the Dead*, and Heiberg was his prophet.

It was just at that time my collection of poems entitled *Fantasies and Sketches* appeared, and on the title page I wrote a motto taken from the *Letters from the Dead* itself; it was my contribution to this vitally important question! I repeated the words of the poet himself:

A judgement there must be, but let him who judges remember that the fruit of genius is but the product of the time; it is born of it and it follows it in its course. If he should chance to praise an occasional work, let him take care of his critical powers; but let him ponder day and night before he condemns. For it is easy to pull things to the ground; nor is it hard to take things away. But it is difficult to restore what has been destroyed and to save what is left.

Letters from the Dead

The first more sober voice to make itself heard above the jubilation was that of Professor Wilster, the poet, who wrote in the monthly *Prometheus*:

Hertz's *Letters from the Dead* is no work of art, but a showpiece, and it is scarcely possible to imagine that a poetic soul possessed of enthusiasm and originality could think of writing a work of this nature and stature: a true poet would scarcely bother himself with such things unless they were intended as parody or irony. The striking manner in which he succeeded in copying the language used by Baggesen in similar polemical publications, a language which at one time swept people off their feet, ensured such publications of exceptional approval, something to which the additional zest of anonymity contributed. They were a success largely on account of their form, which was pleasing enough in itself, but which at the same time had the additional advantage of being a disappointing imitation; so the delight they caused was akin to what we feel when we hear someone imitating the voice of another; nor in such cases do people bother thinking much about *what is* said, but only *how* it is said. So the author, one may almost say in self-defence, was persuaded to sing the praises of form as the only redeeming feature of poetry since form is the only virtue of such a work and of any deliberate and open imitation. But real poetry, ardour, depth or fullness of thought are not to be found in those letters; and if they were to be found there, then the work would be a failure, not a success, for these qualities are lacking even in Baggesen's own satires.

After *Fantasies and Sketches* I published yet another little book, *Vignettes to Danish Poets*, in which I sought to characterise in a few lines the best sides of each of the poets both living and dead. It attracted some attention, and a little poem dedicated to me appeared in *The Day* and ran as follows:

"To the Author of the Vignettes, in the Name of the Poets."

> Obedient to the Muses' high command
> A place thou seekest in the hall of fame!
> Now laurel branches seek to kiss thy hand;

A laurel wreath shall soon enhance thy name.
Fear not the satyrs, fauns, which roam the earth;
Alone by evil can ill's death be hastened;
The finest gold by fire and blows is chastened
And when the diamond's cut 'tis double worth.

It was signed "Knud from Funen". People made fun of this admirer and champion I had found, but they would scarcely have done so had they known, as I soon learned from the author himself, that it was honest old Wegener, the Principal of Jonstrup Training College and the publisher of the periodical *Huusvennen – The Family Friend.* He was held in great respect and honoured by all. My *Vignettes* were copied by other writers but the critics didn't think them worth mentioning; not a single friendly word, not a single expression even of tempered praise came my way. But on the other hand a re-hash of all the old criticism was forced upon me both early and late. I was not criticised, I was chided, and this went on for many years. But this was the time when things were at their worst for me.

Hertz admitted it was he who had written the *Letters from the Dead*, and he was given a bursary on which to travel abroad. I had also applied for one. I looked on King Frederik the Sixth with true veneration and profound gratitude; I had grown up with this feeling and I felt compelled to express it. The only way I had of doing this was to present him with a book, *The Twelve Months of the Year*, which he allowed me to dedicate to him. Now I was told by someone who meant well by me and knew the way things worked, that in order to increase the possibility of being granted a bursary, I ought, on presenting the King with my book, to tell him briefly and clearly who I was. I should tell him that after taking my school-leaving examination I had made my own way without any support from anyone, but that a journey abroad would probably contribute to my education more than anything else. The King was then almost sure to say that I could write an application to him. I should already have one on me and should hand it to him. I thought it dreadful that I should ask the King for something in return for something I was giving him. "Well, that is the way it is," came the reply. "The King knows perfectly well that you are giving him the book in order to get something in return." I was in despair at this, but I had to do it. "That is how it is done," I was told.

My entrance must have been extremely amusing; my heart was beating with anxiety, and when the King stepped quickly towards me in his characteristic manner and asked me what sort of book it was I had brought for him I answered, "A cycle of poems."

"Cycle, cycle, what do you mean?" I was obviously disheartened at that and said, "They are a few poems about Denmark". He smiled and said, "Oh, I see. That is excellent! Thank you very much." And then he bowed to dismiss me. But I had not even started on my actual errand and I said that I had a lot of other things I wanted to say. And without more ado I told him of my studies and how I had managed to complete them. "That is extremely praiseworthy," said the King and when I came to the stage of telling him that I would like to have a travelling bursary he gave me the answer I had been told to expect:

"Well, then bring me an application."

"Yes, Your Majesty," I burst out with all my natural ingenuousness. "I have it with me already. And that is what I myself think is so dreadful, that I have to bring it along with the book; but I have been told I had to and that was the way to do it; but I think it is so horrible, and I hate doing it." And my eyes filled with tears.

The good King laughed out loud, nodded kindly to me and took the application. I bowed and rushed out in great haste.

It was the general opinion that I had reached the peak of my career; so if I were to go abroad it had to be now. I felt that a life of travel was the best education for me, and this has since been generally recognised. But in order for me to be taken into consideration I was told I would have to obtain recommendations from our most important writers and experts, a sort of declaration that I was a poet, for that year many excellent young men were applying for scholarships. I realised the implication that among all these it would be difficult for me to be taken into consideration unless I had some extremely good references.

I obtained all the references, and I believe I was the only Danish poet until then and perhaps since then who has had to submit a written guarantee from others that I was a poet. As far as I know, H. P. Holst, Paludan-Müller, Thisted and Christian Molbech had all received financial support to travel abroad without any such recommendation, which they certainly didn't need. The peculiar feature in my case, however, was that each of the men who recommended me stressed specific characteristics in me. Thus Oehlenschläger talked of my poetical talent and Ingemann of my understanding of the life of the ordinary people, while Heiberg declared that in my various works he thought he could detect a humour closely akin to that of our famous poet Wessel. H. C. Ørsted pointed out that however many different opinions people expressed about my work, everyone agreed on one thing: that I was a poet. Thiele expressed his warm admiration for the spirit within me which he could see fighting against life's hardships and deprivation. He wanted to see my problems overcome, "not only for the sake of the poet but for the sake of poetry in Denmark".

These recommendations had a positive effect, and I was awarded a travelling bursary. Hertz was given a large one; mine was smaller.

"Be content now," said my friends, "and realise how extremely fortunate you have been. Enjoy the present moment, for it will probably be the only time you are given the opportunity of going abroad. You should just hear what people are saying because you are going to travel. You should know how we have to defend you, and unfortunately we have not always been able to do so and have had to admit those people are right." Those words went right through me. I longed with all my heart to get away. I did not remember those true words of Horace that sorrow travels behind the rider on his horse. More than one sorrow weighed down my heart. There is a song in *Agnete and the Merman* called:

"Behind the alder thickets down where the mill wheel turns".

The depths of a human soul can often be reflected in a short poem. As the time for my departure approached, the images of my friends arose in my heart, and among the few I have mentioned earlier there were two who at that time had a significant influence on my own personal development, on my life and on my writing, and whom I must now discuss.

The first was Mrs. Læssøe, the daughter of Abrahamson, the writer of the poem "My son, if you will make a name", and whose beautiful and heartfelt verses at the grave of the fallen, "Peace be with you all as one", once touched the hearts of everyone. She was the mother of the hero of Isted, the glorious, brave, ardent Colonel Læssøe. She, the fondest of mothers, one of the finest intellects I have met among women, had thrown open her comfortable home to me. With deep sympathy, she often shared the sorrows I found comfort in confiding to her. She was full of compassion, helpfulness and reassurance; she opened my eyes more and more to the beauties of nature and the poetical qualities in what we call the small things in life. And when almost everyone gave me up as a poet, she supported me when I was in danger of sinking. If there is any understanding of woman or any purity in any of the things I have written, she is one of those to whom I am particularly indebted.

The second person, also someone who had a great influence on me, was one of Collin's sons, the present Privy Councillor Edvard Collin. He had grown up in happy surroundings and was the son of a highly respected and influential father, and he was possessed of a boldness and determination which were completely lacking in me. I was conscious of his profound liking for me. I had never yet known what it was to have a friend of my own age; gently and with all my heart I inclined towards him. He was the opposite of the almost feminine qualities that were to be found in me. He was the sober-minded and practical one of the two of us and although younger in years he was the older as far as understanding was concerned. He was the leader, the one who took decisions, as was only to be expected. How often I misunderstood him and felt upset and daunted, while his well-intentioned zeal was misunderstood by others. Something I was fond of doing and which made me blissfully happy was to recite either my own or other people's poems. Once when I met my friend in some family circle, I was asked to recite some poems and was prepared to do so. However, he knew the atmosphere and the feelings of the company towards me better than I did. I was undoubtedly a figure of fun in their eyes, and he stepped across to me saying that if I recited even a single poem he would leave. I was upset, and our hostess and the ladies present overwhelmed him with reproaches for his behaviour. Only later have I understood how from his point of view and with his understanding of the situation he acted as a good friend to me; but at that time it cost me tears, although I was profoundly aware of the interest he took in me. What he desired and strove for was to give me, a figure as yielding as a reed, something of his own independence and strength of will. In practical life he stood actively beside me and assisted me with anything from Latin exercises before my examination to making all arrangements with publishers and printers, and even reading proofs. Throughout all those years during which I was developing, from the time when I patiently had to give way and suffer everything until the time when I possessed a free spirit, a strong will and an opinion of my own, he remained ever my true friend.

It is only as you leave mountains that you see them as they really are; thus it was with me and those whom I loved as I left on my travels.

A little album with verses by many people whose names meant much to me was one of my most prized possessions. They went with me and have since grown into a great treasure:

> To Paris hasten o'er the Rhine,
> Then see beyond Italian vine
> And hear the gracious music fill
> With subtle tones the evening air,
> Blending sound with perfumes rare
> Beneath the pine-tree's top so still.
> Remember God, His nature, art,
> Exclude not longing from thy heart;
> It is a sacred candle
> And ever shall its flame enfold
> The pearl of love and friendship's gold –
> A loyal pang and gentle;
> I know that then you will depart
> For Zealand's fields in rich attire
> With priceless treasure for your lyre
> And with an unchanged heart.

Copenhagen, 19th April 1833   Christian Winther

Let now your poet's fantasy
Buzz round us like a busy bee
And bring a pot of honey home.
Forget us not as far you roam.

Copenhagen, 19 April 1833   Adam Oehlenschläger

There must be depth to bear the lofty;
The finest ship needs more than shallow waves;
It must plough deep, or ne'er it swings
Towards the twinkling stars its billowing wings.
In kindly remembrance
                                        B. S. Ingemann

Think, and forget not Denmark's pleasant land
Yonder, 'neath the warm skies of the South;
Forget not Denmark, when, by foreign strand
You wander, or by Seine's or Arno's mouth.
Accept some warm advice from one
Who honours you and all the gifts you have;
Think not I wish to burden you on
This your day of taking leave: –
Use your fancy as a poet should
And understanding like a man;
Whatever goal we aim at would
As in a mist be difficult to scan
If zeal and knowledge sought in vain
Our deeds to follow 'neath life's skies.
Fare well, my friend; go forth, and then
Content and glad return again.
And scorn not my advice.

The Naval Academy, 20th April 1833   Wulff

Eines schickt sich nicht für Alle;
Sehe jeder, wie er's treibe,
Sehe jeder, wo er bleibe,
Und wer steht, dass er nicht falle!

The same thing isn't right for all;
Let each man make his way alone,
Let each man look after his own,
And if he stands, then not to fall.

With these words of Goethe I wish you great benefit from the journey upon which you are about to embark.

Copenhagen, 22nd April 1833.   J. L. Heiberg
                          (Johan Ludvig Heiberg)

Go not so far that you forget Molbech's Dictionary
                          Yours,
                          J. L. Heiberg
                          (Johanne Luise Heiberg)

Reason in reason = the truth.
Reason in the will = the good.
Reason in the imagination = the beautiful.
Remember this text in many conversations

Copenhagen, 21st April 1833
                          Yours sincerely,
                          H. C. Ørsted

Greet Mignon in the orange grove,
And say, though far from her I move,

I merry am and that I love,
When lonely and in thought I rove,
To think of her, that gentle dove,

And of our meeting in the orange grove.
Surprised she'll be, but then she'll smile
And burst out, "Oh".

From Just Thiele

Go and taste just
Of joy beneath the palm tree
And yet remember what you see,
For behold it is on trust.
While you're away –
As a lawyer I must enjoin –
You must pay back another day
In many a lovely poem.

Your friend
F. J. Hansen

On Monday, the 22nd of April 1833 I left Copenhagen. I was deeply emotional on leaving, and my heartfelt prayer to God was that while I was away I might gain so much in maturity and skill that I might produce a fine and true work of art, or that I might never return, but die in some foreign country far from Denmark.

I saw the towers of Copenhagen disappear. We were approaching the cliffs of Møn when the captain came to me with a letter and said in fun, "It has just come down out of the air." It was a few extra lines and a fond greeting from Eduard Collin. By Falster there came yet another letter from one of my friends and at bedtime a third appeared. Then early in the morning, just off Travemünde yet a fourth arrived, "All out of the air," said the captain. My friends had been kind and understanding enough to supply him with a pocketful for me.

"Noch ein Sträusschen! und wieder noch ein Sträusschen!"
"Another posy! And then another posy!"

V

The Danish poet Lars Kruse lived in Hamburg. He was the writer of the tragedies *Ezzelin*, *The Widow* and *The Monastery* which I had seen performed in the Royal Theatre. His novel *Seven Years* was much read and highly considered, and the German *Musenalmanach* boasted of his stories every year. Now he is more or less forgotten both there and at home in Denmark. I found him to be a friendly person, kindly disposed, good natured and just a little plump in appearance; he spoke of his love for his native country and in my album he wrote,

> Be what you are and to your nature true,
> Your soul keep pure, your heart keep happy, too,
> A Dane when far from Dana's land you roam,
> A European when you come back home.

Hamburg, 25th April 1833   L. Kruse

That was the first poetical greeting I received in a foreign country, and so it remained fixed in my memory. The next rather vivid impression that has remained with me from that journey was the sight of a half-obliterated name in Cassel. There, on a street corner, the name of Napoleon could be distinguished through the paint covering it, the street or square having once been called after him. That fascinated me more than all the splendour of the Wilhelmshöhe with its artificial ruins and fountains. For Napoleon was the hero of my childhood and my heart.

Here in Cassel I met Spohr for the first time and was kindly received by him. He knew something of the works of Weyse and Kuhlau and asked me a lot of questions about music in Denmark and Danish composers. A little theme from *The Raven* which Hartmann had written down in my album he found extremely attractive, and I know that several years later he started a correspondence with

Hartmann and, although without success, did his best to arrange a stage performance of *The Raven* in Cassel. He asked which of his own works had been produced in Copenhagen, and I was forced to answer, "None at all". Unfortunately I would still have to say the same today. He seemed to be most interested in his opera *Zemire and Azor*, and he particularly recommended it. As for Danish literature, he knew only a little Baggesen, Oehlenschläger and Kruse. Otherwise, he expressed great admiration for my native country and for the many fine achievements of which this tiny area could boast. He was in particular impressed by Thorvaldsen. When we parted I felt quite moved, for I thought I was saying goodbye for ever to a man whose works will be admired for generations to come. I didn't think we should ever meet again, and yet it was to happen many years later in London when we met as old friends. But more of that anon.

Nowadays it is easy to travel through Germany to Paris, but that was not the case in 1833. There were no railways then, and we crept slowly forward; day and night, tired and dusty. There we were, packed into great, clumsy coaches. After this prosaic part of the journey I discovered sheer poetry on arriving in Frankfurt, the birthplace of Goethe and the childhood home of the Rothschilds, where in deep faith and for the sake of her children's happiness, the mother of those wealthy, powerful sons refused to leave the little house in the Jewish quarter where she had born and brought up her rich and fortunate sons. The old, gabled Gothic houses and the medieval Town Hall constituted an entire volume of pictures for me. Aloys Schmitt the composer, famous for his opera *Valeria*, was the first person outside Denmark to ask me to write the libretto for an opera. He said that my short poems, which Chamisso had translated, had convinced him that I was just the poet he needed. I saw the Rhine. Its banks are at their least impressive in spring, for the vines are only short beside the castle ruins. I had thought it would all be far more impressive, and what I saw failed to fulfil my expectations; and there must be many others whose experience was the same as mine. The most beautiful spot is without doubt the Loreley near St. Goar. The River Danube has banks that are far more romantic than the Rhine, and even the Rhône has stretches that surpass it. The legends are the greatest glory of the Rhine; the lovely songs that Germany's poets have sung of the mighty, sea-green river are its most beautiful feature.

From the Rhine I think we travelled for three days through Saarbrücken and the chalky district of Champagne to Paris. I had been looking out for this "city of cities" as I then called it, and had been asking for such a long time whether we were not soon to be there that I finally gave up and found myself crossing the Boulevard itself before I realised that we had reached that mighty city.

All the impressions from my journey from Copenhagen to Paris are presented in what I have written above, so little was I able to capture as I flew along in this way. Yet there were people at home who expected some kind of development to have taken place in me even after these few days of travelling. They did not realise that just because the curtain has risen, the audience has not necessarily seen and understood the sight confronting it. So I was in Paris now, but I was tired, worn out and sleepy, and even the task of finding a place to stay had been an effort for me. Finally, I arrived at the Hôtel de Lille in Rue Thomas, not far from the Palais Royal. To go to bed and have some sleep was the first and most welcome experience I sought and found; but I did not sleep for long, for I was awakened by a terrible clamour. There was brightness all around me and I leapt over to the window. Just across the narrow street from where I was standing there was a large building, and through the window I could see a crowd of people rushing down the steps. Outside, everyone was shouting and crying. There were roars and flashes and crashes, and, half asleep as I was still, I naturally thought that all Paris was in revolt. I rang for the waiter, "What is all this?"

"*C'est le tonnerre,*" he said.

"*Le tonnerre,*" said the chambermaid, and as they could see from the look of amazement on my face that I could not understand them they rolled their tongues, "*tonnerre-re-rrrr,*" and showed me how the lightning was striking; and all the while it went on, lightning and rumbling and making a terrible din. It was indeed thunder, and the building opposite was the Vaudeville Theatre where the performance had just finished and people were pouring down the steps. Such was my first awakening in Paris.

Now I was to see its splendours.

The Italian Opera was already closed, but the great Opéra was still

114

ablaze with brilliant stars. Madame Damoreau and Adolphe Nourrit were singing there. Nourrit was at the height of his powers and the favourite of the Parisians. It was he who during the July Revolution had fought so bravely at the barricades and sung patriotic songs with such fervour that the fighters' enthusiasm was greatly increased. I heard him, and everyone spoke in praise of him. Four years later I received the news of his despair and death. He went to Naples in 1837, and his reception there was not what he had expected; indeed he was even hissed at a little, something that distressed this singer who had always been lionised wherever he went. Sick at heart he appeared once more, in *Norma*, and one person hissed at him again in spite of the deafening applause from the rest of the audience. Nourrit was deeply shaken; he stayed up all night and early in the morning of the eighth of March he flung himself out of a third-floor window. His widow and six children now mourn for him. As I say, it was in Paris in all his splendour and happiness and feted and admired by all that I heard him in *Gustav the Third*. Everyone was talking about this opera. The widow of the real Anckarström was living in Paris as an old woman. In one of the most widely read newspapers she declared that the love affair Scribe portrays between her and King Gustav was completely false, and that she had only once seen the king.

In the Théâtre Français I saw the tragedy *Les enfants d'Edouard*. Old Mademoiselle Mars took the part of the young sons' mother, and although I understood but little of the French language, everything was made so plain to me by her acting that tears came to my eyes. Neither before nor since have I heard a more beautiful voice in a woman. During the first years I spent in Copenhagen the renowned Miss Astrup still appeared on the Danish stage; the people of Copenhagen admired her and especially emphasised a sort of eternal youth in her. I had a feeling of reverence for her when she appeared in the tragedy *Selim, Prince of Algiers*, in which she played the mother. But for me she was an aged, tightly corseted maiden lady, as stiff as a poker, with an unpleasant, screeching voice; I could not judge her acting. In Mademoiselle Mars in Paris I saw true youth. This was not someone strutting about in tight corsets, but here were youthful movements and a voice of great musicality. Without having to be told, I could myself understand that she was a true artist.

There were quite a number of Danes in Paris that summer. We lived together in the same hotel, went together to cafés, restaurants and theatres and always spoke our beloved native language, in particular to tell each other the contents of the letters we received. It was a pleasant and cordial way of passing the time, but scarcely the right way of occupying yourself while abroad. Yet at that time I enjoyed it with all my heart, and at one of the festive dinners we arranged I expressed some of the feelings we were experiencing in Paris at that time:

> When Danish beech leaves saw the day,
> We too sprang out, though o'er the sea,
> And where we went, the spring in bride's array
> Revealed herself and wondrous fair was she.

It was a life devoted to meetings and shared experiences, and the latter went on and on. Everything was seen and had to be seen; that was what we had gone abroad to do, of course. I can still remember that one of my dear friends quite seriously thanked God one evening when he came back wearied after visiting some museums and palaces which he had found particularly boring. "But you've got to see the damned things!" he said. "It would be a pity to go home and have to say you hadn't been there when your friends asked you. Now I have only the odd place left, and when I have finished with them I am really going to enjoy myself." That was the sort of thing that was said, and it will probably often be repeated.

On this, my first journey abroad, I went with the others and saw and saw the sights, but most of what I saw has been erased from my memory again. The impression made on me by the mighty Palace of Versailles with its richly ornamented rooms and great pictures was immediately pushed into the background for me by the Trianon. I entered Napoleon's bedroom with feelings of piety and elevation. Everything was as it had been when he was alive, the walls were covered with yellow tapestry, and yellow curtains hung round the bed. A small set of steps led up to this bed, and I placed my hand on one of them that his foot had touched, and then on his pillow. Had I been alone I should doubtless have knelt down. For Napoleon

116

was my childhood hero and my father's idol, and I looked up to him as a Catholic to a saint. I visited the farm in the little garden of the Trianon where Marie Antoinette, dressed as a peasant girl, had tended the dairy and everything belonging to it. Here I plucked a honeysuckle blossom that was resting against the window of the unfortunate queen's room. For the sake of contrast I plucked a humble daisy from the splendid gardens at Versailles.

I only saw, or rather only spoke to, a few of the famous persons in Paris; one of these, to whom I was introduced by a letter from the ballet-master Bournonville at home, was Paul Duport, the writer of so many vaudevilles. His drama, *The Quaker and the Dancer*, had been performed in our theatre; it was an excellent production and had had a great success. The old man was quite delighted on hearing this, and because of this news and the letter I had with me I was a welcome guest. However, there was immediately quite an amusing scene between us: I spoke French badly; he thought he could speak German, but the way in which he pronounced it rendered it completely impossible for me to understand it. He thought this was because of his choice of words and so he took out a German dictionary, put it on his knee and kept looking up in it. But to converse by means of a dictionary is a slow business and suited neither a Frenchman nor me.

Another person I visited was Cherubini, for whom I actually had a message from Weyse. Many people will still remember how little general recognition was accorded at home to the brilliant Weyse's operatic compositions, and yet among them there were such melodious works as *The Sleeping Potion* and *Ludlam's Cave*. However he lived and composed exclusively for his native land, though without becoming fashionable there either. Only as a composer of church music did he gain serious recognition, and his *Ambrosian Song of Praise* was particularly well known and held in high esteem. It was a piano version of this that he had asked me to give to Cherubini, the immortal composer of *Les deux journées* and the creator of so many wonderful Requiems. Just at that time the attention of the Parisians was directed to him as after a long period of silence and at a great age he had just produced a new work for the Opéra, *Ali Baba* or *The Forty Thieves*. It was not a success, but was received with deep respect and reverence.

I went out to Cherubini's house. The old man was very much like the portraits I had seen of him, sitting at his piano with a cat on each shoulder. He had never heard of Weyse, not even by name, and he asked me to tell him something about the music I had brought with me. The only Danish composer of whose existence he knew was Claus Schall, who wrote the music for Galeotti's ballets. He had lived together with Schall for a time, and he was interested in him. Weyse never heard from Cherubini and I never saw him again.

One day I went into the "Europe Littéraire", a sort of a Parisian Athenæum to which Paul Duport had introduced me. A small man of Jewish appearance came towards me in a friendly manner. "I hear you are Danish," he said. "I am German. Danes and Germans are brothers, and so may I offer you my hand."

I asked him his name, and he answered, "Heinrich Heine".

So he was the poet who during the recent erotic period of my young life had filled my thoughts and so completely expressed my moods and feelings. There was no one I would rather have seen and met than he; and I told him as much.

"You cannot mean that," he smiled. "Had I interested you as much as you say, you would surely have come and visited me."

"I could not," I answered. "You have such a sense of the comical, and you would have thought it comical if I, a writer completely unknown to you from the little known country of Denmark, came and introduced myself as a Danish poet. I know, too, that I would have behaved clumsily, and if you had laughed at me then or perhaps even mocked me, I would have been infinitely upset simply because I hold you in such high esteem. And so I preferred to omit to see you."

My words made a good impression on him, and he was extremely kind and pleasant. The very next day he came to visit me in the Hôtel Vivienne where I was living. We met quite often and went for a stroll occasionally on the Boulevard, but at that time I still didn't really trust him. Nor did I feel the more cordial manner he revealed when we met several years later, by which time he knew my novel *The Improvisatore* and some of my fairy tales. When we parted, and I left Paris for Italy, he wrote to me:

*Ich möchte Ihnen gar, werthester Collega, einige Verse hier
auf's Papier kritzeln, aber ich kann heute kaum leidlich in
Prosa schreiben.*

*Leben Sie wohl und heiter. Amüsieren Sie sich recht hübsch
in Italien; lernen Sie recht gut Deutsch in Deutschland, und
schreiben Sie dann in Dänemark auf Deutsch, was Sie in
Italien gefühlt haben. Das wäre mir das Erfreulichste.*

   Paris, 10 August 1833   *H. Heine*

I would very much like, my esteemed colleague, to scribble
down a few lines for you, but today I can hardly even write
reasonable prose.

Fare you well and happily. Have a really good time in Italy;
learn German really well in Germany and then in Denmark
write down in German about what you felt in in Italy. That
would be what would please me best.

   Paris, 10th August 1833   H. Heine

The first French book I tried to read in the original was Victor Hugo's
novel, *Notre Dame*. I could visit the cathedral itself every day and see
the entire setting for the book. I was captivated by these impressive
descriptions and dramatic characters, and so what was more natural
than that I should visit the author, who lived at the corner of the Place
Royale. His apartment was old-fashioned and on the walls there
hung prints and wood-cuts and paintings of Notre Dame. The author
himself was wearing a dressing-gown, underpants and an elegant
pair of slippers when he came to greet me, and when I left I asked
him, greatly pestered though he must have been by chance visitors,
to write his name on a sheet of paper for me. He did as I wished, but
he wrote his name right up at the top of the paper in such a way that
the thought immediately occurred to me that he did not know me
and was ensuring that there was not room for a single line above it
to which his name could appear to be a signature. This made a bad
impression on me. Only when I was staying in Paris again at a later
date did I come to know the poet better, but more of that anon.

Throughout my journey to Paris and during my first month there I received not a single word from home. No one wrote to me. In vain did I ask for mail in the Post Office; there was none. I thought that perhaps my friends had nothing cheerful to tell me, or did people perhaps still envy me the bursary I had received for my journey as a result of the numerous recommendations I had been given. It worried me. At last a letter arrived, a thick letter; there was no stamp on it, and it cost me rather a lot, but it was so big, and my heart leapt with joy and impatience to read the contents. It was my first letter from home. I opened it, but there was not a written word in it, merely a printed newspaper, a *Copenhagen Post* with a lampoon about me:

A Farewell to Andersen

> So you will leave this Danish clime,
> Where yet some eyes on you did fondly dwell,
> When scarcely you had reached your prime
> Before you quite had left your shell.
> It is not mete the son should leave
> His home to visit foreign lands.
> Yet still no native tongue commands
>
> Nor is it right and fair that you
> So soon our little Denmark will forsake
> While still you give us verses new
> And read them while our hearts do break.
> It was your constant happiness
> To read your poems for those you met.
> And now – why, whom can you address?
> Be sure, for home you'll oft times fret. etc. etc.

It was sent to me in print, presumably by the author himself. Unstamped, it came all the long way from Copenhagen to Paris. That was to be my first greeting from home. I was deeply shocked, distressed to the core. It was completely wicked. I have never discovered the identity of the author, but his verses seem to have been written by a skilled pen. Perhaps he was one of those who later called me his friend and gave me his hand. People have unpleasant thoughts; I, too, have mine!

I stayed in Paris until the end of the July festival. It had just started when I arrived, and on the first day I was present at the unveiling of Napoleon's monument on the Place Vendôme. The previous evening, while the workmen were still up there and the monument was covered with sheeting, I was standing in the square along with many other groups of people, when a strange, thin old woman approached me. Laughing, and with an insane expression on her face she said to me, "They've put him up there now. They'll tear him down again tomorrow, ha, ha, ha! I know the French". I went away with an uncomfortable feeling. The following day I sat in the crowd, high up on some scaffolding at the corner of the square. Louis Philippe together with his sons and generals stopped in front of me; the guard marched past to the sound of a brass band and with bunches of flowers stuck in the barrels of their guns. There were shouts of hurrah, but there were also many angry cries of, "à bas les forts!" In the Hôtel de Ville there was a grand ball for the people. There were folk there from all classes, from the royal family down to fishermen's wives. The crowd was so dense that Louis Philippe and his queen had difficulty reaching the places assigned to them. It gave me an unpleasant feeling that just as the royal family entered, the orchestra was playing the dance music from the scene in *Gustav the Third* in which King Gustav is shot. I believed I could see on Queen Amélie's face that it made a similar impression on her. She was also deathly pale and clung tightly to Louis Philippe who acknowledged people all around with a jovial smile and shook a number of people by the hand. The Duke of Orleans, young and full of life and extremely handsome, danced with a poorly dressed girl who apparently belonged to the lowest classes. For several days there was festivity and splendour. In the evenings funereal torches were lit by the graves of the fallen, which were adorned with wreaths of everlasting flowers. There were tournaments in boats on the Seine, and there was the same gaiety and merriment on the Champs Elysées as were to be seen in the Deer Park at home. All the theatres in Paris were open, even in the middle of the day, and performances were given with the doors open so that people could come and go as they

121

wished. In the middle of tragedies and operas people would suddenly interrupt and sing "La Parisienne" and the Marseillaise. In the evenings the sky was ablaze with rockets and fireworks; there were impressive illuminations and churches and public buildings could be seen in the bright light from them. This was how my first visit to Paris ended; the finale could not possibly have been more brilliant and festive than it was.

As far as my French was concerned I had made little progress during my stay, which had lasted for almost three months; for, as I have said, we Danes spent too much time together. However, I felt it was necessary to learn a little more of the language and so, although I was told such a stay would be expensive, I decided to spend some time at a *pension* in Switzerland where I would have to speak nothing but French.

"If you could be satisfied with staying in a small town high up in the Jura Mountains snow is already falling in August, it will not be so expensive, and you will be able to make friends there." This I was told by a French-speaking Swiss whose acquaintance I had made through relatives of his in Copenhagen. After Paris the isolation up in the mountains would be doubly welcome to me, and I hoped to be able to complete a work that I was busy with. So we made plans for the journey. I was to travel through Geneva and Lausanne to the small town of Le Locle in the Jura Mountains.

Among the Danes I left behind in Paris there were two very famous men. Both had received me as kind friends and I must pause for a moment to consider them. One of them was the poet Peter Andreas Heiberg, the author of *The Von's and the Van's* and the *Laterna Magica*. At a time that was so different from the present he had been exiled from Denmark and chosen Paris as his new home. All Danes know his story. I went to visit him. He was living in one of the smaller hotels, an old man and almost blind. His son, Johan Ludvig Heiberg, had just married Johanne Luise, who can almost certainly be said to be one of the most highly honoured and valued actresses of the day. The elderly Heiberg was very keen to hear about her, but I could understand that he still held old-fashioned or perhaps Parisian views of actresses. What he liked least about it all, he said, was that his son's wife could be ordered about by the manager of a theatre, a person he seemed to regard as something of a tyrant. However, he told me he was glad to hear from me, and indeed from all Danes, that she was such a highly respectable young lady who was endowed with real talent. It is a pity that he never came to know her outstanding qualities, her importance for the Danish theatre and her noble character. Apart from this he felt lonely, and it was pitiful to see him, half-blind and feeling his way forward through the well-known arcades of the Palais Royal. When I left he wrote in my album:

Receive a blind man's friendly farewell.

Paris, l0th August 1833   P. A. Heiberg

My other famous compatriot was Brøndsted, the Councillor of State whom I had met on occasion at the home of Admiral Wulff. He came to Paris from London, and in Paris he read *The Twelve Months of the Year*. He had not read any of my work before, and my verses appealed to him. He took a liking to me and was an inspiring guide and companion. One morning, shortly before I was due to leave, he gave me the following poem which he had written for me:

My thanks for all those poems about the months;
I see our dove of tender years in flight
Has brought forget-me-nots from native climes
A rich Amalthea's horn from Nordic lands.
And now the dove must fly to regions south
To view the wonders of Italian skies
And climb to Etna's giant flame aloft,
And when we welcome it back home anew,
When it has dreamt in Mnemosyne's grove
When it has seen the ardour of the South,
My friend, a laurel wreath 'twill bring for you.

Paris, Midsummer 1833   Brøndsted

I travelled now for several days and nights, squeezed tight in the overloaded stagecoach. The small, arabesque-like adventures of a life of travel turned up as we progressed. I can still remember a couple of them, and I will recount one of them.

We had left the flat part of France and reached the Jura Mountains. In a tiny village, late in the evening, when I was the only passenger in the coach, the conductor allowed two young peasant girls to join me. "If we didn't let them travel with us," he said, "they would have to walk along deserted roads for over two hours at this time of the night." They whispered and giggled to each other and they were obviously curious. They knew there was a gentleman in the coach, but they could not see me. Finally they summoned up courage and asked whether I was French, and when they heard that I was from Denmark, they turned out to be well informed. They could remember from their geography books that Denmark was the same as Norvège. They couldn't say Copenhague, but always said Corporal. And now they went on to ask whether I was young or old, whether I was married and what I looked like. I pressed myself deep into my dark corner and gave them as ideal a description as I could. They understood the joke, so when I asked about their appearance they described themselves as veritable beauties. They urged me to let them see my face at the next stop, but I would not agree to this, and so when they got out it was with handkerchiefs over theirs. They laughed and shook hands with me; they were very young and had beautiful figures. These two merry girls whom I didn't know and never saw are like a smiling image from my travels.

The road ran beside deep precipices; down below the farm-houses looked like toys and the forests like fields of potatoes. Suddenly, between two cliffs, there was revealed to me a view of – why, to me it looked like floating mountains of cloud, an illusion created by the mists, but it was the Alps and Mont Blanc which I was seeing for the first time. The road led downhill, still alongside the precipice, and it was as though we were flying down through the air; we had a bird's-eye view of everything. A thick mist gathered before us; I thought it must be from a coal-mine, but it was a cloud rising towards us, and by the time it was above us Geneva and Lake Geneva were in sight, together with all the panorama of the Alps. The lower slopes were hidden in a bluish haze, while the black outlines of the highest mountains were clearly defined. The glaciers were shining in the sunlight; it was Sunday morning, and my heart was filled with the sanctity of Sunday devotions here in the great church of Nature.

I knew that old Puerari and his family were living in Geneva. He had come to Copenhagen as an immigrant and had stayed for some time; all Danes were welcome guests in his house. I asked a man in the street where he lived. It happened to be one of his friends, and he immediately took me to those kind-hearted people. The daughters of the house spoke Danish, and we talked of nothing but Denmark. Henrik Hertz had been Puerari's pupil and we discussed the great attention and success his *Letters from the Dead* had enjoyed at home. Puerari told me about his stay in Copenhagen where he had made a living as an ironmonger and by giving lessons in French. He talked of Louis Philippe's stay there at the home of a merchant called de Coninck; he went under the name Mr. Müller, a botanist on his way to the North Cape. As a compatriot of Louis Philippe, Puerari was invited by him one day to dinner in the Hôtel Royal. There was no waiter in the room, and Louis Philippe himself took charge of arranging the table and serving.

The Alps looked so close to the town that I decided to take a morning stroll out there, but they appeared to recede all the time. I walked on and on, and it was midday before I reached the foot of the first mountains and evening before I arrived back in Geneva.

By way of Lausanne and Vevey I reached Chillon, the picturesque old castle famed for the murders that took place in it and in which my interest had been awakened through Byron's poem, *The Prisoner of Chillon* The entire countryside gave me the impression of being in the South despite the mountains of Savoy being covered with snow and shining in front of me. But vineyards and fields of maize stretched in all directions down by the deep, green lake where the castle was situated. Splendid old chestnut trees cast shadows along the ground, and a few spread an abundance of green branches over the water's edge. I stepped across the drawbridge and entered the murky courtyard, and up in the walls I saw the narrow openings from which oil and boiling water used to be poured down on attackers. In the rooms there were trapdoors which gave as soon as you stepped on them, hurtling the unfortunate victims down into the deep lake or impaling them on iron spikes set in the rocks below. Down in the dungeons the iron rings to which the prisoners' chains had been fixed were going to rust. A flat stone had served as their bed. Byron had engraved his name on one of the pillars in 1816, and the woman who was showing me round told me that she had not known who that man was and had tried unsuccessfully to prevent him from doing it. And now everyone looked at those letters, for "he was an unusual sort of person, that gentleman," she said, nodding meaningfully.

From Chillon we went on to the Jura Mountains; up and up we went until I reached my new home, the little town of watchmakers, Le Locle.

It is situated high up in the Jura in a valley that had been a lake in prehistoric times, and where fossils of fish are still to be seen. The clouds are often below this level. It was peaceful here and quite silent beneath the dark spruce trees. The grass was green and fresh and there were succulent, violet crocuses shining in it. The peasants' houses were white and neat, and every one of them was filled with the clocks that were made here. The mountain ash with their red clusters reminded me of pictures in an A B C book and the berries themselves were a pretty red colour that reminded me of home. Le Locle itself is quite a considerable market town. And here it was that I found a delightful place to stay in the home of some good and kind people, the Houriet family. The husband was the brother-in-law of that gifted man, the late Urban Jürgensen. I was welcomed like some dear relative; there was no question of my boarding there or paying for my keep: "We are inviting you to stay here," said both the man and his wife, shaking my hand in a kindly fashion. The children, even the little ones, soon took to me and we became good friends. There were two splendid old aunts in the house there, Rosalie and Lydia. It was good practice for me to have to tell them in French all about Denmark and about their dear sister there whom they had not seen since she went away with her husband while still quite young. Up there in Le Locle people spoke nothing but French, which was the only language they knew; I only spoke it badly, but they understood me quite well, and I understood them. It was August, but my stove was already lit both morning and evening even at this time of the year. It even snowed occasionally, but I knew that below the Jura

Mountains summer was still there in all its warmth and loveliness, and within a couple of hours I could be in it. In the evenings there was something wonderfully peaceful about the countryside here, and from the French border on the other side of the river we could hear the evening bells ringing. Some distance outside the town was a lonely house; it was painted white and looked extremely inviting. You could go in and up through two cellars, and then you found yourself facing an otherwise unseen river that turned the great wheels of a mill. I visited this spot fairly often as well as the more distant but picturesque Doub waterfall. In my novel *O.T.* I have recalled and preserved memories of these places and of all my delightful stay in Le Locle.

Political unrest, however, had come even to this little town situated so high up in the mountains and so completely surrounded by forest, a place at the heart of silence itself. As is well known, the Canton of Neufchâtel is Prussian territory, and now there were some who favoured Prussia and some who favoured Switzerland. They had long been good neighbours, but now they suddenly found themselves in opposition to each other, avoiding meeting and each singing their own songs. It all found expression in small incidents, one of which I heard being about a true Swiss who lived there. Framed behind glass in his parlour he had the picture of William Tell shooting the apple off his son's head, but it had been destroyed by one of the Prussian party. During a visit, this man had pressed his elbow against the glass, breaking it and spoiling the picture. "He did that out of malice," he said. All these political differences, however, passed me by without affecting me. I lived with a happy family as a welcome guest. I gained an insight into family life there and the country's customs and traditions, far better than travellers normally achieve. Apart from this I was also engaged on a new work.

Throughout my entire journey from home and stay in Paris my thoughts had been fixed on an idea for such a work. As the idea became more and more firmly fixed in my mind and all the details became clearer I began to hope that through this work I might be able to win over my enemies and be recognised as a true poet by them. I wanted to treat the old popular ballad of *Agnete and the Merman*. I completed the first part in Paris and the second in Le Locle, and both of them I sent home from Le Locle with a brief introduction. I would not have written that now as I did then, but nor would the adaptation of Agnete have been the same as it was. This introduction is typical of me as I was then:

"Even as a child I was fascinated by the old ballad of *Agnete and the Merman*, representing, as it does, the dual world, the earth and the sea. Now that I am grown up I can see in it the great image of life, the never satisfied yearnings of the heart and its strange longing for a new and a different form of existence. I have long had the idea of expressing this as it lives on in my heart. This old ballad from my native land resounded in my ears amidst all the surging life of Paris. It pursued me on the cheerful boulevard and among the treasures of the Louvre. The child took shape below my heart before I was aware of it.

Agnete was born far from Paris, high up in the Jura Mountains, in surroundings that are Nordic in their grandeur, among gloomy pine forests and in deathly silence, but she is Danish in spirit and thought. And now I send my beloved child to my native country where she belongs. Receive her kindly; she brings with her a greeting to you all. When we are abroad, every Dane is a friend and brother to us, so she is going to her relatives and friends.

Snow is falling outside my window, and heavy, wintry clouds cover the forest, but below the mountains there is summer with its grapes and fields of ripe maize. Tomorrow I am to fly across the Alps to Italy. Perhaps I shall dream some beautiful dream there and then send it to my Denmark. For a son must tell his mother of his dreams. Farewell."

H. C. Andersen
Le Locle in the Jura Mountains, 14th September 1833

My work reached Copenhagen; it was printed and published. People laughed at the introduction to *Agnete*: "The child took shape below my heart before I was aware of it." It was given a cold reception, and it was said that I was unfortunately trying to copy Oehlenschläger, who had sent masterpieces home while he was abroad. Almost at the same time as *Agnete* appeared, Paludan-Müller chanced to publish his *Cupid and Psyche*, a work that gave delight to all and occupied everyone's thoughts. It was as though the weaknesses in my book were more noticeable because of this; it was reviewed in the periodical *Maanedsskriftet for Litteratur*, but it received no praise. Nor did it make the same impression on H. C. Ørsted as I had thought it would. In a rather long, friendly letter, dated 8th March 1834, which I received in Italy, he expressed himself frankly and, as I have since realised but did not then admit, correctly about my work.

Despite all its faults, my play *Agnete* was a step forward. My purely subjective poetical nature was trying here to reveal itself in an objective form. I was undergoing a form of transition, and this play rounded off what can be called my purely lyrical period. Years later the critics spoke better about this work and said that although it aroused less attention on being published than my earlier, less mature work, it showed a fuller and more profound and powerful sense of poetry. My subsequent exercise in shortening and altering it a little and then putting it on the stage was an attempt to attract an audience to a summer performance. The play was indeed performed a few times, but then, too, I was abroad. However, although, as people have said, Mrs. Heiberg gave a brilliant and moving performance as Agnete, and Niels Gade had composed some beautiful music for the occasional songs and choruses, there was no saving it.

Yet all I have written down and told here belonged to the future, both my own and that of my works. *Agnete* was sent off home, to me a beautiful statue then, seen only by me and God. Hopes and dreams went with this work. It travelled north, and the following day I went south, down into Italy, where what might be considered a new period in my life was to begin.

My departure from those dear people in Le Locle was truly sad. The children wept, for we had become good friends even though I could not understand their patois. They used to shout in my ear, thinking I must be deaf when I failed to understand them straight away. Even the servants shook hands with me with tears in their eyes, and the old aunts had knitted me some woollen mittens to protect my hands against the cold in the Simplon Pass.

For me, *Agnete* and the stay in Le Locle round off one period of my life as a poet.

VI

At exactly the same time of year as I had gone to Copenhagen as a poor child, but fourteen years later, I was to set foot in Italy, the land I had longed to see and where I expected to find happiness.

I travelled by way of the Rhône Valley and over the Simplon. What an imposing landscape there was around us! Our overloaded coach with its team of horses looked no bigger than a fly on a mighty block of stone. It was as though we were creeping along the rocky road, which had been blown out of the very backbone of the earth at the command of Napoleon. Glass-green glaciers glistened just above us, and it became colder and colder. The shepherd boys went wrapped in cow-hides, and the inns kept roaring fires in their stoves. It was like the middle of winter outside, but only a few hours later the coach was bowling along under the chestnut trees whose long green leaves were glittering in the warm sunshine. The market place and the streets of Domo d'Ossola presented a picture of Italy with all its bustling life. Lago Maggiore shone among the dark blue mountains, and there were lovely islands scattered like bouquets on the water. But the sky was not clear. There was a greyish cast to it, just as there is in Denmark, and only in the evening did the breeze blow it away. And then the air shone transparent and clear, and it seemed to stretch three times as far up as it does at home. Garlands of grapes hung along the road, as if for some festival. I have never seen Italy look more beautiful.

Milan Cathedral was the first artistic miracle which Italy placed before me. Towering above me in the moonlight, I saw this mountain of marble which the hands of artists have hollowed out, arched and formed into towers and statues. And from up there I had a view of the Alps with their glaciers, and the fertile, green countryside of Lombardy. The Porta Sempione, which people called after Napoleon, was still under construction. La Scala was staging operas and ballets. I visited and saw all these things, but it was Milan Cathedral that was at the centre of it all; it was an elevating experience to hear the sound of sacred music and sense the stillness of prayer.

I left this magnificent city along with two compatriots of mine. With our *vetturino* we drove through the Lombard countryside, which was as flat as the green islands of my native land, and just as fertile and beautiful, too. The rich fields of maize and the lovely weeping willows were new to me; on the other hand the mountains we had to cross seemed small after we had seen the Alps. Before us at last lay Genoa and the sea, which I had not seen since leaving Denmark.

We Danes have undoubtedly the same love of the sea as the mountain dweller feels for his mountains. From my balcony I gazed out across this deep blue expanse which was so new to me and yet which I knew so well. In the evening we were to go to the theatre. It was situated in the main street, the only wide street in Genoa, and as it was a great public building we thought it must be easy to find. Such, however, was not the case. Palace after palace, the one more magnificent than the other, stood there side by side. At last, a huge marble Apollo, as radiant and white as snow before it touches the ground, showed me that this was the place. A new opera, Donizetti's *Elisire d'amore*, was being performed for the very first time. It was followed by a comic ballet, *Il flauto magico*, in which everything, finally even the supreme council and indeed all the pictures on the council chamber walls, joined in and started to dance to the sound of the flute. I have since included that idea in the comic fairy tale *The Sandman*.

A written permit from the Admiralty admitted us to the Arsenal where the galley slaves, then about 600 in number, lived and worked. We visited the inner prisons and the dormitory in which there were large plank beds along the walls; there were iron chains hanging from the walls, and to these the prisoners were shackled when they went to rest in the evening. Even in the sickrooms a few lay in chains. Three of them, with yellowish brown faces and glazed eyes, were on the point of death, and they made a powerful impression on me. This must have been obvious, for one of the criminals there stared at me with an evil look in his eyes. I understood him, for I had merely come out of curiosity, to see them suffer, and he burst into a ghastly laughter, half raised himself up in bed and fixed his evil eyes on me in a quite diabolical fashion. Here, too, lay a blind old man with silvery hair, completely weighed down by the burden of his chains. Down in the courtyard there were various workrooms. Several of the galley slaves were chained together two by two, perhaps for the rest of their lives. I noticed one of the prisoners, dressed indeed like the others in white trousers and a red shirt, but in this case of an extremely fine material. He was young and bore no chains. We were told that it was a local man who had lived in plenty but had stolen huge sums of money and defrauded the town. Now he had been condemned to two years in the galleys. Admittedly he did no work, and neither was he chained during the day, but at night he was locked in with the others and like them chained to the bunk. He regularly received large sums of money from his wife, and he lived in plenty, but what was this when he constantly had to be together with these criminals and be chained in the same place at night and forced to listen to their contemptuous, evil tongues?

The first day's journey south from Genoa along the lake is one of the loveliest you can embark on. Genoa itself stands out on the mountain slopes among blue-green olive groves. There were both sweet and bitter oranges hanging in the gardens and shining, grass-green lemons looked almost spring-like, while people in northern lands were thinking of winter. Beautiful motifs for pictures came one after the other; everything was new and unforgettable to me. I can still see the old ivy-covered bridges, the Capuchins and a crowd of Genoese fishermen with red bonnets on their heads. The whole of this coast with its lovely villas and the sea with its white sailing ships and its smoky steamers shone brilliantly in the sunlight. Later, some hazy, blue mountains could be glimpsed out there: Corsica, the birthplace of Napoleon. Beneath an enormous tree by the foot of a tower sat three old women with long, silvery hair hanging down over their golden brown shoulders, spinning on distaffs. There were huge aloes growing close to the side of the road.

I will perhaps be reproached for allowing my thoughts to linger here over the natural beauty of Italy when I am telling the story of my life. Indeed some will justifiably fear that these pages will be crammed with descriptions of the many journeys that are to follow. However, it will be seen that later on it was the people I came into contact with who made the deepest impressions on me. On the other hand, during this my first visit to Italy it was the countryside and the art that overwhelmed me. These were what I really experienced during this time, and so this period of my life can scarcely fail to make me linger over the outward impressions I received. I just revelled in the luxuriant nature of this countryside. What an enchanting evening we spent in Sestri di Levante. The inn stands close to the sea, which was washing up over the beach in huge waves. The sky was streaked with fiery red clouds and the mountains were variegated with strong colours. The trees themselves resembled great baskets brimful of grapes which had been lifted up there by the vines. And then the scene was suddenly transformed as we reached the mountains. Here everything was dry and ugly for some considerable distance. It was as though, when Fancy had made Italy into a gigantic garden of great beauty, it had thrown all the weeds and garden rubbish just in this place. The few trees were bereft of leaves; it was neither a rocky landscape nor fertile soil; no, there was nothing but mud, gravel and broken boulders. And then, as though by the wave of a wand, everything was once more transformed into Hesperian beauty, and we saw the Bay of Spezia lying before us. Lovely blue mountains surrounded the most fertile and beautiful valley imaginable, a veritable horn of plenty. The vines were heavy with juicy fruit about the leafy trees; orange and olive trees mingled their branches with them and the heavy, juicy vines hung from tree to tree, while black pigs with shiny skins and no bristles jumped around like frolicking kids, causing an ass to kick out in annoyance even though it was carrying a Capuchin monk holding up a gigantic, grass-green umbrella.

We arrived in Carrara just on the birthday of the Duke of Modena. The houses were decorated with garlands, the soldiers had sprigs of myrtle in their caps and the cannon rumbled. But it was the marble quarries we wanted to visit; they are outside the town, and a sparkling little river close by the roadside ran over the glistening white fragments of marble. It was a large quarry containing both white and grey marble in which crystals are to be found. To me it was like an enchanted mountain where the gods and goddesses of antiquity were imprisoned in the blocks of stone, waiting for some great magician, a Thorvaldsen or a Canova, to free them and give them back to the world again.

Despite all the new things we saw and all the beauty of its countryside my companions and I generally had some serious reservations about Italy. The mode of travelling was so different from what we had known elsewhere. We were constantly cheated at the inns, continually asked to show our passports (within a few days they had been inspected and inscribed more than ten times), and our *vetturino* did not know the way and took the wrong road, so that instead of arriving in Pisa in daylight we did not reach it until the middle of the night. After a long and troublesome inspection we drove in through the dark, unlit streets; the only light we had was a large, flaming torch that our coachman had bought at the town gate and now held out in front of him. We finally reached our destination, the Albergo del Ussaro. "Like Jeppe, one day we sleep on a midden and the next in the baron's castle," I wrote home in a letter. This was the baron's castle. We were really in need of a rest and a little *dolce far niente* before going out to see the town's interesting features, the Church, the Baptistry, the Campo Santo and the Leaning Tower. It is the Campo Santo the theatre painter usually reproduces for the backcloth to the monastery hall in *Robert le Diable*. There are monuments and bas-reliefs in the cloister, one of them by Thorvaldsen representing *Tobias Healing his Blind Father*, in which the artist has portrayed himself as the young Tobias. The Leaning Tower was not exactly inviting to ascend, but we went up it nevertheless. It is in the form of a cylinder surrounded by columns, and there are no railings at the top. The wind from the sea is spoiling the side facing the coast; the iron is decaying and the stones are becoming loose; the whole construction is a dirty yellow colour. From up there I could see right across a flat countryside as far as Livorno; getting there means only a short journey by rail these days, but then it was different. It was a case of going by vettura and what we discovered there was in our opinion not worth the journey. Our guide knew nothing and showed us nothing we could not have done without. "A Turkish merchant lives across there," he said. "But his shop is shut today. There is a church with a beautiful painting in it, but it has been taken away. That man who just passed is one of the richest in the town." Those were among the most interesting things

135

he told us. Then he took us to the Synagogue: "the most beautiful and the richest in Europe". The impression it gave was of anything but a religious building, for inside it resembled a stock exchange in every detail. The fact that people here all wore their hats and tried to drown each other out made a very unpleasant impression on me. Filthy Jewish children were standing on the chairs. Some rabbis were grinning from a sort of pulpit and laughing at a couple of aged Hebrews; up by the Tabernacle people were pushing and jostling. There was a dreadful bustle and confusion. There was no thought of devotion here, and nor could there possibly be. Up above us all, the women were almost hidden from view behind a fine grating in a big gallery. The only beautiful thing I saw in Livorno was the sunset: the clouds glittered like tongues of fire, the sea shone and the mountains were resplendent. This was the frame surrounding this filthy town, the setting that imparted Italian splendour to it. But that splendour was soon to reveal itself in all the glory of its art when we reached Florence.

Before this, I had never had any appreciation of sculpture. I had virtually seen none at home, and in Paris, like most other people, I had merely stared at it as I passed by. No painting had so far really inspired me or filled me with enthusiasm. It was in Florence during my visits to the splendid art galleries and the churches with their monuments and wonders that my appreciation of art suddenly seemed to awaken within me. I stood before the Venus di Medici, and it seemed as though the marble eyes had the power to see; I felt myself curiously lost in something approaching pious wonderment and I could not tear myself away:

> From ocean foam, so white and light,
> So fair as must a god delight,
> Ever youthful there she'll stand;
> New generations plough the land,
> But ne'er will love's fair deity die
> The goddess lives for aye.

I visited the galleries every day, and it was always the Venus di Medici and the Niobe group which most occupied my attention. There is a truth, some undying truth in this magnificent group, and as the individual figures stand some way apart from each other it is possible to walk among them in the midst of the action, so to speak. This mother hewn out of marble is portrayed spreading her robe over the head of her last surviving daughter, but you can see from the child's head that the arrow is coming and from the position of the hand that it will find its mark.

What a treasure of wonderful pictures there was here to open up a new spiritual world before me. I saw Raphael's Madonna del Seggiola and the Madonna del Granduco; one wonder after the other was revealed to me. Prior to this I had certainly made the acquaintance of much of what I found here through prints and plaster casts, but none of it had had any great effect on me, and none of it had impressed itself on my spirit, and so I felt like a new being. I visited the most important churches, mainly Santa Croce with its great marble monuments. The personifications of Sculpture, Painting and Architecture are seated around Michelangelo's sarcophagus. Dante's tomb is at Ravenna, but the monument to him is in Santa Croce. Italia points to the poet's colossal statue while Poetry weeps over his sarcophagus. There is also a monument by Canova in honour of Alfieri; it is adorned with masks, a lyre and a laurel wreath, and Italia weeps by the grave. Less imposing are the tombs of Galileo and Machiavelli, but the spot itself is no less sacred.

One day we three Danes went looking for a fourth, the copperplate engraver, Sonne, and had already reached the district where he was said to live. We were talking to each other in loud voices when a man in shirtsleeves and wearing a leather apron came towards us and asked us in Danish, "Who are you looking for, gentlemen?" He was a Copenhagen locksmith who had settled here, married a French girl and had now been away from Denmark for nine years. We heard his story and in return told him what things were like at home. He was living in affluent Florence, but missed the little Copenhagen street called Møntergade.

The day for our departure arrived. We were going by way of Terni to see the waterfall and then on to Rome. It was a wretched journey; scorching sun by day and poisonous flies and midges in the evening and at night, and then we had a poor *vetturino* and all the inconveniences such a man can inflict on people. We considered all the expressions of admiration for the beauties and wonders of Italy we found scratched on the windows and walls in the inns to be sheer travesties. Little did I realise then what love my heart was one day to feel for this land of great beauty and wonderful memories.

Our torments began in Florence as soon as we had climbed into the otherwise excellent coach our *vetturino* had brought with him. Outside the door of the coach there stood a figure who looked like Job when scraping himself with a piece of broken pottery. We shook our heads when he took hold of the door; then he went round to the other side and was given the same signal to go away. When he came back and was once more sent away the *vetturino* came up to us and said that he was a fourth passenger, a distinguished gentleman from Rome. That impressed us, and we allowed him in. But the filth on his body and clothes soon made us decide to tell the *vetturino* at the first stop that we would not continue our journey to Rome with him if this gentleman was to sit in the carriage with us. After much discussion and gesticulating we saw our distinguished gentleman climb up to the coachman. It started to pour with rain and I felt sorry for the poor fellow, but it really was impossible to share a room with him, let alone a coach, and so we let the rain wash him. The road was romantic and beautiful, but the sun burned down on us and the flies buzzed all around us. We defended ourselves with branches of myrtle. Our horses looked like carrion, so covered were they with masses of flies. We spent the night in a dreadful hole in Levane. I saw our distinguished gentleman standing by the chimney drying himself by the fire and helping the innkeeper to pluck the chickens we were to eat and at the same time expressing his fury with heretical Englishmen who one day would be punished for their deeds. And so we were that very night. In order to have some fresh air, we left all our windows open with the result that during the night we were so thoroughly bitten all over our faces and hands by flies and midges that we were all swollen and bleeding. One of my hands alone could boast of no less than fifty-seven bites; I was in pain and was running a temperature. The following day we passed through Castiglione, driving through lovely, fertile countryside full of olive groves and vines. Pretty, half-naked children and old matrons with silvery hair were tending coal-black pigs with shiny skins. By the side of Lake Thrasymene, where Hannibal fought, I saw my first wild laurels by the roadside. We entered the Papal States, and after we had been through a customs examination of our passports and luggage we continued our journey to the accompaniment of the most beautiful sunset. I saw a wealth of colours I shall never forget, but the inn was dreadful. The floor was all broken and there were cripples outside the door; the landlady, who was wearing a filthy blouse, grinned like an ugly witch, spat every time she brought us a fresh course and then went out of the door again.

I thought of this place when describing in *The Galoshes of Fortune* how horrible it can be in "bella Italia". The following morning we reached Perugia, the town where Raphael studied under Perugino. We saw pictures by both the pupil and his master; from the top of the hill we looked out across extensive olive groves and saw the same beautiful landscape that was reflected in Raphael's eyes, just as it was once in the eyes of the Emperor Augustus when the triumphal arch of ashlars was raised for him; it still stands as though it were finished only yesterday. Towards evening we were in Foligno which presented us with the sight of an extremely dilapidated town. Almost all the houses in the main street were supported by means of beams stretching from each house to the house opposite. There had been an earthquake here only a short time before, and great cracks could be seen in the walls, while some houses were mere heaps of rubble. It began to rain and blow a gale. It was anything but comfortable in the inn, and we found the food uneatable, hungry though we were.

"Kennst Du das Land!" mocked a young German as the wind and the rain rattled the shaky windows. "Now there is probably going to be another earthquake, and then the whole lot will collapse," we thought. But it did not collapse, and we slept well, and the next afternoon we were at Terni, standing in front of the magnificent waterfall, which is situated among laurels and rosemary, high up above extensive olive groves, amidst all the beauty of Italy. A little river plunges down from the cliff, and that is all there is, but it was so infinitely beautiful to see, and the spray rose high in the air like steam. The sun lit it all up with dark red beams, and then it sank, and dusk fell suddenly; the night was completely dark as I went back through the black olive grove. I had lost the rest of my party, so I walked together with a young American who talked about Niagara, Cooper and the great prairies.

The following day was wet. The road was bad and the surroundings did not present us with anything new, so we merely felt how tiring and difficult it all was. We found a filthy hotel in dirty little Nepi. The only experience that provided me with anything beautiful to remember was an evening stroll here during which I by chance went out of the town and found some ruins where a waterfall was pouring down into an abyss. I have worked it into my novel *The Improvisatore.* This is where I have let Antonio see Fulvia's face for the last time. Finally, the day came when we were due to arrive in Rome. We left amid drizzle and rain, passed Monte Soracte of which Horace wrote, and proceeded into the campagna outside Rome. But none of us felt its beauty or was enthralled by the colours and beautiful outlines of the mountains. We thought only of the goal and of the rest we should find there. And I admit that when we arrived on the hill at La Storta from which travellers from the North catch their first glimpse of Rome, where the pilgrim kneels in devotion and where many who tell of their travels talk of their delight and elevation at this sight, I was also pleased. However, my exclamation was scarcely the exclamation of a poet: on seeing Rome and St. Peter's for the first time I shouted out loud, "Thank goodness! Now we shall soon be able to have something to eat!"

Rome!

It was midday on the 18th October when I arrived in Rome, that city of all cities in the world where I soon felt as though I had been born and belonged. On that very day I arrived in time for one of the rarest occasions, the second burial of Raphael.

For many years a skull had been kept in the Accademia di San Luca and exhibited as belonging to him, but since some doubt had recently arisen as to whether it was genuine, Pope Gregory the Sixteenth gave permission for the tomb in the Pantheon, or as the church on this spot is now called, Santa Maria della Rotunda, to be opened. The complete skeleton was found there. Now the body was to be reburied. When the tomb was opened and the bones taken out Camuccini, the painter, and no one else had been given permission to paint the whole picture. Horace Vernet, who was then living in the French Academy in Rome, knew nothing of all this, so he took out his pencil and made a sketch. The Papal police who were present forbade him to do this; he looked at them in amazement and quite calmly said, "But I suppose I may make a little souvenir of it from memory at home." They could scarcely object to this, and so between twelve noon and six in the evening he painted a lovely oil painting of the scene. After this he had a plate made in order to make prints of the scene, but this was immediately confiscated by the police. Horace Vernet wrote a furious letter and demanded that the plate should be returned to him within twenty-four hours, since art could not be subjected to a monopoly like salt and tobacco. He received it, too, but he broke it in two and sent the pieces along with a letter written in robust language to Camuccini, saying that with this he wanted to show him that it was not his intention to use it to his disadvantage. Camuccini had the plate put together again and returned it to Horace Vernet together with an extremely friendly letter in which he declared that he had completely abandoned all thought of publishing his painting. Everyone was allowed to sketch the grave now, and so there was soon a host of representations of it.

Our compatriots obtained tickets for us to attend the ceremony, and so our first experience in Rome was to be present at Raphael's funeral. The mahogany coffin covered with a golden cloth stood on a dais draped in black. The priests sang a Miserere; the coffin was opened and the reports which had been read out were put into it; an unseen choir sang with great beauty and moved everyone's heart as the procession began to move around the church. All the most important artists and men of rank followed. It was here in Rome that I saw Thorvaldsen for the first time; like all the others in the procession he walked slowly forward holding a wax candle in his hand. The solemnity of the occasion, however, was spoiled for me by something earthly and unpleasant; when they were putting the coffin in through the narrow opening they had to raise it up on end, so that the bones, which had been carefully arranged, all fell to one end. We could hear how they rattled.

So I was in Rome now and felt very much at home there. Of all my fellow countrymen a medallist by the name of Christensen gave me the heartiest and liveliest welcome. We had not known each other personally before, but he had taken a liking to me as a result of reading my poems. He immediately took me out to visit Thorvaldsen who was living at his old home in Via Felice. He was working on his bas-relief *Raphael*, in which the painter is sitting amidst some ruins where the Muses and Harmony are to be seen in bas-relief. He is drawing from nature. Love is holding his tablet for him and at the same time reaching a poppy to him, a symbolical reference to the artist's early death. Genius, holding a torch, is looking sadly at him and Victory is holding a garland above his head.

Thorvaldsen talked of his idea with great vivacity and enthusiasm and then told us about the previous day's ceremony and about Raphael, Camuccini and Vernet. I was allowed to see a collection of wonderful paintings by living masters which he had bought and said he would leave to Denmark on his death. The simple straightforwardness and the gentle cordiality of this great artist impressed me, remarkably sensitive as I was, so that I was almost in tears when I left him, even though, as he said, we should be seeing each other every day.

Among the others of my compatriots who immediately gave me a delightful and cordial welcome was Ludvig Bødtcher who has written several beautiful works portraying the Italian countryside. He lived a quiet life in Rome, devoted to art, nature and a quick-witted *dolce far niente*. As one who had lived in Rome for many years he knew everything of interest and beauty, and in him I found a guide endowed with both intelligence and knowledge. Another person who became a warm and faithful companion to me was Küchler, the painter, who was still young in both body and spirit. He was not without humour and always had a witty remark on the tip of his tongue. In those days I had no idea of what would become of him later and that he was to end his days as a mendicant friar in a little monastery in Silesia. He was so jovial and kind-hearted, and as far as I could see such an intellectually vigorous young man who painted those beautiful Italian pictures which always contained a roguish touch of the erotic. When I went to Rome for the second time several years later his youthful freshness was gone, and there was only the occasional flash of humour; then, when I visited Rome for the third time in 1846 he had become a Catholic and painted nothing but altar pieces and religious pictures.

Now, as we know, he was invested as a mendicant friar a few years ago by Pius IX, and thus he wandered barefoot through Germany to a poor little monastery in the Prussian States, no longer Albert Küchler, the painter, but the Franciscan monk, Pietro di Santo Pio.

May God grant him there that peace and happiness which, no doubt because he misunderstood the all-loving God, he is now seeking on a misguided path and yet will find.

In the weeks and months we were together he was a vivacious, caring friend. I like best to remember him from those early days which, although I was in Rome, the goal of my longings, also had heavy and bitter times in store for me. But before I go on to reveal these there are still a few beautiful days in mountain air amidst the most beautiful countryside imaginable. It was still like the most wonderful summer weather at home, and although Rome was new to me, this lovely weather had to be enjoyed in all its glory. We arranged a trip to the mountains, to be led by Küchler, Blunck, Fearnley and Bødtcher, who were as though at home there. Not only did their knowledge of the Italian people and the customs of the country make it extremely cheap, but everything was so thoroughly and clearly impressed on me that I, so to speak, became intellectually acclimatised there, and the seeds of most of the descriptions of the Italian countryside and the life of the people that I have given in *The Improvisatore* were planted in me. I still had no thought of writing such a book or even of writing any sort of travel account at all. This week spent walking in the countryside was without doubt the happiest time I had in that lovely country; it was a time of unmixed delight.

Across the Campagna, past tombs dating from antiquity, past picturesque aqueducts, groups of shepherds and their flocks, we went to the Alban Mountains, whose lovely, blue, wave-like contours seemed so close to us in the clear air. At Frascati, where we ate lunch, I had my first sight of a really popular *osteria* filled with peasants and clerics. There were hens and chickens running around on the floor; a fire was burning in the hearth and the ragged youngsters dragged our donkeys right up to it. We mounted them, and off they

143

went at a constant trot, just as it pleased them, on and on into the mountains, past the ruins of Cicero's villa to ancient Tusculum, which had now nothing but cobbled streets to show us. There were no houses, only traces of walls between the laurels and chestnuts. We visited Monte Pozio, where there was a deep well which resonated as though all the wealth of music were hidden in it. It was this resonance which the laughing and jubilant Rossini drew on and in which Bellini shed his tears and gave the world only sad melodies. By evening we were back in Frascati. The brilliant moon shone down on the velvet black cypresses around the Cenci castle where Beatrice lived and defended herself against her brutal father. Under the heading *Italy* in my *Collected Poems* there is a poem called *Beatrice Cenci* that dates from this visit. There was a firework display at Frascati; rockets rose above the dark trees and the town resounded with joy and delight. Early the following morning we went on foot into the mountains. The campagna lay beneath us and we caught a glimpse of the Mediterranean. Before long we reached the Grotta Ferrata, where Domenichino fled to the monastery on account of a murder and there in gratitude painted four superb pictures and gave them to the monastery. The path on which we were walking took us close to a great tree, the top of which spread and arched in the shape of a chapel. The very uppermost part had been cut in the form of a cross surrounded by a wreath; the huge lower branches formed a great dome, and in the hollow trunk a cabinet had been hung behind the glass door of which a figure of the Virgin was to be seen. The whole of this walk was as though through a rich and luxuriant garden with constantly changing views and scenes. We went through Ariccia to Genzano, the town famed for the Festival of Flowers, and not until the evening did we reach Nemi, where there are great plane trees and cacti growing on the slopes of a mountain that was once a crater and now form a flower-strewn barrier around the deep and clear Lake Nemi. How wonderful it was to linger there, to breathe the Italian air and to hear of the festival and of the life of the people. Every day of this expedition was a lovely fairy tale in the midst of nature. One overcast morning when we were riding on donkeys at the side of Lake Albano, we passed a huge, picturesque cave. Its walls were covered with a tapestry of the loveliest greenery. Fine, fresh maidenhair, a type of fern of infinite delicacy and beauty, formed a sort of hanging curtain inside the cave itself. It was filled with a distinctive fairy-like radiance, and even if he could, no artist would dare to paint it, for no one who had not seen it in reality would believe it to be true. That day we were making for the monastery of Monte Cavo, where it was as cold as on a day in autumn. The monastery garden, surrounded by a hedge of magnificent laurels, covers the ground where the temple of Jupiter Stator used to stand and where a few massive blocks of stone are still to be found. A thick cloud stretched out before us, hiding most of the campagna and Rome, but suddenly it dispersed and before us lay Rome, the campagna and the mountains. At our feet we could see Lake Albano and Lake Nemi, radiantly blue, like a little girl's two beautiful eyes. What wonderful evenings we experienced, what beautiful, dreamy walks to the accompaniment of merry chatter and singing in all this luxuriant landscape. It was as though fortune allowed us to see several scenes from the life of the people which are nowadays extremely rare. We saw a real, gold-braided dulcamara on the carts containing his medicines, proclaiming his wares and accompanied by servants who looked as though they were dressed for a masquerade. We met some bandits chained to a cart pulled by oxen and surrounded by gendarmes. We saw a funeral where the uncovered corpse was carried on a stretcher; the red evening sun shone on the pale cheeks and on boys with paper cones catching the wax dripping from the monks' candles. The bells rang out, there were sounds of singing, the young men played at morra and the girls danced a saltarello to the sound of tambourines. I have never since seen Italy so festive and beautiful. It was as though Pinelli's pictures had come to life; I saw them in nature and reality.

We returned to Rome, to the grandeur of the churches, the wonderful art galleries and all the art treasures, but the summer weather, which continued even though it was now November, summoned us to the mountains again, this time to Tivoli.

However, the chill of autumn began to make itself felt in the early morning air; the peasants lit bonfires by which to warm themselves; we met village folk riding past wearing big, black sheepskins, just as though we were in the land of the Hottentots. But as the sun rose higher it grew warm. Everything around Tivoli was green and fresh;

the town was perched above cascading waterfalls, among olive groves resplendent with bouquets of cypresses and red vine leaves. The great waterfalls plunged like masses of white cloud down into the green depths. It was a warm day, and we all felt the desire and the need for a shower bath beneath the fountain at Villa d'Este.

This is where Italy's biggest cypresses grow, as huge as those in the East. We went down to the foot of the steep waterfall in the evening twilight; our torches conjured up strange shapes in the thick laurel hedges. The nearby precipice, where we could hear the water thundering as it rushed down, seemed both nearer and deeper than it really was. At a given signal some wisps of straw were lit above us, lighting up the ancient Temple of the Sibyl which was outlined with its row of columns in the flickering light.

We returned to Rome, where people still lived and behaved as in Goethe's day and where artists kept together more like members of the same family and in a more pleasing way than I have ever seen since.

Scandinavians and Germans formed one circle while the French, who had their own Academy under the leadership of Horace Vernet, formed another. At dinner in the "Lepre" osteria each nationality had its own table. In the evenings, Swedes, Norwegians, Danes and Germans joined company, and a few figures from the older generation were also to be seen there. The two old landscape painters Reinhart and Koch went there, as did Thorvaldsen. Reinhart, who had seen the Italian countryside through the eyes of a poet, had put down roots in that country and exchanged it for ever for Bavaria. He was old, and yet he appeared so young as he sat there with his shining eyes and his silvery hair; his laughter resounded through the whole room; a velvet jacket and a red, woollen cap were characteristic of his dress. Thorvaldsen used to wear an old coat with the Order of Bajoko hanging on the lapel, this being the order one received on joining the regulars forming the company.

The new member would once and for all give drinks all round for the evening. This was known as doing a "Ponte molle", and the new member was given the Order of Bajoko, a copper coin which was to be worn in the button hole on all such occasions. Then there was a lot of dressing up and dramatic scenes; the elected "General", at that time a young German artist, arrived in a sort of military uniform with a golden cardboard star pinned to his breast and accompanied by the Executioner carrying an axe and a bundle of arrows. He was dressed in a tiger skin. After them came the minnesinger, who to the accompaniment of a guitar sang an extempore song about the evening's "Ponte molle". It had previously been the custom when one of our countrymen came to Rome to meet him out by the Pons Aemilius, which in everyday language was called the "Ponte molle", and drink to him in welcome in the inn there. Now this had been changed and made a part of the general taverna life, and the real reception was held in Rome itself.

There was a knock at the door, just like the Commandant's knock in *Don Giovanni*; the expected guest arrived, and now began a duet between the General inside and a soloist and chorus outside. Thereupon the newcomer was allowed to enter and was dressed up in a sort of blouse and long curls, and long paper nails were glued to his fingers. In addition he was painted and garbed in the most fantastic manner. The long hair and nails were now cut off and the ragged blouse taken off, and he was cleaned and dressed so as to be worthy of taking his place among the others. But first he had to listen to the Ten Commandments, among which was one stating that "he should not covet his neighbour's wine and he should love his General and serve no other than him". A big white banner carrying an image of a bottle of wine and an inscription *"Viva la fogliette"*, a pun on Lafayette, waved above him. Now the procession marched around the tables, all the time singing the same song about a "traveller-man", and this was followed by songs in the different languages of the assembly. A merry "Snitzelbank" was put on, starting with "Monte Cavo" and "Kleiner Bravo". Sometimes there followed some pre-arranged practical joke, as for instance on the occasion when one of the peasants from the street rode right into the room on his donkey, to everyone's great consternation or when the real gendarmes had been persuaded to come in and pretend they wanted to arrest some honourable member of the company, all of which resulted in bewilderment and much amusement and ended with the policemen's being given their fogliette, too.

Christmas was our most beautiful festival. I have written of it in

A Poet's Bazaar, but it was scarcely ever again as festive, fresh and bright as in 1833. On the sacred Christmas Eve itself we were not allowed to make merry in the city, but we could do so outside it so we hired a large house in the garden of the Villa Borghese near the amphitheatre. Jensen, the flower painter, Christensen, the medallist, and I were out there from early morning, and in the warm sunshine we went around in our shirt-sleeves making wreaths and garlands. A great orange tree with the fruit still on it was our Christmas tree. I was the lucky one who won the best prize, a silver cup inscribed "Christmas Eve in Rome, 1833." Each of the guests contributed a present, and it was a condition that we should choose something, or at least make it amusing by the way in which it was wrapped up or by the inscription on it. I had with me from Paris a few garish yellow collars, which were of no use for anything but a carnival dress. I decided to use these, but the whole thing took a turn which, as will be seen, could quite easily have ended the evening in quarrelling and bitterness. It never occurred to me that there was anyone who did not believe that Thorvaldsen was the most important among us, and so I thought that I could present him rather than anyone else with the wreath. So the collars, which bore the colour of envy, were an element in the joke. I was ignorant of something that we now can read in Thiele's *Life of Thorvaldsen*, that there had been some differences between Byström and Thorvaldsen as to each other's skill. Byström had expressed the view that Thorvaldsen was better than he in bas-reliefs, but not in groups. Thorvaldsen had then become angry and exclaimed, "You can tie my hands, and I'll bite marble better with my teeth than you can carve it!"

Both Thorvaldsen and Byström were present at our Christmas party. I had made a wreath for my great compatriot and written a little verse to go along with it. The present was for him, but at the side of it lay the yellow collars, which were to go to whoever happened to draw the winning lot. Chance had it that it went to Byström, and the inscription to the winner of it was, "You can keep the yellow collars of envy, but you must present the wreath to Thorvaldsen." There was immediate consternation at this lack of tact or this bad joke. However, as soon as it was realised that it was pure chance that it had fallen to Byström, and when it was learnt that it was I who had done it, and no one attributed any evil intentions to me, everything was smoothed over and good humour was restored.

I had written a song. It was my first really Scandinavian poem. Christmas was a natural Scandinavian festival in Rome, but there was no sign of Scandinavian sympathies. As a title I had called my poem *The Scandinavians' Christmas Song in Rome, 1833*, and it was written to the tune of *Young Athelstane stood by the Judgement Seat*:

> Sweet is the scent of the Christmas tree,
> Though its home is the laurel grove;
> Let us like children enjoy the spree,
> To be called a child is what we love.
> The only difference that I can see,
> Is that children know rather less than we.
>
> Think of the lovely Christmas, when
> We were at home as children small;
> We stood by a door that was locked, and then
> We peered through the crack at the fairy tale hall.
> The neighbours' children were often there;
> And now the same is happening here.
>
> Norwegian and Danish and Swedish are we,
> With the freshness and truth of a loyal friend.
> Though parted we were, we brothers three
> Have met here in Rome at our journey's end.
> One language, one home to us has been given,
> And brothers we are 'neath our Nordic heaven.
>
> For king and our home flows our heart's precious blood,
> What the heart holds in love it will e'er sing and praise.
> Hail, monarch of Denmark, King Frederik the Good.
> Hail, monarch of Sweden, Carl Johan the Wise.
> This health we will drink to each others' king,
> For brother with brother, this Christmas, we sing.

When the song had been sung there was a pause; each wanted to drink the health of his own king first; finally they were drunk together. With a natural sense of tact and without any thought of politics I appeared to have said the right thing; but across the table I was reproached for the "many kings". And later I heard from Copenhagen that people in high positions thought it strange that I, who was travelling abroad for Danish money, should sing the praises of the King of Sweden. It seemed to me that it would have been extremely inappropriate in a gathering of Danes, Swedes and Norwegians if the two kings, just like the three peoples, were not also mentioned at the same time; we were neighbouring children of the North and each of the guests was host as well. But as I say, my opinion was not shared by everyone at that time. Now they have changed their attitudes, as is right and proper, but I was criticised because I came too soon and yet at the right time and in the right place.

After leaving the party together with Thorvaldsen and some of the others at about midnight and knocking on the gate of Rome it reminded me of *Ulysses von Ithacia* where Chilian knocks on the gate of Troy. *"Chi é?"* they asked. *"Amici,"* we replied, and now a gate was opened that was so tiny that we had almost to crawl through it. The weather was lovely, just like a summer night in Scandinavia. "It is different from what it is at home," said Thorvaldsen. "My cloak is really getting too heavy for me."

I rarely received letters from home, and with a few exceptions those that came were written with the object of educating me and were often petty and inconsiderate. Of course they distressed me, and they always had a noticeable effect on me, so much so that those of my compatriots with whom I mixed here in Rome and of whom I was fond, used to exclaim, "Have you had a letter from home again? I wouldn't read those letters, and I'd have nothing to do with friends who only think of tormenting and worrying you." I certainly needed educating, and I was being educated, but in a harsh and unkind manner. People did not realise how the dead words from what had been written could afflict my heart. While enemies lash with whips, friends lash with scorpions.

So far I had heard nothing of *Agnete*. The first comment I received was from a "good friend". His judgement of the work gives us a picture of the Andersen I was then:

"With what I might almost call your unnatural sensitivity and childishness you are very unlike me – I must admit that I had expected something very different from you here – a different spirit, different ideas and images, least of all a character like Henning. In short, Agnete seems to me to be just like your poems (N.B. the best of your poems), although I had hoped in some respects to see signs of a mental change in you as a result of your travelling. I have talked to ** about this, and he agrees with me, and as he, who is both your friend and in a way your mentor, has written to you at some length on this subject, you shall be spared advice and reminders from me.

My dear friend, forget your financial worries and thoughts about home, and derive all the benefit you can from your journey. A little more manliness and strength, and a little less childishness, exaggeration and sentimentality. Study your subjects more and make sure you understand them completely, and then I will congratulate Andersen's friends on his return and Denmark on having found a poet."

That was from someone of whom I was fond, one of those who were my true friends, younger in years but cleverer and in happier circumstances, one of those who expressed his opinion as gently as possible, for of course I was "so sensitive and childish". What a strange thing that he and other sensible folk could expect to see any great change in me in *Agnete* as a result of my travels, which, as I have already said, consisted in sailing by steamer to Kiel and going by stagecoach to Paris and later to Switzerland, whence I dispatched the work less than four months after leaving home. The effects of the journey could not be expected until a considerable time had elapsed, and then I produced *The Improvisatore*.

But the words of another friend, one of those on whom I could best rely, disturbed me far more deeply. He wrote:

"I have no hope of your deriving any real benefit from this subscription. You simply do not know, Andersen, as I and the others who wish you well and are genuinely fond of you

151

know, how people – indeed almost everyone – it is dreadful how few exceptions there are – how people put things: 'Oh, has he managed to string something together again?' – 'I grew tired of him long ago.' – 'He always writes the same sort of thing.' In short it is unbelievable how few friends your Muse has now. What is the reason for this? – *You write too much!* When one work is being printed you are half way through the manuscript for the next, and as a result of this furious, this deplorable productivity you are reducing the value of your work to such an extent that soon no bookseller will even have it as a gift. Are you not already thinking – according to your letter to ** of writing yet another travel book?" – (This was *The Improvisatore* which I began in Rome) – "Who do you think will buy a book in several volumes dealing with your journey, a journey which a thousand others have made; and two thousand eyes can scarcely have missed so much that you can fill two volumes with things that are new and interesting to them. Fundamentally it is a sign of enormous egotism to think that people are so interested in you. The fault must be your own; for the public, at least the critics, have certainly not given you any reason for this. If I know you rightly, Andersen, you will answer quietly and complacently, 'Yes, but once people read my *Agnete* they will change their minds, and then they will want to see how my travels have influenced me and made me more mature, etc.' This is just about what you say in your last letter. But you are wrong, Andersen, pitifully wrong. *Agnete* is so completely the work of the old Andersen, both in the beautiful, child-like passages and in what we already know from his earlier works. I have often been on the point of tears on seeing how much of *Agnete* I recognised and did not want to see; my tears were usually stifled by annoyance. When you have read this you will say that I am unreasonable and so on. So I will tell you something: I discussed my worries concerning the proofs with a man who is very interested indeed in you, a man for whom you have great respect and whose judgement you trust. I asked him to go through the manuscript with me so that

Agnete might be made more or less acceptable to people. I gave him the manuscript to look through and received the following answer from him: 'I had intended spending this evening in the company of Andersen's *Agnete*, but I cannot stomach it. It hurts me to read such a mediocre work by him, and I ask you to show mercy on me; for it is not possible for me to think of correcting minor errors as I read it through when what I have already read only extremely rarely reveals any sign of brilliance. If it is a case of helping our absent friend then there is nothing to do but to keep the entire work back. In my opinion, that will be an act of true friendship to him. The pity is that Oehlenschläger once sent masterpieces home from Paris; so this has presumably been put together at breakneck speed. I am sending the manuscript back to you and I wash my hands of it. I advise you to do the same. We should perhaps one day regret having been godfathers to that child'.

From that you will see that what I said before is not solely my opinion; unfortunately you will soon realise it is the opinion shared by almost everyone. For heaven's sake and for the sake of your honour as a poet, stop writing for a time, for six months at least. Spend one half of your travels studying and enjoying yourself, and the other half doing the same thing. By that I do not mean that you ought to study history from Millot's *History of the World*, as you say you are doing. You will answer that you have to write to earn money and to live. All right, I will admit that, hard though it is. But if there is to be any time when you can manage without writing, then it must be during the two years, probably the only two years of your life, when you have a grant of 600 *Rigsdaler*, although I can quite well understand that it is difficult for you to manage on that."

He then goes on to say that I cannot expect any extension of my bursary, and neither can I hope to obtain what is called the "Lasson Scholarship", and the letter ends as follows:

"And now I am at the end of the unpleasant things I have to say. In the next letter you receive from me I shall try to write in a quieter and friendlier tone; for I have been a little acrimonious in this. And so I will not give you a lengthy report on a review of your *Collected Poems* which recently appeared in *Maanedsskrift for Litteratur*, and where you are dealt with rather meanly in comparison with Hertz, Hansen, Holst, Christian Winther and *Love at Court*. I think it is by Molbech. Apart from being full of criticism as usual, he is witty in his way. But in truth, you lose nothing by being criticised in this manner."

The review was indeed by Molbech.

People will understand the pain this letter gave me. Now, many years later, when everything has resolved itself and I can look calmly back on it all, I can well understand the deep sympathy people showed me! It is obvious how even the person who took my part more than any other was carried away by the general scorn and rejection which was my lot at home. I was so overwhelmed by this letter that I was in danger of forgetting my God, of turning my back on both Him and humanity. I thought of death in a way a Christian ought not to do. But, it might be asked, was there not a single person who even then had some more kindly and encouraging words to say about *Agnete*, the work that had sprung from my heart and had not, as people were saying, "been strung together at breakneck speed"? Yes, there was one, and that was Mrs. Læssøe. I will just quote a few lines from her letter:

"I must admit that *Agnete* has not been a great success, but it can only be evil tongues that can say that it is being torn to pieces as you have heard. It contains many beautiful passages, but I think you made a mistake in dealing with this subject. I think, too, that this was my opinion before you started on it. For us Danes, the ballad of Agnete is a butterfly to be looked at but not touched. You have dealt with Agnete herself in such a delightful way, but her surroundings are too heavy and her world is too small for her to flutter in elegantly."

Shocked both in heart and mind by the criticism I had received at home and by the rejection of my work at large, I then received the news of the death of my old mother. It was Collin who told me about it, and my first exclamation was, "Thank God! Now there is an end to her suffering which I have been unable to do anything to ease." I wept, but yet could scarcely accustom myself to the thought of not having anyone in the world to love me because of the bonds of blood and nature. This new impression filled my eyes with tears; I wept profusely and had a feeling that this was the best thing that could happen to her. For I would never be able to ensure that her final days were bright and carefree. She had died in the happy belief in my good fortune, convinced that I *was something*. Mrs. Læssøe wrote of it:

> "It must have been a heavy blow to receive such sad news while away and among strangers: I mean the news of your mother's death. With God's help she is now in a better land, a land where the heart is given the place it deserves, and then, as far as I can judge from what I know of her, she will come to occupy – not *a lofty* position, for that is a horrible, worldly expression but a good and secure place, for she deserved that by virtue of her love. May she rest in peace. But it is not true to say that there is no one here who 'is fond of you', for I feel a maternal affection for you. I cannot but count you among my sons. You must suffer that!"

How I blessed these comforting, loving words; what a great support they were to me in my infinitely bitter suffering. My compatriots, too, were all full of heartfelt sympathy, though mainly on account of my mother's death. That was what they understood best. Among the most recent arrivals was the poet Henrik Hertz, the man who had attacked me in *Letters from the Dead*. Collin had written and told me that Hertz was coming, and that he would be glad to hear that we met as friends. I was sitting in the Café Greco on the first day Hertz appeared there. He offered me his hand in a friendly manner.

155

I derived much pleasure from his company, and as soon as he saw my sadness and understood what I was suffering he spoke to me in quiet and comforting words. He talked to me about my works and about his views. He mentioned *The Letters from the Dead*, and, curiously enough, asked me not to take unjust criticism to heart. He was of the opinion that the Romantic plane on which I was moving led me to excesses, but on the other hand he thought my descriptions of nature, in which my real nature was revealed in a remarkable manner, were very good, and it was they that he had found most attractive. Moreover, he believed that I ought to console myself with the thought that all true poets had probably gone through the same crisis as I, but that their works had not been known at the time and that once I had been through this purgatory I would come to be truly recognised in the realm of art!

A few days before this Hertz together with Thorvaldsen had heard me read *Agnete* at my home and on that occasion he said that hearing it read was not really sufficient for him to form an impression of the work as a whole. However, he thought the lyrical passages were good and that what people at home called faults in the form were due to the fact that the ballad lost much of its power in a dramatic presentation. Oehlenschläger had spoiled the *Aage and Else* motif with his story *The Pale Knight* in just the same way. Of course I was able to object that *Axel and Valborg* was a beautiful tragedy all the same; but, he said, that was possible because of its enormous length, which really placed it outside the realm of the ballad. Thorvaldsen said little on this occasion but sat looking serious and wise and listening attentively as I read. If his eyes happened to meet mine he nodded kindly and appeared to be pleased. He pressed my hand and praised the music and the harmony both in the work as a whole and in the separate sections. "And then it is so Danish," he said. "It is straight from the forests and the sea at home."

It was thus in Rome that I really got to know Thorvaldsen. When I went to Copenhagen as a boy in 1819, he happened to be there. It was the first time he had been home since leaving as a poor artist. We met in the street. I knew that he was an important man in the world of art, and I looked at him and raised my hat. He went on, but suddenly turned round, came back to me and said, "Where have I seen you before? I seem to think we two know each other."

"No, we do not know each other at all," I answered. Now we were in Rome I told him this story, and he smiled, pressed my hand and said, "Yes, I must have had a feeling then that we should become friends." What pleased me about his opinion of *Agnete* was that he had said it came from "the forests and the sea at home". One day when he noticed how distressed I was he put his arms round my neck, kissed me and told me to cheer up, and when I told him of the lampoon that had been sent to me in Paris, he gripped his teeth intensely in immediate anger and said, "Yes, I know what they are like at home. It would not have been a scrap better for me had I stayed there. I might perhaps not even have been allowed to have a model sit for me. Thank goodness I don't need them. If one has a need of them, they know how to torment and irritate." And he bade me take courage; it would all be all right in the end, and could not be otherwise; then he told me about the darker aspects of his life and his youth, and how he had been insulted and judged harshly at home in Denmark.

The Carnival began in all its festivity. It had not been so relaxed or attracted so many participants for the past three years. There were illuminations again now, and "moccoli" were allowed; I saw them in all their splendour and magnificence, just as I described it in *The Improvisatore*. Personally, however, I did not enjoy them; my good humour had been spoiled, and it was as though my youthful freshness had been washed away by the heavy seas from home. My mood during the carnival is expressed in the following poem which I wrote then:

> In Rome you are, the centre of the ancient world,
> where dwell the treasures and the gods of old.
> You drink the southern air 'neath laurel boughs.
> Then be content!
> Bethink, these never will return.
> Yet, bowed by grief I look towards
> My Nordic home;
> A letter from my friends I beg – a letter, please.
> But not one filled with spiteful murderous words

157

As reached me here
Though from the hands of friends.
Fair here it is – scare not this dream away,
But grant it me, brief as it is.
My distant native land soon calls me home,
And if my foes refuse to be placated,
They surely will lay down their whips
For friends use scorpions to lash me.

After the carnival I went on to Naples. Hertz and I travelled together. I had learned much from his company, and I had reason to believe that I had a more lenient judge in him now than before.

We passed through the Alban Mountains and the marshes in lovely spring weather and reached Terracina where oranges grow and the first palm trees are seen in the gardens by the roadside. The Indian fig spreads its heavy leaves over the cliff on which stand the ruins of Theodoric's castle. Cyclopean walls, laurels and myrtles were soon everyday sights. The open Garden of Hesperia was to be seen from Cicero's villa in Mola di Gaeta. I strolled in the warm air beneath the great lemon and bitter orange trees, and I threw the radiant fruits out into the lovely, blue sea, which was glittering and rocking in the sun. We stayed there for a whole day and arrived in Naples just in time to see Vesuvius in full activity, its lava flowing down the dark mountain sides like long roots of fire from a pine tree of smoke. Together with Hertz and a few other Scandinavians I went to see the eruption at close quarters. The path up the mountain goes through vineyards and past lonely buildings, and soon the vegetation was limited to plants that looked rather like rushes. The evening was one of infinite beauty and enchantment:

Set among the mountains bleak
Fair Naples dreams all clothed in white.
Ischia lies far off, a streak
Of purple in a cloud of light.

Like a flock of swans on high,
On the mountains lies the snow.

>   Black against the radiant sky
>   Vesuvius stands with fiery show.

From the hermitage, I ascended the mountain on foot, walking through a deep layer of ashes. I was in a blissfully happy mood and sang one of Weyse's melodies aloud, and I was the first to reach the top. Suddenly the moon stood right above the crater from which jet black smoke was rising. Glowing rocks were flung into the air and fell almost vertically down again; the mountain shook beneath our feet. At each eruption the moon was hidden by smoke, and the night became intensely dark, so that we had to stand still and keep to the great blocks of lava; then we gradually began to notice the heat beneath us. The new stream of lava burst out from the mountain towards the sea. That was the direction in which we wanted to go, and in order to do so we had to walk over a lava stream which had only just solidified. Only the top crust had been made hard by the air, and through the cracks in it we could see the fiery red beneath the surface. With our guide ahead of us we stepped out on to this expanse; it warmed us right through the soles of our shoes, and if the crust had given we should have gone through into a sea of fire. Silently we went on and reached the great blocks of lava strewn across the mountain side. There we met a group of strangers and together with them we gazed out across the torrent of fire that had burst out and was flowing down the slopes like a sort of fiery porridge. There was an overpowering smell of sulphur, the heat under our feet was almost too much to bear, and we only managed to stay there for a few minutes. But the scene we saw during this time seemed to burn itself into our minds for ever. There were gulfs of fire all about us, and there was a rushing noise from the crater as when a huge flock of birds flies up in the woods. We could not ascend the cone itself since glowing rocks were still raining down upon it. It had taken us about an hour to do this short but difficult journey up the cauldron of ashes to the place where we were now standing, but the journey down took scarcely ten minutes. We flew over the ground and were constantly forced to dig in our heels to prevent ourselves from falling on our faces, but rather to fall on our backs in the soft ashes. The way down was a merry descent through the air. The weather was beautiful, and there was no wind; the lava shone against the black earth like gigantic stars. It was far lighter in the moonlight than it is at home in Scandinavia at noon on a dull autumn day. All houses and doors in Portici were locked when we arrived there. We saw no one and it was impossible to hire a coach, and so the whole company went home on foot in the lovely weather. However, they walked more quickly than Hertz could manage, who had twisted his foot on the way up. I stayed behind with him; we walked slowly and were soon quite alone. The white houses with their flat roofs shone in the clear moonlight. We neither met nor saw a living soul, and Hertz said he felt as though we were walking through the deserted city in the *Arabian Nights.* We talked about poetry and – food. Yes, we were terribly hungry, but every osteria was closed and we had to manage until we reached Naples. The undulating outlines of the mountains glowed in the moonlight like blue fire; Vesuvius flung its column of fire into the sky and the lava was reflected as a dark red streak on the calm sea. We stopped several times in admiration, but each time our conversation returned to the subject of finding a decent meal; late at night that was the high spot of all the splendours.

Later we visited Pompeii, Herculanum and the Greek temples at Paestum. There I saw a poor, blind girl, dressed in rags but a picture of great beauty, a statue come to life, little more than a child. She was fixing some blue violets in her jet black hair, and that was the only decoration she wore. She made an impression on me as though she were a revelation from the realm of beauty. I could not give her money and stood gazing at her with some strange sort of respect, as though she were the very goddess from the temple on the steps of which she was sitting amid the wild figs. The memory of her lives on in Lara.

It was only March, but it was like a beautiful summer's day in Scandinavia. The sea was so tempting as it lay there, and together with some companions I sailed in an open boat all the way from Salerno to Amalfi and Capri, where, a few years before, the Blue Grotto had been discovered or rather visited and turned into the destination of all those who travelled here. The Witches' Hole, as it was called, had been turned into the wonderful Fairy Grotto. I was one of the first to describe it. Many years have passed since then. I have been back to Italy and Capri, but storms and high seas have always prevented me from seeing this wonderful spot again. Yet once seen, it can never be forgotten.

Ischia was the island that impressed me least, and repeated visits have failed to raise it to the level of Capri, the island of Tiberius, the island shaped like a wooden clog.

Malibran was in Naples, and I heard her in *Norma*, *The Barber of Seville* and *La Pruova*. So from the world of music, too, Italy revealed a miracle to me. I wept and I laughed; I felt uplifted and carried away, and in the midst of all the fervour and all the enthusiasm I heard someone hiss; one single person hissed her. Lablache appeared and sang the role of Zampa in the opera *Zampa*, but he was most unforgettable as Figaro because of his liveliness and gaiety.

On the 20th of March we went back to Rome to spend Easter there. The mountains were covered with snow, and it was suddenly winter. We visited Caserta to see the big royal palace with its magnificent halls and its pictures from the time of Murat, and to see the amphitheatre at Capua with its subterranean vaulting and the great openings that were used for machinery to enable people to get up and down; we saw it all.

Easter kept us in Rome. During the illumination of the dome I was separated from my companions, and the vast crowd of people dragged me with them over the Sant'Angelo Bridge, and while at the middle of it all I felt as though I were going to faint. I started to tremble, and my feet began to give way under me and could not carry me. The crowd pressed on; everything went black before my eyes; I felt that I was going to be trodden under foot, but by a great effort of body and soul I managed to remain standing. This was a dreadful few moments, and I remember them better than the splendour and magnificence of the festival.

However, I managed to get across the bridge, and then I felt better. Blunck's studio was not far away, and from there, with the Castel Sant'Angelo in front of me, I watched the splendour of the grand girondole which seemed to be Rome's farewell, and which surpassed all other firework displays I have ever seen. The fireworks in the July festival in Paris were minute in comparison with the shimmering cascades of fire in Rome. In the osteria my compatriots drank to me on my departure and sang the farewell song. Thorvaldsen clasped me in his arms and said that we should meet again in Denmark or in Rome.

Ludvig Bødtcher, the poet, my friend, wrote for me:

If now sans poetry and sweet thought you leave the South,
Then go instead and write a serenade at home;
Receive your kisses from the critic's icy mouth,
Embraces, too, from watchmen as they nightly roam.

I celebrated my second April abroad in Montefiascone where I drank Est! Est!! Est!!! A charming Italian couple were my companions; the young wife was very afraid of robbers, for the district was reputed to be unsafe. The burned stretches of forest with their short stumps did not exactly liven things up, and the mountain roads were narrow with deep, black caves. And soon a storm arose, so violent that we had to wait for several hours at a little inn near Novella.

The storm raged and the rain lashed against the windows. The whole scene was a splendid setting for a story of robbers, but the robbers were missing, and the story is that we reached Siena and then Florence quite safe and sound. Florence was an old acquaintance for me, and I knew everything it had to offer, right from the metal pig to the churches and art galleries.

Filippo Berti, the poet who wrote the comedy *Gli Amanti Sessagenari*, introduced me to his friends among some of the most important artists. Bartolini, the sculptor, had just finished his statue *The Bacchant*, which is now owned by the Duke of Devonshire. Stretched out on her marble pillow the hefty woman lies holding a tambourine in her hand; a snake is wound around her arm and ivy leaves trail from her head. We visited Santarelli and saw his beautiful bas-reliefs of *The Triumph of Bacchus and of Silenus*.

In Vieusseux, the director of the Cabinet Littéraire, I discovered a man who had been in Denmark sixteen years previously and had visited the authoress Frederika Bruun. He knew Oehlenschläger and Baggesen, and he talked of these two and of Copenhagen and life there. When we are abroad and hear people talk of our native country

162

we feel how much we belong there; our hearts always belong to the land of our birth. Yet I did not feel homesick, and nor had I at any time during my travels. I feared the time for my arrival home, as if I were going to awake from a beautiful dream to harsh reality, awake to endurance and suffering.

And I was on my way home. Spring went with me, and the countryside around Florence was resplendent with laurels in flower. Spring was all around me, but it was as though it did not really dare draw breath within me. Northwards I went, across the mountains to Bologna. Malibran was singing there; and I had to see Raphael's *St. Cecilia*, and then on again by way of Ferrara to Venice, the withered lotus of the sea. If you have seen Genoa with its magnificent palaces and Rome with its monuments from antiquity, and if you have wandered about in smiling, sunlit Naples, then Venice is the stepchild. And yet that city is so remarkable and so different from all other cities in Italy. It ought to be seen; but first, and not like a sad *vale* on leaving the country. Even Goethe talks of the funereal effect of the Venetian gondolas. They are as swift as arrows, floating biers, jet black with black fringes, black tassels and hung with black curtains. At Fusina we stepped into such a gondola, and flanked by endless rows of poles, through muddy water and clearer water we entered the silent city. Only St. Mark's Square before the variegated cathedral with its oriental architecture and the fairytale Palace of the Doges with its gloomy memories and prisons and the Bridge of Sighs were alive. Greeks and Turks sat puffing at their long pipes, while pigeons in their hundreds fluttered around the triumphal poles from which the great flags fly. Especially by day I felt as though I were on the wreck of some gigantic phantom ship. It has to be evening there, and the moon must shine; only then does the whole town seem to come to life. Then the palaces are seen more clearly in all their grandeur and majesty. Venice, the Queen of the Adriatic, by day a dead swan floating in muddy water, is suddenly possessed of life and beauty. A scorpion sting in my hand made my stay there physically painful; all the veins right up my arm swelled up and I had spasms of fever. Luckily the weather was cold and the sting was not very severe, and without regret I left Venice in the black, funereal gondola only to go to another city of tombs, Verona, where the Scaligers lie buried and the tomb of Romeo and Juliet is to be found. The painter, Bendz, a compatriot of mine, and like me born in Odense where I had seen him as a child, had left Denmark as a healthy young man; his talents were recognised there and he had a faithful wife. He set happily out on a journey to Italy, crossed the Alps and saw the Canaan of art before him; and then he died suddenly in Vicenza. I went to seek his grave. No one could tell me where it was. How clearly I remembered this Odensean brother, if I may be allowed to call him that. His fate seemed to me to be a happy one, and I wished mine could be the same! It became more and more depressed in spirit as we journeyed north, towards the Alps, towards home. I was travelling together with a young Scot by the name of Jameson, who came from Edinburgh; he found the mountains of the Tyrol reminiscent of the highlands in his native country, and tears came to his eyes at this thought, and he felt homesick. I did not know what it was to be homesick, and thought only of the bitter cup I would probably have to drain and of how many trials I should have to bear. I felt certain that I should never see these beautiful lands again now that I was leaving them, and in this mood I wrote:

A Farewell to Italy

I saw that heavenly, that lovely land
Where children play beneath the lonely pine,
Where tongues of fire escape from mountain's breast
And where the ancient cities breathe again.

Where elevated gods stand dressed in marble robes
Where gentle breeze is filled with scent and song
The sea is smooth as oil and azure-blue
With many-coloured mountains all along.

My eyes were filled with paintings manifold
Here God's creative love's disclosed so fine.
Look at the farmyards hedges: laurels' gold
Midst lofty cacti and grape-laden vine.

My heart became a child's, my thoughts a man's;
I learned to love your nature and your art.

164

You precious land of colour and of form
Good-bye – how sad that I from you must part.

Now the Alps lay behind me, and the spreading Bavarian highlands before me. On the last day in May I reached Munich.

I found a room at the home of a respectable comb-maker. I had no acquaintances in Munich, but they soon came of their own accord. Almost immediately I met a fellow countryman in the street, a man by the name of Birch, who was married to Charlotte Birch-Pfeiffer, the well-known authoress and actress. She was at that time away in Zurich, where she was the director of the Stadttheater, so I did not make her acquaintance. Birch himself I had often seen at Siboni's; he knew me and was extremely attentive and friendly towards me. We now met quite frequently and he was always very frank and open in his conversation. Schelling, the philosopher, was living in Munich at that time. I had no letter of introduction and no one who could take me to meet him, and so I went to his home without more ado, made myself known to him and was given a cordial reception by the old gentleman, who discussed Italy with me for a long time. I did not speak German well, and produced one Danish phrase after the other, but that was itself of interest to him. He said the Danish element could clearly be heard, that it sounded so strange to him, and yet like something distantly related. He was kind enough to invite me to meet his family, and talked to me in a charming and cordial manner. Several years later, when I had made a name for myself in Germany, we met again in Berlin as old friends.

He wrote the following words in my album:

> *Was sich stets und immer hat begeben,*
> *Das allein veraltet nie.*

> What has always and ever happened
> That alone never goes out of date.

During my stay I gradually came to find Munich a pleasant and homely place, but the days pointed more and more towards my real home, Copenhagen. By means of strict economy I tried to lengthen my stay a little, for I felt afraid of settling down at home again and having to bear the heavy seas. I received letters telling me that I had been entirely given up and erased as a poet. The periodical *Maanedsskrift for Litteratur* had made a public statement to this effect, written by Molbech. It was my *Collected Poems*, published during my absence – and previously acclaimed when published separately – that together with *The Twelve Months of the Year* served as proof of my intellectual demise. A friend travelling through Munich brought the review and gave it to me: it was a good thing, of course, that I should read this sort of thing myself.

In it there was a review of the "most recent Danish poetry". I was considered along with other young poets such as F. J. Hansen, H. P. Holst, Christian Winther and Paludan-Müller; and I was pulled up like a weed from among these healthy plants and discarded. On the subject of *The Twelve Months of the Year*, the critic exclaims that he finds it "impossible to see what benefit to art and poetry might emerge from such a formless and futile mixture of immature elements". It is "a hotchpotch of rhymes of which one soon tires"; it is "nonsense"; it "lacks reasonable arrangement"; and it is "more than patience can bear, to see this slovenly use of language year in and year out". There is a reference to my having been "taken to task" in *Letters from the Dead* and it is stated that it would be a soul-destroying undertaking to go through my lyrical works in this manner. He says that I have been disappointed at the reception given to my poems by "those around me". As for the poems I have dared to call "humorous", he says that "the word is used here in a more physical sense than the one normally attributed to it in aesthetics", and he finishes by advising me "henceforth to study more and scribble less".

Then the other authors are dealt with. In F. J. Hansen the critic admits to recognising "a certain sort of wit and humour", citing examples and stating that he is "a poet with unmistakable signs of talent".

H. P. Holst is "more serious in his poetic effects, and he shows what must be considered praiseworthy efforts in a young artist at least to mould and polish the external form".

The critic then goes on to consider Christian Winther, "a linguistically educated, correct and urbane lyrical muse", but abandons himself into true dithyrambic ecstasy in his consideration of Paludan-Müller's *The Dancer*. Molbech apologises at considerable length for being unable to be measured enough, going on to recall that, "When I first read this poem, it had such an effect on me that I seemed to be carried away by the power of the imagination to some faraway part of the heavens where the scents of southern flowers mingled with the fresh morning breezes in our beech groves and with the invigorating gusts of wind from the Danish coasts. And while I felt this freshness being poured into my soul I heard familiar tones that found their way right into my heart from the world of poetry that had suddenly been conjured up around me. There was a sound as though the warblers of spring and summer were mingling their trills with the melancholy sounds of nature which are sometimes to be heard in the forests when the autumn blast whistles through the leafless treetops. Soon it was to be heard again like the muffled roar of the angry sea when the tempest laughs aloud and whips it into still higher waves" etc. etc. That is a sample of Molbech's style and criticism, both the sweet and the bitter sides of it. I received the latter, the bitter side of it, a cup brimming over. And yet two or three years before the very same critic had said of my *Poems* that they contained "the mark of a distinctive poetical nature", "a youthful freshness" and that I had "a sense for a humorous joke and an ability to produce it that no one would call ordinary, for everyone knew how rarely it is found at all, and how much more rarely it is to be seen in a young poet".

That was his judgement then, but the man had forgotten it, and those around me had forgotten it, too. I was trodden underfoot and erased from the ranks of Danish poets. Like a blunt and rusty knife, every word went through my mind, my soul and my nerves, so my fear of coming home will readily be understood. It is quite obvious why I put my return off and let the varied scenes I met on my travels distract my attention as far as possible from the future which was so soon to arrive. I could stay abroad for one more month. From Munich I decided to go by way of Salzburg to Vienna and then finally home.

I left Munich. I had obtained a seat in a "Hauderer". Together with me in the coach there was a lively gentleman on his way to the spa at Gastein. At the city gate the poet Saphir came and shook hands with him and made some jokes about Thor-Schein and Schein der Thoren. My companion was extremely interesting and we soon began talking about the theatre and the latest performance of *Götz von Berlichingen* in which Eszlair played the title role and had to make several curtain calls. I did not like him, and said that the actor I liked best was Mr. Vespermann, who had played the part of Selbitz. "Thank you for the compliment," exclaimed my unknown travelling companion, who turned out to be Vespermann himself. I had not recognised him, and my joy at being together with this skilful actor drew him closer to me, and the journey made us friends.

We reached the Austrian border. My passport from Copenhagen was in French; the frontier guard looked at it and asked my name, so I replied, "Hans Christian Andersen."

"That is not what it says in your passport. It says you are called Jean Chrétien Andersen. So are you travelling under a false name?" Now I had to undergo an interrogation bordering on the comical. I, who had neither any cigars nor any sort of contraband with me, was the only one to have my trunks unpacked, while I myself was rigorously checked. All my letters from home were scrutinised, and I was asked to say on my honour whether they contained anything other than family affairs. Then they wanted to know what my top hat was. "A hat I use when I am in society," I replied.

"What sort of society?" they asked. "Not a secret one?" My ivy wreath from the Christmas festivities in Rome was terribly suspicious. "Have you been to Paris?" they asked. "Yes." And now they told me that everything was as it should be in Austria, that there were to be no revolutions there and that they were happy with their Emperor Franz. I assured them that so was I, and that they had not the slightest cause for alarm; I hated revolutions and was an exceedingly loyal subject. It didn't help. I was subjected to a far stricter examination than anyone else, all because the police in Copenhagen had translated the Danish name Hans Christian into Jean Chrétien.

In Salzburg, not far from where I stayed, there was an old house adorned with some pictures and an inscription. It had belonged to Doctor Theophrastus Bombastus Paracelsus, and it was there he died. The old servant at the inn told me that she, too, had been born in that house and knew a little about Paracelsus. She knew he was the man who could cure the illness called gout, from which only distinguished people suffer. But the other doctors were angry about this and gave him poison. However, he realised it and was clever enough to be able to purge himself of it. So he shut himself in his room after telling his servant not to open the door before he called him. However, the servant was dreadfully curious and opened the door too soon. His master had only got the poison up as far as his throat, so when the door was opened Paracelsus dropped down dead. That was the popular story as it was told to me. Paracelsus has always seemed to me to be a romantic and attractive personality and it must be possible to make use of him in some Danish work of literature since his travels brought him here to Denmark. We hear of him as an army surgeon tending the foreign troops here, and he is mentioned during the reign of Christian the Second as being in Copenhagen and giving Mother Sigbrith some sort of homunculus in a bottle, which rushes out with a noise like thunder when the bottle is broken.

Poor Paracelsus! He was called a quack, and yet he was a genius and his methods were far in advance of his time. But everyone who proceeds ahead of the coach of time is either kicked or trodden underfoot by the horses pulling it.

When you are in Salzburg you have to go to Hallein, bump along through the salt mines there and cross the lid of the gigantic iron cauldron in which the salt is boiled. The waterfall at Golling cascades down over the great rocks, but I have forgotten what effect it had on me, and all I can remember is the smile on a child's face. I had as a guide a quiet little boy, and to a remarkable extent he possessed the adult earnestness that some children can have. There was a quite special understanding and earnestness about the little fellow, and there was not a trace of a smile on his face. Only when we were standing just in front of the foaming water plunging down with a great rumbling sound did his eyes light up; then the little fellow gave a proud and blissfully happy smile, saying, "That is the Golling Waterfall." The water still plunges on and on. I have forgotten it, but I have not forgotten that little boy's smile.

In many other places as well as this there can be something that many people would call unimportant or accidental, but which we notice and keep in our memory. From the magnificent monastery of Mölk on the Danube with all its marble grandeur and wonderful

169

view I have only one vivid recollection, and that is a big black patch that has been burnt in the floor. It happened during the war of 1809: the Austrians were on the north bank of the Danube, and Napoleon had his quarters in the monastery. A dispatch which he set fire to and flung down in anger burned a hole in the floor.

At last I caught sight of the tower of St. Stephen's Cathedral, and soon I was in the Imperial City. The Sonnleithners' house was a true home and place of refuge for all Danes there. Here I met my fellow countrymen, among whom there were at that time several gifted people, Captain Tscherning, for instance, two doctors called Bendz and Thune, and the Norwegian Schweigaard. The whole company would meet in the evening, but I did not join them regularly as the theatre attracted me. The Burgtheater was quite excellent and there I saw Anschütz as Götz von Berlichingen and Frau von Weissenthurn as Madame Herb in *The American*; that was indeed comedy acting. During those very days a young lady who has since established a name for herself as an actress made her *début;* this was Mathilde Wildauer. I saw her *début* as Gurli in *The Indians in England*. Several of Kotzebue's plays received excellent performances here. Kotzebue was clever but not very imaginative; he was the Scribe of his day. He could write works with very few poetical qualities, but his intelligence enabled him to provide them all with brilliant dialogue. In Hitzing I saw and heard Strauss; there he stood in the midst of his orchestra like the heart in that great positive organ of the waltz. It was as though the melodies flowed through him and out of all his limbs; his eyes shone, and it was quite obvious that he was the life and the central figure here. It was in Hitzing that Frau von Weissenthurn had her summer residence, and there I made the acquaintance of that interesting woman; since then, in *A Poet's Bazaar* I have provided a sort of a silhouette of this charming and gifted lady. Her comedies *Which is the Bride* and *The Manor of Sternberg* have met with great success on the Danish stage. I do not believe the younger generation here will know Johanne von Weissenthurn. She was the daughter of an actor and appeared on stage even as a child. In 1809 she played Phaedra before Napoleon in Schönbrunn and received a gift of 3000 francs from him. At the age of 25 she won a wager by writing the tragedy *Die Drusen* within the space of a week, and later she wrote about 60 plays of various kinds; and after a career of 40 years she received "Die goldene Civilehrenmedaille" from the Emperor Franz. This honour, which had never been given to any actress before, led to her being awarded the Prussian Gold Medal for Art and Science. In 1841 she left the theatre and died in Hitzing on the 18th of May, 1847. Her plays have been published in 14 volumes.

It was at her country residence in Hitzing that we talked together for the first time. She was a great admirer of Oehlenschläger; "that great man" as she always used to call him. She had met him and come to admire him while he was in Vienna as a young man. She never tired of hearing me talk about Italy. She thought that my words gave such a lively and vivid impression of the country that she said she felt she was there together with me, and in my album she wrote:

Länder hast Du geschaut, erforscht die Tiefen der Menschen!
Doch aus dem eigenen Born, schöpfe jetzt Weisheit und Licht.

Hietzing, 6ten Juli 1834   *Weissenthurn*

Lands you have seen, explored the depths of mankind!
But from your very own spring, draw now wisdom and light.

Hietzing, 6th July 1834   Weissenthurn

At the Sonnleithners I made the acquaintance of Grillparzer, who had written *Die Ahnfrau* and *Das Goldne Vlies*. In the frank Viennese fashion he shook hands and greeted me as a poet by saying:

> *Gleicher Stamm erkennt sich wieder,*
> *Läg' inmitten eine Welt!*
> *Gleiche Treue, gleiche Lieder,*
> *Nennen Dän' and Teutsche Brüder,*
> *Leugnet's murrend gleich der Belt.*

> The same stock recognise each other,
> Even if there's a world between them.
> The same loyalty, the same songs,

Proclaim Danes and Germans brothers
Though the sullen Belt at once denies it.

The person I saw most frequently was Castelli. He is undoubtedly typical of the true Viennese. All their excellent and exceptional qualities are combined in him: good nature, humour, loyalty and love of the Emperor. "Dear Emperor Franz," he used to say. "I have written a petition to him, a little verse asking him not to take off his hat to us in the cold weather when we Viennese meet him and greet him." I saw all Castelli's curiosities, his collections of snuffboxes, one of which, shaped like a snail, had belonged to Voltaire. "Bow down and kiss it," he said. In *Only a Fiddler* when Naomi appears in Vienna I have let Castelli be one of those taking part. The verse which stands at the head of the chapter is one the poet wrote to me before we parted:

> *Es ist eine seltsame Sache:*
> *Ich sprach Deutsch und Dänisch Du,*
> *Und doch verstanden wir uns im Nu!*
> *Ja Freund! im Aug' liegt die Sprache*
> *Und im Herzen der Schlüssel dazu.*

> It's a strange business:
> I spoke German and Danish you,
> And yet we understood each other in a trice!
> Yes, my friend, language is in the eye
> And in our hearts the key to it.

After spending a month in Vienna I made my way home via Prague. And now that the journey is a thing of the past I can say that there was no lack of what is called "the poetry of travel". Lots of us were packed together; the coach jolted and jerked; but chance had made up for this a little and had introduced humour into the coach in the form of a number of comical characters. For instance there was an old gentleman there who was dissatisfied with everything; he had been the victim of extortion and was continually working out how much he had spent, and it was always too much. At first

172

he was furious about the price of a cup of coffee which he didn't think worth the money, and then about the way in which modern youth was spoiled: it had far too much of a say in everything, even in the fate of the world. A dirty Jew was sitting at the side of him, chattering incessantly. He was a real Gert Westphaler and told us all about his journey to Ragusa in Dalmatia at least ten times. He said he would not like to be a king, for that was too difficult a life, but he fancied being a king's valet. He knew one who had grown so fat that he was unable to walk and so in his turn also had to have a valet. As I say, he was rather grimy, even down to his fingernails, and yet he talked incessantly about cleanliness. It annoyed him to think that the Hungarians used cow dung to heat the ovens in which they baked their bread. He served up a number of old anecdotes for us. Suddenly he became thoughtful, took a piece of paper out of his pocket, rolled his eyes and then wrote something down. It was just a few ideas he had had, he said, and asked me to read out what he had written down.

We did not have individual seats allocated to us in the coach, but had to arrange things among ourselves. However, the best two were stolen from us by two fresh travellers who joined the coach in Iglau and were wise enough to get in while the rest of us, tired and hungry, had gone to supper. It was a young lady with her husband; he was already asleep when we came back, but she was sufficiently awake for both of them and was talkativeness personified. She chatted about art and literature, about good breeding, about how to read a poet and understand him, about music and sculpture, about Calderon and Mendelssohn. Now and then she would stop and sigh to her husband, who was resting his head on her: "Lift your angelic little head, it's crushing my bosom." And then she went on to talk about her father's library and of how much she was looking forward to seeing him again. When I asked her about Bohemian literature she said she knew all the best authors in the country. They would come to visit her father, and all the most recent literature was to be found in his library, etc. etc… When day broke I could see that she and her husband were a fair-haired Jewish couple. He woke up, drank a cup of coffee and then fell asleep again. He laid his angelic little head on his wife's bosom and only opened his mouth once, to make an age-old joke, after which the angelic little thing fell asleep again. She

173

wanted to know all our professions and conditions, and on hearing I was an author she became extremely interested, though only until we reached the gate of Prague and had to give our names. A deaf old gentleman gave his as "Professor Zimmermann." She uttered a little cry: "Zimmermann on Solitude! Are you Zimmermann?" It did not occur to her that the author she was thinking of had been dead for many years. The deaf gentleman repeated his name, and now she expressed her profuse regrets that it was only at the hour of parting that she had discovered who it was she had been travelling with. I had said that I was to go on to Dresden the very next morning. She said she was sorry about that, for otherwise she would have invited me to visit her at her father's house, inspect his library and perhaps meet a fellow author. "We live in the biggest mansion in the square," she said, pointing to it. I saw her and her husband go into it, and on taking my leave of them he gave me his card. The following morning I decided to spend two whole days in Prague. Then I would also be able to pay a visit to my travelling companions and have a look at the library there with all the Bohemian literature. I went to the big house which I had seen the couple enter. No one on the ground floor had heard of this family, nor had anyone on the first floor. When I came to the second floor I mentioned the large library the father was supposed to own. No, no one knew anything about it. I went up to the third floor, but with no better result, and they told me there were no other families there apart from the ones I had already tried. There was certainly an old Jew who had a couple of rooms in the attic right at the top of the house, but it could not possibly be he. However, I went up to see. The walls on to the staircase were of hewn planks, and there was a low door with a piece of paper on it. I knocked, and an old man in a dirty dressing gown opened the door and revealed a low room. A large clothes basket full of old books could be seen in the middle of the floor. "Does this family live here by any chance?" I asked and showed the visiting card. "Mein Gott," came a shriek from a little room at the side. It was the young lady's voice. I looked towards where the sound came from, and there I saw her in her negligée, juggling above her head and trying to put on the dress of fine, black silk in which she had been travelling, while in the bedroom opposite her husband gave a sleepy yawn and lifted his "angelic little head". I stood in amazement; the lady came in with her dress unbuttoned at the back, and with an untied bonnet on her head, blushing deeply at the surprise. "Von Andersen," she said, and asked for forgiveness. Everything was in a state of disorder, her father's library – she pointed to the clothes basket. Thus all the talk in the coach resolved itself into an "attic and a bag of books".

From Prague I went home to Copenhagen by way of Töplitz and Dresden.

It was with mixed feelings I went ashore, and not all my tears were tears of joy. But God was with me.

Actually I had had neither the mind nor an eye for Germany. My heart longed for Italy as for some lost paradise to which I was never to return. I looked forward to the approaching time at home with fear and anxiety. It was as though I was simply drifting onwards, ever nearer to Copenhagen. The Italian countryside and the life of its people filled my very heart, and I longed for that country. It seemed to become one with my own being, and in a quite extempore manner led to a novel. It grew and grew, and I was forced to write it, although I was convinced it would result in more sorrow than joy if the pressure of circumstances at home made me publish it. I had written the first two chapters while still in Rome, and I had continued them later in Munich. This was my novel *The Improvisatore*. A letter I received in Rome had told me of a remark made by J. L. Heiberg to the effect that he regarded me as a sort of "improvisatore", and those words were the spark that gave a name and a character to my new work.

When I first went to the theatre in Odense as a little boy, the performances were, as I have already said, all in German; I saw *Das Donauweibchen*, and the audience shouted with joy for the actress who played the leading part. She was applauded and honoured, and for me she seemed to be the happiest creature on earth. Many years later, when I paid a visit to Odense as a student and went into the hospital I saw a room in which poor widows lived, and where, just as in Vartou, bed stood beside bed, with a little cupboard and a table or a chair as all their furniture. There, in a gilt frame over one of the beds, hung the picture of a woman; it was of Lessing's Emilia Galotti plucking the petals off the rose. But the picture was a portrait, and it stood out strangely amidst all the poverty surrounding it. "Who is that?" I asked. "Oh," they replied, "that's the picture of the German lady." And then a thin, delicate little woman came in; her cheeks were wrinkled, and she was wearing a silk dress that had once been black. This was the highly honoured singer whom I had seen in *Das Donauweibchen*, and whom everyone had applauded at that time. It made an unforgettable impression on me, and I often thought about her. In Naples I heard Malibran for the first time; her voice and acting were far superior to anything I had ever heard before, and yet I immediately thought of my poor singer in the hospital in Odense. These two figures were united in Annunziata in the novel I was writing. Italy was the background to both what I had experienced and what I had imagined.

My journey was at an end. I arrived back in Denmark in August 1834, and soon, during a visit to Ingemann at Sorø, I completed the first part of the novel in a small attic surrounded by the scent of the lime trees. The second half I finished in Copenhagen.

Even my best friends were inclined to give me up as a poet: "They had mistaken my talents," how often I heard this said. I almost failed to find a publisher for my book, but finally, out of kindness to me, Reitzel risked doing it. However, it was necessary to raise a subscription, and I had personally to persuade my friends to subscribe to it. In the introduction I said I was not offering my readers a description of my travels, but a sort of spiritual result deriving from them. Of course I received an incredibly small fee, for there was not the slightest prospect of the book being sold and read. I dedicated it:

To Privy Councillor Collin and his noble wife, in whom I found a mother and father, his children, in whom I found my brothers and sisters, the home of homes, I herewith dedicate the best I have.

The book was read, sold out and published in a second edition. The critics were silent, and the newspapers said nothing, but I heard from various sources that there was some interest in my work, and that many people were delighted with it. Finally Carl Bagger, the poet, who was then the editor of the Sunday newspaper *Søndagsbladet*, wrote a review of it which began as follows:

> " 'Andersen no longer writes as well as he used to; he must have worked himself out, and indeed that is what I have long expected!' Thus has the poet been spoken of here and there in some circles in the capital, perhaps in those very circles where he was most spoiled and even almost deified on making his first appearance. However, that he has not worked himself out, and that he has on the contrary reached heights previously quite unknown to him, he has demonstrated in the brilliant novel *The Improvisatore* which has just been published."

People will perhaps laugh at me, but I must openly admit that I wept my eyes out. I wept myself happy, and I felt gratitude towards both God and men.

VII

Many who had previously been against me changed their opinions now, and among them was one in whom I believe I won a friend for life. This was the poet Hauch, one of the noblest figures I know. After several years abroad he had just returned home from Italy at a time when the people of Copenhagen were completely obsessed with Heiberg's vaudevilles. My *Journey on Foot* was a success, and as I have said before, Hauch embarked on a polemic with Heiberg in which he passed some strictures on me. As he has since told me, no one had at that time drawn his attention to the better lyrical works I had written. People spoke to him of me as nothing but a spoiled, confused child of fortune. In my *Journey on Foot* he found only barren entertainment, but now he had read *The Improvisatore* and realised that I possessed both poetry and depth, something which he had not previously believed. He felt that there was more in me than he had imagined, and so he thought it natural to write me a cordial letter saying that he had done me an injustice and that he offered me his hand in reconciliation; and from that time we became friends. He was keen to speak out on my behalf, and he has followed all my progress with great understanding and interest. But some people had been so unwilling to appreciate his excellent qualities and the noble relationship existing between us that when he some time later wrote his novel *The Castle by the Rhine* in which he drew a caricature of a real poet who is so vain he ends in the lunatic asylum, people here in Denmark thought he had behaved extremely unjustly and badly towards me by revealing all my weaknesses in this way. It should not be believed that these were the words of a single individual – no it went so far as to be generally taken for granted and even openly stated, so that Hauch himself felt moved to write an article on me as a poet in order to show what position he accorded me in the world of art. It is to be found in Schouw's weekly periodical, *Ugeskrift*.

As for Sibbern, of whom everyone thought highly and whose enthusiasm for Paludan-Müller's *Cupid and Psyche* was counted among the proofs of the excellence of this poem, I had been told that he was very critical indeed of my efforts, and did not approve of me as a poet. So it was a pleasant surprise for me to see in a little book he had written in defence of Ingemann, that he thought well of me, since he expressed a wish that someone would say a friendly word on my behalf, too. He read *The Improvisatore* and wrote a heartfelt letter to me, which apart from Carl Bagger's short review was the only piece written in recognition and kindness. It was so much like him that I could almost hear his voice. Sibbern wrote:

I have read your *Improvisatore*, and have done so with both truly great pleasure and delight. Pleasure on account of the book itself, and delight because it is you who have written it. Once more a hope fulfilled; once more a true acquisition. When I made a silent comparison between this and what I knew of your earlier poetry, the difference seemed to me to be the same as that between the young Aladdin we saw hiding behind the pillar and romping in the market-places and the Aladdin who, at once older and younger, steps out of the bath. I read your *Improvisatore* right to the end with the same exclamations of 'That is good, that is very good!' with which I had read the first 24 pages. And the day after I finished it, I could not bring myself to read anything else. You surely know what this means. It means one is completely satisfied.

And what filled me was both delight at the book and delight on behalf of you. We know you as what the Germans call 'eine gute Seele'; it was with great joy that I now realised you are also a thorough soul. In the society of others you are open, good-natured, willing, lively and easily moved. I can see that at home you can be profound, warm, full of feeling and possessed of a sound imagination. Make sure that you preserve both sides of your nature. And in order to be able to do that, do not concentrate all your heart and mind on criticism, or what is called by that name. Rather read none at all, and let no critic approach you. You have a Muse, a deity who is at your side. Do not frighten her away, and take care that others do not do so.

You have been in Italy, and you have lived in Italy: in order to experience it, not to paint it. The painting came later of its own accord, and the picture you have presented to us is a great one indeed.

There will come a time, or has it perhaps already come, when you will venture forth into and reside in another great region: the realm of history. I look forward to seeing what it is you will bring home with you then.

Then yet another time will come later when you will be attracted to another great realm: the realm of philosophy. Then, too, I hope you will bring us reflections of it, showing us that your Muse has been your close companion.

I write these lines from the bottom of my heart. I truly wish you well. But should these lines reach you just at a moment when your mind and your living room are sacred places, then let not this letter disturb you, but put it quietly aside. And if it be not so, then may your mind and your home soon be sacred places. And if anything should come to disturb or distract you, then say, *'Abitote, nam heic Dii sunt'*.

And now receive the heartfelt wishes of your sincere friend, Sibbern.

Copenhagen, 12 Sept 1835   To Andersen the poet.

But to return to *The Improvisatore*. This book raised my sunken fortunes, gathered my friends around me again and indeed even increased their number. For the first time I felt I had won real recognition.

The book was immediately translated into German by Professor Kruse and given the long title of *Jugendleben und Träume eines italienischen Dichters*. I said I did not approve of this title, but, although I now know he was wrong, he insisted that such a title was necessary in order to attract attention, something the plainer title of *The Improvisatore* would have failed to do. As we already know, Carl Bagger had reviewed the book. No actual criticism appeared until every aspect of it had been discussed, and then at last a review did appear, in *Litteraturtidenden*, I believe. It was certainly more polite than I was accustomed to, but little was said about the book's good qualities. "It is as usual," it ran, concentrating on its faults and listing all the Italian words and expressions I had got wrong. Indeed, as Nicolai's well known book *Italien wie es wirklich ist* appeared at the same time, placing the natural beauty of Italy below that of Germany, seeing Capri as nothing but a "*Meer-Ungeheuer*" (sea monster) and rejecting all beauty on the other side of the Alps except that possessed by the *Venus di Medici*, the beautiful shapes of which Nicolai thereupon gives according to his own measurements with a piece of string, people at home in Denmark began to say that now they could see what sort of a book Andersen had written.

No, Nicolai was quite a different proposition, and his book gave an impression of Italy as it really was.

I presented my book to Christian the Eighth, then Prince Christian. In the antechamber I met one of our lesser poets, who is classed as an extremely high-ranking person in the State Calendar. He was condescending enough to speak to me. Why, he said, we both belonged to the profession, we were both writers. He then went on to give a lecture on the subject of the word "*Collosseum*" to a person of rank who was present: all for my benefit, of course. In my book it was spelt differently from in Byron, where it is wrongly spelt "*Coliseum*". That was dreadful, he said; it was again all this slovenly use of language, because of which one was inclined to forget what talent there was in the book. The lecture was delivered in a loud voice so that the whole assembly could hear it. I sought to point out that I had spelt the word correctly, whereas Byron had not, and this gentleman of rank shrugged his shoulders, smiled, handed the book to me, and deplored "that bad misprint in such a nicely bound book!"

"Oh, it's all about yourself," people said in the various circles where "they were ruining Andersen with their eternal praise". *Maanedsskrift for Litteratur*, the review which all readers who were considered intelligent looked up to, and which was the Supreme Court in the realm of beauty, discussed many a little pamphlet and comedy that has long been forgotten, but it did not deem *The Improvisatore* worthy of a single word, perhaps because it had already won a large readership, a second edition now having appeared. Only when, encouraged by the firm ground on which I had established myself,

I had written a new novel *O.T.* did this periodical in 1837 publish a review of this and *The Improvisatore*. And how I was criticised and taken to task – but more of that later.

The first real – or perhaps exaggerated – appreciation of my work came from Germany, and like a sick person I leaned over towards the sunlight, full of joy and gratitude, for my heart was indeed filled with gratitude! I was not an ungrateful person, showing in my book a lack of gratitude towards those who had helped me, as *Maanedsskrift for Litteratur* stooped to insinuate and more or less openly stated in its criticism of *The Improvisatore*; for I myself was poor Antonio who complained of all the pressure I must and ought to bear, I, the poor lad who had lived on charity!

A translation also appeared in Sweden, and all the Swedish newspapers I saw expressed praise and admiration for my work. In England, too, the book was translated by the Quaker Mary Howitt, and all its important features were noted and admired.

"This book is in romance what *Childe Harold* is in poetry," these were the words with which it was reviewed there, and when I visited London for the first time some thirteen years later I heard of a generous criticism it had received in *The Foreign Review*. This was attributed to Walter Scott's son-in-law, the accomplished and stern critic, Lockhart. I knew nothing of it; I could not read English in those days, and although it was in one of the most widely read and best known London reviews that came here to Copenhagen, it was not mentioned in a single Danish newspaper, all of which otherwise report every time the name of any Danish writer is mentioned in England. My reviewer says:

The Improvisatore is… a work originally composed in the Danish language: the language in which Hamlet spoke and thought – that melancholy "Prince of Denmark" whose doubtful existence Shakespeare's glorious dream has taught us to look upon as a familiar reality… A friend of ours… told us that *Corinne* was grandmother to *The Improvisatore*; perhaps she was; there is at all events a starched high-flown grandmotherliness in her pages, when compared with her descendant, which makes the Italian grandson (to our fancy) a much pleasanter companion.

A German critic has said of *The Improvisatore*:

> It would not be uninteresting to draw a parallel between Andersen's *The Improvisatore* and Madame de Staël's *Corinne*. Both authors have found heroes for their novels in the figure of Italian improvisatores, and both have tried to combine this with a portrayal of the splendours of Italy. But the Dane is naïve, the Frenchwoman sentimental. Andersen gives us poetry, de Staël rhetoric.

The Dansk *Maanedsskrift for Litteratur* also mentioned *Corinne* but here the tone was different: "It is probable that Madame Staël-Holstein's novel *Corinne* was a model that led the author astray," etc.

How different is the way in which we see the English and German reviews comparing *The Improvisatore* and Corinne from that in which I am briefly dismissed in respect of the same book by the Danish review.

In North America, too, a couple of English translations appeared, and the Swedish edition was followed – although not until 1844 – by a Russian version published in St. Petersburg and then by a Bohemian translation. The book also attracted attention in Holland; a very warm endorsement of it was published in the periodical *De Tijd,* which was very widely read there. In 1847 it appeared in French, translated by Madame Lebrun, and received extremely positive reviews in which its "purity" was especially emphasised. In Germany there have been seven or eight different editions of this novel in addition to several impressions. In this connection I must refer to the well-known Hitzig edition of Chamisso's works, where, in one of his letters to me, the poet expresses his delight at my book, which he ranks higher than *The Hunchback of Notre Dame*, *La Salamandre* etc.

As I say, the most clearly expressed recognition came to me from abroad during the following years, and this kept my spirits up. If Denmark has found a writer in me, it is not because I was ever encouraged to be one here at home. While parents normally tend every little shoot they think might be a sign of some sort of talent, most people did more or less all they could to stifle it in me. But God desired it thus for the sake of my development, and so He sent rays of sunshine to me from outside and let what I had written make its own way. At the same time, there is some power in the public greater than all critics and individual cliques.

With *The Improvisatore* I had after all gained a foothold at home in Denmark, and indeed in the eyes of some people I had struggled for and gained a respectable place. My spirits knew some moments when they could spread their wings. Only a few months after *The Improvisatore* appeared I published the first volume of my Fairy Tales, though it would be wrong to believe that they were immediately accorded a good reception. People who maintained they wished me well expressed their regret that after *The Improvisatore* had recently given reason to hope that I would be able to produce something "worthwhile", I had now once more resorted to "childishness". *The Maanedsskrift for Litteratur* never deigned to mention them, and in Dannora, a critical review which was then widely read, they begged me not to waste my time writing fairy tales. The writer looked in my work in vain for the elements normally to be found in this sort of writing, and I was given models to study. But of course, I would not do so, they said. And so I stopped writing fairy tales, and while I alternated between melancholy and sanguinity, I now published my second novel, *O.T.*. I felt some sort of a mental compulsion to produce, and I thought I had found my right element in the novel. So, in quick succession, I produced *The Improvisatore* 1835, *O.T.* 1836, and *Only a Fiddler* 1837. Many people were impressed by *O.T.*, especially H. C. Ørsted, who greatly appreciated the humorous element in it. He encouraged me to continue in this manner, and from him and his circle I derived both joy and recognition.

After receiving the letter on *The Improvisatore* I had made the personal acquaintance of Sibbern, and at his house I read *O.T.* aloud. Poul Møller, who was on a visit from Norway and had not been enthusiastic about my *Journey on Foot* was present one evening when I was reading, and he listened with great approval. The scenes set over in Jutland, on the heath and by the west coast, interested him, and he praised them warmly and sincerely. A couple of translations of *O.T.* in German were later rendered into Swedish, Dutch and

English. My compatriots from Copenhagen had taken offence at some Italian words in *The Improvisatore* which had been spelt wrongly or missed when the proofs were read. In order to avoid a similar charge, one of the professors at the University offered to read the proofs when *O.T.* was about to be published. "I am used to it," he said, "and have always been praised for my accuracy, so people will not be able to dwell on less important faults like spelling when it is criticised." He read it page by page and in addition to him two other competent men went through it all very carefully. The book appeared, and the criticism I received at home ended with: "The grammatical carelessness that is always to be found in Andersen, is also evident in this book."

"That is going too far," said the professor. "I have been just as careful as in my own books. They really are unfair to you."

O.T. was read and re-read. My readership increased, but the critics in newspapers and reviews still gave me little encouragement. They forgot that as the years pass, the boy becomes a man, and that one can acquire knowledge by other means than what is normal. People continued with the old assertions and accusations. Many who had perhaps never read my latest and best works were those who expressed themselves in the sternest tones, but they were not all as honest as Heiberg, who, when I asked him whether he had read these novels, gave me the jocular answer, "I never read long books."

The tone adopted by *Maanedsskriftet for Litteratur* can be seen from the attack Paludan-Müller made on this group of people when, now a recognised and highly esteemed young poet, he received a harsh criticism from the same review. He wrote his polemical poem Trochees and Iambs and in a note to this he told how far the review dared go in its criticism of a poet. These are Paludan-Müller's own words:

In which reputable review, either at home or abroad, have we ever seen a critic take such liberties against the person of the author he is criticising? The author's lack of understanding, higher education and real studies is not only made the subject of discussion, but an objection is raised against his lack of interest in undertaking such studies. Good advice is passed

185

on concerning future application and study; criticism is threatened, and finally the author is offered the hope of being able to produce something satisfactory if he will bear the critic's advice in mind. These and many other grave assertions against the poet (among which there is even an indirect accusation of ingratitude towards his benefactors), none of which have anything whatsoever to do with the works they are reviewing (*The Improvisatore* and *O.T.*), the editors of the review allow an unnamed critic to publish unchecked, and at the same time, by casting a veil of anonymity over him, they protect this person from the censure which he justly deserves from the person he has insulted.

It is typical that while the names of most of the critics were printed by this review, the author of this has never since dared to reveal who he is.

The following year (1837) saw the publication of *Only a Fiddler*, a spiritual flower springing from the hardship I suffered in this mighty battle between the poet in me and the harshness with which I was surrounded. Nevertheless, I had made some progress: I understood both myself and the world better than before, but I was on the point of giving up all thought of receiving any sort of true recognition in Denmark for the qualities with which God had endowed me. In another world it would surely be revealed, and in that thought I sought my consolation. If *The Improvisatore* really was an improvisatore, then *Only a Fiddler* was struggle and suffering as I understood them. This work as a whole was carefully planned and, seen from outside, it was as though every detail in it was born of my own experience. The opposition stirring within me to the injustice, foolishness, triviality and pressure by which I was surrounded created moods which are revealed in the figures of Naomi, Ladislaus and the godfather.

This book, too, was a success at home; but I received no thanks for it, and no encouragement. The critics merely admitted that I was often guided in some strangely fortunate manner by *my instinct*. They chose the expression used of animals, but for the quality that in the world of human beings and poetry is usually called *genius*. It was to be called instinct as far as I was concerned. It was as though they were constantly treading on all that was good in me. The occasional gifted person might speak to me and say that I was being treated too severely and unfairly, but no one said it in public. For a short time the novel *Only a Fiddler* occupied the mind of one of the country's highly gifted young men: Søren Kierkegaard. One day when we met in the street he told me that he would write a criticism of it that would satisfy me more than previous ones had done, for, he admitted, people misunderstood me.

A long time passed; he read the book again, and the first good impression was erased. And I believe that the more seriously he considered the work, the more full of faults it became to him, and when the criticism finally appeared, it was not one that was likely to please me. It appeared in the form of a whole book; I think it was the first that Kierkegaard wrote, rather difficult to read, with a certain Hegelian ponderousness in the phrasing. And people said in fun that Kierkegaard and Andersen were the only people to have read the book right through. It was called *From the Papers of One Yet Alive*. At that time I understood from it that I was no poet, but a poetical figure who had run away from my group, and that it was the task of some future poet to put me back into that group or to use me as a character in some work in which he was creating a better version of me. Later I was better to understand this author who has shown me kindness and discretion as I have progressed.

I neither found nor won anyone at home who would publicly defend or review my novels, and something that helped to overshadow them was the general enthusiasm for the *Everyday Stories* that Heiberg had edited. The language in them, the contents and, most of all, the enthusiastic recommendation given to these works by Heiberg ensured them the top place in the literature of the day in the eyes of Danish readers.

Yet, however scornfully I was dismissed, I was read, and I had now reached the stage when there were many at home who no longer doubted my poetic talent, that talent that had been completely dismissed before my journey to Italy. But no Danish review commented on the ideas, the freshness, the humour or all the special features in my novels. Only when they were published in Swedish did a few Swedish newspapers undertake a more thorough and open-

187

minded appraisal of them. They read and understood them positively and honestly. And the same was the case in Germany. It was from this that I gained the courage to continue.

The *London Literary Gazette* made the following comment on *O.T.* and *Only a Fiddler*:

> ...one of the most interesting publications which has been issued from the press for years. Its pictures of Danish life are most natural and most admirable; its illustrations of superstitions, its descriptions of scenery and external objects, its touches of truth in character and incident, its exquisite drawing of children and children's minds, its naiveté and lively sallies, its world-wisdom and imaginativeness, all briefly set before us, as if in flashes of light and intellect, possess so entire a charm, that we do not for a moment hesitate to say that this is a book which will afford the utmost gratification to every class of readers, and deserve a place among the most sterling works of fiction that ever were produced.

It was only several years later that a man of note in Denmark commented on the novels and with a few strokes drew people's attention to what was characteristic in them. This was Hauch, in the article I have already referred to in Schouw's *Ugeskrift*. He writes:

The main feature in Andersen's best and most thoroughly planned works, in those where the richest imagination, the most profound feelings and the most deeply moved poetic spirit are to be found, is a talent, or at least a noble nature that seeks to fight its way forward out of narrow and oppressive circumstances. This is the case in his three novels, and in this area, he really has a significant life to portray, an inner world which no one knows better than one who has himself drunk of the bitter cup. There is suffering and loss, there are painful, deep feelings closely related to those he himself has experienced. And in these, memory, who in the meaningful ancient myth is the mother of the Muses, comes to meet him hand in hand with her daughters. What he can tell the world in these works must surely deserve to be heard attentively; for despite the fact that on the one hand it is only the innermost personal life of one individual, it is at the same time the normal lot of talent and genius (at least when they are in difficult circumstances) with which we are presented. Insofar as in *The Improvisatore*, in *O.T.* and *Only a Fiddler* he not merely reveals himself in his separate individuality, but at the same time portrays that significant struggle which many have experienced, and which he, too, knows, because his life has developed through it, he is not in any way portraying something belonging to the world of illusion, but only something which bears witness to truth, and which, like any such evidence, has a general and lasting value. Indeed, he not merely champions the cause of talent and genius, but, as I have already said, also the cause of abused and unjustly treated humanity. And since he himself has suffered so much in this struggle where the snakes of Laocoon crush the hands held aloft, since he himself has been forced to drink of the wormwood beaker which an indifferent and arrogant world so often offers to one oppressed, he is also in a position in this respect to impart to his portrayal an element of truth and seriousness, indeed of tragic and distressing pathos that can scarcely fail to make an impression on a sensitive human heart.

Who can read that scene in his *Fiddler* in which the 'dog of rank', as the author calls him, turns in disgust from the food with which the poor boy has to be satisfied, without recognising at the same time that this is not a game in which vanity is seeking to triumph, but on the contrary that it is human nature, wounded in its innermost depths, which is expressing its pain!

That is what was said of me in Denmark nine or ten years later; that is what was uttered by a noble, an honourable man. For me the same has applied to criticism as is applied to wine: the more years passing before it is served, the better it tastes. The same year as the *Fiddler* appeared I visited the country nearest to ours and travelled by canal to Stockholm. No one in those days felt what we now call Scandinavian sympathies. We still felt a sort of suspicion of our neighbour as a result of wars long past. In winter, when ice linked the two countries together and the Swedes came over to us in sleighs, the street lads in Copenhagen never failed to shout coarse invectives at them. Very little was known about Swedish literature, and it only occurred to a small number of Danes that with very little practice we could read and understand the Swedish language. Tegnér's *Frithiof* and *Axel* were known, but only in translation. Times change.

I had read a few Swedish authors, and of them it was especially the late, unhappy Stagnelius, who appealed to me. I much preferred his work to that of Tegnér, who at that time was the main representative of poetry in Sweden. Having only travelled south, in doing which to say farewell to Copenhagen is to say farewell to our mother tongue, I felt half at home throughout the whole of my visit to Sweden. I could speak my own language and hear the language of that country simply as a kind of Danish dialect. It seemed to me that Denmark was expanding; I saw similar features in the two peoples plainly revealed, and I understood how close Danish, Swedish and Norwegian are to each other. I met kindly, friendly people, and it is my nature quickly to take to such folk. This journey was and remains one of my happiest. The picturesque Swedish landscape with its spreading forests, its great lakes, the grand Trollhättan and the picturesque archipelagos: all this was new to me. And now Stockholm itself; the setting of which is almost as impressive as that of Constantinople and certainly on a level with Edinburgh, came as a great surprise to me.

For the uninitiated, the canal journey sounds almost like a fairy tale when it is told how the steamship sails from the lakes and across the mountains from where there is a wonderful view of the spreading forests of spruce and birch. By means of ingenious locks the ships are raised and lowered while the passengers go for a stroll in the forest. To this journey and especially to the huge Lake Vänern I owe a very interesting acquaintance which was not without influence on me. It was with the Swedish novelist, Fredrika Bremer.

On the canal between Trollhättan and Vänersborg I had just asked the captain and some of the passengers on board which Swedish authors lived in Stockholm, mentioning my desire to meet Miss Bremer. "You won't be able to meet her," said the captain, "She's away on a visit to Norway at the moment."

"Then she is certain to come back while I am there," I joked, adding, "I'm always lucky when I'm travelling, so that most of the things I wish for come true."

"But I hardly think you'll be lucky this time," said the captain. Three hours later, when we were about to leave Vänersborg, where we had taken goods and passengers on board, he approached me with a smile, holding the list of new passengers in his hand, and said, "You are in luck. Good fortune has come your way after all. Miss Bremer is here, sailing with us to Stockholm." I thought this was a joke. He showed me her name on the list, but I was still not convinced that it was the writer herself. Among the people I saw going on board I saw no one who looked to me as though it could be she. Evening fell, and by about midnight we were on the great expanse of Lake Vänern.

At three o'clock in the morning I got up to see the sunrise. Apart from me, one other person appeared from the cabins. It was a lady, not young, and not old, wrapped in a shawl and a cape. She too, wanted to see the sunrise. I thought that if Miss Bremer were on board then it must be this person. I began talking to her. She answered politely but distantly, and when I asked her if she were not the writer of the famous novels she gave me an evasive answer and asked me my name. She knew it but admitted that she had not read any of my works and asked if I had any of them with me. I happened to have a copy of *The Improvisatore* which I had intended to give to Beskow. I lent it to her and she went down into her cabin and did not reappear for the rest of the morning. But when I saw her again her face was radiant and affable. She pressed my hand and said that she had read most of the first part of the book and that now she knew me. The ship flew over mountains with us, through quiet lakes and forests and out into the Baltic archipelagos where rocky islands are strewn all over the water and form strange abrupt transitions from bare rock to islands covered with green meadows and others again with trees and houses. We went through surf and whirlpools; twice all the passengers had to sit still in their seats while the pilot concentrated all his attention on one spot. We could feel the hand of nature in all its power for a moment as it grasped and then relaxed its hold on the ship. Miss Bremer told me many a legend and many a story connected with one or other of the islands and with such and such a large farm inland. The journey was richer and happier for this.

Our acquaintance continued in Stockholm, and letters exchanged between us have strengthened it over the years. She is a woman of noble qualities, filled with the consoling truths of religion and the poetry to be found in the quiet things in life, and she is possessed of sufficient genius to give expression to this.

As yet none of my novels had appeared in Swedish translation. I was only known as a writer in Stockholm by a few people who had read my *Journey on Foot* and my poems, and these few were mainly people with literary interests, who also received me cordially and with Swedish courtesy and attentiveness. Dahlgren, the cleric known and honoured for his humorous poems, and now long dead, wrote a song in my honour. I encountered hospitality and kindness, and I became fond of Sweden and the Swedes. H. C. Ørsted had given me an introduction to the famous Berzelius whose acquaintance I now made for the first time. Thanks to him I was given a splendid reception in Uppsala where I spent some days and where Professor Rudberg, who was still alive at that time, took me up the ancient burial mound where, from the great silver horn presented by King Carl Johan, we drank to the North in champagne.

I took a liking both to the country and to its people, and as I say, I felt as though the borders of my own country were being extended. Only now did I understand how closely related Swedes, Danes and Norwegians really are, and filled with this feeling I wrote on my return:

One folk we are and Scandinavians called

I was not thinking of politics in this poem, for they are alien to me. A poet must not work in the service of politics but calmly precede movements, like a prophet. This Scandinavian poem was created at a time when no one talked of Scandinavians. It was born of the awareness of the relationship between the three peoples, of the affection which I felt and wished they might share with me for each other in their spirits and hearts instead of being divided like rushing streams, dominated by enmity and a lack of understanding.

"It's obvious the Swedes made a fuss of him," was the first comment I heard on my poem at home. A few years passed and the neighbours understood each other better: Oehlenschläger, Tegnér and Fredrika Bremer persuaded them to read each other's literature, and people began to feel and understand the relationship. The foolish old remains of enmity, which had persisted because they did not appreciate each other's good qualities, disappeared, and Swedes and Danes came to regard each other with a charming, cordial mutual understanding.

Pan-Scandinavianism blossomed in Copenhagen, perhaps in Sweden as well, but I do not believe it has established itself in Norway. We were given a "Scandinavian Club", that is to say a society in Copenhagen where fraternal speeches were given about the three peoples of the North, where there were lectures on history and Scandinavian concerts with songs of Bellman and Rung, Lindblad and Gade, and of course that was all excellent. Now my poem was held in high esteem, and people said that it would outlive everything else I had written. Indeed one of the important figures in public life assured me that that was the only poem that gave me the right to be called a *Danish poet*. Now it ranked so high, and yet only a year ago it was seen as merely the product of flattered vanity.

In both Sweden and Denmark, composers set my poem to music, and it has become a song to be sung at concerts, but it has not become what one might call popular.

After my return from Sweden I began to make a thorough study of history and to make myself increasingly acquainted with foreign literature. Yet the book I read most and from which I derived the most profound impressions was, as always, the book of Nature. That summer I was given the kindest of receptions and the most comfortable of refuges in stately homes in Funen. This was especially the case with Kai Lykke's old mansion of Lykkesholm in its romantic setting close to the forest and Glorup, where Walkendorf, the powerful enemy of Tycho Brahe, had lived and which was now the home of the fine old Count Moltke-Hvitfelt. And on my quiet walks there I think I learnt more than I ever could have gained from the reflected wisdom of academic teaching.

In Copenhagen Collin's house was already then, as it still is, the "home of homes" to me, a term I had already used of it in the dedication in *The Improvisatore*. There I found both parents and siblings. The humour and the gaiety found in the novel *O.T.* and the dramatic works I wrote during those years, for instance *The Invisible Woman* of Sprogø, derive from Collins' home, which had a good effect on me and prevented me from being dominated by morbid, unhealthy moods. Especially Collin's eldest daughter, Mrs. Ingeborg Drewsen, with her lively humour, her wit and gaiety, had a great deal of influence on me. When the mind is soft and elastic like the surface of the sea – and mine was – then, like the sea, it will reflect its surroundings.

I was quite productive, and my works were among those which were always bought and read at home. For every new novel I wrote I received a larger fee, but it must be remembered how far afield Danish books are bought, and that I had not been proclaimed one of the great poets of the age from the palace balcony of Heiberg and the *Maanedsskrift for Litteratur*, so the fee remained small. However, I managed to live, although of course not in the way people in England imagined when they talked of the author of *The Improvisatore.* I remember Charles Dickens' amazement later on hearing the fee I was given for that book.

"How much did you receive for it?" he asked. I answered, "£19."

"Per quire?" he repeated.

"No," I said, "for the whole book."

"Let me see, I think we must be misunderstanding each other," he went on, "You cannot have been given £19 for the whole of *The Improvisatore*; that must be what you have received for a quire!"

I had to say I was sorry, but that was not the case. The price per quire was about ten shillings.

"Good Heavens," he exclaimed, "I would not believe it if you had not told me yourself." To be sure, Dickens was not familiar with conditions in Denmark and based my fee on what he was given in England; but it is probable that my translator there earned more than I did as the author. But enough of that; I survived, though admittedly I suffered some want.

I felt that to produce and produce all the time would be terribly damaging to me, but the attempts I made to find myself some sort of employment or some other honest means of earning a living failed. I applied for a situation in the Royal Library; H. C. Ørsted warmly supported my application to the director of the library, A.W. Hauch.

194

After discussing Hans Christian Andersen's "merits as a poet" Ørsted concluded his written recommendation by saying "that he is characterised by honesty and a sense of order and accuracy which many do not expect of the writer, but which cannot be denied him by those who know him." However, these words about me written by Ørsted achieved nothing. The director rejected me with the greatest courtesy by saying that I was possessed of far too much talent for him to be able to offer me such a trivial post as was to be found in the library.

I sought to contact the Society for the Freedom of the Press since I had plans for a Danish popular almanac like the widely known German one by Gubitz. At that time there was still no Danish equivalent. I believed that in *The Improvisatore* I had shown a talent for nature descriptions of this kind. And a couple of slender volumes of my fairy tales had already appeared, so they must show that I could tell a story. Ørsted approved of my plan, and also gave it his best recommendation, but the members of the committee were of the opinion that this work would entail too many and great difficulties for the Society to be able to take it on. That is to say they did not think I was good enough to do it. Later a similar almanac, edited by someone else, did appear and was supported by the Society.

So, in order to live I always had to think of the next day. Yet another hospitable home was thrown open to me at that time by an old lady whose peculiarities were more easily perceived by people than her many other excellent characteristics. She took great joy in reading my works, and she showed her good will towards me with a maternal affection. She was old Mrs Catharina Nigel, née Adzer. She is now dead. Collin was moreover also a help, comfort and support to me at that time, but in my modesty I only resorted to him in the most difficult instances. I experienced want and poverty, which I do not feel any desire to write about here. Yet, just as I thought during my childhood when things are really difficult, God will help. I have a lucky star, and it is God.

One day as I was sitting in my little room in Nyhavn – then on the Charlottenborg side – there was a knock on the door, and a stranger with kindly, distinguished features entered.

I had never seen him before. It was the late Count Conrad

Rantzau-Breitenburg, a native of Holstein and at that time the Prime Minister of Denmark. He was fond of poetry. His thoughts were filled with the beauty of Italy, and he wanted to pay a visit to the author of *The Improvisatore*.

He had read my book in the original language and felt deeply moved by it. He had spoken warmly of it at Court and among his acquaintances. He enjoyed a fine reputation and was recognised as a man of taste, with a knowledge of literature and of a truly noble mind. In his youth he had travelled a great deal and had spent some time in Spain and Italy, and so his judgement was of great importance. This was the man who visited the writer. He came quietly into my little room and expressed his thanks and his appreciation of my book; he invited me to go and visit him and quite openly asked me if there was no way in which he could help me. I told him how difficult it was to be forced to write in order to live and not to be able to develop and work without concern for the necessities of life. He pressed my hand fondly and promised to be an active friend for me; and so he was. I believe that Collin and H. C. Ørsted must also quietly have spoken on my behalf to King Frederik the Sixth.

For several years of this King's reign a sum from the state finances had already been used to provide support for young scholars and artists to travel abroad; indeed some who still had no fixed employment received a sort of annual salary, or "support" if you will. One such writer was Oehlenschläger, and previously there had been Ingemann, Heiberg and so on. Just at this very time Hertz had been granted an annual sum, so that his future had been more or less secured. It was my hope and wish that the same good fortune might come my way, and that is what happened: King Frederik the Sixth granted me 400 *Speciedaler* a year from now onwards.

I was filled with gratitude and joy. Now I was no longer forced to write in order to live, as I had been such a short time ago. Now if I fell ill I had an assured support; I was less dependent on the people around me.

A new chapter in my life was beginning.

VIII

It was from this day as though a more constant spring sunshine entered my life. I felt more secure since, on looking back, I could see more clearly that a loving providence was watching over me, and that everything was directed for my wellbeing, as though by the action of some higher power. And the firmer such a conviction becomes, the more secure one feels.

"In the British Navy a red thread runs through all the rope, both thick and thin, to show that it belongs to the Crown. Throughout every human life, in both great things and small, there is an invisible thread showing that we belong to God." This conviction, which I have felt and written down in the novel *The Two Baronesses*, still lives in me and fills my very being.

I had lived the life of a child, and the life of a young man really only began from this time. Before this, I merely swam against the waves and struggled against the heavy, gigantic breakers. In my thirty-fourth year the proper spring of my life began, but springtime also has its overcast days and storms before turning into bright, warm summer, and these storms are needed in order to develop the later fruits.

We were going to look ahead to what we call the grey days and storms, which, of course, afterwards, in a brighter and calmer season, make us smile at having been so easily frightened.

But let us get to the point!

Something that one of my dearest friends later wrote to me during a journey abroad, can serve as an introduction to what I am about to tell. He wrote in his own peculiar style:

It is that exquisite imagination of yours, which immediately makes up stories, that persuades you to believe you are despised in Denmark. This is completely untrue. You and Denmark get on admirably and would get on still better if there were no theatre in Denmark: hinc illæ lacrimæ! That accursed theatre! Is *that Denmark?* And are *you* nothing more than a hack writing for the theatre?

There is a grain of truth in that. For a number of years the theatre was the place that embittered my life. I am told that it is normal all the world over for people of the theatre to be a peculiarly difficult crowd. Almost all of them, from the leading supernumerary to the leading lover place themselves in one pan of the scales and the rest of the world in the other. The wall of the pit is the boundary of this world; the newspaper critics are fixed stars in this universe, and if shouts of bravo and admiration, often only parrot-like and expressing thoughtless admiration inherited from others, are the only things heard in this space, then it is only human to have your head turned more than your real importance justifies.

At that time, when politics played no role whatever for us, the theatre was the most important subject of conversation every day and evening. The Royal Danish Theatre could probably also be counted as one of the leading theatres in Europe, and several people of considerable talent belonged to it. Nielsen was in his youthful prime, and in addition to the thoughtfulness of his acting he was possessed of a voice which spoke his words with true music and enchanted his audiences. Then, too, the Danish stage possessed Dr. Ryge, who by reason of his personality, genius and voice was admirably suited to perform Oehlenschläger's tragedies. In Frydendahl the theatre had a rare example of wit and humour permeated by culture and grace. Gottlob Stage was by looks a true gentleman, but when playing comic roles he also revealed a bold sense of humour. Then even at that time there were talented figures such as Mrs. Heiberg, Mrs. Nielsen, Rosenkilde and Phister. In addition to all this we possessed an Opera, and the Ballet began to flourish under Bournonville.

As I say, our theatre was then one of the best in Europe. However, it would be wrong to assert that *all* actors there were the most outstanding representatives of the age, although some of them behaved as though they were, at least in front of me, for the writer did not rate highly in their estimation. I believe that the Danish theatre has always been too lacking in discipline, and discipline is necessary when a large number of individuals are to be brought together to form a whole, particularly if it is to be an artistic whole. In the course of the few generations through which I have already lived, I have discovered that there has always been the same tendency in the public to complain about the theatre management, especially with regard to the choice of repertoire. And there has been the same periodic dissatisfaction between the management and the actors. The cause surely lies in something in human nature that cannot be changed, and so it is very likely that every young author who is not enjoying the highest favour at the moment any more than I did will have the same things to suffer under and fight against. Even Oehlenschläger often suffered a great deal and was ignored or at least not treated in a manner I considered him to merit. It has been known for the actors to be applauded while he was hissed. And yet in what tones have I heard my fellow countrymen speak of his genius. However, it is probably the same in all countries, though how sad that is. Oehlenschläger himself recalls how, because they had him as their father, his children were insulted by the other boys at school, who merely repeated what they had heard their parents say.

The actors and actresses who either on account of talent, friendship with the press or popular favour are considered to be among the best, see themselves as superior to both management and playwrights. The latter must make sure of being favoured by them lest they should refuse to act a part or – as is often just as bad – should express a rather poor opinion of the play before it is performed. Plays are criticised in cafés before anyone is supposed to know the slightest thing about the new work. It is also typical of the people of Copenhagen that when they are going to see a new play they do not say, "I am looking forward to it," but rather, "It's probably not particularly good. I wonder if we shall have to hiss it?" Hissing is of great importance and is a form of entertainment that always ensures a full house. But a bad actor has never yet been hissed off the stage. No, only the poet and the composer, they alone are the sinners for whom the scaffold is erected. And during the five minutes the hissing usually fills the theatre, the ladies, beautiful and ugly alike, can be seen smiling and enjoying themselves just like Spanish women at their bloodthirsty bullfights. For a number of years the most dangerous time for a new play to appear was November and December; for during the preceding month the young schoolboys and schoolgirls cleared the hurdle of their final school-leaving examination and became very strict judges.

As is well known, all our most important dramatists have been hissed; Oehlenschläger, Heiberg, Hertz etc. have all been hissed off the stage, not to mention foreign classics such as Molière.

However, the theatre was and remains the most profitable field for any Danish author. When I was without any help or support of any kind I had sought to exercise my talent in this field. I had written the opera libretti of which I spoke above and which were so severely criticised, and I tried my hand at vaudeville. The author's fees, which were then not of such size as Collin managed to achieve during his last period as director, were, I really must say, reduced at that time to a level bordering on the comical. I must mention this; there are things which are called facts, and they cannot be erased. A well known and able businessman became the director of the theatre. People expected there would be order in everything now, for he was a good book-keeper. People looked forward to progress in the field of opera, for he had a sense of music as he himself sang in musical circles. People expected vigorous changes, and these came, too, in the regulations governing payment for plays. The value of plays was difficult to determine, and now it was decided that they should be paid for according to length and should be measured in fifteen-minute periods. At the first performance, then, the stage manager stood with a watch in his hand and wrote down how many quarters of an hour it took; these were added together, and the fee was paid accordingly. What was missing in the last quarter of an hour fell to the theatre; this is good business and well planned. Everyone thinks of himself first, and that was the case with me, too. I needed every copper I could get, and so I felt the loss deeply when my vaudeville *To Part and to Meet*, written in two parts with separate titles, was treated as two vaudevilles which, in the opinion of the management could be performed independently of each other. But "we must not speak ill of the authorities", and the theatre management is the authority governing the writer; on the other hand, some of the actors... but I will let them speak for themselves.

"It is no great difficulty to make a success of your plays, when

200

the finest talents in the land are to make them shine," said one of the finest talents who at that time did not want to play a part. "I don't play the part of a man," I was reminded by one actress to whom I had dared give a part she found too mannish. "Just point one single amusing line out to me," thundered one of the actors at a rehearsal of one of my first plays. Greatly upset at this I was later standing over in a corner, when the same great personage came across to me and said, "Do you really take that so much to heart? Do you think I find the part bad? No, because then I would not act it. However, the poorer I make out it is on your part, the better it will appear to be on mine. But if you tell anyone I've said that I shall say you are lying." The actor spoke this line excellently, without thinking of the public hearing it now. Perhaps people will laugh at it and say it is just something to make fun of, but that is not how quite a young author can take it. The strong expressions used in commands in ships are not to be taken literally, and neither are they to be in the great ship called the theatre, but I did so. But why did I bother with the theatre? Because it was there you could earn most by getting a play accepted, and it is impossible to live without money; and then the stage is a great platform where, as Carl Bagger says, "hundreds hear what scarcely ten would read".

Collin was no longer director of the theatre. Molbech was the most energetic and the hardest of the censors. I believe that the censor's reports, which the theatre keeps and in which Molbech has commented both on plays that have been rejected and those that have been accepted, will in time provide us with a most extraordinary character study. And if we then go on to read what he later wrote and published when he was no longer a director of the theatre and Heiberg rejected a play by his son – talking of duties towards young talents – we find the very comments that could and should have been made to him himself when his own capriciousness had free rein. That he would condemn everything I wrote was only to be expected; it should simply have been done in the normal way, the way which was considered correct by the management. When a play is rejected the management usually uses the formula that it: "does not find itself in a position to accept the enclosed work". They do not set about providing their reasons, and what they had to say would in many cases be extremely long-winded. On the other hand I received a letter which could not possibly have been dictated by anyone but Molbech and which was constructed *con amore* in order to say things to me that were less than kind things, something of which he was very capable. So the only way to have a play staged in Denmark was to make it available for the actors' summer performances. In the summer of 1839 I wrote the vaudeville *The Invisible Woman of Sprogø*, to be performed with the *décor* that had been made for Hertz's *The Flight to Sprogø*. People liked the hilarious fun in the play and it won so much public favour that the management included it in the repertoire; and this lightly constructed work was received on the stage with great applause and survived a greater number of performances than I had dreamt of. However, this approbation had not the slightest influence on the Royal Theatre management, and I had the vexation of seeing every new work rejected. Nevertheless, filled with the idea and the action of the little French story *Les épaves*, I decided to adapt it for dramatic performance, to prove at the same time what people had so often denied me, that I possessed a sufficiently steady character to plan a piece of work thoroughly and diligently. So I wrote a play of five acts in rhymed verse, indeed in some parts in the manner of Paludan-Müller in lyrical flights of three or four rhymes. Moreover I believed myself as able to move about in language as a bird in a grove. It was a theme that was foreign to me and contained a rich dramatic action, and my poetry so adorned it with fresh greenery that it almost looked as though it had come from my garden. And if music can be imparted to verse, then I tried at least to subject the whole to the music of the language and thereby to translate another writer's work to the stage. I felt that the original story had been absorbed into my blood before I submitted it to the theatre. I did not think that people would be able to say, as they had done when I used themes from Walter Scott's novels, that I had arranged or cut it to pieces for the stage. The play was written and read for several of my older friends, intelligent men, who thought highly of it. A couple of the actors I hoped would appear in it also heard me read it and became extremely interested in it, especially Mr. Wilhelm Holst whom I hoped to persuade to play the leading role. He was one of the actors who treated me kindly and sympathetically and to whom I owe gratitude and recognition.

Having learned of the contents, one of our more high ranking officials from the West Indies attacked the play while waiting in Frederik the Sixth's antechamber, saying that this was not a play suitable for the Royal Theatre as it would have a damaging influence on the black population of our West Indian islands. "Yes, but it is not going to be performed in the West Indies," was the reply he received.

The play was submitted to the theatre and of course rejected by Molbech. It was well known to the public that what he encouraged for the stage soon withered, but, like so many weeds, what he threw aside often turned into fine flowers in the garden. So his rejection did not have an unfortunate effect, and that was always a consolation. Another of the directors, the Cabinet Secretary J.G. Adler, a man with taste and a sense of fairness, became the advocate for my work, and as the public was favourably disposed towards it, thanks to those who had heard me read it, it was decided after some discussion to perform it. But before it was finally accepted there was a little scene which is both characteristic and amusing, and which I here will preserve.

There was a man, an excellent person, but not one versed in aesthetics; nevertheless, his opinion would have a considerable effect on the outcome of the performances. He told me that he meant well by me, but that he had not yet read my play; there were so many who spoke in its favour, but Molbech had written reams against it. "And then," he said, "I must point out that it is based on a novel. You write novels yourself, so why do you not invent a story for your play? Then I must say that it is one thing to write novels and another to write plays, for they must contain theatrical effects. Are there any in *The Mulatto*? And are they new?" I tried to satisfy the man's demands and ideas and answered, "There is a ball."

"Yes, that is excellent, but so there is in *The Bride*. Is there nothing quite new?"

"There is a slave market," I said.

"Hm, a slave market. That is probably something new. Yes, that is something. I will be fair to you. That slave market appeals to me." And I believe it was the slave market that won the final and necessary approval for the play's being accepted.

After the first stage rehearsal Holst sent me a delightful poem expressing his thanks and appreciation.

Two evenings before the first performance was to take place I had the honour of reading the play for Prince Christian and his wife, who gave me a kind and gentle welcome and from whom I have since received many tokens of favour and cordiality.

The day arrived; it was the third of December, 1839. The bills were posted outside, and all the previous night I had not slept a wink for excitement and anticipation. People were already standing in a queue in front of the theatre to buy their tickets. Then royal messengers were seen hurrying through the streets, and people began to assemble in serious groups. The sad news had been received that King Frederik the Sixth had died that morning. It was proclaimed from the Palace of Amalienborg, and people cheered for Christian the Eighth. The gates of the city were shut and the army was sworn in. Frederik the Sixth had still belonged to the patriarchal age. The rising generation had never before lost a king, and the sorrow and seriousness were great and clearly to be seen.

For two months everything was like a house in mourning, and only after this did the Theatre open for the first time in the reign of King Christian the Eighth with my drama *The Mulatto*. I wrote the following dedication to the King, who, of course, already knew the book and had approved of it:

> You listened kindly to my songs
> Proclaiming victory to the spirit due.
> You prize the spirit that to God belongs.
> And so, oh King, I dedicate my song to you.

The play was well performed and was received with great enthusiasm, but I could not at first feel any joy at this. I only felt relief from the tension under which I had suffered, and now I could breathe more freely. My play received the same acclamation throughout a whole series of performances. Most people rated this work far above anything else I had ever written and were of the opinion that my real career as a poet would now begin. None of my poems or *The Improvisatore*, *The Fiddler* and so on were of any importance at all compared with this work. In short, a great many people accorded it the sort of praise I had only experienced once before, on the publication of my first work, *The Journey on Foot*. So far these two were the only works which had been really valued, perhaps overvalued. The play was soon translated into Swedish and received with great applause in the Royal Theatre in Stockholm. The Swedish poet Ridderstad wrote a sort of epilogue to it in which Paléme seeks revenge on his master. Travelling players performed my play in the smaller towns in Sweden, and the Danish troupe led by Mr. Werligh performed it in Danish over in Malmö, where a great crowd of students from Lund received it with great acclamation. Friendly greetings in verse and prose echoed across the Sound to me:

> Young swan of Denmark, Northern lyre,
> In singing drown a brutal time;
> Rebuild a glittering Palmyre,
> But on Parnassus, fair, sublime.
> Fill us with beauty now as though
> To lead us back from darkness' power.
> And bathe us in the morning's glow,
> Reveal once more the Nordic flower.

C. Adlersparre

The week just before this, I had been on a visit to Baron Wrangel in Scania. These Swedish neighbours received me so cordially and with such heartfelt kindness that the impression of it has never been erased from my memory. It was there that I received the first mark of honour from abroad, something that made a profound and unforgettable impression on me. I was invited by the students at Lund to visit their ancient city, where a banquet was arranged in my honour, speeches were made and my health was drunk; and later that evening, while I was visiting some acquaintances, I learned that the students intended serenading me. The mere news of this so surprised me that I began to tremble in every limb. I became quite feverish on seeing the tightly packed throng, all wearing their blue caps, approaching the house arm in arm. Indeed I felt so humble and so aware of my weaknesses that I almost felt I was being pressed to the ground rather than elevated. When they all bared their heads as I stepped forward, it was all I could do not to burst into tears. Feeling that I was unworthy of such homage, I watched them closely to see if there were smiles on the lips of any of them, but I saw nothing but friendly faces. A dubious smile at this moment would otherwise have wounded me grievously. They cheered me, and of the speech that was made I clearly remember that they said, "When your own native land and the nations of Europe pay homage to you, we ask you not to forget that the first to do so were the students of Lund." When our hearts are warm, we do not weigh the strength with which we express ourselves; I felt this deep within me and answered that from this moment I felt that I *must* make a name for myself so as to show myself worthy of the honour they did me. Those nearest to me I shook by the hand and thanked them as profoundly and heartily as it is possible to thank people. And when I went into the drawing room again I found a corner where I could weep after this excitement and these overwhelming feelings.

"Don't think any more about that, but be happy along with us," said a couple of my Swedish friends. They were all so cheerful, but my soul was filled with serious feelings. The memory of that evening has often come back to me, and no generous person reading these lines will see vanity in my lingering so long over this great event in my life, which eradicated pride rather than gave it nourishment. My drama *The Mulatto* was to be produced in Malmö after this. The students wanted to see it, but I hurried my departure so as not to be present in the theatre on that occasion. I think back on the Swedish university town with joy and gratitude, though I have never been there since. The young men who showed their enthusiasm for me that day are now scattered all over the country. My greetings will reach them, just as my deepest homage is linked to the old university town.

The Swedish newspapers carried reports of the honour done to me, and *Dagen* of 30th April, 1840 contains a summary of an article in *Malmö nya Allehanda* on Andersen, who, in a way that did credit both to him and the Danish nation, was honoured by the students in Lund on Good Friday; the newspaper also contains a report on the dinner that had been arranged in the Great Hall at the Town Hall. The Swedish correspondent finishes by saying:

We well know the harsh voices which out of envy and comradeship are raised in the neighbouring capital against one of the nation's finest sons. But these voices must be silenced. Europe is placing its opinion on the scales, and its judgement has never been rejected. As a writer, Andersen belongs not merely to Denmark, but to Europe as a whole, and the honour done to him by Swedish youth in Sweden's southern university might, we hope, be able to render harmless the sting with which pettiness and envy in his native land seek to turn his laurel wreath into a crown of thorns. And with this we bid a hearty farewell to the delightful bard, and we assure him that we shall always meet him with true admiration and fraternal loyalty wherever he sets foot in our beloved homeland of Sweden.

When I arrived home in Copenhagen, a few of my old and tried friends met me with profound delight; I saw tears in their eyes. They said that they were especially pleased to see how I received the honour that had been done me. For me there is but one way: in the midst of all my joy my thoughts fly up to God, gentle and humble, and pray that He will grant me the strength and ability to deserve such honour.

A few people smiled at the enthusiasm. There was the occasional person who would have liked to make fun of it. The poet Heiberg said ironically to me, "When I go to Sweden you will have to come with me, so that I, too, may enjoy a little homage of that sort!" I did not like the quip and replied, "Just take your wife with you, and you will find it comes to you much more easily."

From Sweden I heard of nothing but enthusiasm for *The Mulatto*, whereas a few voices at home spoke out against it. They said that the action had been taken from elsewhere, though this was not stated on the title page. That was because of an unfortunate coincidence: I had written an acknowledgment on the last page of the manuscript, but as the drama, when printed, finished on the very last page of a quire it meant starting a new one to include this note, and so the printers asked me if it could not be omitted. One of our writers whom

I consulted on this was of the opinion that it was quite unnecessary, since *Les épaves* was widely read. When he had adapted Tieck's *The Elves* even Heiberg himself had not indicated his rich source. This was where they started to get at me. The French story was scrutinised thoroughly and compared with my play. Someone sent a translation of *Les épaves* to the editor of the periodical *Portfeuillen* with the urgent request that he should publish it. The editor told me, and of course I said he should accept it. On the stage the play continued to be a great success, but the critics reduced the value that had been accorded to my work. The overwhelming praise I had received made me sensitive to what I thought was unfair criticism. I could take it less than I could before and believed that it derived less from an interest in artistic value than from a desire to annoy me and once more to consign me to the slough of poetic mediocrity. In the recently published novella by the author of *An Everyday Story* the enthusiasm for *The Mulatto* was also ridiculed, and the idea of the triumph of the spirit, to which I had given expression in it, was considered to be sheer nonsense. As everyone knew that it was J. L. Heiberg who was responsible for the publication of these stories, almost everyone thought that they must have been written in his home, and that he must have some close relationship with the author. We saw how Heiberg had his name on the posters for the drama *Might and Cunning* when it was first performed, but when the play was a failure he retracted this and said it was by the author of *An Everyday Story*, in the works of whom it has since been included. So I assumed that the side-swipe at me must derive from, or at least have the approval of Heiberg. I became more and more convinced that he simply disliked me, and this upset me. I liked his company, and recognised how gifted he was, and then I was often brought into contact with him in the circles in which I moved. Modestly and fervently I had attached myself to him, the man who was the star of the day here in Denmark, but now I felt I had been coldly repulsed. At least that is how it appeared to me, and once I had become suspicious, how easy it was to build on every thoughtless or careless word and to see it through the microscope of an angry eye. Perhaps it was I who was most unjust. The admiration my closest associates had for Heiberg as a poet and aesthetic judge naturally influenced their opinion of me, and I was often on the point of giving up, as I did not believe anyone had any confidence in me. It is not envy and vanity, but a wound that bleeds when only one's enemies are continually quoted and admired.

But my mind was pliable and fresh, and just at that time I had the idea for *A Picture Book without Pictures*, and I wrote it. It is only a small book, but judging by the reviews and numerous impressions of it that have appeared in Germany, it must be the most successful of all my books, even more than the fairy tales, and it has become incredibly widely known. One of the first to write on it added: "Many of the pictures contain the stuff of short stories and novellas, and indeed a gifted person might even create novels from them." A novel was in fact later based on one of them: the gifted Frau von Gören admits that she borrowed the idea for her first novel, *Die Adoptivtochter*, from the third evening of *A Picture Book without Pictures*, when the moon tells of its "Rose from the Parsonage Garden".

My book was also translated into Swedish and dedicated to me in an extra "evening". It attracted less attention at home, and as far as I remember Mr. Siesbye in the *Copenhagen Morning Post* was the only person who deemed me worthy of some friendly remarks.

In England a couple of translations appeared, and the English critics praised it highly, calling it "an Iliad in a nutshell". From England I have seen a proof of a deluxe edition of the same work; but of course the result, as in a later German edition, was that it was turned into a *Picture Book without Pictures* containing: pictures.

As I have said, no great attention was paid to the little book in Denmark. On the other hand people were still talking about *The Mulatto*, though they were mostly saying that I had borrowed the idea, something of course that also applied to Oehlenschläger's *Aladdin*, based on the Arabian Nights, and Heiberg's *The Elves*, which derived from Tieck's fairy tale; but Tieck was not well known, and Heiberg was above criticism at that time.

The fact that people were constantly pointing out that I had not invented the plot myself prompted me to invent one, and I now wrote the tragedy *The Moorish Girl*, hoping through this to silence all those evil tongues and at the same time secure my position as a dramatist. Moreover it was my plan that for the proceeds from this work together with a small sum of money I had collected and saved

209

from the fee for *The Mulatto* I would once more be in a position to go abroad and indeed undertake a longer journey, not merely to Italy but to Greece and Turkey. My first travels had contributed more than anything else to my intellectual development, as everyone was prepared to admit. I felt that life and the world were my best school. I was filled with the urge to travel and to acquire more knowledge of our natural surroundings and of mankind in general. In thoughts and feelings I was still very young indeed.

Heiberg, who was now the censor at the Theatre, disliked my play, and indeed he did not approve of any of my dramatic activities. Mrs Heiberg, for whom I thought I had written the part, refused to act it, and I knew that the public were not keen on going to the theatre if she was not appearing. So the fee I received would be small, and I would not be able to extend my journey. I said this to her, without thinking of any lofty considerations she might have towards art, but she refused in no uncertain terms.

Deeply hurt, I went away and complained to a few friends. Whether because of the way in which my complaints were repeated or because it is a crime to complain about the public favourite, I do not know, but Heiberg became my enemy for a number of years, though I hope the relationship is better now. This was only on a small scale of course, for in the eyes of the Danish public I was not an opponent worthy of him. I understood this and suffered it in this spirit. I was soon given clear indications of his aversion for me. But there was never a sign from Mrs. Heiberg, and if I have said here that I was once rather less than pleased with her it is my desire and duty not to be misunderstood here by her or anyone else. I must also express my ardent and lasting recognition of her. I consider her to be such an excellent artist that if the Danish language were as widely known as French and German she would have a European reputation. In tragedy she is extremely interesting by virtue of the understanding and brilliance with which she conceives her role, and in comedy she is unsurpassed in truth and naturalness. In later years I have also learned to see in her one of the noblest and best of women, and she has treated me with the greatest sympathy and cordiality, so that the only reason for my saying all this is that it has already been said in *Das Märchen Meines Lebens* and is very much part of what I experienced in the past. But now back to my mood at that time.

Whether or not I was unjust, certain people were against me and the public did not favour me. I was conscious of being continually overlooked and badly treated. I felt insulted and was exposed to several unpleasant confrontations. I no longer felt comfortable in Denmark. I was more or less ill and could stand it no longer, so I left my play to its fate and, suffering and depressed, I hurried to leave the country. In this mood I wrote a preface to *The Moorish Girl* which only too clearly revealed how sick at heart I was; and naturally people made fun of that. If I were to begin to deal here with all the aesthetic cliques we had, I would have to reveal many mysteries, and I would have to introduce many people who do not belong to public life if I wanted to make this section clearer and more precise. Many others in my place would have become ill as I did, or furiously angry, which would have been more sensible. The best thing for me was to leave the country, and that was what my friends wished me to do.

"Be of good heart and make sure you get away from all this nonsense as soon as you can," Thorvaldsen wrote to me from Nysø. "I shall probably see you here before you leave, but otherwise we shall see each other in Rome."

"For heaven's sake go away for a time," said my honest and sympathetic friends. H. C. Ørsted and Collin, too, urged me to carry out my plan, and Oehlenschläger sent me a poem in which he gave me his best wishes for the journey.

My friend, the poet H. P. Holst, was also due to go abroad. His poem *Oh, land of my birth, what hast thou lost?* was on everyone's lips. Its simple, heartfelt words seemed to express what everyone felt. The death of King Frederik the Sixth was both a national and a family loss, and so the first natural and beautiful poem of mourning which expressed these feelings captured the hearts of all. Holst was the fortunate poet of the moment, and without any difficulty or need for recommendations – this is not said out of any bitter feelings towards him – he had been awarded a travelling bursary. His many friends in the Students' Union arranged a farewell dinner for him, and this prompted a few of my younger friends to get together and arrange a farewell dinner for me, too. These were young students and a few older men including Reitzel, the publisher, Collin, Adam

Oehlenschläger and H. C. Ørsted. That brought a little sunshine to my poor and gloomy poet's life. Songs by Oehlenschläger and Hillerup were sung, and I felt cordiality and friendship here just as I was leaving my home in deep distress. That was in October 1840. I was going to pay my second visit to Italy, and then continue to Greece and Constantinople, a journey which I have described in my own way in *A Poet's Bazaar*.

On the outward journey I spent some days in Holstein at the home of Count Rantzau-Breitenburg, whose parental mansion I now visited for the first time. I saw the rich scenery of Holstein, its heaths and its marshlands. Although it was late autumn, the weather was beautiful, and one day we visited the churchyard in the nearby village of Münsterdorf, where the author of *Siegfried von Lindenberg*, Müller von Itzehoe, as he is also called, lies buried. He was Germany's most widely read novelist in the last century, and wrote *Komische Romane aus den Papieren des braunen Mannes*. Once the most widely read novelist, he was nevertheless almost forgotten by the time he grew old. Nevertheless, he received a pension from the King of Denmark until his death (on the 23rd of June 1828) enabling him to live, and suffer, as he had what is known as a "sensitive nature".

The railway between Magdeburg and Leipzig had been opened, and I saw and tried it for the first time. It was a great event for me to see and feel the speed with which it travelled, and the profound impression it made on me can be seen in *A Poet's Bazaar*.

Mendelssohn-Bartholdy lived in Dresden, and I owed him a visit. Collin's daughter and son-in-law, Mr. Drewsen, had brought me greetings from him the previous year. During a trip on the Rhine they had heard that he was on board, and since they knew and loved him as a composer they spoke to him. He heard that they were from Denmark, and one of his first questions was whether they knew Hans Christian Andersen, the poet. "I consider him my brother," said Mrs. Drewsen, and now they had found a point of contact. Mendelssohn told them that while he had been ill he had had *Only a Fiddler* read aloud to him. The book had interested him very much indeed and had awakened his interest in the author. He asked them to convey his sincere greetings to me, adding that if ever I were in Leipzig I must certainly visit him.

Now I was there, but only for one day. So I immediately went to find Mendelssohn. He was at a rehearsal at the Gewandthaus. I did not say who I was, but that a gentleman who was passing through the town was very keen to speak to him. He came, but I could see he was rather irritated at being disturbed in his work.

"I have very little time and can't really talk to strangers here," he said.

"You have invited me yourself," I answered. "You said I was not to travel through your city without making myself known to you."

"Andersen," he exclaimed now, "That's who it is." And he beamed all over his face; he embraced me and took me into the hall, and I had to listen to the rehearsal; they were playing Beethoven's Seventh Symphony. Mendelssohn wanted me to stay to dinner, but I had to go and visit my elderly friend Brockhaus, and immediately after dinner the coach was due to leave for Nuremberg, my next destination.

So I had to promise to stay a few days in Leipzig on my way home. And I kept that promise. Now Mendelssohn gave me pen and paper and asked me for my signature. I wrote:

> Through the church the organ's tones rang out:
> A child is born, and Felix is its name;
> Aye, "Felix" then the heavenly host sang out,
> Within him burns sweet music's sacred flame.

It was in Nuremberg I saw daguerreotypes for the first time. These pictures, I was told, were the work of only ten minutes; it seemed like magic to me. This art was new, and nothing like what it is in our days. Daguerreotypes and railways: these two new flowers of the age were already two experiences I had gained from my journey. I flew away by train to Munich to visit old friends and acquaintances.

There was a host of my compatriots there: Blunck, Kiellerup, Wegener, Holm the animal painter, Marstrand, Storch, Holbech and the poet Holst with whom I was to travel on to Italy. The two of us stayed in Munich for a couple of weeks and shared accommodation. He was truly a good friend, sociable and understanding. Together with him I visited the Artists' Inn a few times. This was a Bavarian copy of life in Rome, but it was beer and not wine that sparkled there. Nor did I feel at home in all this merriment, and none of my fellow countrymen really appealed to me. And as for my qualities as a poet, their judgement of me was probably based on standards in Copenhagen. On the other hand they were friendlier towards Holst, and so I went about mostly on my own, sometimes full of joie de vivre, but more often doubting my own ability. I had a peculiar talent for lingering over the more gloomy sides of life, of finding bitter memories and savouring them again. I was an adept at torturing myself.

I stayed in Munich for a couple of weeks, and even if I did not meet with any interest on the part of my compatriots I found all the more from foreigners. *The Improvisatore* and *Only a Fiddler* were familiar to quite a number of people. The famous portrait painter, Stieler, came to visit me and threw his home open to me, and there I met Cornelius, Lachner and Schelling, whom I already knew. Soon several homes were open to me. My name reached the ears of the manager of the theatre, where I was given a free seat just beside Kaulbach. In *A Poet's Bazaar* I have described my visit to Kaulbach, the artist whom other artists then thought insignificant, but whom the world at large has since learnt to consider a great painter. There I saw a cartoon of his *Destruction of Jerusalem* and his sketches for *The Battle of the Huns*, and he showed me the lovely drawings – which we have all seen since then – for *Reynard the Fox* and Goethe's *Faust*.

I was looking forward like a child to going to Italy together with my friend H. P. Holst and to showing him that lovely country and all the wonders it had to offer. But our compatriots in Munich, especially Blunck and Storch, would not let go of him. He had his portrait painted. Days passed, and at last, as he himself could still not say when he would be able to leave, I was forced to go alone and give up the pleasure of travelling with him in the country I loved and knew as the beautiful land of art. However we decided to find apartments together in Rome when he arrived, and agreed that from there we would go on to Naples together.

I left Munich on the second of December and went by way of the Tyrol, Innsbruck and the Brenner Pass to Italy, the goal of all my longings and the home of my most cherished thoughts. So I was to go to Italy again after all, and it was not to be "probably the only time I should be so fortunate", as someone had once said to me. I was moved and happy, and for a time that feeling completely replaced the sorrows which oppressed my mind, and I prayed fervently and earnestly to God for health and strength to be able to follow the calling of a poet.

I arrived in Rome on the 19th of December. The events and impressions I encountered on that journey are described in *A Poet's Bazaar*. On the very day of my arrival I found a good apartment at the home of some respectable people in the Via Purificazione. It was a large apartment, a whole floor to myself and Holst, who would soon be arriving.

But a long time passed before that, and I had to live alone in the big, empty rooms which I had acquired for a very modest rent since there were few visitors in Rome that winter on account of the bad weather and because a dangerous fever was raging there.

A small garden containing a huge orange tree full of fruit went with my flat, and up against the walls there was an abundance of roses in flower. And then I could hear the singing of the monks in the Capuchin Monastery, the very place which I used as the setting for the childhood of my "improvisatore".

Once more I visited churches and art galleries and again I saw all the art treasures. I met several old friends and spent Christmas Eve together with them, and even if it was not as festive as the first time, it was Christmas in Rome. The Carnival and Moccoli followed. However, not only was I myself physically ill, but there was also something wrong with the air. There was not the peace and the freshness that there had been the first time I had lived there. The earth trembled, and the Tiber ran through the streets. People sailed about in boats, and the fever took a heavy toll. Within the space of a few days the Prince of Borghese lost his wife and three sons. There was sleet and a cold wind, and it was not at all pleasant. Many an evening I sat in my large drawing room in a draught from the windows and doors. The thin twigs in the hearth blazed up, and the heat from them burned me on one side, whilst the other side of me felt the cold air. I sat half wrapped in my cape and wearing my boots indoors. And in addition, for nights and weeks on end I had a most violent toothache, the one I have tried to laugh at in the story entitled *My Boots*.

Holst did not come until well into February, just before the Carnival. I was sick, both in mind and body, but what a sincere friend he was, gentle and kind, and that was a blessing, for I was suffering a great deal. And in that state of mind old memories often appear. Many a little poem from those days has blown away, and I have only a few left:

> I gave all my heart and my youthful blood,
> And then she commented, "He's ever so good,"
> Yet handsome enough I was not.

> A sorrow it was for my faithful friend,
> All poison he gathered and to me did send:
> "Now this you must drink, for strength it will give."

> I sang what I felt, all faithful and true,
> But then all the critics said that wouldn't do.
> "Oh, that he has taken from Heine."

Every day was wet and raw, and letters started to arrive from home now, and they were not very different from the ones that had come during my previous visit to Rome. They contained no good news: *The Moorish Girl* had been produced, and had been quietly performed a few times, but, as I had foreseen, since Mrs. Heiberg was not acting the main part, no one went to it, and so the management had taken it off. My fee for the evenings it had been performed would probably be reduced because of the new system, according to which only plays taking three hours were considered as lasting all evening. One of my fellow countrymen received a letter telling him that *The Moorish Girl* had been hissed off the stage, which was completely untrue. Nevertheless, the news was passed on to me, and it had its unpleasant effect on me, so the object was achieved. Later I learnt for certain that the play had been well received, but as I have said, it did not play to full houses.

The principal part was played beautifully and with much feeling by Madame Holst, and Hartmann's music was very distinctive indeed, but the staging had been such as to spoil everything. This was bad, tasteless and distracting; indeed the dramatic section in Alhambra was very clumsy and completely ridiculous, for all of which of course the crowd blamed the writer. In the role of Lazaron, I was told that Mr. Phister had acted so splendidly and had been so full of humour that everyone was drawn down into a torrent of laughter. People had laughed until they could laugh no more.

However, the worst thing for me was that Heiberg wanted to get at me. In Copenhagen at that time he was both Allah and his prophet in Danish literature, and he had just then published a new work which occupied everyone's thoughts. It was *A Soul after Death*, and, as someone wrote to one of my compatriots, Andersen "was really and truly ridiculed in it". Even one of my most affectionate friends told me that it was an excellent play but that I was lampooned it. That was all I heard and all I knew. No one told me exactly what the satire had said about me, or what was the reason for its being so laughable and amusing. "Andersen is really and truly being made fun of," was all people said. It is doubly awkward to be mocked when we do not know what it is people are mocking in us. The bits of news were like melted lead being dripped into an open wound.

It was not until after my return that I saw the book. Only on my arrival in Copenhagen did I read it and discover that what had been said about me was nothing to take so much to heart. It was a joke about my being famous from "Scania to Hundsrück" that Heiberg did not like. From "Scania to Hundsrück" was about as far as Heiberg had travelled, and he had heard everywhere that I was famous, he didn't like that, and so he let me go to Hell. However I found the play so excellent that when I had read it I was tempted to write to him and thank him for the enjoyment I had derived from it. But I slept on this idea, and when I awoke I had reflected and was afraid he might misunderstand my thanks. As far as my being sent to Heiberg's Hell is concerned, I am told by people who originally heard him read the work that I was not in it then, and so I must have been damned by him and put in at a later date.

As I say, I still did not know the book while I was in Rome. I only heard the rush of the arrows and felt them wound me without knowing the strength of the poison that might have been put on them.

And so my second visit to Rome, like the first, was spoiled for me. I had a feeling that this metropolis that I loved so dearly and where so much appealed to me and filled my thoughts did not bring good fortune to me. The days that passed there were gloomy and bitter, none of them much better than during my visit in 1833. I felt physically ill and was eager to get away.

Holst had arrived at about Carnival time, and with him came our mutual friend Conrad Rothe, who was now a clergyman in Copenhagen Cathedral. The three of us left for Naples in February. There is a legend and a superstition among foreigners in Rome that on the evening before departing you must go to the *Fontana di Trevi* and take a drink of its water in order to be sure of coming back to Rome again. The first time I left I was prevented from going to the fountain that evening. I thought about it all night long, and then a porter came to fetch my luggage. I went with him, and quite by chance we went past the *Fontana di Trevi*. I dipped my finger in the water and tasted it, believing that I would come back to Rome, and so I did. On this occasion I ignored this superstition before leaving. We drove off, and suddenly the carriage turned off from the Corso: we were to pick up a priest from a monastery, and we came to the *Fontana di Trevi* and so I came to Rome for the third time.

The priest we fetched was a choirmaster, a jolly man who took off his clerical dress at Albano and was transformed into a cheerful, amusing gentleman who sang for us. H. P. Holst has included this man whose acquaintance we made in this way in his *Italian Sketches*.

It was cold in Naples, and Vesuvius and the mountains around it were covered with snow. I was feverish and suffering both physically and mentally. My toothache, which had lasted several weeks, had put me in a very nervous state. I took as firm a grip on myself as I could and drove with my compatriots to Herculanum. However, while they were walking about in this excavated city I simply sat, ill and feverish, and it was a fortunate mistake for me that we took the wrong train, and instead of going to Pompeii were taken back to Naples. I arrived there mortally ill, and only by allowing myself to be bled without delay, as I was urged to do by my assiduous Neapolitan landlord, did I escape death. The following week I felt noticeably better and left Naples on a French warship, the Leonidas, for Greece. Down on the shore people sang out, "*Evviva la gioia.*" Yes, long live joy; if only we could capture it.

A new life was to be revealed to me, and indeed that is what happened. If it is not to be read in my writings, it certainly made its presence felt in my view of life and in my entire intellectual development. It was in the afternoon of the 15th of March that I left Naples, the city I knew and where I had friends, and it seemed I was now leaving my European home behind. I felt young and light at heart, and it was as though a river of forgetfulness flowed between me and all my unhealthy and bitter memories. I felt health in my blood and health in my thoughts, and I raised my head boldly and fearlessly.

Naples lay bathed in sunshine, clouds hung over Vesuvius as far down as the hermit's hut; the sea was like a millpond. The following night I was called up to see Stromboli in eruption, the light from it reflected in the water. In the morning we passed Charybdis and could see the surf at Scylla and the low cliffs of Sicily, while Etna, covered with snow and with smoke rising from it, towered before us.

In *A Poet's Bazaar* I have described this journey along the coast, the brief visit to Malta and the lovely days and nights on the motionless Mediterranean, its swell luminous at night, and the magnificence of the stars which shone with a brilliance that amazed me. The rays from Venus were like those from the moon in Scandinavia, it even cast shadows. Great dolphins romped on the surface of the water. On the ship itself there was quite a social life; there was music, singing and dancing; we played cards and carried on a lively conversation. There was a mixed company of Americans, Italians and Asians, bishops and monks, officers and tourists.

A few days' life at sea attaches people to each other. I had come to feel quite at home, and so it was a sad moment when I had to leave the vessel at Syra. The French line from Marseilles to Constantinople meets that from Alexandria to Pyræus at the island of Syra, and there I had to change to a ship from Egypt, and apart from a Persian from Herat I was the only one to leave the Leonidas.

The town here looked like a city of tents, like a whole encampment, as huge canvas sheets were hanging from house to house to protect them from the sun. The shore shone white and red, and a large crowd of people was standing on it, Greeks in red shirts and white *fustanellas*. The Greek steamer that normally sailed between here and Pyræus was undergoing repairs, and so I travelled on the one from Alexandria, which had just arrived and was only to spend a couple of days in quarantine with us when we reached Pyræus. For more about this journey I refer my readers to *A Poet's Bazaar* where I have presented a series of pictures of this journey, and so I can fly through the countries here more quickly.

In the harbour at Pyræus, where we lay at anchor in quarantine, a boat immediately appeared full of Germans and Danes. The *Allgemeine Zeitung* had announced my arrival, and they rowed close to the ship to wish me welcome. When our quarantine was at an end they called for me in Pyræus and, taking with us a hired Greek servant in national dress, we set off through the olive groves for Athens, where I had already from afar caught sight of the Mount Lycabettus and the Acropolis.

The Dutch consul, Travers, was also the Danish consul and spoke Danish. Among my new friends was the Court chaplain, Lüth, a Holsteiner married to a young Danish lady from Fredensborg. He told me that he had learnt Danish by reading my *Improvisatore* in the original. Our fellow countryman, Køppen, the architects the Hansen brothers, and the Holsteiner Professor Ross were among those whom I met there. The Danish language resounded in the royal city of Greece, and the champagne popped for Denmark and for me.

I remained in Athens for a month. There had been hopes of arranging a visit to Parnassus for me on my birthday, the second of April, but winter came, and a good deal of snow fell, so I spent most of my birthday up in the Acropolis.

Among the most interesting acquaintances and one of those to whom I became most attached in Athens was Prokesch-Osten, who was the resident Austrian minister, already familiar to us through his memoirs from *Egypt and Asia Minor* and his *Journey in the Holy Land*.

Consul Travers presented me to the King and Queen. We went out on several extremely interesting excursions. I was there for the Greek Easter and the "Festival of Peace" which I have endeavoured

220

to describe.

Greece lay before me like a Switzerland with loftier and clearer skies than Italy. The natural scenery made a profound and solemn impression upon me. I had the feeling that I was going about on the great battlefield of the world, where nations had fought and been destroyed. No single work of poetry can encompass such greatness; every dried-up river bed, every hill, every stone had great memories to tell. How small the difficulties of everyday life appear to be in such a place. A wealth of ideas filled my mind, but in such abundance that none were committed to paper. I felt a desire to express the feeling that the Divine has its battle to fight here on earth, and that it is rejected and repelled, but yet advances victoriously over the centuries, and in the legend of The Wandering Jew I found a suitable motif. It seemed to me that the interpretation I gave him contained the truth, and yet it was all quite different from the way in which many other poets have treated the same theme. The German poet Mosen, the Dutchman Ten Kate, the Frenchman Eugène Sue, and in Denmark Ingemann have all treated the legend, and in a smaller way we have examples from Schubart, Lenau, Karl Witte, Paludan-Müller etc. This material had been in my mind for a couple of years, but I was never really able to shape it into a work of literature. I experienced what we are told often happens to treasure-seekers: just as they think they have raised the treasure, it suddenly sinks deeper. I doubted whether I should ever be able to bring the gold up into the light. I felt what a great deal of knowledge of various kinds I would have to acquire, and so I read diligently, carefully choosing the works to which I turned.

At a time when most of the critics were complaining of a lack of knowledge on my part I was studying diligently. However, one person wrote and said the same as the next, and everyone had their own idea of study, as I had learnt at the home of a rather didactic old lady who once told me that people were right in saying that I did not study sufficiently. "You don't know anything about mythology," she said. "In all your poems there is not a single god or goddess. You must read some mythology, Corneille and Racine for instance."

I had read and made notes for the first part of my *Ahasuerus*, but it only came together when I began writing it here in Athens. I soon put it aside again, but the desire to tackle it kept returning, and when it had lain untouched for some time I comforted myself by saying that it was the same with children of intellect as with ordinary children: that they grow while they sleep.

On the 21st of April I sailed again from Pyræus to Syra where I boarded the French steamship Rhamses en route from Marseilles to Constantinople. We ran into rough weather in the Archipelago. I thought of shipwreck and death, and once I came to the conclusion that all was over now I became remarkably calm, and lay down in my bunk while people all around me wailed and prayed. Everything was creaking and cracking, but I fell asleep, and when I awoke we were safe and sound in the bay off Smyrna. – Another part of the world lay before me. And in truth, on looking at it I felt the same sense of reverence as I had felt as a child on going into old St. Knud's Church in Odense. I thought of Jesus Christ who shed His blood in this part of the world. I thought of Homer, whose songs for all time rang out across the world from here. The coast of Asia preached its sermon to me, and it was perhaps more enthralling than any sermon I have ever heard in a church built by Man.

Smyrna looked magnificent, but it had pointed, red, Nordic roofs, and only a few minarets. The streets are narrow like those in Venice. An ostrich and a camel happened to pass by, and people were obliged to step out of the way into the open houses. The streets were swarming with crowds of people, Turkish women of whom one could see nothing but their eyes and the tips of their noses, Jews and Armenians with white and black hats, some of which were rather like inverted cauldrons. The flags of their respective countries were flying outside the houses of all the consuls. In the bay there lay a smoking Turkish steamship with the crescent moon on its green flag.

We left Smyrna towards evening. The new moon was perched above the tomb of Achilles on the Trojan plains. At six o'clock in the morning we sailed into the Dardanelles. On the European side lay a red-roofed town with its windmills and a handsome fortress, on the Asiatic side a smaller fortress. The distance between the continents seemed to me to be about the same as between Elsinore and Hälsingborg; the captain said it was two and three quarter leagues. Gallipoli, near which town we entered the Sea of Marmora, has quite a gloomy, Nordic appearance. There were old houses there

222

with bay windows and wooden balconies. The town was surrounded by cliffs which were low but of a naked, wild appearance. The sea was rough, and it began to rain towards evening. The weather was cold and Nordic, and in this weather the next morning we saw the magnificent city of Constantinople, like a Venice rising out of the sea. Mosque after mosque appeared, each more wonderful than the last. The Seraglio lay before us, light and elegant. The sun came out and shone upon the shores of Asia, the black forests of cypress and the minarets of Scutari. It was an absolutely wonderful sight! The air was full of the shouts and cries of folk in the tiny bobbing boats swarming around. Honest Turks carried our luggage for us.

I spent eleven interesting days in Constantinople. The Danish minister, who was living at his country residence at Bujukdereh, a few miles from Constantinople, invited me out there, but I preferred to stay in the city, where the Danish consul, an Italian called Romani, took care of me. The good fortune which usually accompanied me on my travels did not desert me here either, and it just happened that the birthday of Mohammed (the fourth of May) occurred during my stay. I saw Abdul-Meschid drive to the mosque. The troops were on parade, and all the streets and squares were thronged with people in their many-coloured oriental costumes. That evening there were magnificent illuminations; all the minarets in Constantinople were lit up, and above them and the whole city there seemed to be a network of small lamps, sparkling in competition with the bright, twinkling stars. All the ships and boats were outlined in light. It was an Oriental, starlit evening. Mount Olympus in Asia Minor glowed in the sinking sun. It was the most fairy-like moment I have ever experienced.

I was given a warm reception by the Greek minister, Christides, to whom I had a letter of introduction from Athens, and also by the Austrian Internuntius, Baron Stürmer, and at the house of this delightful man I found a German home and German friends.

I had intended travelling home by way of the Black Sea and the Danube, but I was told that part of Roumelia and Bulgaria was in revolt, and that several thousand Christians had been murdered. All my fellow travellers at the hotel simply gave up their plans for sailing up the Danube, but I had a deep-seated desire to try it. Everyone advised me to do as they were going to do and to return through

Greece and Italy. I was in a dreadful dilemma. I am not one of the bravest, as I have often been told and as I believe, yet I will maintain that it is only small dangers that really scare me. On the other hand, when the dangers are big and there is really something to be gained, my will asserts itself, a will which has become stronger year by year. I tremble; I am fearful; but I still do what I consider to be right. And I should imagine that when a man is born a coward, and yet fights against it of his own accord, then he has done what he can, and he need not be ashamed of the weakness with which he has been born.

With all my heart I wanted to get to know something of the interior of the country and to see the whole length of the Danube and the banks which were then so little known to foreigners. I was really in a great moral conflict. In my imagination I fancied the most dreadful happenings. I spent a heavy, sleepless night, but in the morning I went to Baron Stürmer and asked his advice. And as he thought I could risk it, especially since two of his military officers were themselves to travel by that route to Vienna carrying dispatches and would if necessary be able to obtain help and escort on the way, I decided on the journey up the Danube. From the moment I had made up my mind, my fear was gone, and I was completely secure in my faith in God and my devotion to Him.

In the evening of the fourth of May I boarded the ship, which was lying off the gardens of the Seraglio. When we raised anchor early the following morning we heard the sad news that the large Austrian steamship that was to have met us had struck a rock in the Black Sea in the fog that very night and was a total loss. Now we sailed quickly through the wonderfully beautiful Bosphorus. We experienced both mist and heavy seas, and spent twenty-four hours off the town of Kostendsche close to the decaying ramparts built by Trajan, and there, in great basket-work carriages drawn by white oxen, we drove out across the desolate landscape where wild dogs roamed and where only the overturned gravestones of two cemeteries showed there had been large towns which the Russians had burned to the ground in the war of 1809. This was Dobrudscha. It took us a couple of days to pass over the scene of this remarkable war between the Russians and the Turks. In my mind I have a splendid map of the reaches of the Danube, and an extremely clear picture of the miserable villages and the decaying fortresses, or at least that is how they appeared then: I saw whole ruins or fortifications of earth and basket-work.

The first sign of the unrest in the country came when we were approaching Rustschuk with its many minarets. The shores were swarming with people, and two young men in Frankish dress were thrown into the Danube. They swam towards the bank, and one went ashore while the other, whom the crowd began to stone, swam out to us and shouted, "Help, they are murdering me." We stopped in the middle of the stream and took him aboard. Guns were fired from the ship as signals and answered from land. The local pasha came on board and took the poor Frank under his protection.

The next day we could see the snow-capped Balkan mountains from the ship. The revolt was raging between them and us. We heard of it the following night. An armed Tartar who was taking letters and dispatches from Widdin across the country to Constantinople had been ambushed and killed, and, I believe, another had not fared any better. A third had seen his escort killed, though he himself had escaped and reached the Danube. There he had hidden in the reeds and waited for our ship to arrive. Dressed in sheep-skins, coming up out of the mud and then armed to the teeth as they say, the man was a terrifying sight when we saw him in the light of the lamps on board. He went with us up the Danube for about a day. In Widdin, the powerful Turkish fortress, we went ashore after first being thoroughly fumigated so as not to spread the plague from Constantinople. Hussein Pasha, who resided there, sent us all the latest issues of the German newspaper *Allgemeine Zeitung*, so it was from the Germans we received the best information on the state of the country.

Serbia opened up before us like a primeval forest. We travelled in small boats through many miles of torrents and cascades in the stretch of the Danube known as the Iron Gates. This took a couple of days, and I have tried to paint a picture of it in *A Poet's Bazaar*. Quarantine awaited us at Old Orsova. The building was only intended to house Wallachian peasants and other travellers who were used to nothing better. Almost all the rooms had stone floors. The food was absolutely awful, and the wine, if possible, was worse. I shared a room with an Englishman by the name of Ainsworth (the brother of the author) who was just on his way home from a journey

225

to Kurdistan.

When *A Poet's Bazaar* subsequently appeared in London, Ainsworth was asked by the editor of *The Literary Gazette* to write an article for its issue of the tenth of October 1846 on the time we had spent together in quarantine. The view of my person contained in it reveals a kindly disposition that portrays me in too flattering a light. Ainsworth then goes on to tell readers that I was "very skilful in cutting out paper. The drawings of the Mewlewis, or Whirling Dervishes, in my Asiatic travels, are from cuttings of his".

When our quarantine was at an end, we passed the military border beneath magnificent chestnut trees and past relics from Roman times, ruined bridges, towers and the great Trajan's Tablet in the cliff face. Picturesque groups of Wallachian peasants alternated with large numbers of Austrian soldiers and gypsy bands encamped in caves. Picture after picture followed, but when we returned to the ship we found it so overcrowded that it was almost impossible to move. Everyone was going to the great fair to be held at Pesth. It was a difficult, sleepless and long journey, but it gave an impression of Hungarian peasant life. The countryside gradually became flatter and was no longer as varied as it had been and was again to be when we came nearer to Pressburg. The town of Theben was in flames as we sailed past. We had spent twenty-one days in all on the Danube when we went ashore at the Prater and drove into the imperial city. I visited old friends and soon, by way of Prague and Dresden I was travelling homewards. It seemed to me to be typical that while my trunk had only been examined twice – at the Austrian and German frontiers – during the whole of my journey from Italy through Greece and Turkey to Hamburg, it was inspected no fewer than five times before I was again in my sitting room in Copenhagen. First it was examined when I entered Holstein, then at Ærøsund, then again when I went ashore on Funen, again when I left the coach in Slagelse, and finally when I arrived by stagecoach in Copenhagen. That was customary in those days.

The great music festival was taking place in Hamburg when I arrived there. I met a number of my compatriots there at the table d'hôte. While I was talking to friends sitting beside me about the beauty of Greece and the riches of the East, an old lady from

Copenhagen turned to me with the words, "Well, Mr. Andersen, have you ever seen anything while you have been out travelling which is as beautiful as our little Denmark"

"Yes, indeed I have," I answered, "I have seen many things which are more beautiful."

"Shame on you," she exclaimed. "You are not a patriot."

I passed through Odense just at the time of St. Knud's Fair. "It was nice of you," said a respectable lady from Funen, "to have arranged your long journey so that you could visit the Fair. Yes, you are fond of Odense; I have always said so."

So there… I did look like a patriot!

It was a strangely moving experience when, just outside Slagelse, where I used to go to school, I chanced to meet some old acquaintances. While I was a pupil at the school I used to see that fine old man, Pastor Bastholm, take the same walk every evening with his wife: out of the back gate of their garden, along the path through the cornfields, and home along the main road. Now, several years later, driving down the Slagelse road on my way home from Greece and Turkey I saw the old couple taking their usual walk through the cornfields. It affected me in a strange way. There they were, still walking along that path, year in and year out, and I had been so far afield. The great contrast between us occupied my thoughts in a quite remarkable manner.

It was in the middle of August I arrived in Copenhagen, this time without anxiety and suffering, as was the case on my first return from Italy. I was glad to see all those I was fond of, and it was quite natural for me to exclaim, "The first moment at home is the crowning moment of the whole journey".

A Poet's Bazaar, which soon appeared, is divided into different individual parts, Germany, Italy, Greece and so on. In these different places as well as at home, there were certain persons to whom I felt bound in gratitude, and whose names I especially associated with these regions. A poet is like a bird, he gives what he has. A bird gives a song, and that is what I wanted to do to each of these people of whom I was so fond. That was an idea that had suddenly appeared and was born purely and simply of a grateful heart.

In the collected edition of my works I have omitted all former dedications, and this is also the case with the many in *A Poet's Bazaar*, although they had their significance, as will be understood.

To Rantzau-Breitenburg, who had lived in Italy, loved that country, and through my *Improvisatore* he had become my friend and patron, I dedicated the part of the book that dealt with Italy. I gave the section on Greece to Prokesch-Osten, our Minister in Greece, a learned man and a poet, and to the archeologist Professor Ross from Athens. The dedication in the part I wrote on the East ran: "To the Austrian Internuntius, Baron von Stürmer of Constantinople, through whose hospitality I found my beloved Scandinavia in the Orient, and Scandinavia's great poet Adam Oehlenschläger through whose *Aladdin* and *Aly and Gulhyndy* I early found the Orient in the North, I dedicate these pictures with a grateful heart". Before *The Journey on the Danube* I wrote: "To the princes of the piano, my friends, the Austrian Thalberg and the Hungarian Liszt I dedicate and perform this *Danube Theme with Coastal Variations*. *The Journey Home* was dedicated to "the charming author of *Sketches from Everyday Life*, Fredrika Bremer of Stockholm, and my benefactor, Jonas Collin's gifted daughter, Mrs. Ingeborg Drewsen of Copenhagen, whose true, sisterly help and understanding for me often caused me to think of home."

My intention with these dedications will probably be understood now, but it was not in those days. People dwelt on them and considered them to be fresh evidence of vanity, saying I wanted to boast of names and connections and refer to important persons as my friends. But there was no real review of it. Only a couple of the daily papers commented on it. The main object of criticism was that there was too much in the book: "This book ought to have been published in smaller sections, so that it could be digested more slowly," said one clever, calculating author to me. "And then it would have had a better reception."

Newspaper reviews of *A Poet's Bazaar* in Copenhagen were infinitely stupid. People thought it terribly exaggerated that I could write that when I saw the new moon in Smyrna I could see the entire round, blue outline of the moon. Our Danish critics have not usually a keen eye for natural phenomena; even the very distinguished *Maanedsskrift for Litteratur* once criticised me for talking of a lunar rainbow in one of my poems. That, too, was supposed to be my imagination driving me too far. I complained of this to Ørsted. A man who is now a country dean, and who I suspect had written the criticism, overheard me and exclaimed, "But it is daring of you to create a lunar rainbow like that."

"Yes, but I have seen it myself."

"Where?" he asked.

"One evening on Vesterbro," I answered.

"Vesterbro!" he laughed aloud. "Oh, of course, in that theatre with all the pantomime and magic." The man thought I meant Casorti's Theatre.

"No, up in the sky, in God's own sky; that is where I saw it." And now Ørsted came to my aid.

What a lot of idiotic sagacity I had to put up with, both spoken and written. I was simply the scapegoat whom people neither would nor could understand. When, in *A Poet's Bazaar*, I tried to vary my style in describing Nuremberg and said "if I were a painter I would paint this bridge and this tower", and then used the opportunity to describe the scene, and then again, in order to have so to speak a new link, I continued: "but I am not a painter, I am a poet", and sought to vary the style in a more lyrical manner, they said, "He is so vain that he himself tells us he is a poet."

There is something so wretched and pitiable in such criticism that one is not hurt by it. But even the most peaceable of human beings feels a desire to thrash such wet dogs that come into our sitting rooms and lie down in the best places. A complete *Narrenbuch* could be written about all the ridiculous and shameless things I have been forced to hear from the first time I appeared and until then.

Meanwhile, people read *A Poet's Bazaar*, and it was what is called a success. Only once in my life have I spoken to the brilliant historian, Professor Finn Magnussen, though we did not know each other personally at all. One day he stopped me in the street, and this man, who was normally so serious, was friendliness and cordiality personified. He thanked me with all his heart for my book, which he ranked highly, and which, he said, it annoyed him that the public did not value sufficiently. And he was not the only one. Several of the most capable men in the country, H. C. Ørsted and Oehlenschläger among them, commented warmly and appreciatively on this work, and thanked me for it and encouraged me.

Several editions of the book have subsequently been published in German, and it has also been translated into Swedish. An extremely beautiful edition has appeared in England where the critics have reviewed it in very warm terms. The English edition in three volumes and including a portrait was published by Richard Bentley in London, and was highly praised in English newspapers and periodicals. The English publishers sent a beautifully bound edition of this book along with my earlier works to King Christian the Eighth. The same thing had happened in Germany, and the King was pleased at the recognition I enjoyed abroad. I know he told H. C. Ørsted and several others, at the same time expressing his surprise at the opposition I was encountering here at home, the constant efforts to point out my weaknesses and erase the true impression of my work, the desire to mock and belittle my activities. It did me good to hear it, coming, as it did, from H. C. Ørsted, the only man among all the closer, understanding friends around me who clearly and firmly expressed his recognition of my poetical gifts, and with great conviction gave me courage by prophesying a better time for me at home. It would and must come, a time when I would be recognised and satisfied with the judgement I received at home, just as now I could be satisfied with what I received abroad. We often discussed what the true cause of my having to struggle so much and so long really was, and we agreed on several likely reasons. Some of the problem was surely my original poverty and my dependence on other people. As has also been remarked abroad, people could not forget that they had seen me running about as a poor lad. And as my biographer in the *Danish Pantheon* has also remarked, it was probably also partly due to my not knowing how to make my way by getting on with others. In addition, as H. C. Ørsted was sorry to admit, there was the severity and lack of good will towards me in the highly respected *Maanedsskriftet for Litteratur*. Finally, there was the derision in the *Letters from the Dead* and the criticism in the papers that went along with the mood of the moment, in short, public opinion in print, which still exercised its power over those of us who bowed to authority. To all this could be added the fact that

230

we are all very receptive to anything amusing and laughable, and I had suffered the fate of being presented in this way in several clumsy though extremely well-meaning articles. There was a time when the Odense newspaper always called me "the child of our town" and provided a good deal of information on me that could have been of no interest whatever to the general public. Of my private letters from abroad, passages were extracted that were ridiculous when put in a newspaper. For instance, once when I had written home from Rome that I had seen Queen Christina in the Sistine Chapel, adding that she reminded me of Hartmann's wife in appearance, this was reported in the Funen newspaper, in order to avoid naming Mrs Hartmann, as: "Queen Christina resembles a certain lady in Copenhagen". People had to laugh at this.

From that time to the present day, I have been afraid of talking about anything at all to a thoughtless newspaper editor, and yet I have not been able to avoid it. Here I was once more made a laughing-stock through no fault of my own.

Once when I was away travelling and the coach stopped for half an hour at Odense Post Office, an editor came and asked me, "Are you going abroad now?"

"No," I replied.

"Are you not thinking of doing so?"

"That depends on whether I can find the money. At the moment I am writing a play, and I can only think of travelling abroad if that is a success."

"Where will you go to then?"

"I don't know yet. I shall go either to Spain or Greece."

And the same evening it was stated in the paper that Hans Christian Andersen was working on a new play, and that if it was a success he would be going abroad, either to Spain or Greece.

Of course people laughed at this, and a Copenhagen newspaper wrote rightly enough that there were no immediate prospects of that journey. The play, they said, had yet to be written, to be accepted and to be a success, and then it was not even certain yet whether I would be going to Spain or Greece. People laughed; and if you are laughed at, you have already lost your cause. I had become mentally thin-skinned, and I was not cautious enough to hide it.

When boys throw stones at a dog swimming against the current, it is not sheer cruelty but because it amuses them; and people derived the same sort of amusement from me. No one came to defend me; I belonged to no clique; I had no friends on the newspapers, and so I had to suffer as I suffered. And yet it was said and repeated later that I was living in a couple of circles of people who did nothing but admire me. How little people know! What I recount here is not a complaint. I do not want the faintest trace of a shadow to be cast over the many people I am fond of, for I am convinced that had some great need or misfortune befallen me they would have spared no effort to prevent my being overwhelmed. But there is another kind of sympathy which is necessary for a poet's character, and that is what I missed. The circle of my closest friends expressed amazement at the recognition my works received abroad just as much as did any severe critic. Fredrika Bremer received an insight into this, which came as a curious surprise to her. We were together in Copenhagen in one of the places where people said I was merely spoiled. She thought she was saying something nice when she told them, "It is quite amazing how popular Andersen is in Sweden. All the way from Scania up to the north. There are some of his books in almost every home."

"Don't give him ideas," was the reply she received, and in all seriousness at that.

Much is said about the fact that being of noble birth is no longer of any importance. Such talk is nonsense. A clever but poor student does not normally encounter the same politeness and kind welcome in good homes, as they are called, as is given to the elegantly dressed son of a nobleman or high-ranking official. I could quote many examples to illustrate this, but I will only give one, which must suffice for them all; it is one from my own life. The guilty person shall not be named. He is, or, to put it further into the past, he was a highly esteemed person.

When Christian the Eighth went to the theatre for the first time as king, it was to a performance of *The Mulatto*. I was sitting in the stalls beside Thorvaldsen, and as the curtain fell he whispered to me, "The King is bowing to you."

"No, it must be to you," I answered. "He can't mean me." I looked up at the royal box, and the King bowed again, and it was to me. But I felt that a possible mistake on my part would give people the opportunity of criticising me mercilessly; so I remained quietly seated. The following day I went to visit the King to thank him for the unusual honour, and he joked with me for not having accepted it in the theatre.

A few days later there was to be a great ball in Christiansborg Palace for all classes of society. I had received an invitation.

"What are you going for?" asked one of our older professors when I mentioned the ball in his drawing room. "What do you want in such places?" he repeated.

I answered in fun, "It is in those circles I am best received."

"But that is not where you belong," he replied angrily.

The only thing left for me was to answer lightly and with a smile, as though I did not feel any resentment:

"The King himself has bowed to me from his box in the theatre, so I imagine I am entitled to go to a *bal paré*."

"Bowed from his box indeed," he exclaimed. "But that does not entitle you to push yourself into the foreground."

"But there are people of the class to which I belong coming to this ball," I added in a more serious tone. "There are some holders of the students' examination coming."

"Oh, who," he asked.

I named a young member of the man's own family.

"Well, of course," he answered, "but he is the son of a Councillor of State. What was your father?"

My blood boiled. "My father was a craftsman," I said, "and it is through my own efforts and with the help of God that I have won my position, and I thought you would respect that."

I never received an apology for what had been said.

When we do not wish to do someone else an injustice or to hurt someone who might unintentionally have hurt us, it is very difficult to avoid or to renounce telling what it is that has wounded us to the bottom of our hearts. Throughout all this book I have felt how difficult this is, and therefore I have discarded many a bitter cup and have only retained a few single drops. My dwelling on the subject in these pages will perhaps serve as an illustration of some things in my writings which ought to be given space here because just after my arrival home from my long journey and after the publication of the

Bazaar there was, if not a halt to the arrogance of the critics, at least a change in the judgements expressed about me. There were still rough seas ahead, but from that time I progressed steadily towards calmer waters, towards the recognition I could desire and expect at home in Denmark, and which Ørsted had comforted me with by prophesying for me.

IX

Political life in Denmark at that time was developing rapidly, and had both its good and bad sides. Eloquence, which had previously half unconsciously been practised in the manner of the philosopher, by putting pebbles, the pebbles of everyday life, into one's mouth, now began to deal more freely with subjects of greater interest. However, I felt neither the ability nor the need to take part in such things, and likewise I believe that politics are a great misfortune for many a poet in our time. Madame Politics is the Venus who entices them into her castle, where they are destroyed. The same thing happens to their songs as to the daily papers; they are grabbed, read, praised and forgotten. Everyone would like to rule these days. Subjectivity asserts its power; but most people do not remember that in practice it is impossible to carry out much that is possible in theory. People forget that things look different when viewed from the top of the tree and not from the bottom. Anyone who is moved by some noble conviction, be he a prince or a man of the people, anyone who only desires what is best and has the ability to achieve it, to him will I bow down. Politics are not my business, and I can achieve nothing in that area. God has given me another task; I felt it then and I feel it now.

At the homes of what are called the leading families in the country I met a number of cordial, friendly people who valued the good qualities they found in me and accepted me in their circles, allowing me during the summer to share in their good fortune. There, I was quite independent and could devote myself entirely to the beauties of nature, to the silence of the woods, and to life in the great mansions. It was there I really got to know the Danish countryside. It was there I wrote most of my fairy tales and later the novel, *The Two Baronesses*. By the side of the silent lakes in the woods, in the green meadows where the game sprang past me and the stork strutted about on its red legs I heard neither politics nor polemics, and I heard no one talk about Hegel. Nature, both around me and within me, preached to me and showed me my calling. Through Baroness Stampe from

Nysøe I was introduced to the Danneskjold family from Gisselfeld.

The Christmas celebrations in this ancient mansion, once a monastery, were so fine and so Nordic, and the old Duchess Danneskjold was a splendid, affectionate woman. Here, I was not a poor child of the people; no, I was a guest who received a kindly welcome.

The beech trees cast their shadows now over her grave out in the generous woods to which her heart was related. From Gisselfeld I went to the splendid, charming manor of Bregentved, where I was invited by Count Wilhelm Moltke, then Minister of Finance, of beloved and blessed memory. The hospitality I met there, the happy domestic life in which I shared, brought sunshine into my life. During several fairly prolonged visits to Nysøe I lived happily in the company of Thorvaldsen, for whom a studio had been built in the garden there. I came to know him properly as an artist and as a human being. This was an extremely interesting time for me, and I shall have more to say about it.

My becoming accustomed to life in these various circles had a great influence on me. I have found the same noble qualities of human nature in princes, nobility and the poorest members of society. We all resemble each other in the good things, the best things.

However, most of my time was spent in Copenhagen, at the home of His Excellency, Jonas Collin. I was also a regular figure in the homes of his married sons and daughters, where a number of children were growing up. My friendship with the gifted composer Hartmann became firmer and firmer, and his lively, intelligent wife enchanted their home, filling it with blessings and sunshine. She herself was an ardent, gifted, and at the same time curiously innocent and charming person. Collin was my adviser in practical matters, while Ørsted advised me on each new work I produced, and we came ever closer to each other and understood each other better and better. I shall later have the occasion to say more about his influence on my character and his importance to me. Meanwhile, if I may put it this way, the theatre was my clubroom each evening. I went there regularly. I had that very year been given a seat in what was known as the "Court Stalls", which were only separated from the rest of the stalls by an iron bar. It was the custom at that time that every author who produced one play for the theatre should be given a free seat in the pit; two plays gave him a seat in the stalls, and three gave him admittance to the "Court Stalls". Of course, they had to be three plays each lasting a whole evening, or as many shorter plays as would take three whole evenings when put together. And then we were given admittance to the part of the stalls where the King gave seats to his courtiers, diplomats and leading officials. It is said that when a certain poet, who at the same time was an actor, was given a seat here on account of his dramatic works, someone said to him, "Yes, you may have that seat, but please be modest, because there are always so many fine folk there."

I, too, was given this honour. Thorvaldsen, Oehlenschläger, Weyse and several others were there as well at that time. Thorvaldsen wanted me to sit by him, talk to him and explain various things to him, and as long as he lived that is where I usually sat. Oehlenschläger, too, often sat beside me and, although probably no one had the slightest idea of it, a reverent sense of humility filled my soul on many an evening as I sat in the company of these great men. The different periods of my life passed through my thoughts, from the days when I used to sit up in the upper circle box reserved for the ladies of the *corps de ballet* and from the time when in childish superstition I had knelt up there on the stage and recited my "Our Father" just opposite the seat where I was now seated among leading figures. If any of my fellow countrymen at that time sat in his seat thinking, "There he is, among the great, filled with pride and arrogance," then he will be able to see from this how wrongly he judged me. I was filled with humility, and from my heart a prayer went up to God for strength to deserve my good fortune. May God let me always preserve these feelings. I saw Thorvaldsen and Oehlenschläger there every evening. Both showed friendship towards me, and both belong to the brightest stars on the Nordic horizon. I must emphasise here how they were reflected both in and around me.

When he was not together with a large number of people, when he was quiet and reserved, there was something so frank and child-like about Oehlenschläger's character that it was impossible not to become attached to him. His significance for this country and for the whole of Scandinavia is well known; he was one of those who

237

are born true poets. He seemed to be ever young, and even as an old man he produced more than that of any of the younger authors. He listened kindly to my first lyrical outbursts, and he followed my career with great interest. And although for a long time he never expressed any great enthusiasm, when critics and the public judged me harshly and mercilessly it was he who registered a vehement and heartfelt protest. One day he found me downcast after far too harsh and bitter a treatment and he pressed me to his heart.

"Take no notice of those vociferous critics," he said, "I tell you, you are a true poet." Then warmly and passionately, he voiced his opinion of poetry and poets, and of the judgements one received here in Denmark while at the same time according me his full recognition as a poet. He spoke out seriously and whole-heartedly on behalf of the poet who told fairy tales, and I know that one day when someone sought to belittle me by talking of what he considered the orthographical sins he had found in one of my books, Oehlenschläger eagerly exclaimed, "But they *must* be there. They are tiny idiosyncrasies that are part of him; that is not the main point. 'Let that little beast stay there,' said the great poet Goethe of such a little mistake, and he would not even correct it." Later I shall once more describe a few of his characteristics and tell something more of our friendship during the last years of his life, when we became even more attached to each other. My biographer in *Dansk Pantheon* has referred to one point of contact between me and Oehlenschläger, saying in his introduction:

Nowadays it is becoming increasingly rare for a man to become an artist or a poet purely because of some innate impulse that is soon revealed to be an irresistible urge. They are more often created by fate or circumstances than destined to this calling by nature. In most of the poets of our time an early acquaintance with passion, early experiences or outward circumstances are to be thanked, and not the primitive voice of Nature, and such can scarcely be shown with the same certainty in our literature in any other writer than Oehlenschläger and Andersen. This explains why the first of these two has so often been the object of criticism and attacks here in Denmark, while the latter has really only gained full recognition abroad, where an older civilisation has already learned to nourish a dislike of the compulsion to conform to what is taught in school, while we Danes still retain a pious respect for the yoke imposed by schools and the out-lived wisdom of reflection.

Thorvaldsen, whom, as I have already explained, I met for the first time in Rome in 1833 and 1834, was expected in Denmark during the autumn of 1838, and great preparations were made to welcome him. A flag was to fly from St. Nicholas' Church Tower at the approach of the ship carrying him. It was a national festival. Boats decked with flowers and pennants were bobbing on the water between Langelinie and Trekroner. Painters and sculptors each had their emblems in their flags; the students carried one with Minerva on it and the poets one with a golden figure of Pegasus. A hint of it all is still to be seen in the painted frieze on Thorvaldsen's Museum. In the boat full of poets that is painted there it is possible to recognise Oehlenschläger, Heiberg, Hertz and Grundtvig; I am standing on the thwart, holding on to the mast and swinging my hat.

On the day of his arrival the weather was misty, and the ship could not be seen until it was quite near the city. The signals were fired and people poured out to the Customs House to meet him; and the poets who had been invited there by Heiberg, who was then the leading figure and decided who should come, stood by their boat which was moored by Larsens Plads, but Oehlenschläger and Heiberg himself had not yet arrived. The poets waited, and cannon shots were heard from the vessel which had already dropped anchor. I realised that Thorvaldsen would already have gone ashore before we got out there. The sound of singing was born in on our ears on the breeze; the festive reception had begun; I wanted to take part in it, and so I said to the others, "Let us row out there."

"What, without Oehlenschläger and Heiberg?" said the others.

"But they are not coming, and it will soon all be over."

One of the poets said that surely I would not sail out under that flag if they were not with us? And he pointed at Pegasus.

"Then we can throw that down into the boat," I said and took the flag down. Now the others went along with me, and we arrived

239

on the spot just as Thorvaldsen was sailing ashore. Heiberg and Oehlenschläger met us out there in a boat they had borrowed for themselves, and now they came on board to us. The sun came out and a lovely rainbow spanned the Sound:

A triumphal arch for Alexander

And it was in truth a procession fit for an Alexander, far finer than it is described in the periodical *Dansk Folkeblad*. Sounds of jubilation could be heard from the shore where the people themselves drew Thorvaldsen's coach to his residence in Amalienborg. Everyone poured over there; and everyone and anyone who had the slightest acquaintance with him pushed their way forward. All that day and evening groups of sightseers stood on the square just to look at the familiar red brick walls of Charlottenborg, for *Thorvaldsen* was in there. In the evening the artists came to serenade him, and the light from their torches burned beneath the trees in the Botanical Gardens. Young and old alike streamed in through the open doors, and the kindly old man to whom everyone was paying homage, pressed those he knew to his breast and kissed them and shook their hands. There was in everyone's eyes a halo around Thorvaldsen, and this made me shyly hold back. My heart was beating with joy at seeing the man who had met me abroad with comforting and gentle words and who then had pressed me to his heart and said, "We two should always remain friends." But here, amidst all this homage and jubilation, where thousands were watching every movement he made, and where I would be noticed and condemned by all of them, yes, condemned as a vain person who wanted to show that I, too, knew Thorvaldsen and that he was kind and friendly towards me.

I stepped wisely and quietly aside, remained hidden in the dense crowd and avoided being seen by him.

Not until several days later, when no one saw me and he had no visitors, did I go to visit him, and I found in him the unchanged simple, affectionate and frank nature, the friend who embraced me with delight and said how surprised he was he had not seen me before.

In Thorvaldsen's honour a sort of festival of poetry and music had been arranged in which each of the poets had written a poem, which he now read out in praise of the returning artist. Every author, except Heiberg, read his own poem. I had written about Jason going to fetch the Golden Fleece, Jason-Thorvaldsen going to capture Golden Art. A festive dinner and a little dancing ended this charming and lively event, which was attended by people of all classes. A beaming Thorvaldsen personally danced a polonaise with the young Miss Puggaard who later married Orla Lehmann and is now dead. That evening was a festive occasion on which, for the first time in Denmark, I saw reflected a kind of popular life and a great interest in the realm of art.

Thorvaldsen was made an honorary member of the Students' Union. On this occasion I, too, wrote a song which was highly acclaimed and seems to be one of my poems that people remember:

> There you stood, a student bold,
> It must have been in October's cold
> You made your way, as people say,
> All Homer's works you've put in clay.

From this time I saw Thorvaldsen every day, either in society or in his studio. For several weeks on end I shared his life at the home of Baroness Stampe at Nysø where he seemed to take root like a welcome guest and indeed like a close relative to be looked after, amused and inspired to activity. Most of the works he made in Denmark were created there. He had a robust character and was not without humour, and so Holberg was the author he loved best. He did not bother himself with the troubles and disturbances in the world, and so he did not really like the character of Byron. One morning at Nysø when he was at work on the statue of himself I went in to him in the little studio which Baroness Stampe had had built for him down in the garden, close to the old moat. I wished him good morning, but he seemed not to notice me, so intent was he on what he was doing. Now and then he stepped back and bit his bright, strong teeth together, as he always did when he was looking closely at his work. I tiptoed silently away. At lunch he was even more silent than usual, and when we asked him at least to say something, he replied dryly, "I talked a lot early this morning, more than I have talked for

241

several days, but there was no one to listen to me. Then I noticed Andersen standing behind me, for he said good morning, and so I went on to tell him about a lengthy business I once had with Byron; I thought it merited a comment in return, so I turned round, and then I discovered I had been talking aloud for more than an hour to the bare walls." We all asked Thorvaldsen to tell the story again, and we were given a very brief version.

"Oh, it was in Rome," he said, "when I was to do Byron's statue. He sat down in front of me, but immediately started to pull a different face from how he usually looked. 'No, will you please sit still,' I asked him. 'You mustn't pull faces.' 'That's my expression,' said Byron. 'Very well, then,' I said, and I sculpted him as I wished. When I had finished, everyone said it was an extremely good likeness, but when Byron saw it he said, 'It is not at all like me; I look unhappier than that.' You see, he simply had to look unhappy," added Thorvaldsen with a humorous expression on his face.

After a meal the great artist delighted in listening to music with his eyes half closed, and his greatest joy was when the Baroness took out the bag filled with counters and began a game of lotto. Everyone living near Nysø learned to play lotto; they only played for glass beads, and so I can tell you that he just *had* to win, and everyone let him win. And this could totally preoccupy the great man. Playing lotto bored me in the long run, and many a moonlit evening I made for the woods, although I could hear them calling for me to come and play lotto.

Thorvaldsen could take the side of those he believed were suffering injustice with great warmth and intensity. Irrespective of who he was upsetting, he always opposed unfairness and mockery when it began to verge on the malicious. It was Baroness Stampe, née Dalgas, who with daughterly devotion to the great artist ensured that everything was good and cosy for him there. All her thoughts and efforts were directed at this.

I wrote a couple of my fairy tales, for instance *The Sandman*, while in his company at Nysø and he listened to them with delight and interest. At that time my fairy tales were not yet of any particular interest in Denmark. In the twilight as the family sat in the open room overlooking the garden, Thorvaldsen would often come across to me and quietly pat me on the shoulder, saying, "Won't you read a fairy tale for us children?"

In his own natural manner he always praised me for the truth my works contained. He loved to listen to the same fairy tales time and time again, and often, while he was in the midst of one of his own most poetical works, he would stand with a smile on his lips and listen to the story of *The Top and the Ball*, *The Ugly Duckling* and so on.

I have some sort of talent for improvising small poems and songs, and this talent provided Thorvaldsen with much amusement. When he had modelled the bust of Holberg in clay at Nysø and everyone was lost in admiration of it, I was given the task of saying some words in verse on his work, and I recited the following impromptu:

> No more shall Holberg see the day;
> I'll break the clay his soul contains
> 'Twas thus Death spoke; but from cold clay
> Thorvaldsen said, 'He shall be born again.'

One morning when he was making his great clay bas-relief, *The Road to Golgatha*, which now adorns Copenhagen Cathedral, I went into his studio. "Tell me," he said, "Do you think I have dressed Pilate correctly?"

"You mustn't say anything," shouted Baroness Stampe, who was still by his side. "It is quite right; it is excellent. Be off with you." Thorvaldsen repeated his question.

"Well," I answered, "since you ask me I must say that I do think that your Pilate is dressed more like an Egyptian than a Roman."

"That's just what I think," said Thorvaldsen, and he plunged his hand into the clay and pulled the figure to pieces.

"Now you are to blame for his ruining an immortal work," exclaimed the Baroness.

"Then we can make another immortal work," he said merrily, and went on to model Pilate as he is now to be seen in the bas-relief in the Cathedral.

In the summer months he went every day to a bathing-hut some distance from the mansion, far out on the beach.

"I could quite easily have been drowned today," he said merrily one day when I met him on his way home, and he went on to tell me that he had dived under the water and then come up again, but right underneath the bathing-hut so that he had nearly lifted it from its hinges with his head. "It turned a little black in front of my eyes," he said, "but it soon went off again. Had I fainted you would perhaps have found me floating out there on the water."

His last birthday was celebrated at Nysø. Heiberg's vaudeville *The April Fools* and Holberg's *The Christmas Party* were performed for him. I had written a song to be sung at table, but in addition to this I had also improvised another one. Early in the morning the Baroness sent for me and told me that Thorvaldsen was still not up, and that it might be amusing to awaken him to the sound of music played on the gong, the fire-tongs, bottles, knives and forks. But, she said, we also needed a song. It didn't matter what it was like, provided it was amusing, and as I say, I was literally forced to improvise it on the paper from which I sang the solo whilst the ink was still wet, and the others joined in the chorus to the noisy accompaniment and to the tune of "What says the noble baron?"

> A little song, oh listen then,
> For one we deem immaculate;
> And that, dear friend, is Thorvaldsen,
> As well as a piece of chocolate.
> Sing now aloud
> That we may be proud,
> And let it sound
> Out all around.
> To sing his praise the whole world throngs;
> He's heard all that so often.
> So we will sing some clownish songs,
> Yet ne'er our praises soften.
> Chink with your cup,
> Raise your head up;
> That's if it'll be fun
> For the great one.
> Before our singing falls far too far

244

> We'll stop our playing clever,
> And may his ever lucky star
> Shine on our friend for ever.
> Dance now and jump,
> Bumpety bump.
> Thorvaldsen live for ever,
> Hurrah.

And we danced and beat on the tongs and rubbed the cork up and down the bottle. Thorvaldsen emerged in a dressing-gown, slippers and drawers, swinging his Raphaelian night-cap in the air, dancing round the room with us and singing the chorus:

Dance now and jump, Bumpety bump.

There was plenty of life and humour in the powerful old man. I sat by his side at dinner on the last day of his life. The Stampe family had their winter residence in Kronprinsessegade in Copenhagen. In addition to Thorvaldsen, the guests included Oehlenschläger, Sonne and Constantin Hansen. Thorvaldsen was unusually lively and told us some of the jokes from *Corsaren* that had amused him; he talked of the journey he intended making to Italy the following summer. It was a Sunday, and that evening Halm's tragedy *Griseldis* was to receive its first performance in the Royal Theatre. Oehlenschläger was going to stay with the Stampe family and read something for them, but Thorvaldsen preferred to go to the theatre and asked me if we could go together. However, as I had no free seat that evening and the play was, I think, already advertised to be performed again the following evening, I said I would wait until then. I shook hands as I said good-bye. When I went out of the door he was sitting in an armchair close by the sofa and had shut his eyes to doze a little. I went out quietly but when I turned round he opened his eyes, smiled and nodded to me. That was his last farewell.

I stayed at home all evening. The following morning the waiter in the Hôtel du Nord, where I was living, said to me, "It was a curious thing, Thorvaldsen dying all of a sudden yesterday."

"Thorvaldsen!" I shouted in amazement; "He's not dead; I had dinner with him yesterday."

"They say he died in the theatre yesterday evening," said the waiter.

"He must just be ill," I said, and I really believed that this must be the case, but yet I felt strangely anxious. I immediately took my hat and hurried off to his home. There lay his body, stretched out on the bed. The room was filled with strangers who had forced their way in. The floor was wet from the snow on their boots; the air was stuffy. No one said a word. Baroness Stampe was sitting on the edge of the bed weeping. I stood there, shocked and deeply moved.

Thorvaldsen's funeral was a day of national mourning. Men and women dressed in black stood at the window in all the streets, and all involuntarily bared their heads as the coffin was carried past them. There was perfect silence; even the wildest lads, the poorest children, stood holding each other by the hand and forming rows as the great procession went past from Charlottenborg to the Cathedral where King Christian the Eighth came to receive the procession. From the organ there thundered a funeral march by Hartmann; it was so mighty that it was as though one could feel the great, unseen spirits joining the procession. I had written a song wishing him a calm repose. Hartmann had written a melody to this, too, and it was sung by the students beside Thorvaldsen's coffin.

> Approach this mournful coffin, oh mankind,
> Of you this man was born, yet you may say,
> That for our land he was an honour unconfined
> And gave to us art in fine array.
> Oh sorrow, change to song, a last farewell,
> And now in Jesu's Name, sleep well.

X

In the summer of 1842 I wrote a little play called *The Bird in the Pear Tree* for performance during the summer. It was received with so much applause that the management included it in the Royal Theatre repertoire, and indeed Mrs. Heiberg showed so much interest in it that she decided to play the leading lady. People had enjoyed it and found the choice of melodies excellent. I knew that it had stood the test when suddenly one of the winter performances was hissed. It was some young men who took the lead and started it. To people who asked why they were doing it, they are supposed to have said, "that bagatelle was too big a success and Andersen was becoming too self-confident".

I myself was not in the theatre on the evening when they hissed it and had no idea they had done so. The following day I visited some friends. I had a headache and looked rather serious, and as the lady of the house was quite certain that the expression on my face was the result of the evening's occurrences she came over to me, took my hand in sympathy and said, "Is it worth taking it so much to heart? There were only two who hissed, and all the rest of the audience took your side."

"Hissed? My side?" I exclaimed. "Has someone hissed me?" And now she became quite afraid because she was the first person to tell me.

I stayed at home for the next performance, and when the play was over I had quite an amusing scene in my sitting room with some sympathetic friends. The first to arrive assured me that the hissing the previous evening had, to use his words, been a sheer triumph for me. Everyone had applauded heartily, and only a single person had hissed. Now another man arrived, and when I asked how many had hissed he said, "Two." The next said, "Three, definitely not more." Then came one of my most honest friends, the gifted, naive and magnificent Hartmann. He had no idea of what the others had said, and when I now asked him to tell me on his honour how many people had hissed, he laid his hand on his breast and said, "Five at the very most."

"Oh, no," I burst out. "I won't ask any more now; the number increases every time I ask, just as in the case of Falstaff. There is someone here who even maintains there was only a single person who hissed."

To make up for what he had said before, Hartmann said rather amusingly and in all honesty, "Well, there might only have been one, but he made a confounded noise with it."

The following day Bournonville, the ballet master, sent me a lovely poem which he had written, called *The Poet's Tree*. It is printed in the appendix to his memoirs. This is how the poem finished, talking about my poet's tree:

> Your pears refreshed us in the summerscape.
> They say they now have lost their taste.
> Perhaps in years the fruit will turn to grape
> To bring refreshment with a juice so chaste.

> So let not sadness ever gnaw your heart;
> Nor sorrow force a sigh from you.
> How many men whom God gives gifts of art
> Remember to give God the praise He's due?

> Be not ungrateful to your God;
> You have many blessings from His hand.
> No poem can e'er to naught be trod,
> All evil will it evermore withstand.

A rhymed epistle to my friend Hans Christian Andersen from his sincere and faithful August Bournonville
Copenhagen, 13th Nov 1842

The Pear Tree was lampooned in several newspapers, and they began to make fun of *A Poet's Bazaar* again. On this occasion I remember that Oehlenschläger expressed his heartfelt praise and admiration for both. On the other hand, Heiberg wrote the following on my dramatic bagatelle in his *Intelligensblade*:

> It is one of those small creatures, the inclusion of which in our theatrical cage it would be pedantic to oppose, for it can be said of it that even if it does no good, neither does it do any harm. It is too small, too insignificant and too innocent for that. It is the fill-in often needed by the theatre, and as such it can perhaps amuse many and it can certainly not upset anyone at all. Indeed, it must be said that it is not entirely devoid of the odd trace of naive and lyrical beauty.

Although at that time Heiberg was a friend neither of me nor my work, there was, as in the case of every able antagonist, something to which he did justice, and that was the fact that I really suffered only from the attacks of certain coteries. In the above review he wrote:

> *The Bird in the Pear Tree*, to which it is only after the third or fourth performance that the public shown a harsh judgement which could have been more justly applied to the paths which are seen by the Lord, (but at which the Lord will scarcely condescend to look) and to the dowry that is given to the unfortunate Suzette, but which is so clumsy and poor that it cannot bring happiness to any girl. The bird in the pear tree is in fact such an innocent little bird that it cannot possibly provoke to fury anyone who is at all sober-minded and gentle, not even a person who does not savour its poetry. The violent hissing and whistling which to the thunderous accompaniment of the gong put an end to the life of this poor and weak bird, an opposition as violent as though it were a matter of principle, cannot therefore be regarded as anything but an outburst of tame Danish fanaticism.

Ten years later, when he was director of the Royal Theatre, to which the play still belonged even though it had been shelved, Heiberg gave permission to the Casino Theatre to perform it. By that time I was moving in a more benevolent generation than before. The little work was received with great and lively acclamation, and it has often been performed since then.

The eighth of October 1842 saw the death of Weyse, the first of my noble benefactors. We had certainly often met at Wulffs in the early days and had worked together on *Kenilworth*, but we did not really become intimate friends. His life was as solitary as mine, and yet people liked to see him, as, I believe, they like to see me. However, I am a bird of passage by nature and fly out all over Europe. His longest journey was to Roskilde where he felt at home with a certain group of friends, and where he could improvise on the organ in the Cathedral. He is buried near Roskilde. He just could not be persuaded to go farther afield; I can remember his humour when I visited him after returning from Greece and Constantinople. "You see, you have come no further than I have," he said. "You have come to Kronprinsessegade and can look out across Kongens Have; but so can I. And *you* have used all that money. If you *must* travel, then go to Roskilde; that's far enough. Just wait until people start travelling to moons and planets!"

I still have a letter he wrote at the time of the first performance of *Kenilworth* and which is typical of him. It begins:

> "*Carissime domine poeta!*"

> "O dearest Sir Poet"

> The dull people of Copenhagen cannot understand the meaning of the finale of the second act in our opera etc.

It was decided that *Kenilworth* should be performed in memory of him in the Theatre. It was Weyse's last work and so perhaps the one of which he was most fond; he had chosen the subject himself and had even written parts of the libretto. I am certain that if his immortal soul in another world had still retained the same feelings for his compositions as he had nourished on earth, its greatest delight would have been to see this composition, rather neglected during his lifetime, dedicated to him as a token of honour. However, the idea was abandoned, and it was decided to perform Shakespeare's tragedy *Macbeth*, to which Weyse had written incidental music which, at least in my opinion, is not the most characteristic of his compositions.

Strange to say, on the day of the funeral the corpse was still not quite cold in the pit of the stomach. When I arrived at the house of mourning together with the other mourners I asked the doctors for heaven's sake to examine him and do all they could to bring him back to life, but after giving him the minutest examination they assured me that he was dead and would remain dead. This sort of warmth was nothing unusual, they said. I asked them at least to sever his arteries before the coffin was closed, but this was not done. Oehlenschläger heard of this and came across to me: "What is this I hear? Do you want him dismembered?" he said with a vehemence that was characteristic of him in certain situations. "Yes, that is better than that he should wake up in his grave, and you would presumably prefer that, too, when you die."

"I!" exclaimed Oehlenschläger, and stepped back. Alas Weyse was dead. I wrote a song that was sung at his grave:

> To the silent grave his weary dust has come;
> His mighty spirit now is gone to higher things.
> In this world he was a silent, lonely man;
> Alone he was when death his eyelids closed.
> Alone he was; when suffering in his heart
> He softened pain with tender melodies;
> His youthful love in music is preserved;
> Resounding still in "sparkling waves on high".
>
> When seated at the organ, power he had
> To raise our thoughts aloft, high o'er the earth;
> He gave us all a treasury of song,
> His music spoke the spirit of the North.
> Bounteous was his speech, so firm and rich;
> His soul was young and now tastes Heaven's joys.
> Alas, our Weyse's dead! What elegy
> Has power like these sad words? We weep for him.

As a result of my last works and by means of prudent economy I had collected a small sum of money which I decided to use on a journey to Paris. So I left Copenhagen at the end of January 1843.

On account of the time of year I went by way of Funen, Schleswig and Holstein. I had more than my fill of winter travelling and the poetry of bad highways which people so seem to regret having lost through the blessings of the railways. It was a difficult, tiring journey until we reached Itzehoe and my beloved Breitenburg.

His Excellency Count Rantzau was delighted to see me and gave me a hearty welcome, and I spent several delightful days together with him in his old castle. Spring storms were raging, but the sun came out with its warm rays. The larks sang above the green fields, and I visited all the places I knew in the area. Our dinners and evenings were extremely festive.

Whereas I had always lived without thought of politics and matters political, I now noticed for the first time a sort of tension between the Duchies and the Kingdom reflected in a few people here. I had paid so little attention to the relationship between these countries that I had had no hesitation in dedicating *A Poet's Bazaar* to "my fellow-countryman, Professor Ross of Holstein". However, as to our being fellow-countrymen I soon realised that all was not as I had imagined. "*Unser Herzog*," I once heard a lady say, meaning the King. "Why do you not call him the King?" I asked in political ignorance. "He is not our King; he is our Duke," she replied. Small political differences occurred, but Count Rantzau, who loved the King, Denmark and the Danes, and at the same time was an extremely attentive host, smoothed over what had been said with a kind word and a joke.

"*Es sind närrische Leute*," he whispered to me, and I thought it must be a couple of eccentrics I had met, failing to appreciate that this was the increasingly popular opinion.

As we all know, Hamburg had been devastated by fire. All the area of the city near the Alster had been burned to the ground. A few new buildings were certainly beginning to make their appearance, but most of the district still lay in ruins with charred beams and crumbling towers. Rows of small brick-built shops had been erected on the Jungfernstieg and Esplanade, and there the many shop-keepers whose businesses had been burned down were now selling their wares.

It was difficult for travellers to find a place to stay. However, just because of this I found one of the best and most comfortable places: Count Holck, who was the Danish postmaster, welcomed me to his home as a revered guest.

I experienced many delightful hours together with that able man Speckter. He had just begun drawing illustrations for my fairy tales which were so enchanting, so brilliant and so full of humour. They can be seen in one of the English editions as well as in one of the less fortunate German editions in which "*grimme Ælling*" (ugly duckling) has been translated by "*grüne Ente*" (green duckling), and from that has found its way into French as "le petit canard vert".

There was still no railway across the Lüneburg Heath, and we travelled day and night in the slow mail coach along poor roads from Hamburg through Osnabrück to Düsseldorf, where I arrived on the very last day of the Carnival and so was able to see in German guise what I had already seen in Roman dress. Meanwhile, Cologne is said to be the German city in which the most magnificent processions wind through the streets. The merriment in Düsseldorf was, as it would be put in a newspaper report, "favoured by the most enchanting weather". I saw an amusing procession, a cavalry troop of boys who walked along on their own two feet, leading the horses on which it looked as though they were riding. There was a comical "Narhalle", the opposite of "Walhalla", which was open to visitors. I was told that the arrangements for the festival were by Achenbach, the painter, whom I also came to know and esteem. Among the masters of the Düsseldorf School I recognised several old acquaintances from my first visit to Rome.

I also met a fellow countryman of mine, a son of Odense; it was von Benzon. At home in Denmark, he had painted my portrait as soon as he started painting. It had never been done before and this first one was simply dreadful. It looked like the brightly illuminated shadow of a man or like someone who has been in a press between folios for years on end but has now been taken out and put on show even though he is as dry as a mummy. Reitzel, the bookseller, bought it off him. Here in Düsseldorf Benzon had risen to be a true artist and had just completed a beautiful picture of the murder of Saint Knud in St. Alban's Church in Odense. However I felt the absence in it of one figure who ought to have been there and who would surely have added a painterly shadow on the scene; I mean "false Blake". How strange that he did not know this figure who has become proverbial even in the Funen dialect; but now it was too late to include him.

Through Cologne and Liege, sometimes by coach and sometimes by the railway, which was only partly finished, I reached Brussels, where I heard Alizard in Donizetti's *La Favorita.* I was bored in the Art Gallery looking at Rubens' fat, blonde women with their plain faces and faded dresses. I felt uplifted by the magnificent churches, and, full of memories and visions, I lingered before the old City Hall, in the shadow of which Egmont was beheaded.

The tower rises aloft delicately ornamented and full of pointed decorations: a magnificent, fairy tale piece of Brussels lace.

In the railway train from here to Mons I leaned on the window in the door to look out. The door was not properly shut, and it opened, and if the person sitting next to me in the compartment had not seen it and held me back with all his strength I should have fallen out head first; as it was I escaped with a fright.

Spring had come to France; the fields were green and the sun warm; I caught sight of St. Denis, passed the new entrenchments outside Paris and was soon sitting in my own room in the Hôtel Valois in Rue Richelieu just opposite the library. In the *Revue de Paris* Marmier had already written an article on me entitled "*La vie d'un poète*". Martin had translated a few of my poems into French and indeed had even honoured me with a poem which had been printed in the revue I refer to above. My name had thus reached the ears of some of the literary world there like a sound from afar, and so this time I was given a surprisingly warm welcome by these people in Paris.

I visited Victor Hugo several times and was given a friendly reception, just the sort of reception that Oehlenschläger complains in his memoirs that he did not experience, so I must feel flattered. At the invitation of Victor Hugo and with a ticket he gave me I went to the Théâtre Français to see his latest and much abused tragedy *Les Burgraves* which was hissed every evening and parodied in the smaller theatres. His wife was very beautiful and in addition possessed of the charm of all French women, which is always so enchanting to foreigners. A little poem I had written in Danish and which had been

translated – by Marmier, I think – was all she knew of me as a poet
at that time:

To the Wife of Victor Hugo

> Not far from here, a few days' journey,
> Lies Denmark, land of beech and golden corn,
> The land that drove out Tycho Brahe
> But still owns Thorvaldsen – and woods and shores.
> It is the Northern kingdoms' lyre.
> There I was born; that tongue is mine;
> There oft I sang for tender Danish maidens;
> There free my Muse was to explore the heavens.
> And oft a welcome guest came to my room
> Your Victor's songs, *Notre Dame*, *Hernani*,
> *Angelo* and *Fenilles d'automne*.
> I love him and admire him as a poet;
> I know his Muse, her glance, her speech.
> As dear she is to me as is my own.
> To you, his wife, his youthful love, to you
> I dedicate this song bouquet.
> Through it and from your lips may he be told
> That in the North he won my love
> – And surely that of others manifold.

Monsieur and Madame Ancelot opened their home to me, and there
I met not only French artists and authors such as Louis Blanc, but
also foreigners such as the German author and critic Rellstab and
the Spanish Martinez de la Rosa. I had been talking to de la Rosa
for a long time without knowing who he was. The impression his
conversation had made on me prompted me to ask Madame Ancelot
who this gentleman was.

"Have I not introduced you to each other?" she said. "He is the
statesman and poet, Martinez de la Rosa." She brought us together
again and told him who I was, and he inquired after old Count Yoldi
in Copenhagen and told the people gathered there how kindly and
sympathetically King Frederik the Sixth had treated the Spaniard

when he had asked him for advice as to which party he ought to adhere to at home, and when the one he supported lost, he was given an appointment and a home by the Danish king.

Soon the conversation was entirely about Denmark, and as there happened to be a young diplomat present who had been sent to the coronation of Christian the Eighth, we were given what seemed to me as a Dane a peculiar but well-intentioned and enthusiastic description of Frederiksborg and the festivities there. He talked of the great oak forests, the old Gothic castle surrounded by water and the brightly gilded chapel. And he told, rather comically, as he seemed to assume that it was the everyday custom, how all high-ranking officials went about in golden and white silk garb with feathers in their birettas and wearing long, flowing velvet robes which they had to throw over their arms when walking in the streets. He had seen it himself, he said! And I had to admit that it had been the case during the coronation celebrations.

Both in the life he lived at home and in his personal demeanour Lamartine seemed to me to be the prince of them all. And when I apologised for speaking his native language so badly he answered charmingly and with French politeness that it was he who ought to be censured since he did not understand the Scandinavian languages. He had heard that a great deal of sparkling, lively literature had been written in them, and that the poetical soil was so remarkable that you merely needed to stoop down to pick up an ancient golden horn. He asked me about the Trollhättan Canal and expressed a desire to travel through Denmark to Stockholm. He could remember Christian the Eighth, to whom he had paid his respects in Castellamare. Moreover he revealed a knowledge of people and places in Denmark that surprised me in a Frenchman.

His wife seemed to be one of those cordial and yet determined characters in whom one soon feels confidence. There was something loyal and wise about her eyes. Before my departure from Paris Lamartine wrote the following little poem for me:

> *Cachez-vous quelquefois dans les pages d'un livre*
> *Une fleur du matin cueuillie aux rameaux verts*
> *Quand vous rouvrez la page après de longs hyvers,*

Aussi pur qu'au printemps son parfum vous ennyvre;
Après les jours bornés qu'ici mon nom doit vivre
Qu'un heureux souvenir sorte encore de ces vers!

> Paris, 3 Mai 1843
> *Lamartine*

Sometimes if you hide in the pages of a book
A morning bloom picked from the green branches,
When you open the page in the long winter night
Its pure perfume is still as heady as in spring;
After these few days may my name live on here,
May these lines still exude a sweet memory.

> Paris, 3 May 1843
> Lamartine

I normally found the jovial Alexandre Dumas in bed, even if it was long past midday. There he lay with paper, pen and ink, writing away at his latest drama. One day when I found him thus, he gave me a friendly nod and said, "Just sit down for a moment; my Muse is here on a visit, but she will be going before long." And he went on writing and talking to himself. Then he shouted "Hurrah," sprang out of bed and said, "That's the third act finished." He lived at the Hôtel des Princes in Rue Richelieu; his wife was in Florence, and his son, Alexandre Dumas fils, who later followed his father's literary footsteps, had his own apartments in town. "I just live the life of a bachelor," said Dumas. "And you must take me as you find me."

One evening he took me to several different theatres so that I could see life behind stage there. We were in the Palais Royal where we talked to Déjazet and Anaïs, and then we wandered arm in arm along the colourful boulevard to the Théâtre St. Martin. "They are just in their short skirts now," said Dumas, "Shall we go up?" We did so, and behind the curtains and scenery we stepped through the sea in *The Thousand and One Nights*. There was a crowd of people, machinists, chorus girls and ballet dancers, and Dumas led me on in the midst of them. On the boulevard on the way home we met a quite young man who stopped us. "This is my son," said Alexandre Dumas; "I had him already when I was eighteen, and now he's that age but without a son." He was the man who was later renowned as "Dumas fils".

To Alexandre Dumas, too, I owed my acquaintance with Rachel. I had not yet seen her act when he asked me one day whether I would like to meet her. There was nothing I wished more. One evening when she was appearing in *Phèdre* he took me back stage in the Théâtre Français. In the other theatres he had taken me into the wings without more ado, but here he asked me to wait a moment, and then he came back to lead me to the queen of the stage. The play had started. He went with me to one of the front wings, behind which a screen had been used to set up a sort of room in which there was a table laid with refreshments and a few stools.

There sat the young girl who, as a French author has said, can carve living statues out of Racine's and Corneille's blocks of marble. She was extremely thin, finely built and looked very young. Both here and later at her home she seemed to me to be a picture of melancholy. She was like a young girl who has just finished weeping over her afflictions and is now letting her thoughts gently linger over what is past. She spoke to us quite cordially; her voice was deep and masculine. In the course of her conversation with Alexandre Dumas she forgot me. It was as though she felt this and she turned to me as he said to her, "He is a true poet and a true admirer of yours. Do you know what he said to me as we came up the stairs?

He said, 'I feel almost ill because my heart is beating so fast now that I am to meet the lady who speaks the most beautiful French in France'." She smiled and uttered a few friendly words, and now I gained sufficient courage to take part in the conversation. I said that I had seen and heard many interesting and wonderful things in this world, but that I had not seen Rachel, and that it was largely for her sake I had come to Paris and used all the income from my latest works on the journey. However, I apologised for my bad French, she smiled and said, "Whenever you say something to a Frenchwoman that is as gallant as what you have just said to me, she will always think you speak it well." I told her how famous her name was in Scandinavia. "If," she said, "I ever come to St. Petersburg and to your city of Copenhagen, then you must be my protector, for you are the only person I know there. But so that we may come to know each other better, and since you say it is largely for my sake you have come to Paris, we must see each other more often. You will be welcome at my home. I always receive my friends on a Thursday. But duty calls," she exclaimed, gave us her hand, nodded to us in a friendly fashion and then she was standing a few paces away from us on the stage, larger, quite changed and with an expression as though she were the tragic Muse herself. We heard the jubilant applause for her.

As a Scandinavian I cannot accustom myself to the French manner of acting tragedies. Rachel acts like all the others there, but it is as though this manner is natural to her while the rest were merely trying to imitate her. She is the French tragic Muse herself, and the others are only poor human beings. When we see Rachel perform we think all tragic acting should be like that. There is truth and reality in it, but revealed in a different way from what we know in the North.

At her home I found everything magnificent and sumptuous, but perhaps a little too artificially arranged. The outer room was in a shade between blue and green, with subdued lighting and small statues of French authors. In the actual salon, crimson was the dominant colour in the coverings, curtains and book-cases. She herself was dressed in black, almost as she is dressed in the well-known English steel engraving of her. The company was made up of gentlemen, mostly artists and academics, but I also heard a few titles. Splendidly dressed servants called out the names of the guests as they arrived. We were given tea and refreshments, more in the German manner than the French. I also heard her speak German. Victor Hugo had told me that he had heard her speak it to Rothschild. I asked her whether she could, and she answered in German, "I can read it; I was born in Lorraine, and I have some German books; look!" And she showed me Grillparzer's *Sappho*, but after that she immediately continued the conversation in French. She said that she would like to play the part of Sappho. Then she talked about Schiller's *Mary Stuart* in which she had acted the part of Mary. I saw her perform it, and her regal splendour in it is especially unforgettable, she became almost taller and more commanding in the scene with Elizabeth when she said:

Je suis la reine! – tu es – tu es – Elisabeth!

I am the queen! – you are – you are – Elizabeth!

The scorn which lay in the word Elisabeth was more than long verses and words could convey. However, it was especially her performance in the last act that surprised me. She played it with the truth and tranquillity that a genuine Nordic or German artist would have put into it, but this was the very act the French liked rather less. "My compatriots," she said, "are not used to this manner, and yet it is the only way in which it can be played. It is impossible to storm and rave when your heart is breaking with anguish and you are saying farewell to your friends for ever."

Her salon was for the most part decorated with books, and these, all of them magnificently bound, were displayed in ornate glass bookcases. On the wall there was a painting representing the interior of the theatre in London, where she was standing at the front of the stage while people showered her with flowers and wreaths. Beneath this picture there was a lovely little bookcase containing what I call "the high nobility among poets" – Goethe, Schiller, Calderon, Shakespeare, etc. She asked me many questions about Germany and Denmark, about art and the theatre, and with a friendly smile on her serious lips and nodding cordially, she encouraged me when I stopped for a moment in my stumbling French in order to collect my thoughts or to find an expression. "Just carry on," she said. "Your French is not good. I have heard foreigners who can speak my language better, but it has often not interested me so much as this. I completely understand the spirit of your words, and that is the main thing. That is just what interests me in you."

When we parted for the last time, she wrote in my album:

"L'art c'est le vrai."
J'espère que cet aphorisme ne semblera paradoxal à un écrivain aussi distingué que Monsieur Andersen.

    Paris, le 28 Avril 1843   *Rachel*

"Art is what is true."

I hope that this aphorism will not seem paradoxical to as distinguished a writer as Monsieur Andersen.

Paris, 28th April 1943   Rachel

I discovered a charming personality in Alfred de Vigny. He was married to an English lady, and their home seemed to represent the best in each nation. Towards midnight on my last evening in Paris, this man, who by virtue of his intellectual standing and earthly riches was at that time most likely to be found in the wealthy salons, came up the many flights of stairs in the Hôtel Valois. He came right up to my room on the top floor, carrying in his own arms all his works, which he brought to me as a parting gift by which to remember him. There was so much deep feeling in his words, and so much heartfelt sympathy in his eyes that the tears came to my eyes when I parted from him.

I also quite often met and talked to David, the sculptor. There was something about his character and directness that reminded me of Thorvaldsen and Bissen. It was during the last few days of that visit to Paris that we came to know each other; he said he was sorry we had met each other so late and asked if I could not stay longer, as he would like to model my bust as a medallion. "But you do not know me as a poet; you do not know whether I deserve such an honour." He looked me straight in the face and patted me on the shoulder; "I have read you, before reading your books," he said with a smile. "You are a poet."

At the home of Countess Bocarmé, where I met Balzac, I saw for the first time an elderly lady whose countenance, if I may call her soulful expression by that name, particularly attracted my attention. There was something so intelligent and sincere about her; and her portrait, which was in the Louvre that season, had also caught my attention. Everyone gathered around her, and the Countess introduced us to each other; she was Madame Reybaud, the author of *Les épaves*, the little story I had used in my play *The Mulatto*. I told her about it, and told her what success the play had had. This interested her so

261

much that from that evening she became my especial protectress. We spent an evening together exchanging ideas. She corrected my French for me and made me repeat anything which did not sound quite right to her, and she was quite maternally kind to me; she is an extremely gifted lady with a sharp eye for the world.

Balzac, whom, as I say, I met at the same time at the home of Countess Bocarmé, was an elegant, exquisitely dressed gentleman with front teeth shining white between his red lips. He seemed quite jovial, although he spoke little, in this circle at least. A lady who wrote verse attached herself to him and to me, drew us over to a sofa and sat between us, seeking to maintain her position by saying how insignificant she felt between us two. I turned my head, and behind her back I met Balzac's satirically laughing face, his mouth half open and rather artificially pulled out of shape. That was actually our first meeting.

One day I was walking through the Louvre when I met a man who in build, walk and features resembled Balzac, but this man was dressed completely in poor, ragged, indeed quite filthy clothes. His shoes needed brushing, and there was dried mud on his trousers; his hat was dented and badly worn. I started; the man smiled at me. I passed him, but the resemblance was simply too striking. I turned round, ran after him and said, "You are not Monsieur Balzac, are you?" He laughed and showed his white teeth, and simply said, "Monsieur Balzac is going to St. Petersburg tomorrow". He pressed my hand; his was fine and soft, then he nodded and went off. It had to be Balzac. Perhaps he had been out on some authorial exploration of the mysteries of Paris. Or was this man perhaps someone else who on account of his resemblance to Balzac had often been mistaken for him and was now enjoying mystifying a stranger in this way. A few days later when I was talking to Countess Bocarmé, she said that Balzac had sent me his best wishes. He had gone to St. Petersburg.

I also met Heinrich Heine again. He had married here in Paris since the last time I had been there. I found him rather ill but full of energy, and he was so cordial towards me and so natural that this time I was not afraid of being myself in his company. One day he had told my story *The Steadfast Tin Soldier* to his wife in French, and he took me to see her, telling her that I was its author. "Are you going to publish an account of your journey?" he asked first, and when I said not, he went on, "Very well then, I will show you my wife." She was a lively, neat little Parisienne; a flock of children were playing round her in the sitting room: "We have borrowed them from the neighbours," said Heine, "for we have none of our own." His wife and I played with them while Heine wrote in an adjoining room:

> *Ein Lachen und Singen!*
> *Es blitzen und gaukeln*
> *Die Sonnenlichter.*
> *Die Wellen schaukeln*
> *Den lustigen Kahn.*
> *Ich sass darin*
> *Mit lieben Freunden und leichtem Sinn.*
> *Der Kahn zerbrach in eitel Trümmer,*
> *Die Freunde waren schlechte Schwimmer,*
> *Sie gingen unter, im Vaterland;*
> *Mich warf der Sturm an den Seinestrand.*
> *Ich hab' ein neues Schiff bestiegen,*
> *Mit neuen Genossen; es wogen und wiegen*
> *Die fremden Fluthen mich hin und her –*
> *Wie fern die Heimath ! Mein Herz wie schwer.*
> *Und das ist wieder ein Singen and Lachen –*
> *Es pfeift der Wind, die Planken krachen –*
> *Am Himmel erlischt der letzte Stern –*
> *Mein Herz wie schwer! Die Heimat wie fern!*

Diese Verse, die ich hier in das Album meines lieben Freundes Andersen schreibe, habe ich den 4ten Mai 1843 zu Paris gedichtet.   *Heinrich Heine*

> Laughter and song!
> The sun's beams
> Flicker and flash.
> The waves rock
> The merry boat.
> I was sitting in it

With dear friends and a light heart.
The boat was wrecked
My friends were poor swimmers
They were drowned in our native land;
The storm cast me up on the banks of the Seine.
I have embarked on a new boat,
With new comrades; the foreign waters
Rock and toss me to and fro –
How far off is home! How heavy my heart.
And once more there is laughter and song –
The wind whistles, the planks creak –
The last star in the sky goes out –
How heavy my heart! How far-off my home!

These lines, that I have written here in my friend Andersen's album, I wrote on the 4th of May 1843 in Paris.

Heinrich Heine

On account of the many people I have named here, and to whom a list of others could be added, such as, for instance, Kalkbrenner, the composer, Gathy, the co-editor of the *Gazette musicale*, and Ampère, who was well acquainted with Denmark, Norway and Sweden, my stay in Paris was full of interest and was most encouraging, and I no longer felt like a stranger. I was given the kindest reception in the homes of the greatest and finest people. It was as though they were giving me credit for works for which they were still waiting, so that in them they would be able to see that they had not judged me wrongly. In addition, I lived in a circle of extremely gifted young compatriots, among whom were Læssøe (who later fell in the Battle of Isted), Orla Lehmann, Krieger, Buntzen, Schiern and one of the dear friends whom I saw every day at home, Theodor Collin.

Here in Paris I was also given a happy and encouraging sign of interest in me as a writer in Germany, where several of my works had already been translated and read. A German family, among the most cultured and charming I know, had read my translated works with great pleasure, including the short biography of me in the introduction to *Nur ein Geiger*. They had developed a sincere interest in me; although they did not know me personally, they wrote to me to express their thanks and their delight in my works. And they suggested I should go home by way of the town in which they lived and spend some time with them as a welcome guest if I felt at home there. There was something so sincere and so natural about their letter, which was the first I received on this journey. It reached me immediately after my arrival in Paris; and it was a remarkable contrast to the letter I received there in 1833 as the first greeting from my native land. There was also a reference to this in their letter. People knew what sort of a greeting I had first received from home, and they wrote, "This time, we hope that this heartfelt and well-intentioned letter will bring you a more pleasant greeting from German soil". I accepted their invitation, and thus, through my works, I found in Germany that I was adopted by a family which I have since been glad to visit, and where I now know that it is not merely the poet, but the person, of whom they are fond.

And what a lot of similar signs I have since received while abroad. I will mention one on account of its being so striking. There lives in Saxony a rich, noble-minded family. The lady of the house read my novel *Nur ein Geiger*, and the impression this book made on her was such that she promised that if ever during the course of her life she should meet a poor child with great musical talents, then they should not be wasted as in the case of the poor fiddler. The musician, Wieck, the father of Clara Schumann, had heard her say this, and shortly after this he brought her not one, but two poor boys, two brothers. He pointed out their talents and reminded her of her promise. She discussed the matter with her husband, and she kept her word. Both the boys came to live at her home, received a good education and were sent to the Music Conservatoire. The younger of them has played for me, and in him I have seen a happy, joyous face. I believe they are now in the theatre orchestra in one of the biggest cities in Germany. It could probably rightly be said that the same thing would have been done for these two children, and by the same excellent lady, whether or not my book had existed, and whether or not she had read it. But it did happen, and it is a fact, and a link in the chain of events which have given me joy.

On the way home from Paris I travelled along the Rhine. I knew that the poet Freiligrath, to whom the King of Prussia had just awarded a pension, lived in one of the towns there. I had always been very attracted by the painterly quality of his poems, and I wanted to meet him face to face. So I stopped in a few of the towns on the Rhine and asked about him. In St Goar I was shown a house in which I was told he lived. I went in; he was sitting at a writing desk and seemed to be irritated at being disturbed by a stranger. I did not say who I was, but merely said that I could not travel through St. Goar without paying my compliments to Freiligrath. "That was very kind of you," he said in a rather cold voice, and asked who I was. When I answered, "We have both one and the same friend, Chamisso," he sprang up in delight; "Andersen!" he said, "That's who it is," and he fell on my neck and his honest eyes shone with joy. "Now you will stay a few days here with us, won't you?" he said. I told him I could only stay for two hours as I was in the company of some fellow countrymen who were to continue the journey. "You have a lot of friends in this little place called St. Goar," he said. "I have recently read your *O.T.* to a large group of people. I must at least have one of my friends here, and you must meet my wife. Of course, you don't know that you are partly responsible for our marriage." And he went on to tell me how my novel *Nur ein Geiger* had caused them to correspond with each other, and how at last they had really become man and wife. He called to her and told her who I was, and I was like an old friend in their home. Before I left he took out a manuscript: "This was intended for you before we met," he said. "I heard you were travelling, and I would have sent it to you, but I was prevented from doing so, and the poem was put away again." Now he wrote on a sheet of paper:

(ErsteStropheeinesunvollendetenGedichtesanH.C.Andersen,
als er Ende 1840 seine Reise in den Orient antrat.)
   St. Goar, 18 Mai 1843   *F. Freiligrath*

> *Du bist gewiss den Störchen nachgezogen;*
> *Dass Du sie liebst, ich wusst' es lange schon.*
> *Sie schwirrten auf, sie sind davon geflogen;*
> *Auf und davon – das ist ein luft'ger Ton!*

266

Du sahst empor; die weissen Federn wallten;
Sie blitzten flockig in der Sonne Strahl;
Da stand es fest! "Was lass ich hier mich halten?
Fort in den Süden wiederum einmal."

(First verse of an unfinished poem to H. C. Andersen when he set off on his journey to the East at the end of 1840.)
St. Goar, 18 May 1843   F. Freiligrath

Surely you have followed the storks;
I have long since known you love them.
They swooshed up, they flew away;
Up and away – an airy note!
You looked up; the white feathers rippled;
They glittered like snowflakes in the sun's rays;
Your mind was made up. "Why should I stay here?
Off to the south once again."

I spent the night in Bonn. The following day I visited old Moritz Arndt, who later became such a bitter opponent of us Danes. At that time I only knew him as the poet who had written the beautiful and inspiring song:

"*Was ist des Deutschen Vaterland!*"

"What is the German's fatherland?"

I found in him a powerful, rubicund old man with silvery hair. He spoke Swedish to me; he had learnt that language when staying in Sweden as a refugee from Napoleon. There was an air of youthful freshness about the old man. I was not unknown to him, and it seemed that the fact that I came from one of the Scandinavian countries increased his interest in me. During the course of our conversation a stranger was announced; neither of us heard the name properly. The visitor was a handsome young man with a confident, sunburned face. He sat down quietly inside the door, and only when Arndt was showing me out and the visitor got up, did the old man delightedly

267

exclaim, "Emanuel Geibel."

Yes, that is who it was, the young poet from Lübeck, whose lovely, cheerful songs were sung for a short time throughout Germany, and to whom the King of Prussia had also given a sort of pension, just as he had to Freiligrath. Geibel was actually on his way to Freiligrath in St. Goar with the intention of spending several months there. Now I did not leave immediately, and I had made the acquaintance of a new poet. Geibel was so handsome, powerful and lively; and as he stood there at the side of the hale old poet, I could see in these two men both old and young poetry, both of which were equally robust. Rhine wine was brought up from the cellar; there was green woodruff floating in it; that was our *Maitrank*, and in honour of May, in praise of May and of spring, the old bard gave me a verse to take with me on my way:

> *Drum mein Lenz sollst Du nicht schweigen,*
> *Klinge, Mai, mit Freudenschall!*
> *Klingt mit Pfeifen, Flöten, Geigen,*
> *Kukuk, Lerch und Nachtigall!*
> *Deutschlands Frühling, er wird kommen!*
> *Für die Welschen klingt Schaff ab!*
> *Allen Guten, Tapfern, Frommen,*
> *Leg ich diesen Wunsch auf's Grab.*

Mit diesem meinem letzten Vers grabe ich einem frommen, kindlichen, nordischen Mann meine Erinnerung ein.
    Bonn den 19 Mai 1843   E. M. Arndt aus Rügen

> So, my spring, thou shalt not remain silent,
> Ring out, May, with peals of joy,
> Ring out with whistles, flutes and fiddles,
> Cuckoo, lark and nightingale.
> Germany's spring, it will come.
> For the French there rings out an 'Abolish!'
> This wish I place on the graves
> Of all good, brave, pious people.

With this my last lines I engrave my memory on a pious, childlike, Nordic man.

Bonn, 19th May 1843   E. M. Arndt from Rügen

An English author once called me "the child of fortune", and I must gratefully acknowledge all the happiness with which I have been blessed during my life and how fortunate I have been in meeting and knowing the noblest and best people of my time. I tell this in the same spirit as I have already told of the poverty, humiliation and oppression I have experienced. This talk about joy and honours has been called arrogance and vanity by some people, but how completely wrong it is to class it as such.

It is from abroad that all the recognition and honour I have talked about has come to me, so people here in Denmark will perhaps ask whether I was never attacked abroad. And my answer must be, "No". I had not yet encountered any actual attack on me. No one at home had told me of one, and so there can scarcely have been any. There was one exception, which was certainly delivered in Germany, but it had been inspired in Denmark, inspired while I was in Paris.

A German by the name of Boas was travelling in Scandinavia at that time, and he wrote a book about his experiences in which he gave a sort of survey of Danish literature. He had this survey printed in the periodical *Grenzboten*, and, it seems to me that I am treated rather harshly in it both as a poet and a man. Several Danish authors, including Christian Winther, also had cause to complain. Mr. Boas had drawn on the petty gossip of everyday life in Copenhagen. His book attracted attention here, but no one would admit to having been his informant. Indeed, the poet H. P. Holst, with whom it appears from the book that Boas had travelled in Sweden and who received him in his home in Copenhagen, issued a declaration on account of this in the newspaper *Fædrelandet*, saying that he had no connection with Mr. Boas. I am told that while in Copenhagen this young man had spent much of his time in the company of some young people belonging to a certain clique. Mr. Boas then went home and in his book repeated all he had heard them say about Danish poets in the course of their merry, frivolous conversations. There is, however, some truth in what he says; he does express the opinion which, if

269

not all Danes, at least the common run had of me at that time. It is somewhat unkind and harsh, not only towards me as a poet, but also as a person. That it was also my compatriots abroad who were the first to draw my attention to what Mr. Boas had said, is of course quite typical.

On the other hand, Germans, among whom was Ludwig Tieck, did their best to erase the bad mood this article created in me. I was assured that I already had a large readership in Germany and that the good opinion they had of me could not suffer because Mr. Boas belittled me with reports from Copenhagen. In *Das Märchen meines Lebens* I discussed this and added a comment which I can repeat here, that I am certain that had Mr. Boas come to Copenhagen a year later, his opinion of me would have been different. Much changes within a year, and the tide turned for me that very next year. This was when I published my *New Fairy Tales*, resulting in a fresh and favourable opinion of me in my native land that has lasted until this day. Since that time I have had nothing particular to complain of. I have gradually come to receive all the recognition and favours I deserve, and perhaps a few more, too.

In Denmark, my *Fairy Tales* have undoubtedly been placed above everything else I have written. So I must linger a little over these works which, on first appearing, were not given an encouraging reception, but, as I say, only later received their proper recognition.

My first real fairy tale is to be found in the section called *Brunswick* in my *Rambles in the Romantic Regions of the Harz Mountains*, where it appears as an ironical little piece together with the drama *Drei Tage aus dem Leben eines Spielers*. Similarly the start of *The Little Mermaid* is to be found in the same book. The description of *The Elves on the Lüneburg Heath* must entirely be considered as constituting fairy tale writing, something which the critic in *Jahrbücher der Gegenwart 1846* already noticed and pointed out.

Only a few months after *The Improvisatore* appeared in 1835, it was followed by the first book of *Fairy Tales*. It was not considered to be of much value, and indeed, as I have already said, people even expressed regret that an author who had just taken such a step forward in *The Improvisatore* should immediately fall back and produce something as childish as these fairy tales. Here, where I surely deserved praise, acknowledgement and encouragement because my productive talents had turned in a fresh direction, I received nothing but disapproval. Several of my friends whose judgement I valued advised me very strongly not to write any more fairy tales.

People in general said that I had no talent for writing that sort of thing, and that they were not suited to the present day. Others were of the opinion that if I wanted to try my hand at it, then I ought to study the French fairy tales. The *Maanedsskrift for Litteratur* made no reference at all to my fairy tales and has never done so to this day. *Dannora*, a review for "criticism and anti-criticism", edited and published by Johannes Nikolai Høst, was in 1836 the only one to consider my work, and what it said sounds extremely amusing now, although it naturally upset me at the time. The critic says that: "these fairy tales could amuse children, but there is no question of children learning anything from them, and your present critic will not guarantee that they are harmless reading. At least no one will surely maintain that a child's sense of what is fitting will be sharpened by reading about a princess who, while asleep rides on a dog's back to a soldier who kisses her, after which, when she is wide awake, she talks of this charming episode as – a strange dream; etc. etc." The critic finds that the fairy tale *The Princess on the Pea* lacks bite, and it seems to him to be, "not only indelicate but even inexcusable, insofar as a child can derive the false impression from it that such a high-ranking lady must always be terribly tender-skinned." The critic ends by expressing the hope that the author "will not in future waste his time on writing *Fairy Tales for Children*". However, these tales forced themselves on me so vigorously that I was unable to stop writing them. In the first volume to appear I had done the same as Musäus, only in my own way, retelling old fairy tales that I had heard as a child. The tone in which they still rang in my ears was the most natural, but I was quite aware that the learned critics would disapprove of this language. So in order to prepare people for it I called them *Fairy Tales, Told for Children*, although it was my intention that they should be both for children and grown-ups. The first volume ended with an original story, *Little Ida's Flowers*. This was the one in which people found least fault, although it is fairly closely related to Hoffmann and already has roots in *The Rambles*.

271

My wish and my urge to write fairy tales increased. I could not stop. The tiny spark of friendliness which a few people showed towards this original tale persuaded me to try my skill at writing more of the same sort. The following year a fresh volume appeared, and soon after that a third was published containing the longest of those I had made up myself so far, that is to say *The Little Mermaid*. Especially this tale attracted attention, and the interest increased with the succeeding volumes. A fresh volume appeared every Christmas, and soon it was an understood thing that my fairy tales should not be missing on a Christmas tree. Mr. Phister and Miss Jørgensen even tried reciting a few of my fairy tales from the stage; this was something new and a change from the surfeit of declamatory pieces with which people were normally served. It was a success, and especially in recent months they have been extremely well received, although this was not the case at first. One of the most important German judges of aesthetics once spoke to me about these readings from the stage; he valued them highly, commenting that the Danish public must be extremely cultured and possessed of good taste to be able to enjoy the kernel without having the attraction of a scintillating shell. I could have replied, although I did not, that it was scarcely the fairy tales people were applauding, but the highly valued actor or actress who was telling them.

As I have already said, in order to give the readers the right impression from the start, I had entitled the first volumes *Fairy Tales, Told for Children*. I had written my stories down in the language and expressions I myself had used when telling them to children, and I had come to realise that people of all ages were happy with this. The children were most amused by what I will call the trappings, while older people on the other hand were more interested in the underlying ideas. The fairy tales became something for both children and adults to read, and that, I believe, is the thing to aim at for anyone who wants to write fairy tales nowadays. They began to find open doors and open hearts, and now I left out *Told for Children*, and published three volumes of *New Fairy Tales*, all of which I had made up myself, and they were received here in Denmark with as much approval as I could wish for. I felt really worried and concerned in case I might not receive such an encouraging verdict on each new volume. It was *Fædrelandet* that was the first of all Danish magazines and newspapers to give me a review full of praise and acknowledgement when the first part of *New Fairy Tales* appeared, the part containing *The Ugly Duckling*, *The Nightingale* and so on. It was *Fædrelandet* that later wrote of the great admiration there was for my work abroad. Thus in 1846 it reported: "In the London magazine *The Athenaeum*, which is known for the objectivity of its criticisms of English literature, the translation of Andersen's *Fairy Tales* is reviewed as follows: 'Fanciful though it seem, we could defend our crochet that the most fitting review of this volume would be a strain of Elfin music; such as Weber wove for his mermaids in *Oberon*, or Liszt can whisper when in a mood of gentle improvisation. Common Cheapside paragraphs are too square, and sharp, and ungraceful to invite gentle readers to pages so full of enchantment as these. Can the world be old? – Can the Poet (as some complain) have degenerated into a moonstruck creature, wasting his life in searching the tombs of his ancestors for their buried wealth, when treasures so exquisite as these are still, from time to time, coming to light?" etc. etc.

What a contrast between the first verdict at home and the first verdict abroad! It was the talented P. L. Møller who was the first in Denmark to speak out warmly in recognition of the fairy tales. Indeed he was virtually the only man at that time who dared to print a favourable opinion of me as a poet. In *Dansk Pantheon*, in which he wrote most of the biographies, he gave me a high and honourable ranking. However, his judgement as a whole and especially of me, was not very much respected at the time. People were against him as his opinions were in many respects not in keeping with the mood of the day. However, it was a voice speaking out publicly in favour of me and not against me! People spoke well of my fairy tales both at home and abroad, and so I gradually won strength to withstand any insults to which I might be exposed. I had firm ground under my feet. Refreshing sunshine streamed into my heart. I felt courage and happiness and was filled with a keen desire to develop even further in that direction and to come to comprehend the very essence of the fairy tale. And still more I wanted to discover the rich natural fountain from which I could drink. If people will follow the order in which my fairy tales were written, I am sure they will sense my progress and see a clearer idea, greater moderation with the means I use, and, if I may say so, more health and natural freshness.

Just as when a man hews a path step by step up some steep cliff, I had at home hewn my path forward, and I now saw myself recognised and accorded a sure place in the literature of my native land. This recognition and gentleness at home had a greater effect on me than any amount of harsh criticism. All became as clear as day within me. Peace descended upon me, and a realisation that everything, even the bitter experiences of life, had been necessary for me for the sake of my development and happiness.

The fairy tales were translated into most European languages. There followed several editions and impressions in German, just as also in English and French, and these have continued right up to the present. Translations have appeared in Swedish, Flemish, Dutch etc., and this has shown me that by going the way God showed me I have done better than by following the advice of the critics and "studying French models". Had I done as they said, I should scarcely have been translated into French and, as is the case in one of the French editions, been ranked alongside La Fontaine, and my fairy tales alongside his "*fables immortelles*": "a new La Fontaine, he makes animals speak amusingly, he associates himself with their suffering and their pleasures, seems to become their confidant and interpreter, and he is able to create for them a language so naïve, so piquant and so natural that it only seems to be a faithful reproduction of what he really has heard." Nor would I have succeeded in having any influence, in one direction at least, on the literature of my native land, which I hope I have had. Even people abroad attribute to my work great significance for their own literature; I am here thinking chiefly of the able critic Julian Schmidt's *Geschichte der Deutschen Nationalliteratur*, Leipzig 1853, in which he speaks of this, and especially emphasises my *Fairy Tales* and *Picture-Book without Pictures*. In view of modern efforts, he says, to picture the real world in specific and attractive outline, it was natural that poetry should turn to the world of the imagination to find some natural beauty in which one could take pleasure and could study in detail, study those things that were lacking in nature and mankind:

It is this delight in detail, this clever and playful eye to the life of the small things in nature and the soul that ensures Andersen a justified and valuable role in the development of contemporary literature. As a rule, poets whose virtuosity is linked to small things find it difficult to make their way in foreign countries, because in their details there are many features that foreign readers will not understand. However, Andersen has found so much good will in Germany that he is almost as much at home here as in his native land of Denmark. His poetry came to Germany at just the right time to show that we can still take delight in these things. His fairy tales have rightly made their way into all groups of the population. Their humorous and fantastic colouring is quite devoid of all affectation, and only rarely is the poet sentimental; his ideas are everywhere both delicate and surprising. His many, colourfully drawn figures express no more of the bitter seriousness of real life than of the colourless idealism of a fairy-tale picture taken from a fashion journal. Best of all is the way in which, with the pantheism of a warm-hearted child-like soul, the poet endows the entire world, from the sun and the planets down to an old slipper and a dirty gas lamp with human qualities. It is not just the easy way of putting words into the mouths of any old object and for better or for worse spinning a dialogue between unreasoning things; we are seriously transported into the souls of tables, chairs, violins, elves and goblins. We feel the psychological gaze of the poet penetrating to the depths of the old, broken darning needle; we have a vivid impression that if this cat, this double bass or this evergreen had thoughts, then they must be these and no others. Andersen even knows how to derive a humorous element from Peter Schlemihl and his lost shadow. Andersen is a true poetical nature, elegantly and gracefully transforming the false world of romanticism into a harmonious image. Etc.

Various slim volumes of *Fairy Tales* followed in several impressions between 1835 and 1852. Then they were published together in an illustrated edition. The later series was given the name of *Stories*, a name which was not chosen arbitrarily – but more of this and of *Stories* and *Fairy Tales* later.

As early as 1846 Dr. K. A. Mayer, the author of *Neapel und die Neapolitaner*, wrote a quite extensive review expressing great interest in my fairy tales in the September-October issue of *Jahrbücher der Gegenwart* under the title of *Andersen und seine Werke*. This article, which in any event does great honour to Danish literature, appears not to have been noticed or known at home. It closes by according to my fairy tales their place in German literature: "When fully developed Andersen's fairy tales fill the gap between the literary fairy tale of Romanticism and the folk tale as preserved by the brothers Grimm".

The significance the critic here attributes to my fairy tales is so great and does me such honour that I hope that in the course of time it will be established as true. However, I will dare to believe that people will always admit that I strove for the position Mayer indicated.

XI

It was at this time that I made a friendship of great intellectual significance to me. I have already written of various public figures who had an influence on me as a poet. No one has done so in a nobler sense than the person to whom I am now going to turn, the person through whom it was as though I learned even more to forget myself, to feel the sacred quality of art and to recognise the mission which God has given me as a writer.

I will go back to 1840. One day in the hotel in which I was living in Copenhagen I saw listed among the visitors from Sweden the name of Jenny Lind. I already knew that she was the leading singer in Stockholm. I had of course been in her country that year and enjoyed much good will and had such honour done to me that I thought it would not be inappropriate to pay my respects to the young artist. She was quite unknown outside Sweden at the time, and I believe that there were very few people even in Copenhagen who knew her name. She received me politely, but with a certain reserve; one might almost say coldly. She said that while she was travelling with her father in the southern part of Sweden she had come over to Copenhagen for a few days to see the city. We left each other as strangers. I had the impression of a quite ordinary person, and she was soon erased from my memory. In the autumn of 1843 Jenny Lind came to Copenhagen again. My friend Bournonville, the balletmaster, whose charming wife was the daughter of a Swedish clergyman and a friend of Jenny Lind, told me that she was in town and that she remembered me. She had read my works, he said, and would be pleased to see me. He asked me to go along with him to visit her and together with him to try to persuade her to make some guest appearances in the Royal Theatre. He said I would be quite enthralled by her singing.

We went to Jenny Lind's apartment, and this time I was not received as a stranger. She cordially shook hands with me, talked about my works and about Fredrika Bremer, who was also her close friend. We soon mentioned the possibility of her performing in Copenhagen, but Jenny Lind said how nervous she would be: "I have never yet sung outside Sweden," she said. "In my own country everyone is so kind and gentle towards me, and suppose I were to perform in Copenhagen and be hissed off stage – I daren't." – I said that of course I could not judge her voice, which I had never heard, and neither did I know what her dramatic presentation was like, but I was convinced that with Copenhagen in its present mood she would be a success if only she had a moderately good voice and reasonably good acting to her name. I said I thought she could risk it.

The fact that Bournonville managed to persuade her gave the people of Copenhagen one of the greatest delights they have ever had. Jenny Lind appeared as Alice in *Robert le Diable*. It was a revelation in the realm of art; her fresh, youthful, beautiful voice captivated the hearts of everyone. Here was truth and natural charm; she gave meaning and clarity to everything. Jenny Lind gave a recital of her Swedish songs. It was so remarkable and enchanting that people forgot it was in a concert hall; interpreted with such pure femininity and with the immortal stamp of genius, the folk tunes exerted their power over everyone present. Copenhagen was wildly enthusiastic. That many gatherings of fine folk neglected her in order to hear the fashionable Italian opera and failed to go to listen to this young woman who was as yet not at all famous was only human. Nevertheless, she awoke great enthusiasm in all those who heard her. Jenny Lind was the first woman singer to be serenaded by the Danish students. From the hotel she moved to the home of the Bournonvilles where she lived together with the family just like a much loved relative and friend. One afternoon they took her to visit Mr. Nielsen, the producer, who was then living in Frederiksberg Allé, and there, as evening came on, she was surprised by the light of torches and sound of singing; there was a song by F. L. Høedt and one by me. – She expressed her thanks by singing a couple of her songs again, and then I saw her hurry into the darkest corner and weep her heart out. "Yes, yes," she said, "I shall work, I shall strive, I shall be much better the next time I come to Copenhagen."

On stage she was a great artist who dazzled all those around her; at home, in her drawing room, she was a modest young girl with the mind and piety of a child. Her appearance in Copenhagen was a great event in the history of our Opera. Her performance and personality showed true art in all its sanctity. I had seen one of its vestals. She left for Stockholm, and soon afterwards Fredrika Bremer wrote to me about her: "We agree entirely about Jenny Lind as an artist. She is as great as any artist can be in our time, and yet you do not know her enough to appreciate her significance. Speak to her of her art, and you will understand her grasp and see her eyes beam with enthusiasm. Then talk to her of God and the sacred gift of religion, and you will see tears in her innocent eyes. She is great as an artist, but she is even greater as a human being."

The following year I was in Berlin. One day when the composer Meyerbeer came to visit me we happened to discuss Jenny Lind. He had heard her sing the Swedish songs and been amazed by her. "But what is her acting like? How does she say her lines?" he asked, and I said how enchanted I was and told him a little about her performance of Alice. He then said that it might be possible for him to get her to Berlin, but that the matter was still being negotiated. It is well known that she did appear there and amazed and delighted everyone, first gaining a European reputation in Germany.

In the autumn of 1845 she came to Copenhagen again, and the general enthusiasm for her was quite unbelievable. The halo of fame makes genius visible to everyone, and people literally camped out outside the Royal Theatre to obtain a single ticket, something which was repeated throughout the cities of Europe and America. Jenny Lind appeared before us, and even to her earlier admirers she seemed to be greater than before, for we now had the chance to see her in more and very varied roles. Her Norma is true plastic art. Every pose could be the most beautiful model for a sculptor, and what might appear to be the result of profound study and thought is in her a moment's inspiration and not something that has been studied in front of a mirror; it is always fresh and always true. – I have seen Malibran, Grisi and Madame Schröder-Devrient play Norma, and however brilliantly each of them was able to portray her, it was Jenny Lind who delighted and carried me away more than anyone else. Her conception of the part seems to me to be profound and true. Norma is no raging Italian woman, but a woman who has been wounded, a woman who has sufficient heart to sacrifice herself for an innocent rival. She is a woman who, in the heat of the moment, can consider killing her faithless lover's children, but who is disarmed as soon as she looks into their innocent eyes. "Norma, high priestess of the temple," the chorus sings to her, and Jenny Lind understood these words "high priestess", as she shows us in the aria, "Casta divina". – She sang all her parts in Swedish in Copenhagen, while the rest of the cast sang in Danish. The two languages, which are so closely related to each other, blended well and no one was disturbed by it. Even in *The Daughter of the Regiment*, where there is a fair amount of dialogue, there seemed to be something characteristic, something charming and fitting, about the Swedish. And what acting! Why the very word is a contradiction, for it was nature itself. Never has there been anything more true on a stage! She portrays for us in every detail the simple child of nature who has grown up in the camp, and yet the grace and nobility with which she has been born are evident in every movement. *The Daughter of the Regiment* and *La Sonnambula* must surely be Jenny Lind's most outstanding roles by far; no one else can compare with her in these parts. People laugh and people weep. It does you good like going to church, for you become a better person. You feel that God is present in her art, and where we meet God face to face, that place is a holy church. Writing to me of Jenny Lind, Mendelssohn said, "A personality like hers has not been born for centuries," and his words express my own conviction. When she appears on the stage we feel that the sacred wine is being offered to us in a spotless vessel. "She would be the right person to act my Valborg," said Oehlenschläger with shining eyes, and he wrote a beautiful and deeply felt poem to her. Thorvaldsen recognised the halo of genius about her head the very first time he saw her on the stage, and when, on that occasion, I introduced them to each other in the stalls, he bowed and kissed her hand. She blushed scarlet, and made to kiss his in return. I stood there terrified, for I knew the public – it is stronger on criticism than on sensibility.

Nothing can obliterate the greatness of Jenny Lind on the stage, except her own personality at home. There, a child-like yet intelligent disposition exercised its remarkable power. She was happy to feel that she, as it were, no longer belonged to the world. All she thought of then was a peaceful, undisturbed home. Yet, loving art with all her soul, she felt her calling in it and was prepared to follow it. A noble and pious mind like hers is not spoiled by homage. – Only once did I hear her express her awareness of her talent and her joy at being so gifted. It was during this, her last stay in Copenhagen. She appeared in operas or gave recitals almost every evening; every hour was taken up by something. Then she heard of the Society for the Care of Neglected Children and was told of the work it did and the progress it made. It had as yet only limited finances. I was among those who spoke to her about this society. "Well, is there not a single evening when I am not performing?" she said. "Let me give a concert for the benefit of these children. But on this occasion we shall have to double the price of tickets." This was something she otherwise insisted should not be done when she sang here. A concert was arranged, and she sang scenes from *Der Freischütz* and *Lucia di Lammermoor*, and the latter especially was so moving that Walter Scott himself can scarcely have imagined a more beautiful and true picture of the unfortunate Lucy. This performance brought in a considerable profit. I told her how much and said that help for these poor children was now assured for a couple of years. Her face lit up, and tears came to her eyes: "Oh, it's so lovely to be able to sing like that," she exclaimed.

I appreciated her with all the feelings of a brother and was happy to know and understand such a soul. Throughout her stay here I saw her every day. She stayed at Bournonville's, and I, too, spent most of my time there. Before leaving she gave a splendid dinner at the Hôtel Royal, to which all those people who, as she put it, had been of service to her were invited, and I believe everyone apart from me received a little souvenir from her. She gave Bournonville a silver cup inscribed, "To Bournonville, the ballet master who has been a father to me in Denmark, my second homeland." In the words of thanks that Bournonville addressed to her he said that now all Danes would wish to be his children in order to be Jenny Lind's brothers. "That would be rather too many," she joked. "In that case I would rather choose one of them as my brother. Will you be my brother, Mr. Andersen?" And she approached me, chinked glasses of champagne with me and drank her brother's health. She left Copenhagen. The carrier pigeon flew from one to the other at intervals; she was infinitely dear to my heart, and we met again, as the following pages will tell. We saw each other in Germany and England. A whole book, the book of a heart, could be written on that subject; I mean of *my* heart, and I think I may say that through Jenny Lind I came to understand the sacred nature of art. Through her I have learned that we must forget ourselves in the service of something higher. For a time no books and no people had a nobler influence on me as a writer than did Jenny Lind, and so it is natural that I must dwell so long and so enthusiastically on my memories of her.

I have made the happy discovery that as I have increasingly come to understand life and art, more and more sunshine has poured into my breast from outside. What blessings came my way after the earlier dark days! Peace and assurance have entered into my soul. Yet such peace can well be combined with an ever-changing life of travel. There was a time when I felt so oppressed and tormented by events at home that to be abroad at least meant a respite from my suffering – and so foreign countries seemed to offer me peace. I came to be fond of being abroad, and since it is my nature quite easily to become attached to people who show confidence and friendliness in return, I took a liking to travel abroad, and did so often.

"To travel is to live."

In the summer of 1844 I visited Northern Germany again. An intelligent and charming family from Oldenburg, the present Minister von Eisendecher and his wife had invited me to spend some time at their home. Count Rantzau-Breitenburg repeatedly told me in his letters how welcome I would be at his home, and that, whatever I did, I must go and visit him in beautiful Holstein. And so I went there. Although not one of my longest journeys, it was probably one of the most interesting.

I saw the fertile marshland in all its summer profusion. Cows with bells hanging from their necks walked around in grass that reached up to their shoulders, just as in the Swiss valleys. Everything was pure idyll. Breitenburg itself lies surrounded by forest on the

River Stör just before it reaches Itzehoe. Steamship traffic from here to Hamburg added life to the little river. There were so many picturesque spots around the place itself; and I felt so much at home and so comfortable in the castle that I really could dedicate my time to reading and writing. I was as free as a bird in the air, and the family looked after me as though their guest was a dear relative. Together with Count Rantzau I went on several short but interesting excursions and became acquainted with the Holstein countryside. However, his health was failing rapidly, and this was to be his last summer. It was the last time I was to come to the comfortable, friendly castle of Breitenburg. He himself had a presentiment of his approaching death. One day when we met in the garden he took hold of my hand and pressed it warmly, expressing his delight at the recognition I had achieved abroad as a writer and speaking of his friendship for me, and finally he said, "Yes, my young friend; God alone knows it, but I have a firm belief that this year is the last time you and I are going to meet here. My days are numbered, I am afraid." He looked at me with such serious eyes that it went right to my heart. There was nothing I could say. We were just standing close to the chapel. He opened a gate between some thick hedges, and there we were standing in a small garden with a grass-covered grave in front of a bench. "This is where you will find me next time you visit Breitenburg," he said. And his sad words came true. He died the following winter in Wiesbaden; in him I lost a friend, a protector and a fine, noble heart.

In 1831, when I visited Germany for the first time and went to the Harz Mountains and Saxon Switzerland, Goethe was still alive. It was my most ardent desire to meet him. It was not far from the Harz Mountains to Weimar, but I had no letter of introduction to him, and at that time not a single verse of my poetry had been translated. Several people had described Goethe to me as a very distinguished gentleman, so perhaps he would not receive me? I doubted whether he would, and decided not to go to Weimar until I had produced some work that would make my name known in Germany. I was successful in this with *The Improvisatore* – but by then Goethe was dead. Later, on my way home from Constantinople, I made the acquaintance of his daughter-in-law, Frau Goethe, née Pogwisch, at the home of Mendelssohn. She told me that she had come by rail from Dresden for my sake, and this intelligent and highly honoured lady met me most cordially. She said that her son Walther had been my friend for several years. As a boy, she said, he had made a whole drama out of my novel *The Improvisatore*, and this play had been performed in Goethe's house. Walther, she told me, had at one time been completely filled with the idea of travelling to Copenhagen to visit me. A Danish visitor he had met in Saxon Switzerland had even given him a letter for me, but had not spoken of me with any great enthusiasm, and had been amazed at the importance the young Goethe accorded to me as a Danish author.

So now I had friends in Weimar. A remarkable desire moved me to see the town where Goethe, Schiller, Wieland and Herder had lived, and whence so much light had shone out over the world. I came to that small country that has been made sacred by Luther, by the Minstrels' Contest in the Wartburg, and by great and noble memories. I arrived at the friendly town on the 24th June, the birthday of the present reigning Duke. Everything indicated the day that was being celebrated, and in the theatre, where a new opera was being performed, the young prince, the Hereditary Grand Duke, was received with true enthusiasm. I had no idea at that time how profoundly dear to my heart all the glories and wonders I saw about me would become, or by how many future friends I was surrounded or how fond I was to become of this town, which indeed was to become my second home in Germany.

I had a letter of introduction to Goethe's distinguished friend, the excellent old Chancellor Müller, and I was received most cordially. On my first visit there I chanced to meet Baron Beaulieu de Marconnay, whom I knew from Oldenburg; he had recently been given a post in Weimar, and was now living there.

There are people one needs no more than a few days to come to know and love; in those days I believe I found a friend for all time in Beaulieu. He introduced me to all the best families. The charming Chancellor Müller looked after me equally kindly, and so whereas when I had arrived I had believed myself to be quite alone as Frau von Goethe and her sons were in Vienna, I suddenly found myself known and accepted in all circles in Weimar.

The reigning Grand Duke and Duchess received me so graciously and warmly that it made a deep impression on me. After I had been presented to them I was invited to dine with them, and it was not long before I was summoned to visit the Hereditary Grand Duke and Duchess, who before marrying had been a Princess of the Netherlands. They were living at the hunting lodge at Ettersburg which lies high up and close to the extensive forest.

I drove out there with Chancellor Müller and Goethe's biographer, Eckermann. A short distance from the castle the coach came to a standstill and a young man with an open face and splendid, gentle eyes stopped us and spoke. "Have you brought Andersen with you?" he asked, and since he was very pleased to see me I shook hands with him.

"It is wonderful to see you here," he said. "I will join you up there soon."

"Who was that young man?" I asked as we drove on.

"It was the Hereditary Grand Duke," said Müller. So I had been presented to him.

We soon met in the castle; it was and still is such a homely and comfortable place. I encountered gentle eyes, joy and vivacity all around me.

After dinner the ducal couple and all their guests went out into the village close by the castle. The young people from the village and the surrounding countryside had congregated there to celebrate the birthday of their beloved Hereditary Grand Duke now he had returned to Ettersburg. Greasy poles with kerchiefs and ribbons fluttering from them had been erected; violins were playing and people were dancing merrily under the great lime trees. There was a holiday atmosphere about it all, a sense of contentment and happiness. The young, newly-married Duke and his lady seemed to be attached to each other with truly deep feelings. If one is to feel happy while spending a considerable time at a court, it is necessary to forget the star for the heart beating behind it. Carl Alexander of Sachsen-Weimar possesses one of the noblest and best of hearts. The passing years, times of happiness and gravity, have granted me the fortune of consolidating my belief. Even during my first visit I went out to beautiful Ettersburg several times. In the park there, from which the Harz Mountains can be glimpsed, the Hereditary Grand Duke showed me an ancient tree in the trunk of which Goethe, Schiller and Wieland had carved their names. Indeed Jupiter himself had decided to add his, and his thunderbolt had imprinted it on one of the branches. The intelligent Frau von Gross (as a writer known under the name of Amalie Winter), the charming old Chancellor Müller, who was able to give us a spirited impression of Goethe's day and accompany an account of his *Faust* with perceptive commentaries, and the child-like and utterly loyal Eckermann all formed part of the circle at Ettersburg where the evenings passed like some amazing dream. Everyone took his turn at reading aloud, and even I was bold enough to read one of my fairy tales, *The Steadfast Tin Soldier*, in German. Chancellor Müller took me to "die Fürsten-Gruft" where Carl August rests by the side of his wonderful Duchess, and not between Schiller and Goethe as I believed when I wrote, "The Duke has created a rainbow-like halo for himself, since he stands between the sun and the rushing water-fall."

Close to the tomb in which lie Carl August and his Duchess, those people of royal family who best understood and valued what was great, the immortal friends rest; withered laurel wreaths lay on the simple, brown coffins whose only embellishments are the immortal names, "Goethe" and "Schiller". In their lives the Duke and the poets went hand in hand, and in death their dust rests beneath the same vault. Such a place is never erased from one's memory, and in such a place one says a silent prayer which God alone is to hear.

Before my departure I wrote at the front of an album for the little Prince Carl August:

(Weimar)

In Thuringia there stands a castle, the home of hearts. It is so homely there, so good, and there I saw a blissful family life. There was marble and coloured splendour all around, and yet I can best remember one room, the throne room of the heart; where I saw the most wondrous sight.

The Princess, the mother, innocent and happy, romped in play with her little son who sat like a horseman on her back. He wanted to gallop and gallop. So beautiful, so gentle, a happy mother, she smiled. What joy it was for her. The angels will one day sing the prayers of this faithful heart.

Oh gentle child with eyes of blue and a charming smile on your lips, may you inherit your father's loving heart, his open mind and his will to strive. Eternal candles shall burn for you in the resplendent lighthouse of science; nature will open its book of stories for you, and all hearts will be opened to you.

Oh Thuringian forest, your name has a lofty sound, and a voice that belongs to the world. There Luther spoke, there Goethe sang; there wondrous things have their home. May God bless the family striving on towards fortune and happiness in great things. In Thuringia there stands a castle, the home of hearts.

When I left Weimar I felt as though I had lived in that city before, and as though it was a beloved home I was now leaving. As I drove through the gate, out across the bridge beside the watermill and took a last look back at the city and its castle, my soul was filled with a profound melancholy. It was as though a beautiful period of my life now belonged to the past. On leaving Weimar I felt that my journey could have no more flowers in store for me. How often have letters from me flown to this place since then, and my thoughts yet more often. From Weimar, the city of poets, sunshine poured into my poet's life.

In Leipzig, where I now went, a beautiful and truly poetical evening awaited me at the home of Robert Schuman. The brilliant composer had surprised and honoured me the previous year by dedicating to me his setting of the four of my poems which Chamisso had translated into German. They were sung there that evening by Frau Frege, whose eloquent singing has brought joy and enthusiasm to so many thousands. Clara Schumann accompanied her, and the poet and the composer constituted the sole audience. A little dinner and a mutual exchange of ideas made the evening seem far too short.

In a letter written in April 1845 Robert Schumann, too, recalls that evening which I had thought so beautiful:

"– *Ein Zusammentreffen, wie das an dem Abend, wo Sie bei uns waren, – Dichter, Sängerin, Spielerin und Componist zusammen – wird es sobald wieder kommen? Kennen Sie* "Das Schifflein" *von Uhland:*

> *– wann treffen wir*
> *An einem Ort uns wieder –?*

Jener Abend wird mir unvergesslich sein."

"– *A gathering, like that one the evening when you were at our house – poet, singer, player and composer all together – will it happen again that soon? Do you know 'Das Schifflein' by Uhland:*

> *– when shall we meet*
> *At some place again –?*

I will never forget that evening."

(*Das Schifflein – the little ship*)

In Dresden I met old friends with youthful minds. My gifted semi-compatriot, the Norwegian Dahl was there, the man who really knows how to make a waterfall cascade and birch trees grow on canvas just as they do in the valleys of Norway. There was Vogel von Vogelstein, who did me the honour of drawing me and including my picture in the royal portrait collection. There was Herr von Lüttichau, the manager of the theatre, who gave me a seat in the directors' box each evening. And the highly honoured Baroness Decken, one of the noblest ladies in leading circles in Dresden, received me like a mother receiving her son; and as such I have always since returned to her home and her circle of delightful children. Oh, how radiant and beautiful the world is! It is a delight to live! That is what I felt and recognised there.

Beaulieu's brother Edmond, an army officer, came one day from Tharandt, where he was spending some months that summer. At his invitation I went there with him, and spent some happy days in the gentle mountain air.

I made new acquaintances everywhere. People saw only my good sides, and they became fond of me. Through Baroness Decken I was introduced to the home of the famous and gifted artist Retzsch, who has drawn those spirited portraits of Goethe and Shakespeare. Retzsch's comfortable and friendly residence is in the idyllic and beautiful, vine-covered hills close to Meissen. Every year he gives his wife a new drawing on her birthday, and it is always one of his best. The collection has grown into a valuable album over a number of years, and if he dies, she is to sell it and live on the money it brings in. Among the many splendid ideas here there was especially one, *The Flight from Egypt*, that caught my attention. It was night, and everything in the picture was asleep, Mary, Joseph, trees and bushes, even the ass that was carrying her. Only the infant Jesus with His round, open face was awake, illuminating everything else. In exchange for one of my fairy tales which I read for him, I was given a beautiful drawing. It is of a young girl hiding herself behind the mask of an old woman, the idea being that the eternally young soul with its radiant beauty is peeping out from behind the old mask of the fairy tale. Retzsch's pictures are all figures of the imagination, born of beauty and talent.

I enjoyed German country life with Major Serre and his charming wife on their sumptuous estate at Maxen in Saxon Switzerland. There are quarries there, great lime kilns, industry and activity, and all is hospitality and kindness. There are few people in the world who could show more generosity than these two delightful people who always gather a circle of interesting and intelligent people about them. I stayed there for more than a week and met Kohl, who has given us such clear and lively descriptions of his travels.

Also on a visit here was the authoress, Countess Ida Hahn-Hahn, whose novels and travel accounts were extremely well known at that time. Since then, as a result of her conversion to Catholicism and her *Von Babylon nach Jerusalem,* she has again been a subject of conversation. I am told that her father was known for his unbounded love of plays, so that at last he was almost always absent from his estates, travelling around with his troupe of actors. She married her cousin, the wealthy Count Hahn-Hahn, but a divorce followed, and after that time she began to appear in print with poems, novels and travel accounts. The dominant aristocratic element and the noticeable distinction in her novels has been underlined, criticised and discussed sufficiently. She herself has been accused of the same thing, but she gave me not the slightest impression of it. During the days we spent together in Maxen I found in her true womanliness and conviviality, in every way a personality that filled one with confidence.

She always travelled together with Baron Bystram, an extremely charming gentleman, and she always stayed under the same roof as he. Everyone was convinced that they were married and said so openly, and it was as man and wife they were received in all the most exclusive social circles. Once when I asked someone why this marriage should be kept secret they said it was probably because, on marrying again, she would lose the large allowance she now received from her first husband, and she would be unable to live without it. – As an author she has been the object of a large number of harsh and scornful attacks; and her activity as a writing nun or, if you will, as a woman writing Catholic propaganda, certainly entails many elements that are both untrue and unhealthy, but she is a noble nature and an unusually gifted woman. It is a pity that the talents she received from God have not produced the blossoms and fruits here on earth which they might have done in different circumstances. She was understanding and kind towards me. It was through the dark glass of *Only a Fiddler* and the world of the fairy tale that she saw me as a poet, and this she expressed in the following verse which she wrote for me one morning:

> *Andersen.*
> *Solch ein Gewimmel von Elfen und Feen,*
> *Blumen und Genien im frölichen Scherz;*
> *Aber darüber viel geistige Wehen,*
> *Aber darunter – ein trauriges Herz.*
> *Dresden, den 14ten Juli 1844.   Ida Hahn-Hahn.*

> Andersen.
> Such a teeming throng of elves and fairies
> Flowers and spirits in joyous play;
> But above it much intellectual birth-pangs.
> But below it – a sad heart.
> Dresden, 14th July 1944.   Ida Hahn-Hahn.

People like to stay where they are received well. I felt inexpressibly happy during this little visit to Germany, and I was convinced that I was no foreigner there. It was the heart and the truth and naturalness in my works that people valued, and however excellent and praiseworthy beauty of form is, however imposing the wisdom deriving from reflection is in this world, heartfelt feelings and naturalness will still be the qualities that are least changed over the years and best understood by everyone.

I went home by way of Berlin, which I had not visited for several years. But the dearest of all my friends there, Chamisso, was dead. The "wild swan which flew so far about the earth and laid its head in the bosom of the wilds"– had flown to a more splendid realm. I saw his children who were left without father or mother. It is in the young people I see around me that I realise I am growing older; I do not feel it within myself. Chamisso's sons, whom I had last seen as boys with open shirts playing in the little garden, now appeared equipped with helmets and swords; they were officers in the Prussian army. For a moment I felt how the years roll by, how everything is changed, and how much we lose:

> Yet it is not so hard as has been said
> To lose a loved one here on earth below.
> Our loved ones are with God, a bridge is spread
> 'Twixt us on earth and heaven, you know

A new family circle was opened to me, that of Savigny, the Minister for Legislation. There I was given a most cordial welcome and made the acquaintance of the extraordinarily gifted woman of genius, Frau von Arnim, or to call her by the name we know best, Bettina, Goethe's Bettina. She and Frau Savigny are the sisters of Clemens Brentano. I first met Bettina's beautiful and intelligent daughters, the youngest of whom has written the poetical fairy tale, *The Moon King's Daughter*. They brought their mother across to me in the salon: "Now, what do you think of him?" they asked. Bettina looked at me closely, touched my face with her hand and said, "Passable". She then went away, but soon came back, eccentric and charming. A single hour's conversation with Bettina, during which she did most

291

of the talking, was so rich in interest that I was struck dumb as I listened to this eloquence, this firework display of ideas.

Later that evening when the company dispersed she sent her carriage home empty and we walked together along Unter den Linden. The Prince of Würtemberg had offered her his arm, and I walked along with her daughters. We stopped outside Meinhards Hotel, where I was staying. Bettina went over and stood in front of the steps, put her hand to her forehead in military fashion and said, "*Gute Nacht, Kamerad! Schlafen Sie wohl*". A few days later I visited her at her home, and there she revealed herself in a different light; she was certainly just as brilliant, but not so superficially witty; she gave me the impression of being a profound and sincere person.

Everyone knows her books, but she possesses one talent which is less known; that is her skill at drawing. Here, too, it is the idea that surprises one. For instance, she had sketched an event that had just taken place: a young man had been killed by wine spirits. She portrayed him half naked, climbing down into the vaults where the wine casks lay around in the shape of monsters. Bacchants and bacchantes danced forth, caught their prey, took him in their arms and killed him. I know that Thorvaldsen, to whom she had once shown all her drawings, had been extremely surprised.

"*Da haben Sie mein letztes Buch, lieber Andersen,*" she wrote at the front of *Brentanos Frühlingskranz*, which she then gave me to take with me.

When we are away from home it is such a good feeling to find a house where all eyes light up like festive lanterns when we appear, a house where we catch a glimpse of a quiet, happy family life, and such a house I found at the home of Professor Weiss, to whom a letter from H. C. Ørsted had introduced me. These were delightfully kind people. But what a lot of new acquaintances I made and old ones I renewed. I met Cornelius from Rome again, Schelling from Munich, my Norwegian compatriot Steffens and Tieck from Dresden, whom I had not seen since my first visit to Germany. He had changed, but his wise, gentle eyes were the same; his handshake was the same; I felt how dear and good he was. I had to visit him out in Potsdam where he lived in beautiful, opulent surroundings. At dinner there I made the acquaintance of his brother, the sculptor. I was told how graciously and kindly disposed the King and Queen of Prussia were towards me, that they had read my novel *Only a Fiddler*, which had appealed to them greatly, and that they had accordingly asked Tieck about me. Their Majesties were absent from Berlin just at that time. I had come to Berlin the evening before their departure, when the dreadful attempt to assassinate them was made.

Just at the last moment before I was due to depart, a poem, a song, was sung to me as a greeting from my German friends. It was from the childlike, popular poet, Kletke, who had already honoured me by dedicating the second part of his *Deutsche Märchen* to me the previous year, while the first part had been dedicated to Tieck. Here is the song, which I keep as a flower of remembrance from Berlin:

> *An H. C. Andersen.*
>
> *Dir haben liebliche Elfen zur Nacht*
> *Ihr schönstes Lied gesungen;*
> *Der Berg, der Strom und die Waldespracht*
> *Sind dir in Lust erklungen.*
> *Wie schimmert die goldene Märchenwelt !*
> *Palläste, marmorne, steigen*
> *Aus dunklem Grunde – am Königszelt*
> *Tanzen die Elfen den Reigen.*
> *Du bist der Zauberer, der sie ruft,*
> *Dir müssen sie alle dienen;*
> *Du bist ihr König, in Wald und Kluft,*
> *In Gold-und Silberminen.*
> *Ich seh' von fern und lausche bang*
> *In die duftige Welt der Träume,*
> *Kaum dass ein leiser Sehnsuchtklang*
> *Durchzittert die rauschenden Bäume.*
>
> *Und weht zu dir solch einsamer Klang,*
> *Mit den Blättern, sturmgetrieben:*
> *So nimm es als einen deutschen Dank*
> *Von Herzen, die Dich lieben!*

To H. C. Andersen.

To you the charming elves at night
Sang their most beautiful song;
The mountain, the river, the forest's splendour
Rang out to you in joy.
How golden gleams the world of faery!
Palaces, of marble, rise up
Out of dark depths – by the kings's tent
The elves are dancing round.
You are the magician who calls them,
They all have to serve you;
You are their king, in forest and gorge,
In gold and silver mines.
I see from afar and hearken fearfully
To the gossamer world of dreams,
Hardly does a soft echo of longing
Make the rustling trees quiver.

And should such a lonely echo wing its way to you
With the leaves, storm-driven:
Take it as German thanks,
From the hearts of those who love you.

I went to Copenhagen by way of Stettin. The weather was rough. Happy and full of life I saw all those I held dear, and then a few days later I went off again, this time to visit Count Moltke-Hvitfeldt in Funen in order to enjoy a few more lovely summer days in the delightful mansion of Glorup. There I received a letter from Count Rantzau-Breitenburg who was taking the waters at Föhr together with King Christian the Eighth and Queen Caroline Amalie.

He had talked to their Majesties about my happy stay in Germany and about the extremely gracious welcome I had received at the court in Weimar, and, he said, since my King and Queen were graciously and kindly disposed to me, they, too, wished to afford me a few days full of life and variety in their company at the remarkable spa at Föhr. Rantzau had been given the task of communicating their gracious invitation to me.

In my novel *The Two Baronesses* I have tried to depict the unusual scenery there and on the low Hallig islands of which Biernatzky has given such a fine description in his short stories, as he did also of Amrum with its sand dunes. So the best and most characteristic descriptions of the countryside in this book I owe to the invitation I received from my King and Queen. I was happy at the gracious kindness they showed me, and I looked forward to once more being in the company of dear, kind Count Rantzau-Breitenburg. It was the last time we met.

It was just twenty-five years since I had gone alone and helpless to Copenhagen as a poor boy. So the anniversary was to be celebrated.

I was to be together with my King and Queen, to whom I remain loyally devoted, and with whom I was then given an opportunity of becoming better acquainted, so that I came to love them with all my heart. Everything around me, both people and the countryside, made an unforgettable impression on me. I felt as though I had been taken up to some high place from which I could look back even more clearly on the twenty-five years with all the good fortune and happiness that had revealed themselves to me in them and see how everything had happened and turned out for the best. Reality often surpasses the most beautiful of dreams.

From Funen I had gone to Flensborg, where for the first time I saw the woods and slopes by the picturesque fjord. I experienced the slow journey across the heath where only the clouds seem to move. Monotonously we progressed across the deep sand. Monotonously an odd bird cheeped in the heather: it was enough to make one fall asleep. And yet progress became even more difficult and slower, indeed almost hazardous when we came to the end of the heath and the marshland began with all the soft mud resulting from the rain. The continuous downpour had turned the cornfields and meadows into huge lakes; the dykes were like quagmires; the horses sank deep in the mud, and in several places the light carriage had to be supported by the peasants to prevent it from overturning on to the low houses below the dykes. Progress was at the rate of a couple of miles an hour at the most.

Finally I reached Dagebüll, and before us lay the North Sea with all its islands along the coast, which is itself a dyke, artificially made and strengthened for miles on end by a sort of straw thatch against which the waves break. I arrived just at high tide; the wind itself was in our favour, and it was hardly an hour before we reached Föhr, which seemed to be a real fairyland after the difficult journey.

The town of Wyck, the biggest on the island, the place where the baths are situated, is built entirely in the Dutch style. The houses are all single-storeyed, with thatched roofs and gables, so the whole town makes a very modest impression. However, the many visitors who were there in the bathing season, the entire Court and everything connected with it, produced a lively, festive atmosphere which was especially noticeable in the main street. There were visitors staying at almost every house, and familiar faces peeped out from all the windows in the parlours and gables. Danish flags were flying and music was being played; it was as though I was arriving in the middle of some festival.

The sailors from the ship took my luggage to the hotel. Not far from the landing stage, near the single-storeyed building in which the King and Queen were living, we could see a large wooden house in which some ladies were moving about near an open window. They looked out and called, "Andersen! Welcome, welcome." The sailors bowed low and took off their caps. I had for a long time been a guest unknown to them. In their own way they had estimated my standing and condition, but now I became a person of importance to them, for the ladies who bade me welcome were the young Princesses of Augustenburg and their mother, the Duchess.

In the hotel I had just been shown my place at the table d'hôte, and as a new guest I was the object of a great deal of curiosity when a royal servant came and invited me to join the party at dinner. The meal had already begun, but the King and Queen had heard of my arrival, and a place awaited me.

"It was only then I really became interesting," said a fellow countryman who was also at the table in the hotel. At the King's command accommodation had been arranged for me. Throughout my entire stay I was together with this elevated company and Rantzau-Breitenburg at lunch and dinner and in the evening. They were wondrous, happy, poetical days, the likes of which could never be experienced again.

It is good to see noble men and women revealed where we otherwise see nothing but a royal crown and crimson robes. Few people could be more charming in their private lives than the Danish King and Queen. May God grant them joy for the sunshine they brought to my heart.

In the evening I usually read a couple of fairy tales. *The Nightingale* and *The Swineherd* seemed to be the two the King liked best, and so they were repeated on several evenings. My talent for improvisation was discovered one evening when, for fun, one of the courtiers produced a sort of rhyme characterising the young Princesses of Augustenburg. I was there, and I added in jest, "You do not recite your rhymes properly. I can do it better. You must say: …and now I produced an impromptu verse. Everyone joked and laughed. This could be heard in the adjoining room where the King sat playing cards. He asked what it was, and I repeated the impromptu verse I had written on behalf of someone else. Now everyone wanted to improvise, and I had to help them out. I did my best, suiting it to everyone's character as far as I could.

"Am I the only one not to have produced a poem then?" asked General Ewald, who was playing cards with the King. "Won't you recite one of my best ones for me?"

"The King and all the country know Ewald's poems," I replied and thus wriggled out of the difficulty. Then Queen Caroline Amalie said, "Can you not remember anything I have thought or felt?"

I wanted to speak some dignified lines and replied, "Yes, Your Majesty; I have it written down so as to keep it, and tomorrow I will give you a copy."

"I hope you will remember it," she repeated. Everyone went on urging me, and I improvised the following strophe which is printed among the shorter verses in my *Poems*:

Prayer

May He who is our stronghold in the storm,
Whose sunlight ever brightens life on earth,
Give succour to our King in every form.

Of peace may Denmark never suffer dearth.
May victory's wreath aloft hang with our flag,
Reflecting love and upright noble will.
When every realm is judged on that dread day,
May Denmark stand with those who did no ill.

I accompanied the King and Queen on a visit to the largest of the Halligen Islands, those grassy runes in the sea that tell of a sunken land. The mighty waves have transformed the mainland into islands, then torn them apart again and buried people and towns. Year after year, pieces are torn away, and there can be no doubt that in less than fifty years there will be nothing there but the sea. The Halligens are now flat islets of dark, sharp greensward grazed by a few flocks of sheep. When the sea rises they are driven up into the lofts of the houses; the waves wash over these small islands that lie miles away from the coast.

Biernatzky has given an admirable impression of this landscape in his stories. I read his accounts on the very spot, and they were so true to life that they were almost like parts of my own notes recording my observations there. It cannot be done better or more faithfully. The fact that I have portrayed the same place and countryside in *The Two Baronesses* must only be regarded as a sort of appendix, the same scenery reflected through the eyes of another poet.

We visited Oland, where we found a small village. The houses stand close together, as though they too are trying to huddle together in their need. They are all built on tiers of beams and have small windows like the cabins on a ship. There, in the small panelled parlour, the mothers and daughters sit alone by their spinning wheels for six months on end. There is always a small collection of books there, and I found some in Danish, some in German and some in Frisian. And as they sit there reading and working, the sea will often rise round the houses, which then lie there like wrecks thrown ashore by the waves. Sometimes during the night, a ship can drift on to the island, run aground and be stranded. In the great floods of 1825, houses and people were washed away. Day and night, they crouched half naked on the roofs until they gave way. No one from Föhr or the mainland could bring help to them. The churchyard is half washed away, and coffins and corpses stick out into the surf; it is a shocking sight. Yet the people of the Halligens love their little home, and they could not tolerate having to remain on the mainland. They become homesick and so they are forced to go back again.

I visited the island together with the royal party. The steamship on which we sailed remained well away from land, and there was nothing but a couple of small boats to take us ashore. I modestly waited so long that I almost failed to go with the last boat, and so I reached Oland just as the King was returning. "Are you only coming now?" he asked kindly. "There is no need to hurry. Take a good look, and let the boat wait. Go and look at the old churchyard, and then go into the house there and see a beautiful young woman."

All the men folk were at sea at the time, sailing either to Greenland or Holland, so only their wives and daughters were there to receive us. The sole man on the island had only recently risen from his sickbed. A gate of honour had been erected in front of the church, covered with flowers they had fetched from Föhr, but it was so small and low that we had to go round it. However, the good intentions were plain to see. They had cut down the only tree on the island, a rose-bush, in order to cover a muddy place over which the Queen had to walk; the good Queen was deeply moved by this.

The girls are beautiful, and their clothes are half Oriental. They consider, too, that they are of Greek lineage. Their faces are almost half covered by veils, and under the linen they wear a red Greek fez, around which their hair is bound in plaits.

I saw the churchyard and I saw the beautiful woman in her house, and when we reached the steamer again we went to dinner. When this was over we were sailing through an archipelago, and in the lovely sunset the deck was hastily cleared so we could dance. Both young and old danced. The servants went to and fro among the dancers with refreshments. Sailors stood by the paddlewheel casing taking soundings and monotonously shouting how many feet deep the water was. The moon rose, big and round, and the sandhills of Amrum seemed to rise up before us like a snow-covered Alpine chain.

I later visited these deserted sandhills. The King went over to hunt rabbits, which swarm over the island in their thousands – only a few years after the Adam and Eve of the family had arrived there, the sole survivors from a stranded ship.

Apart from me, the Prince of Noer was the only person who did not take part in the hunt. The two of us wandered about in the dunes, the appearance of which makes one think of the ash at the top of Vesuvius. Here, too, you sink in at every step. The stiff lyme-grass is not strong enough to hold the loose surface together. The sun burned down among the white dunes; it was like walking in the African desert. In the valleys between the dunes, there grew roses of some kind and the heather was in flower. Other parts were completely devoid of vegetation, and in the wet sand nearby the waves had left marks; as it left, the sea had written some strange hieroglyphs.

The Prince and I sat on one of the highest dunes; the tide was out. We gazed out across the North Sea which on account of the ebb tide was now over a mile further away, and the boats lay on the sand like dead fish waiting for the flood. A few sailors were walking about far out on the sand and looked like no more than black dots. Out where the sea itself still gently touched the white surface of the sand a long sandbank was visible. The account of the Danish waters, *Den danske Lods*, tells all about it. We could see the high log tower on it. This provides shelter for a shipwrecked sailor and holds a barrel of water and a basket containing bread and brandy so that he can keep himself alive for a few days in the midst of the swirling seas until it is possible for help to reach him.

There was now firm land between Amrum and Föhr, and people were driving across the wet sand from one island to the other. We could see a whole row of carriages that looked more than twice their real size as they stood outlined against the white sand and the blue horizon. They looked as though they were gliding through the air. But narrow lines of water, like the strings in a net, could be seen all around in the sand as though holding on to it, this sand which belonged to the sea and would soon be washed over by it.

It was a strange contrast, something almost fairy-like, to return from such a scene to a royal dinner, a beautiful court concert and the various small balls in the salons, and to stroll in the moonlight on the promenade, which was so full of visitors as to resemble a miniature boulevard.

Rantzau-Breitenburg knew what significance the sixth of September had for me; he knew that, as I have said, this very day was the twenty-fifth anniversary of my seeing Copenhagen for the first time. As I sat at the royal dinner table all my life passed through my mind, and I had to summon up all my strength not to burst into tears. There are moments of gratitude when it is as though we must press God to our hearts. How deeply I felt that I was nothing, and that all I had, everything, came from Him.

After dinner their Majesties congratulated me – to say graciously is to use too poor a word – they were so full of heartfelt interest. The King congratulated me on everything I had overcome and achieved. He asked me about the first time I appeared in public, and I told him about a few typical episodes from that time. During the course of the conversation he asked me if I did not have a fixed yearly income. I named the sum for him, 200 *Speciedaler*.

"That is not much," he exclaimed.

"But I do not need much," I answered. "And my works provide me with something, too."

The King asked a number of concerned questions about my life and activities. "You ought to have an easier life now than before," were his words, and he ended the conversation by saying, "If at any time I can be of any help to you in your literary activities, then come to me."

At the court concert that evening the King pursued this conversation further. My heart was deeply moved.

Some of those who had heard the King's words to me that day later reproached me for foolishly failing to make use of such a favourable opportunity. "The King put the very words into your mouth," they said. "He said you ought to ask him for a bit more to live on. He himself made it quite clear that what you have is too little and that you should have an easier, more comfortable life now."

"How could I," I said to them, "at the very moment I am treated as a guest here, if I may use that expression, at the very moment the King and Queen are so understanding and kind towards me, how could I then grasp a word spoken to me in kindness and make use of it? Perhaps I am not acting wisely, but I could not do otherwise. If the King thinks I need a little more than I receive, then he will give it to

301

me of his own accord."

The sixth of September was a day of rejoicing for me, and apart from my King, the German guests at the spa also showed their good will towards me. While I was sitting at the King's table in the hall at dinner, they drank the health of the Danish writer whose works they knew from their homes and whom they had now met personally. One of my compatriots rose and thanked them on my behalf. So much can easily spoil a man and make him vain – but no, you are not spoiled by it, and you do not become vain. Such occasions make you good and better; they purify your thoughts, and you feel the desire and the need to become worthy of it all.

At my farewell audience, the Queen presented me with a valuable ring in gracious memory of these days on the island of Föhr. The King once more spoke words full of good will, nobility and genuine interest. – I became devoted with all my heart to those two exalted beings.

The Duchess of Augustenburg, whom I saw and spoke to every day in the royal home, invited me in the most gracious and cordial manner to go home by way of Augustenburg and spend some days there. The King and Queen repeated this suggestion to me.

So from Föhr I went to Als, which must be one of the most beautiful islands in the Baltic. This little land is like a garden in flower. The rich fields of corn and clover are enclosed by hedges of hazel and wild roses. There are spreading orchards near the cottages and woods alternate with gentle slopes. Sometimes the open sea can be seen with the wooded hills of Angel, and sometimes the Little Belt, looking like a river. And from the beautiful castle the garden stretches right down to the winding fjord. I was given a most magnificent welcome, and found a delightful family life there. Only Danish was spoken, and indeed Danish correctly pronounced. No thought of the dark and evil days that were to come entered my head. I stayed there for a whole fortnight, spending my time in a rich succession of excursions in coaches and country walks; and there I began my novel *The Two Baronesses*. The evenings were delightful, being spent mostly listening to music. Kellermann spent several days there and played his gentle, cradling fantasies, romanescas and Alpine melodies. The Duchess's birthday was celebrated; the "*Liedertafel*" came in a torchlight procession and sang for her, and there was a ball and festivities in the castle. The Augustenburg Races, which were always held in connection with these celebrations and lasted for three days, had assembled a crowd of people both at the castle and in the town. Virtually the entire Holstein nobility was there. At dinner, the Duke rose and spoke of the importance of Danish literature at that time, pointing to the skill and healthy qualities to be found in it in contrast to the more recent German literature, and he took the opportunity to drink the health of the Danish poet who was present. – At Augustenborg on that occasion I saw nothing but friendly, cheerful people and a happy family life. I thought everything was so Danish, and it seemed that the spirit of peace lay over that beautiful place. And that was in the autumn of 1844. – How soon I was to see things in quite a different light!

XII

In the spring of 1844 I had completed the fairy tale drama *The Flower of Fortune*, in which I sought to show that it is not the immortal name of the artist, nor the splendour of the royal crown that makes a man happy.

Happiness is where one is satisfied with little, where one loves and is loved in return. The setting is very Danish, a sunny, idyllic life, in whose sky two images are reflected as in a dream – the life of the unfortunate poet Johannes Ewald and the tragic Prince Buris, whose story is told in the folk ballads.

In the name of truth and in honour of our time I wanted to show that the period which many poets only portray for us in an attractive light, was in fact dark and miserable.

I submitted my play to the management of the Royal Theatre. J. L. Heiberg had been appointed aesthetic judge there, and probably rightly so, as he was a man of importance. But as everyone knows, I was simply not in his favour at that time. After he had used *The Moorish Girl* and *The Mulatto* to torment the damned in Hell in his play *A Soul after Death* I had received a few more gibes in his literary reviews *Dansk Atlas* and *Intelligensblade* and when, to please one of the actors, I had followed his wishes and adapted *Agnete and the Merman* for performance during the summer, Heiberg characterised it as "transported straight from the bookshop to the stage; this work on which Gade has wasted his tender melodies," and then he went on to talk of the author's "usual lack of ideas of his own and any ability to give his characters a reasonable development and clarity to the *idea* he wishes to illustrate. All contrasts, which ought to have an organic relationship to each other, are stirred together into a thin gruel in which neither one nor the other is to be recognised."

I really believe that the fact that I was out of favour with this poet and arbiter of taste subjected my works to a sterner examination than otherwise would have been the case. I believed that he was driven by a personal dislike of me, and this caused me more pain than the news which I soon received that this play, too, had been rejected. It disturbed me to have such a strained relationship with a writer to whom I looked up in so many ways, and with whom I was convinced I had done everything possible to maintain a friendly relationship. Not in order to get my work accepted, but so as to achieve clarity over our relationship and to make a friendly approach to him I wrote to Heiberg, expressing myself openly and, I believe, cordially. I asked for a clear explanation of why he had rejected my play *The Flower of Fortune*, and I asked him to tell me whether he bore me a grudge. Immediately on receiving my letter he was kind enough to pay me a visit, and, as he did not find me at home, I repaid it the following day. He lived out in Frederiksberg, and I received an extremely kind welcome. The visit and our conversation must surely be classified as extraordinary, but it led to an explanation, and, as it turned out, a better understanding between us. He clearly explained to me his reasons for rejecting my play, and on his premises they were entirely justified. However, his opinions were very different from mine, and so we could not reach any agreement on this point. He declared that he bore me no grudge whatever, and that he acknowledged my talents. So I pointed out that he had previously made attacks on me in his *Intelligensblade* and that he denied me any "inventiveness", which I believed I had shown in my novels.

"But you have not read any of them," I said. "You have told me so yourself."

"Yes, that is true," he said. "So far I have not read them, but now I will do."

"And later," I continued, "in your *Dansk Atlas*, you mocked me in my *Bazaar* and talked about my enthusiasm for the lovely Dardanelles, but I state specifically in my book that the Dardanelles are not beautiful. On the contrary, it was the Bosphorus by which I was enchanted, but you seem not to have noticed that, or perhaps you have not read that either. You know you once told me that you do not read long books."

"Oh, it was the Bosphorus," he said with his peculiar smile. "Hm, I didn't remember that, and you see other people don't remember it either; and it was only because I wanted to make a dig at you."

The admission sounded so natural and so peculiar to him that

I had to smile, and then when I looked into his intelligent eyes and remembered all the beautiful things he had written, I could not be angry with him or bear him a grudge. Now the conversation became more animated and lively. He said a few kind words to me and ranked my fairy tales highly, and he asked me to visit him again, saying I would be welcome.

I have come increasingly to understand this writer's personality, and I believe he understands mine. We are utterly different from each other, but we both make for the same goal.

The last few years, during which I have won and achieved so many good things, have furthermore brought me recognition from this gifted genius. But to keep to the correct order of events: my fairy tale comedy was staged and received seven performances that season, and then it was put aside, at least for as long as those people ruled the theatre.

I often asked myself whether it was because my dramatic works were particularly weak or because I was the author of them that they were attacked and so harshly condemned at every opportunity. To discover this I could of course submit an anonymous work to the theatre and see what happened. But could I keep it a secret? No, everyone was agreed that I could not, and that opinion was of great benefit to me. During a short visit to Nysø I wrote *The King Dreams*. No one except Collin knew that I was the author. I heard that Heiberg, who just at that time was treating me severely in his *Intelligensblade*, was especially interested in this anonymous work, and indeed, as far as I remember, it was he who staged it. However, I must add that he later gave it high praise in a charming laudatory review in his *Intelligensblade* even, it appears, after he had begun to suspect that the play was by me, something which almost everyone else doubted.

A fresh attempt provided me with even greater joy and amusement as a result of the situations in which I found myself and the criticisms and judgements I heard. At the very same time as I was having problems getting *The Flower of Fortune* accepted for the stage I wrote and submitted *The New Lying-In Room*. At that time this little comedy was quite admirably played. Mrs. Heiberg was full of life and wit as Christine, and there was a freshness and charm about the whole production. As everyone knows it was a very great success indeed.

Here, too, it was Collin who had been initiated into the secret, as, in fact, had H. C. Ørsted as well. I read the play for him at home, and he was delighted with it, just as he was later delighted with the praise accorded to it, an acclaim that was actually far too great. No one had the slightest idea it was by me. As I was on my way home on the evening of the first performance one of our gifted young critics came up to me. He had been at the theatre and now expressed his delight at the little play in the most enthusiastic terms. I was deeply moved and was afraid of betraying myself either by a word or a look, and so I straight away said, "I know who the author is."

"Who?" he asked.

"It is you," I said. "You are so excited, and much of what you say betrays you. Don't go to anyone this evening and talk as you have talked to me or else you will give yourself away."

He flushed with surprise, put his hand to his heart and assured me that he was not the author. "I know what I know," I said with a smile, and now I excused myself and said I must be going. It was really impossible for me to stand it any longer, and so I was forced to say what I said; and he suspected nothing. A few days later I had to go to Adler, the director of the theatre, to hear what he had to say about *The Flower of Fortune*. "Well," he said, "it is a very poetical work, but it is not the sort of play we can derive much benefit from. You know, you ought to write a play like *The New Lying-In Room*. That is an excellent play, but of course it lies quite outside your talents; you are a lyrical poet and do not possess that man's humour."

"No, I'm afraid not," I replied, and now I, too, proceeded to praise *The New Lying-In Room*. The little play ran for years and continued to receive the same enthusiastic applause. No one knew who the author was. People guessed at Hostrup, and that did me no harm. In time, a few people did suggest me, too, but no one believed it. I myself have seen how many of those who suggested this were put right, and one of the arguments used was: "Andersen would not be able to keep the secret, because the play is such a success."

"No, I would most certainly not," I said, silently promising myself not to reveal that I was the author until years later, when it had had its run and no longer attracted the same interest as a little work of that sort can have when it is new. And I have kept my word.

Only last year did I admit it by including it in my collected works together with *The King Dreams*. Several characters from the novel *O.T.* and a few odd ones from *Only a Fiddler*, for instance Peter Wik, ought to have suggested I was the author. I thought that people would surely have been able to find some humour in my *Fairy Tales* themselves, but no one did. They only found it in *The New Lying-In Room*. This especially amused H. C. Ørsted, who, moreover, was the very first person to discover my talent for humour and point it out to me. He could see it in several of my early works, and in several of my personal characteristics. When, in 1830, I published my first collection of *Poems*, several of which had already been printed and spread around, I wanted to provide the whole collection with a motto, but I could not really find anything suitable, and so I made one up myself:

Vergessene Gedichte sind neue!

Jean Paul

Forgotten poems are new ones!

Jean Paul

And afterwards I had the amusement of seeing other writers, well-read men, quote the same line from Jean Paul. I knew where they had found it, and Ørsted knew, too.

At a time when I was really suffering bitterly from a criticism that was far too harsh and almost personal, so much so that I was often on the point of abandoning everything, there came moments when humour, if I may call it such, raised me up above the distress and misery into which I was sinking. I could see my own weaknesses and deficiencies, but at the same time I could also see how ridiculous and foolish this rather insipid querulousness and arrogance was. At such a moment I wrote a criticism of Hans Christian Andersen as an author. It was extremely sharp and ended with an exhortation to me to study and show gratitude towards those who had educated me. I had not only recapitulated the usual objections to my work, but added a few extra which I myself felt could probably be used by anyone really wanting to get at me. I took what I had written along with me to H. C. Ørsted's one afternoon. There were several people there. I told them that I had with me a copy of a harsh and very rude criticism of me, and I read it out. They could not understand why I wanted to make a copy of that, but they admitted that it was certainly cruel.

"So it is," said Ørsted. "People are too hard on Andersen. But on the other hand, as I sit here I do think that there is something in this piece, a couple of points that are really quite striking and show an understanding of you."

"Yes," I answered. "That's because I wrote it myself." And now there was general surprise, and everyone laughed and joked. Most of them were amazed that I could write that sort of thing.

"He is a true humorist," said H. C. Ørsted, and that was the first time I had realised I had any talent of that kind.

However much we travel the world, there is always one place that becomes a real home to us as we grow older. Even birds of passage have a special place to which they will always return. Apart from H. C. Ørsted's, Wulff's and Mrs. Læssøe's, that place for me was the Collins' home. That was and remains my real home in my native country. I have been treated as a son and almost grew up with their sons and daughters, so that I have become a member of the family. A more intimate sense of unity than in this house I have never known. One link in this chain broke, and just in that hour of loss I felt how much I had become a part of this place and that I was regarded as one of their children. If I were to name an example of a woman who completely sacrificed her own personality for her husband and her children, then I must name Collin's wife, the sister of Hornemann the botanist, and the widow of the philosopher Birckner.

During the final years of her life her hearing had become impeded, and before long she was unfortunate enough to become almost blind. She underwent an operation on her eyes. It was a success, so during the winter she was able to read a book again and was grateful and glad for that blessing. She felt a strange longing to see the first green shoots of spring, and she saw them in her little garden. One Sunday evening I left her well and happy. I was awakened during the night: Collin's servant had brought me a letter in which Collin wrote,

"My wife is extremely ill. All the children are gathered out here." I understood it, and hurried off. She was sleeping quietly, without pain and apparently without dreaming. It was the sleep of the good; it was death approaching quietly and kindly. On the third day she still lay in an uninterrupted, gentle sleep; then a pale shadow passed over her face, and she was dead.

> You closed your eyes in sleep to gather sight,
> In thought your life before you to parade
> We saw a gentle sleep, so child-like light,
> O death, 'tis light you are and never shade

I had never thought that it could be so painless and blissful to leave this world. My soul was filled with reverence, a certainty of God and eternity, which made this moment a great experience in my life. It was the first time I had stood by a deathbed as a grown man. The children and grandchildren were gathered there. At such a moment all around us is sacred. Her soul was love; she went to love, and to God.

At the end of July the monument to King Frederik the Sixth was to be unveiled near Skanderborg. At the request of the committee I had written a cantata to mark the occasion, and Hartmann had set it to music. The Student Choral Society was to perform it. The singers, the composer and the poet were, of course, officially invited to the occasion.

The lake where Christian the Fourth played at sailors as a child is situated near a series of beautiful bays among hills adorned with magnificent beech trees. A church has been built in the castle ruins, and in front of it stands the monument, one of Thorvaldsen's works. I would say the ceremony demonstrated a great measure of enthusiasm but little sense of order. People broke down the barriers so as to hear better; but they could not hear anything at all, for the wind carried the music and the singing away from the actual heart of the proceedings, and the voice of the speaker was lost in the air. What to me was the most beautiful moment came during the evening after the monument had been unveiled. Tarred grommets had been lit around it, and their unsteady light was reflected in the lake. Thousands of lights twinkled in the forest, and the sound of dance music came from the tents. Bonfires had been lit on all the hills around, in the woods and above them, and they shone in the night like red stars. The lake and the countryside were bathed in peace and a scent of summer such as the North possesses on the loveliest of summer nights. The shadows of everyone walking between the monument and the church floated along its red walls as though they were spirits taking part in the celebration.

A royal steamship had been provided to take the students home, and before our departure the citizens of Aarhus were kind and well-meaning enough to arrange a ball for us. We arrived in Aarhus in a long line of carriages, but we were earlier than they had expected us, and as a festive reception was being prepared for us we were asked to wait a little. We had to wait for a long time outside the town in burning sunshine all for the sake of the honour they were doing us, and when we arrived in the market square we were arranged in rows. Each of the good citizens took a student to give him a home and refreshments. Hartmann was among the first to receive an invitation. I was among those waiting my turn. A couple of citizens came along one after the other, bowed and asked my name, and when I told them they asked, "But you are not the poet?"

I said "Yes," and they bowed again and went away. They all went away; not a single one of them would have the poet, or perhaps I should believe what someone politely explained to me later, that they all wanted me to have such a good host, the best there was, that in the end I had none at all. I stood alone and deserted, just like a black whom no one in the slave-market will buy. I alone had to resort to a hotel in the good city of Aarhus.

We went home across the Kattegat to the accompaniment of music and singing, the temperament and courage of youth. Kullen raised its dark cliffs ahead of us, and the Danish coasts with their beech forests were fresh and green. It was a journey of song, a journey of friends for the composer and the poet.

I was going home to literary activity again.

At the beginning of the year my novel *The Improvisatore* had been translated into English by the well-known writer, Mary Howitt, and, as I have already said, it was received with great acclamation. *O.T.*

and *The Fiddler* followed under the joint title of *Life in Denmark*. I had become a widely read author in the great land of England. From there my works had found their way to America. Prior to this, the only translations of my works were in German and Swedish. Now, apart from those I have mentioned, there came a Dutch edition of the novels, and in St. Petersburg a Russian translation was published after the Swedish version of *The Improvisatore*. What I had never dared to think possible had now come about; my works seemed to be under some lucky star.

I cannot explain it otherwise. They flew out to other countries, and everywhere found friends and kinder judges than in my own native country, where they had after all been written and were read in the original language.

There is something at once uplifting and yet terrifying in seeing your thoughts go so far abroad and become part of people. It is almost frightening thus to belong to large numbers of people. What is noble and good becomes a blessing to us, but our errors and the evil sides of our natures also have their germs within us, and without our wishing it they take possession of our thoughts: Oh God, let me never write down a word which I cannot justify to Thee. A strange feeling, a mixture of joy and fear, fills me every time the genius of my good fortune carries my work to a foreign people.

To me travelling is like a refreshing bath for the spirit, rejuvenating me like Medea's potion. I feel the need to travel, but not to find material as one critic believed and said when reviewing *A Poet's Bazaar*, words that have been echoed by other people since. There is a wealth of material within me, and life is too short to exhaust this store. But a mental vivacity is necessary to give it a healthy and mature form on paper, and as I say, for me travelling is this refreshing bath from which I return strengthened and rejuvenated. By virtue of financial prudence and with the help of the income I had from my works I had been away several times during the last few years. Recognition, perhaps overestimation, but especially heartfelt interest, joy and happiness had come my way in full measure while I was abroad. Unfortunately I could not say the same of my native country, yet that is where one's heart truly belongs. Abroad I was bathed in sunshine, only a few beams of which reached me at home where people mainly had an eye for my faults, constantly took the liberty of trying to educate me and stunted many a sound growth in me. Indeed, they would have killed them all off completely had they not been tended by love from abroad, a love that gave me a sense of independence and finally through its expression, understanding and appreciation had surprised people at home and forced them to respect my poetical qualities.

My fate has been the same as that of the man who is an outcast and a scapegoat at home, but elsewhere a much loved and spoilt child; the thought raised my spirits a little, but at home the harshness and suffering were felt all the more.

But to return to my travels: the journey I am about to discuss is one of those on which God granted me the greatest joy and recognition.

I was again going to visit Italy. This was the third time. I wanted to become acquainted with the South in the warmer season of the year, too, and after visiting Italy it was my plan to go on to Spain and to come home by way of France.

I left Copenhagen at the end of October 1845. On previous occasions the thoughts I had had before leaving had been: "God, what will You allow to happen to me on this journey?" This time my thought was rather: "God, what will happen to my friends at home during the long time I am away?" And I felt anxious. A hearse can drive out of the gate many times in the course of a year, and who could know whose names might shine from the coffins?

We have a saying when we feel a cold shiver run down our backs, "Someone is walking on my grave."

The shiver is even colder when we think of the graves of our best friends.

I spent a few days with Count Moltke at Glorup. I was captivated by life out there in the country, and there is something beautiful and poetical about it in the late autumn. When the leaves have fallen from the trees but the sun is still shining on the green grass and the birds are singing, it is often possible to imagine it is a spring day; thus an elderly man will have moments in his autumn when his heart still dreams of spring.

I only spent a single day in my native town, old Odense. I felt more of a stranger there than in any of the great cities in Germany. As

313

a child I was lonely and so I have no childhood friends there. Most of the families I knew there are dead and quite fresh people walk about in the streets, which have also changed their appearance. My parents' poor graves are no longer to be found; others have been laid to rest there. Everything is changed.

I went one of my childhood walks, out to Maria Høi which had belonged to the Iversen family. They, too, had been scattered, and I saw unfamiliar faces at the windows. Many were the youthful thoughts I had exchanged there. One of the young girls, Henriette Hanck, who had listened to my first poems quietly and with shining eyes when I had come as a scholar from Slagelse and later as a student, was now even quieter in noisy Copenhagen where she had already presented the world with her first works, the novels, *Aunt Anna* and *An Authoress's Daughter.* Both of them had already appeared in Germany. The German publisher thought that a few words by me would be of benefit to them, and so I, a foreigner who had perhaps been given far too kind a reception in Germany, introduced the modest girl's writings into that country. I visited her childhood home beside the Odense Canal, the place where the first little group of people had paid me homage and given me pleasure. Now everything was strange to me, and I myself was a stranger. Nor should I ever see her again, for the following year when I arrived home from my travels I received the news that she had died in July (1846). She had grown up as a loving daughter to her parents. She was a deeply poetic nature, and in her I had lost a faithful childhood friend who had followed me in good times and bad with the interest and feelings of a sister.

The Duke of Augustenburg had celebrated his silver wedding, and I was among the several Danes he had honoured with an invitation. However there were certain signs of ferment and strain that made the ducal family rather ambivalent with regard to Danish interests. Although all my work was and remains free from politics, I preferred to avoid hearing possible words or comments that might offend my Danish sentiments. It was also more convenient for me on this journey to go to Gravensteen at a later date and thank them for their kind and gracious invitation rather than to go there, return and then set off again. So now, for the first time, I came to the beautifully situated hunting lodge of Gravensteen and was as before given a gracious and cordial welcome. I noticed nothing that could offend Danish feelings and sympathies, and the fact that one evening they sang *Schleswig-Holstein meerumschlungen* among other songs I took as being of no significance at all. Among themselves, the family spoke nothing but Danish, and they emphasised to me just how Danish the Duke was, and how unjust the people of Copenhagen were in their incorrect judgement of him. Least of all had I any idea then of when the storm would break.

I stayed there for a whole fortnight, and it was as though it was a preparation for me for all the happiness and blessings I was to find when I arrived in Germany. The countryside around the Flensburg Fjord is without doubt one of the most picturesque parts of Schleswig. There are great forests, hills almost like mountains and the ever-varying scenery of the winding fjord and the many quiet freshwater lakes. Even the autumn mists hanging over the landscape endowed it with something yet more picturesque, something foreign for the island-dweller, who only sees such a landscape on a smaller scale at home. It was beautiful outside, and there was a blissful feeling of comfort indoors. And there amidst the festivity and abundance in the ducal home, one of my fairy tales was created, one depicting deprivation and poverty, *The Little Match Girl.* The publisher of a Danish almanac sent me three different woodcuts and asked me to write a story for one of them. I chose the picture of the poor little girl sitting with the matches in her apron and a bundle of them in her hand.

With an invitation to return to Gravensteen and Augustenburg I left a place where I had enjoyed some happy days. Heavy days full of bloodshed were to pass over it. I have not had the heart to visit those parts again. – The last notes I heard there were those of "*Lotte ist todt*", played in youthful merriment by the Princesses of Augustenburg. The memory of that time and its reverberations is painful to me. – "*Todt! – todt!*" – But let us return to my journey.

A new friend, the gifted painter Speckter, was added to the list of the old ones I visited in Hamburg. He surprised me with his delightful, lively illustrations to my fairy tales. He already had a whole collection of them, and they have since been reproduced in one of the German editions as well as an English one. They are undoubtedly the most outstanding illustrations to the fairy tales. The same vivacious, natural freshness that is revealed in each of them, to make it into a miniature work of art, is also expressed in his personality. He was not married at that time, but the family home in which he lived, seemed to me to be a patriarchal one. There was a kindly old father and gifted sisters who loved their brother with all their hearts. Speckter seemed to be entirely taken with my fairy tales, and he was consequently devoted to me. Full of life and humour, he accompanied me one evening when I wanted to go to the theatre. It was scarcely more than a quarter of an hour before the start of the performance when we came to a splendid house.

"My dear friend," he said, "we really must pay a visit here first. The family that lives here is very wealthy, and they are friends of mine and of your fairy tales. The children would be delighted."

"But the performance will be starting in the theatre," I said.

"Just two minutes," he replied, and he dragged me into the house and told them who I was. The children crowded round me. "And now you must tell them a fairy tale – just one."

I told one and hurried off so as to reach the theatre in time.

"That was a curious visit," I said.

"Excellent," he cried. "Simply excellent. The children are full of Andersen and his fairy tales, and suddenly there he is in the midst of them; he tells one of them himself, and then, he is gone, vanished. It's like a real fairy tale for the little dears. They will always remember it."

In the Grand Duchy of Oldenburg my own little room awaited me, where everything had been arranged to make me feel comfortable and at home. I was expected by von Eisendecher, the minister whom I have already mentioned and his brilliant wife, whom I could count as being among the most devoted of all my friends abroad. I had promised to spend a fortnight with them, but my stay turned out to be a little longer. A house in which all the best and most intelligent people in the town meet is always a pleasant place to stay, and such a house I found here. There is a great deal of social life in the little town, and the theatre, where neither opera nor ballet was being performed at that time, was in those days at least one of the most excellent in Germany. Gall was the theatre manager; his ability is well known, and the collaboration given by Julius Mosen, the poet, was also of considerable benefit. Despite his physical ailments, Mosen, who in some ways resembles Alexandre Dumas – having rather African features with sparkling eyes – was lively and intelligent. We soon came to understand each other and met frequently. I owe it to him that I managed to see one of Germany's classical plays, Lessing's *Nathan der Weise*, in which the principal part was taken by Kaiser, who was as excellent and thoughtful at acting as he was at reading aloud.

Here, too, I again met Mayer, who has written such an interesting book on *Neapel und die Neapolitaner*. He made himself acquainted with the rest of my works that had been translated into German, and the following year in *Jahrbücher der Gegenwart* he wrote a detailed article on me entitled *Andersen und seine Werke*; this exudes affection and reveals deep reflection and an understanding of what he has read. The whole article might be said to be in praise of Danish literature and it was something of great importance for me. However, no one at home appears to have noticed it, although the publication was widely read. No reference has ever been made to the review, though I would think it could have been mentioned as remarkable if only for the comparison between Heine, who enjoyed the highest recognition, and me, who enjoyed it only to a very limited extent. So the fact that he named Heine and me together must have appeared remarkable to those who read the article; but that was the case:

Both poets are related to German Romanticism, but in Romanticism, in the wreath of which he is at his best interwoven with the most beautiful of flowers, Heine relapses into the prose of the witticism. Andersen, on the other hand, incorporates the substantial contents which, in contrast to self-centred Romanticism, the most recent school of writing demands, into both kinds of writing, which he mainly pursues in the novel and the fairy tale, without, however, adopting the unhealthy features in this school: the philosophical construction and the political purpose. He knows nothing of Hegel, and nor does he want to know anything of him, because grey theory is contrary to his child-like, genuine poet's nature.

317

August Pott, the conductor, and my fellow countryman Jerndorff, the painter, were among my earlier friends, and in addition I made fresh acquaintances every day. Through Herr von Eisendecher, the minister in whose circle I had my home, all houses were thrown open to me. The Grand Duke received me graciously and with interest, and the very day after my arrival I was invited to a court concert. I later received several invitations to dinner.

In von Eisendecher's home and that of Beaulieu, the Privy Councillor, I had on a few occasions read my fairy tales in German, and as a result of my putting my Danish soul into the expression, and because my soft pronunciation when reading the fairy tale perhaps helped to stress their simplicity, which the translator has at least tried to recapture, people were keen to hear me myself read them. For the Grand Duke and a select gathering which, however, was the largest to which I had yet read aloud, I read my fairy tales in a foreign language, just as I had done once before at the Court in Weimar; and after that I was bold enough to do so more often in the homes of my friends in Germany, and I believe they were always interested in hearing me personally read these little stories. A foreign accent can best be accepted in readings of fairy tales; the foreign element here borders on the childlike, giving the work the atmosphere that is natural to it. Everywhere I was able to watch the most important men and the most intelligent women following me with interest.

The critic in the *Jahrbücher der Gegenwart* says:

Andersen has been accused of vanity because he never tires of repeatedly reading the same fairy tales and talking about his own works. But good-natured as he is, he cannot on the other hand refuse the repeated requests that are made everywhere to him even at the risk of great weariness. To tell or read a fairy tale is of course such a small thing and so easy. Just as a charming song can be sung over and over again, a fairy tale will always be read time and time again, and if a start is made on one, a couple more will easily follow. On the other hand, other poets are also fond of hearing themselves reading, especially if, like Andersen, they read well and meet with approval. Thick manuscripts, however, do not so easily find such a willing public. Other writers, too, are fond of talking about their works, and, showing little sense for anything that is outside their circle, they tend in their conversation to return to themselves. They are merely smarter and are better able to avoid the *appearance* of vanity.

Winter had come already, and I was still in Oldenburg. The meadows were under water and formed great lakes around the town. They were covered with thick ice, and skaters flew across them. It was as though I had taken root in the charming town of Oldenburg where there were so many hospitable friends. Days and evenings passed in an intelligent social life, with readings, music, plays and conversations. I must include in these pages a little anecdote which I had not heard before and which as far as I know has not been written down before, concerning the story of the unfortunate Danish queen, Caroline Mathilda. An elderly lady in the court of the Grand Duke told me that her father had been one of the ambassadors who had accompanied Caroline Mathilda, Christian the Seventh's Queen, from England. On board the ship they ran into a storm on the North Sea. The Danish and English flags, which were flying united on the ship, were torn from the flagpole by a gust of wind and separated into two individual flags. It seemed to be a bad omen, and Caroline Mathilda's eyes filled with tears; but then she quickly took hold of the separated pieces, found a needle and thread and sat down on the deck. And while the sea covered her with spray she personally sewed the flags together and made them into one again.

I was touched by a feature of Mosen's little son. He had heard me read a fairy tale, and so the day before my departure, when I came to take leave and his mother told him to shake hands with me, adding, "It might be a long, long time before you see him again," the little boy burst into tears. That evening when Mosen came over to me in the theatre, he said, "Little Erik has two tin soldiers, and he has sent one of them for you to take with you on your journey."

And it accompanied me all the way. I thought of Erik's tin soldier in the story of *The Old House*. In the front of his *Johan of Austria*, Mosen wrote for me:

Kam ein Vogel einst herüber,
Von der Nordsee wüsten Strand,
Singend zog er mir vorüber,
Märchen singend durch das Land;
Fahre wohl! bring deine Lieder
Und dein Herz den Freunden wieder.

Once a bird came across
From the North Sea's desert shore,
Singing it flew past me,
Across the land, singing fairy tales;
Fare thee well, take your songs
And thy heart back to your friends.

My departure could be postponed no longer. Christmas was approaching, and this year I wished to spend it in Berlin. But what is distance nowadays – the steam train went from Hannover to Berlin in a single day! I had to leave Oldenburg and all those people there who were so dear to me.

As the author of *The Improvisatore* I had been invited on the last occasion when I was in Berlin to the "Italian Club", where only those who had been to Italy were admitted. There I saw Rauch for the first time; with his powerful, masculine figure and his silvery hair he resembles Thorvaldsen to some extent. However, on that occasion I was not introduced to him, and I did not dare make myself known. Nor did I speak to him in his studio, which I visited like other foreigners.

However, when he visited Copenhagen in the company of Ignatz von Olfers, the director of the museum, we met at the home of the Prussian ambassador, and became acquainted with each other. So on this occasion in Berlin I immediately went to visit him. Since our meeting he had read most of my works, and was especially enthusiastic about my fairy tales. He embraced me and expressed far too much praise for me as a writer, although I believe he meant it. Such a moment of esteem, or exaggerated esteem, by a genius can erase many dark shadows from our minds.

It was from Rauch that I received my first welcome in Berlin, and he told me what a large circle of friends I had in the Prussian capital. I soon discovered this to be true. It was those who were blessed with the noblest minds as well as those who were in the highest rank of artists and scholars who came to greet me: Alexander Humboldt, Count Radziwill, Savigny and many other unforgettable figures. The last time I had been there I had sought out the brothers Grimm, but our acquaintance on that occasion had not progressed very far. I had no letter of introduction with me, as everyone told me – and I myself believed – that if anyone in Berlin had heard of me it must be the brothers Grimm. I went out to their home, and a maid asked me which of the two I wished to speak to.

"The one who has written most," I said, since at that time I was ignorant of which of them had been the more active in the publication of the popular fairy tales.

"Jacob is the more learned," said the maid.

"Very well, then take me to him."

I entered the drawing room, and Jacob Grimm, with his wise and characteristic features, stood before me.

"I have come to you without any letter of recommendation, since I hope my name is not entirely unknown to you."

"Who are you?" he asked. I told him, and Jacob Grimm said in a rather embarrassed voice, "I don't know that I have ever heard your name. What have you written?"

Now it was my turn to be embarrassed; and I named my fairy tales.

"I don't know them," he said. "But tell me the titles of some of your other works, and then I shall probably recognise them."

I mentioned *The Improvisatore* and a few other books I had written. He shook his head. I felt extremely uncomfortable. "What must you think of me," I began, "coming to visit you as I do, a complete stranger, and listing what I have written in this way! But you *must* know me. I know of a Danish collection of fairy tales of all nations, edited by Molbech and dedicated to you, and there at least you will find one of my tales."

Good-humoured, but embarrassed, as I was myself, he said, "Hm, I have not read that book. But I am pleased to meet you; let me introduce you to my brother Wilhelm."

"No, thank you," I said, wishing for nothing more than to get away. I had had a big enough fiasco with the first of the brothers and had no desire to experience the same with the other. I shook hands with him and hurried away. In Copenhagen a few weeks later, just as I was packing my trunk to leave for the provinces, Jacob Grimm, in travelling attire, entered my room. He had come to Copenhagen and had just left the boat, and as he was passing my apartment on the way to his hotel he had come up to visit me, for "Now I know you," he said. He shook hands with me warmly, and looked at me kindly with his intelligent eyes. The porter who was to fetch my luggage entered at that moment. I had only a few minutes, and so our meeting in Copenhagen was just as brief as in Berlin. However, we knew each other now; we were old acquaintances who were meeting again.

Jacob Grimm is one of those personalities one cannot but love and become attached to. Now I came to know and cherish his brother, too. One evening I read one of my fairy tales at the home of Countess Bismarck-Bohlen. There was one person in the group who listened with obvious attention, and then he made a number of discerning and interesting comments on it. It was Wilhelm Grimm.

"I think I would have known you if you had come to see me the last time you were here," he said.

I later met these two charming and gifted brothers almost every day; the circles in which I moved seemed also to be theirs, and it was a joy and a delight to me that they listened to my fairy tales and that they followed me with interest, these two whose names will always be known as long as the *Children's and Household Tales* are read.

During my previous stay in Berlin I had been disheartened to discover that Grimm had never heard of me, and so when someone at that time remarked how well known I was in Berlin and how well I had been received there, I shook my head and expressed my doubts with the words, "Grimm has never heard of me."

But now it was different.

Tieck was ill, and I was told that he could receive no visitors, but when he saw my card he immediately sent me a letter and arranged a little dinner in my honour. His brother the sculptor, Raumer the historian, and Steffen's widow and daughter were the only ones there apart from me. It was the last time we were together; a few happy and lively hours flew past. I shall never forget the music there was in his voice, and the warmth radiating from his intelligent eyes, was not lessened with age, but rather increased by it.

Even if Tieck had written nothing else, *The Elves*, one of the most beautiful fairy tales written in our day, is sufficient to crown his name with immortality.

As a teller of fairy tales I had great respect for him, the older man, the master, the man who many years before had been the first German poet to embrace me, as though it were a consecration and a sign that we were to tread the same path.

I had to visit all my older friends, and the number of new ones increased each day. Invitations followed. Real physical strength is needed to deal with so much good will. I stayed in Berlin about three weeks, and time seemed to pass more quickly each day; but I overstrained myself, and at last I was physically and mentally tired. I could only expect to find peace and rest again in the railway train, speeding through the countryside.

And yet, amidst all this hustle and bustle, in all this profusion of kindness and desire to make my stay there a pleasant one there was *one* evening on which I had nothing to do, one evening where I suddenly felt loneliness pressing on me. That was Christmas Eve, the very evening that in all its festive splendour I look at through the eyes of a child, the evening when it is a matter of course that I have a Christmas tree to look at, when I take delight in the children's joy and when I see the grown-ups become children again.

That very evening, when, as I was later told by the many people who showed me hospitality and were always pleased to see me, everyone thought I would long ago have accepted an invitation to visit the home where I most wanted to be, I sat quite alone in my room in the hotel, thinking of home and Copenhagen. Jenny Lind was in Berlin. As he had told me earlier, Meyerbeer had arranged for her to appear there, and she was everywhere extolled and admired. Everyone sang her praises, not only to the praises of the artist, but of the woman, too. The two qualities together awoke such admiration and enthusiasm that the theatre was really and truly besieged when she was to sing.

In all the towns and places I visited people talked about her, but this was not necessary, for she was fixed deeply in my thoughts, and it had long been my fondest dream to spend Christmas Eve together with her. I was convinced that if I was in Berlin at that time, this evening would be spent in her company. I was so sure of this that I refused invitations from my friends in Berlin, and then when the evening arrived, Jenny Lind had not invited me and I sat quite alone in my hotel. I felt terribly forsaken and opened my window to look at the starry sky that was my Christmas tree. My thoughts were so gentle and tender. Other people would perhaps call me sentimental; they know the expression, but I know the feeling. The next morning I was angry, childishly angry at the way in which my Christmas Eve had been wasted, and I told Jenny Lind in what a sad way I had spent it.

"I thought you were spending it in the company of princes and princesses," she said.

Then I told her that I had declined all invitations so as to be together with her, and that I had been looking forward to that for a long, long time, indeed that that was why I had decided to spend Christmas in Berlin.

"What a child you are!" she said with a smile, and stroked my forehead with her hand; she laughed at me and said, "It never occurred to me, and besides I was invited out; but we must have Christmas Eve all over again. Now I'll light the tree for the child. On New Year's Eve there shall be a Christmas tree up in my room."

And on the very last evening of the year, for me alone, a little tree was decorated and lit up in her room. Jenny Lind, her lady companion and I were the only people present. We three children from the North were gathered together on the Eve of Saint Sylvester. I was the child for whom the Christmas tree had been illuminated; we were like children pretending that guests were coming. We had all the different courses just like at a large party, tea, ice cream, and then supper. Jenny Lind sang a great aria and then a couple of Swedish songs. It was quite a festive evening, and I was given *all* the presents from the Christmas tree. Our quiet party that evening was rumoured and reported in the newspapers. The two children of the North, Jenny Lind and Andersen, both beneath the Christmas tree, was just about all that was said.

I was told a little story, something that contributed to her triumph. One morning I looked out of my window and saw a man standing in *Unter den Linden*. He was rather poorly dressed, and took a comb from his pocket, straightened his hair, arranged his cravat and brushed his coat with his hand. I know that self-conscious poverty which feels oppressed by its poor clothes, and my interest was immediately awakened in him. A moment later someone knocked on my door, and the same man came into my room; he was the nature poet, Gottfried Worch, who is only a poor tailor but has a truly poetical temperament. Rellstab, Kletke and other authors in Berlin had spoken of him in the newspapers with considerable respect and said that there was something genuine and deeply religious about his poems. He had read that I was in Berlin and so had come to visit me. We sat together on the sofa, and he radiated such charm and frugality and such unspoiled goodness that I was sorry I was not rich enough to be able to do something for him. I could see that despite his frugality he was in need. He was in need of money, but I was ashamed to offer him what little I could give him. It had at least to come in some more acceptable form. I asked him if I might invite him to go and listen to Jenny Lind.

"I have heard her," he said with a smile. "I had no money to buy a ticket of course, but I went to the leading supernumerary and asked whether I could be a supernumerary one evening in *Norma*, and I was taken on. I was dressed as a Roman soldier with a sword at my side, and I went on the stage where I could hear her better than anyone else. I stood close by her. Oh, how she sang, and how she acted! I couldn't help weeping, but that was not allowed. The leading supernumerary forbade it. He was angry and refused to let me take part again, for you are not allowed to weep on the stage."

Jenny Lind introduced me to Madame Birch-Pfeiffer. "She has taught me German," she said. "She is like a kind mother to me. You must make her acquaintance." I looked forward to meeting her. We took a cab in the street. There are perhaps those who will say, "The world-famous Jenny Lind in a cab!" just as was once said in Copenhagen when someone saw her in a cab together with an elderly friend. "It is not fitting for Jenny Lind to take a cab; you must act in accordance with your status." It is strange how often the idea of what is fitting asserts itself. Such petty concerns of everyday life never occur to truly great characters.

Once at Nysø when I intended to go into town by stagecoach, Thorvaldsen said, "I am coming with you." And there was immediately someone who said that it was not fitting for Thorvaldsen to travel by stagecoach."

"But Andersen is going by it," he said quite innocently. "That is quite another matter," I had to explain to him: people would be shocked to see Thorvaldsen in a stagecoach. It had already shocked people to see Jenny Lind in a cab, but now, in Berlin, she went in one with me. We stopped it in the street and drove off to Madame Birch-Pfeiffer's home. I knew how talented an actress this artist was and was aware that she possessed an ability almost as great as that of Scribe to give dramatic form to something that had originally been fashioned as a novel. I knew how harshly the critics had almost always treated this extremely gifted woman, and at first when I saw her it seemed to me as though this, quite naturally, had added some bitterness to her smile. I could sense it in the way in which she greeted me: "I have not read your books yet, but I know they always receive an extremely favourable criticism – something of which *I* do not have the pleasure."

"He is like a kind brother to me," said Jenny Lind, and she put my hand in her friend's. Madame Birch-Pfeiffer gave me a sincere and cordial welcome, and was full of life and wit. The next time I visited her I found her in the middle of *The Improvisatore*, and I felt that I had found yet another friend.

During my stay in Berlin I had the pleasure of being received several times by the Princess of Prussia, the sister of the present Grand Duke of Weimar. She had a comfortable home which at the same time was like a fairytale palace; the flowering winter gardens with the spring splashing amidst the moss in front of the statue's foot led to the rooms where the friendly children and the intelligent and cordial princess received me. One morning I read a few of my fairy tales for her; her royal husband listened, too, and Prince Pückler-Muskau, the author of *Semilasso*, was also present.

On my departure the Princess presented me with a beautiful album bound in velvet, on the first page of which there is a picture of the wing of the palace where I had stayed and in which she has written her name to commemorate my visit. It is not only what is given to us that is important, but its value is enhanced by the way in which it is given.

Immediately on my arrival in Berlin I had the honour of being invited to dinner at the royal palace. I was given a seat next to Humboldt, whom I knew best and of whom I became still fonder not merely on account of his intellectual standing and his charming, straightforward manner, but because of his infinite goodwill towards me. The King gave me a most gracious reception, and told me that during his stay in Copenhagen he had enquired after me and heard that I was abroad. He expressed great interest in my novel *Only a Fiddler*, and added that after reading that book he always thought of poor Christian when he saw a stork. The episode of the stork's death had moved him deeply. The Queen, too, spoke in the same gentle, gracious tone.

I was later fortunate enough to be invited one evening to the palace in Potsdam, an evening that was rich in experiences and quite unforgettable to me. Apart from the two ladies-in-waiting and chamberlains who were in attendance there, the only people present were the King and Queen, Humboldt and I. I was given a seat at the same little table as they, the very place, the Queen told me, in which Oehlenschläger had sat and read his tragedy *Dina* to them. I read four fairy tales: *The Fir Tree*, *The Ugly Duckling*, *The Top and the Ball*, and *The Swineherd*. The King was full of life and extremely interested, and he spoke wisely and intelligently. He told me, too, how beautiful he had found the Danish forest landscape and how excellent the performance had been of Holberg's play *The Political Tinker* in Copenhagen. There was such a kind and friendly atmosphere in the royal drawing-room, and gentle eyes were turned towards me. I felt that people were kindly disposed to me, indeed, far too kindly.

When I reached my own apartment late at night my thoughts were so filled with the evening's events, and my mind so moved that I could not sleep. Everything seemed to me to be so like a fairy tale. The clock in the tower chimed the hour throughout the night, and the ethereal music was absorbed into my thoughts. When we are happy we become pious and good.

The evening before my departure I was given yet another sign of how gracious and kind to me the King of Prussia was. I was decorated with the Order of the Red Eagle, Third Class. Such an honour delights anyone who receives it, and I will admit that it made me feel happy. I saw in it a clear sign of how kind the noble and enlightened King wished to be towards me. My heart was full of gratitude. It was the first decoration to be conferred on me, and I received it on the sixth of January, the very birthday of Collin, my benefactor. Now that day is doubly significant to me. I was happier than I could express, and I prayed that God would gladden the royal heart which had determined to give me such joy as this.

My last evening was spent together with a group of mainly young men and women. They drank to me, and someone recited a poem, *Der Märchenkönig*. I went home late, only to leave by train early the next morning. I was to meet Jenny Lind again in Weimar.

In my German autobiography, *Das Märchen meines Lebens*, which I wrote and completed during this journey, and where the impressions were accordingly fresh and my feelings still vibrant with excitement, this is what I say on my departure from Berlin; I must repeat the actual words: "I have written a good deal about the countless tokens of graciousness and kindness which I received in Berlin, and I feel like a man who receives great sums of money for some purpose from a large assembly. He feels the need to account for what he has received, to tell people what he has been given. May God give me the strength to do this now that I have received encouragement in such abundance."

After a twenty-four-hour journey I was at the home of the noble Hereditary Grand Duke in Weimar. I have no words to describe the infinite kindness which I was shown every day of my stay in the Grand Ducal home in Weimar, but my heart is overflowing with devotion. At the court feasts and in the charming family life there I learned to appreciate their most gracious and kind intentions towards me. It was like a Sunday that lasted a whole month. Beaulieu saw to my comfort with the heart of a brother; and I shall never forget the quiet evenings at his home, where friend conversed with friend. Both Schober and the erudite, gifted Schöll joined this circle. The alert and dignified old Frau von Schwendler, who had been a faithful friend of Jean Paul since his youth, greeted me with understanding, heartfelt maternal interest and the delightful words that I reminded her of that great poet. She told me many things about him that were quite new and unknown to me. Jean Paul, or, to give him his real name, Friedrich Richter, was so poor during his youth that in order to buy the paper on which to write his first work he had to earn money by transcribing copies of the local newspaper, the *Dorfzeitung*, for the peasants in the village where he lived. She said it was the poet, Gleim, who was the first person to notice him, and he wrote to her about this gifted young man whom he had invited to his home and to whom he had sent 500 *Thaler*, which he thought he probably needed.

Frau von Schwendler had lived here in Weimar in its days of glory. She used to spend the evenings at Court in the company of Wieland, Herder and Musäus. She had a vast store of anecdotes to tell about them and about the relationship between Goethe and Schiller. She made me a present of one of Jean Paul's letters to her, adding the words:

> In view of the direction mainly taken by modern literature in Germany, I hardly expected on my way through life to meet another such beautiful intellectual relationship as that indisputably existing between Mr Andersen and Jean Paul.

Jenny Lind came to Weimar; I heard her at a Court recital and in the theatre. Together with her I visited the places that have been made sacred to us by Goethe and Schiller. We stood by their sarcophagi, to which Chancellor Müller had taken us. The Austrian poet, Rollett, who met us here for the first time later, to mark the occasion, wrote a beautiful poem, which has become a visible sign to me of that hour and that place. We place beautiful flowers of which we are fond in books, and as such I will include his verse here.

> *Mährchenrose, die Du oftmal*
> *mich entzückt mit süssem Duft,*
> *Sah Dich ranken um die Särge*
> *in der Dichterfürstengruft.*

Und mit Dir an jedem Sarge
in der totenstillen Hall,
Sah ich eine schmerzentzückte
träumerische Nachtigall.
Und ich freute mich im Stillen,
war in tiefster Brust entzückt,
Dass die dunklen Dichtersärge
spät noch solcher Zauber schmückt.
Und das Düften deiner Rose
wogte durch die Totenhall
Mit der Wehmuth der, in Trauer,
stummgewordnen Nachtigall.

Weimar am 29 Jan 1846

Fairy rose, who so often
Delighted me with your sweet fragrance,
I saw you twined round the coffins
In the vault of the princes among poets.
Together with you by that coffin
In the deathly hush of the chamber
I saw a wistful nightingale
In rapturous pain.
And I felt a secret joy,
Rapture deep within my breast,
That such magic still adorns
The poets' dark coffins after all these years.
And the fragrance of your rose
Wafted through the burial chamber
With the melancholy of the
Nightingale, mute with mourning.

Weimar on 29 Jan 1846

One evening, at a gathering at the home of the brilliant Froriep, I met
Berthold Auerbach, the author of *Schwarzwälder Dorfgeschichten*,
for the first time. He happened just then to be staying at Weimar. I

had been completely carried away by his *Dorfgeschichten*, and I regard them as the most poetical, the soundest and the happiest work produced by modern German literature. His personality made the same joyful impression on me. There is something so open, so wise and frank in Auerbach's appearance. I am almost tempted to say that he looks like a "*Dorfgeschichte*" himself, healthy in body and soul, and honesty itself radiates from his eyes. We soon became friends. He was open and forthright, and he suggested that we should address each other informally, then adding with a smile, "But you know, I am a Jew."

I laughed, as though learning that he belonged to the oldest race, one of the most interesting, could make any difference.

My departure from Weimar was put off time and time again, and it became almost difficult for me to tear myself away. After the birthday of the Grand Duke and after being present at all the festivities to which I had most graciously been invited, I left. I had to be, and wanted to be, in Rome before Easter. Early in the morning I saw the Hereditary Grand Duke once more, and with a heart overflowing with emotion I bade him farewell. I shall never forget the elevated position his birth gives him in the world, but one thing I dare say, just as the poorest man can say of a prince: I love him as I love those who are dearest to my heart. May God bless him and give him joy in his noble strivings. A noble heart beats behind the princely star.

Beaulieu went with me as far as Jena, and there I found a hospitable home containing cherished memories from the time of Goethe. I spent a few days with Frommann, the publisher, whose sparkling, witty sister had shown much interest in me during my stay in Berlin. I also saw the Hereditary Grand Duke once more; he came to Jena. We met at the home of Schiller's sister-in-law, Frau von Wolzogen, the brilliant author of the novel, *Agnes von Lilien*, and there we took leave of each other.

Professor Michelsen from Holstein gathered a large number of friends of my Muse at his home one festive evening, and in a beautiful and heartfelt toast to me he spoke of the importance of Danish literature at that time and noted the healthy, natural elements that were characteristic of it. Among those guests I was especially interested in the famous theologian, Professor Hase, the author of

331

The Life of Jesus and *The History of the Church*. On hearing me read some of my fairy tales a few evenings before he had taken a great liking to me. What he said about my fairy tales in a moment of warm and heartfelt interest bears witness to this; he wrote down the following on a sheet of paper by which I was to remember him:

> What Schelling – not the man living today in Berlin, but he who lives as an immortal hero in the realm of the spirit – once said, that: "Nature is visible spirit, spirit invisible nature" again became quite obvious to me yesterday evening as a result of your fairy tales. How on the one hand they listen so intently to the secrets of nature, understand the language of birds and know the feelings of a fir tree or a daisy so that everything seems to be there for its own sake and we take part along with our children in joy and sorrow. Yet on the other hand, everything is only the image of the spirit, and the human heart in its infinity trembles and beats through it all. May this fountain from the poet's heart that God has given you continue to gush forth so invigoratingly for a time yet, and may these fairy tales become popular stories in the memories of the Germanic peoples.

What I must strive for as a writer of fairy tales is contained in these last lines. It was also Hase and the gifted improvisatore, Professor Wolff of Jena, who together were largely responsible for ensuring that a German edition of my works' should provide me with an income. They were surprised to hear that I had so far not received any fee at all for the many translations of my works that already existed in Germany. I had been pleased that my books had found translators and readers, and I felt indebted to the publisher when he sent me a few copies. Hase and Wolff said that I should and must ensure that the position which my works already occupied in Germany provided me with an income, and they showed they were willing to help me in this.

And so, on my arrival in Leipzig, I received an offer from Berlin, while in Leipzig itself both Brockhaus and Härtel and then my compatriot, Lorck, all offered to be my publishers, and they proposed to give me a couple of hundred *Thaler* once and for all in recompense for the works which had already appeared. I gave the rights to my compatriot, and we have both derived profit and pleasure from the undertaking. This was arranged during my stay in Leipzig. So my travels were interrupted by a few hours devoted to business.

The city of publishers, too, presented me with a fee, but it also gave me more than this, for once more I met the Brockhaus family and spent some happy hours at the home of the magnificent and gifted Mendelssohn. I heard him play again and again, and it seemed to me that his soulful eyes looked into my very soul. Few men showed more obvious signs of an inner fire than Mendelssohn. A gentle and friendly wife and lovely children made his exquisite and well-arranged house a good and blessed place to be. It amused him to joke with me about *the stork* and the numerous occasions on which it appears in my work. He had grown to like it in *Only a Fiddler* and it delighted him in the fairy tales, and so he would often nod across the table to me in jest and say, "Tell us a tale about the stork."

"Write me a song about the stork."

And his wise, sparkling eyes twinkled mischievously and with child-like gaiety. When my journey was ended we met again, but then no more on earth. His wife, too, has followed him, and his beautiful children, true models for Raphael's cherubs in the Dresden Madonna, are scattered all over the world.

Auerbach, whom I met here again, introduced me into several pleasant circles. I met the composer Kalliwoda together with my gifted fellow-countryman Gade, Mendelssohn's favourite, who was treated almost as the baby of the family all over Leipzig.

Immediately upon my arrival in Dresden I hurried to visit the charming old Baroness Decken, who always shared my happiness with a heart like that of a mother. I received a joyous and heartfelt welcome. A no less sincere one came from Dahl, the painter, and I saw my Roman friend again, the poet of words and colours, Reinick, who has now also joined my departed friends. *Schwanenlied* was his last song. I met the gifted Bendemann, whose *Jews in Mourning* is a true poem in colour. The words of the Psalm, "By the rivers of Babylon, there we sat down, yea, we wept," are here brought to life before our eyes, worthy of a place throughout the ages.

Grahl, the painter, made a portrait of me, one of the most beautifully conceived, and it has been reproduced as a steel engraving at the front of the *Gesammt-Ausgabe*.

I missed one of my older friends Brunnow, the poet, the author of *The Troubadour*, who was now resting in his grave. The last time I was there, he had given me a vivacious and sincere welcome in a sitting room decorated with beautiful flowers, which were now planted on his grave. It gives one a strange feeling to meet on just a single occasion on the journey through life, to understand each other, become fond of each other, and then part for all time, until the journey is ended for both.

I spent what to me was an extremely interesting evening together with the royal family who most graciously received me. There, too, a most happy family life seemed to prevail. A host of attractive children, all of them Prince Johan's, were present. The youngest of the princesses, a little girl who knew I had written the story about *The Fir Tree* began her conversation by confiding in me: "We had a fir tree last Christmas, too, and it stood here in this room." When she was being taken to bed, earlier than the other children, and had said good night to her mother and father and the King and Queen, she turned round once more in the half-closed door where I could see her. She nodded to me in such a friendly manner as though I were an old friend; then she kissed her fingers and gave me a last wave; to her I was "*der Märchenprinz*".

I read a few of my fairy tales, and one of them, *Holger the Dane* led the conversation on to the wealth of legends the North possesses. I told a few of them and stressed the remarkable character of the beautiful Danish countryside. I told how the beech forests virtually burst into leaf within the space of a night and then stood resplendent in their glorious freshness. I told of the sweet-smelling fields of clover with their warriors' barrows, and of the *menhirs* by the open sea. No more than in the others did I feel oppressed by the ceremonial in this royal palace. Gentle, friendly eyes turned to me.

My last afternoon in Dresden was spent at the home of Könneritz, the Minister of Justice, where I was given a most friendly welcome. A few hours later I was in the coach by which I was to travel since there was still no railway from Dresden to Prague. A large number of friends came to see me off, and Frau Serre brought me some lovely flowers; "You have a large family here, Sir," said the guard as we rolled off. My thoughts were full of all those many people who had made my stay so overflowing and so happy. The sun was shining, and the weather was warm; spring was about me, and spring was in my heart.

I knew no one in Prague, but a letter from Dr. Carus in Dresden ensured hospitality for me at the home of Count Thun. The Hereditary Grand Duke of Weimar had given me a letter to Archduke Stephen, in whom I found an intelligent and warm-hearted man. I visited Hradschin and Wallenstein's palace, but these magnificent buildings were all spoiled by the Jewish quarter. It was dreadful. The whole place was swarming with women, old men and children, playing, shouting and bartering, and at every step the street became narrower. The ancient synagogue, shaped like the Temple at Jerusalem, lies squeezed in between the houses. Time has raised a layer of earth against its walls. I had to go down a few steps to get inside, and there the ceiling, windows and walls were blackened with smoke. I was met by a stench of onions and evil smells, so that I had to make my escape into an open square. This was the cemetery which rests on generations of the dead; stone after stone with Hebrew inscriptions stands and lies chaotically here beneath a forest of pygmean elder trees, sickly and almost devoid of sap in their branches. Spiders' webs hung like the ragged remains of mourning crape between the dead, black graves.

My departure from Prague took place just at an interesting moment. The soldiers who had been stationed there for a number of years were leaving by rail for Poland, where unrest had broken out. The entire city seemed to be on its feet to go and say good-bye to their military friends. The street leading to the station was full of people, and it was only with difficulty we could make progress. Several thousand soldiers were to leave, and at last the train started. It was a magnificent sight to see this mass of people filling the whole mountain side, which seemed to be covered with a carpet of rich colours – though the weaving consisted of men, women and children. Head moved beside head; hats and scarves were waved in the air. Never before had I seen such a mass of people; they were grouped magnificently. A scene such

335

as this cannot be arranged on the stage nor all its extent represented on canvas. Here it was the masses that were so impressive; everywhere, for miles along the railway, we could see people gathered to wave good-bye to those who were leaving. All night long we travelled through the spreading Bohemian countryside. Great crowds of people had congregated outside all the towns and villages. The brown faces, the tattered clothes which many were wearing, the light from the torches and the Bohemian language, which was quite incomprehensible to me, gave the entire scene an atmosphere of its own. And on we sped, through tunnels and over viaducts. The windows rattled, the whistle shrieked, the iron horse puffed – I leaned my head back and slept under God's protection.

At Olmütz, where we were given fresh coaches, someone called me by name. It was Walther Goethe; we had travelled together all night without knowing it. We met several times in Vienna. Noble powers and true genius live on in Goethe's grandsons, both in the composer and the poet, but it was as though the greatness of their grandfather put pressure on them.

Liszt was in Vienna. He invited me to his recital, for which it was extremely difficult to get a ticket. Once more I heard his fantasies on themes from *Robert le Diable* and once more I heard him play with the strings like some tempestuous spirit. He can juggle with notes in a way that staggers the imagination. Ernst was there as well. His recital was not to be given until a few days after my departure. I had never heard him yet, and it was not certain we should ever meet again. Once while I was visiting him he took his violin, and to the accompaniment of tears it sang of the secrets of the human heart. Several years later, at home in Denmark, we became good friends in Copenhagen during the first year of the war. It was especially *Das Märchen meines Lebens* that drew him to me, and then my reading of *A Picture-Book without Pictures*: "Your 'Pictures without a Book' – that is what you really ought to call this little work, for one quite forgets that it is a book," he once wrote to me

I saw that wonderful man Grillparzer again and was several times in the jovial company of Castelli. At just about that time King Christian the Eighth had made him a Knight of the Dannebrog. He was absolutely delighted and asked me to tell my countrymen that any of them coming to visit him and saying, "I am Danish!" would be most heartily welcome. There is something so open and honest about Castelli, and it is accompanied by such good-natured humour that it is impossible not to become fond of him. To me he is the picture of a true Viennese, typical of the best of them. He has earned a fortune with his writing and bought himself a country house. He gave me an excellent picture of himself to remember him by, and under it he wrote the following little verse which is quite characteristic of him:

> *Dies Bild soll Dir stets mit liebendem Sehnen*
> *Von ferne zurufen des Freundes Gruss;*
> *Denn Du lieber* Däne! *bist Einer von* Denen
> *Die man immer achten und lieben muss.*

> With loving longing may this picture
> call out to you your friend's greeting from afar;
> For you, dear Dane, are one of those
> Ever worthy of our respect and love.

Castelli introduced me to Seidl and Bauernfeld, neither of whom is known in Denmark, although the former deserves to be on account of his sincere and heartfelt poems, and the latter for his excellent comedies, several of which ought to be produced on the Danish stage, for instance *Bürgerlich und Romantisch*, *Das Liebesprotokoll* and so on. He wrote the following amusing lines for me in my album:

> *Der Eine treibt's,*
> *Der And're schreibt's;*
> *So leben wir ein Jeder:*
> *Der von der Gans, der von der Feder.*

> One man gads about,
> Another writes it out;
> Each leads his life as he will:
> The one Sir Goose, the other Sir Quill.

I saw most of the bright stars of Austrian literature pass by me in rather the same way as we see church towers from a railway train. We can say that we have seen them. And to retain the image of the stars, I can say that in the Concordia Society I saw the entire Milky Way; a host of developing young talents, men of ability and importance.

At the home of Count Széchenyi, who hospitably invited me to visit him, I met his brother from Pesth, with all of whose achievements everyone in Hungary is familiar. I consider this short meeting to be one of the most interesting I had during that stay in Vienna. The man himself was revealed in all his personality, and his eyes told me that I could have confidence in him.

When I left Dresden, Her Majesty the Queen of Saxony had asked me whether I had an introduction to anyone at the Court in Vienna, and I had had to reply that I did not. And then the Queen was gracious enough to write a letter for me to give to her sister, the Archduchess Sophie of Austria. One evening Her Imperial Highness sent me an invitation through Count Széchenyi, and she gave me a most gracious welcome. The Dowager Empress, the widow of Franz the First, was also present, a kind and gentle person. There, too, I found Prince Vasa and his sister, and I saw the Duke and Duchess of Hessen-Darmstadt and several other princes. One of them began a friendly conversation with me – he was the Archduchess Sophie's eldest son, the present Emperor.

The prince's tutor asked me about the Danish branch of his family, whose name was Brun. I was talking to Count Bombelles, whose brother had married Ida Brun, whom Baggesen and Oehlenschläger mention on several occasions in their writings. After partaking of a cup of tea I read a few fairy tales, *The Top and the Ball*, *The Ugly Duckling* and *The Red Shoes*. When I wrote them this was the last place I would have dreamt of reading them. I can truthfully say that people have been kind to me right from the imperial castle down to the modest cottage.

A tasteful breast-pin which I was given by the Archduchess Sophie before leaving is something I shall always cherish with interest as a memory of that evening in the imperial palace.

Before leaving Vienna I still had to visit the brilliant Frau von Weissenthurn. She had recently risen from her sickbed and was still unwell, but she insisted on seeing me. However, as though she were on the threshold of the realm of the dead, she pressed my hand and said that we should never meet again and that this was the last time we would see each other in this world. She looked into my eyes with the kind gaze of a mother, and her penetrating look followed me to the door when we parted as though it were in truth the last time.

And so it was.

The railway to Trieste went as yet no further than to Grätz, and so I had to proceed by coach via Semmering. How dreadful it was after a day in a railway train to have to crawl forward at snail's pace for a night and a day and yet another night before reaching Trieste. At last the town and the Adriatic lay before us. I heard the Italian language ringing in my ears, but I had not yet reached Italy, the land of my longings. I spent only a few hours as a stranger in Trieste.

Our Danish consul, von Oesterreicher, as well as the consuls of Prussia and Oldenburg received me well, and I made several interesting acquaintances, for instance Count O'Donells, Count Stadion, the Governor, and Count Waldstein, this latter being especially interesting for me as a Dane as he is a descendant of Corfitz-Ulfeldt and Eleonore. He had their portraits hanging in his drawing room, and he showed me some interesting Danish relics from their time.

It was the first time I had seen Eleonore Ulfeldt's portrait, and the melancholy smile on her lips seemed to say to me, "Sing away the shadows which a harsh age cast on the man for whom it was my happiness to live and suffer." This material had attracted me even before Oehlenschläger thought of writing *Dina*. I wanted to adapt it for the stage and had already collected a good deal of historical material when I was told that it was too close to our own time and that King Frederik the Sixth would not allow any of his forefathers after Christian the Fourth to be represented on the stage. Count Rantzau-Breitenburg confirmed to me that this was the case. However, Christian the Eighth, who was still Prince Christian at that time, encouraged me to go on with the work. "It can be read," he said. But I abandoned the idea. When Christian the Eighth came to the throne these considerations were no longer necessary, and one day Oehlenschläger came to me and said, "Now I have written a

Dina, just as you were once thinking of doing." Both in plan and character his drama was quite different from mine. From this it will be quite obvious that anything about Ulfeldt and his family was of great interest to me. Count Waldstein told me that in his father's castle in Hungary or Bohemia – I cannot quite remember which it was – there was still a whole collection of letters and papers concerning Corfitz and Eleonore. I had made the acquaintance of another branch of Ulfeldt's family in Scania; this was Count Beck-Friis. The picture of Christian the Fourth, the founder of the family, hangs in the dining room there. I had to tell all about this family together with all the traces of it in Copenhagen, from the Blue Tower to the Pillar of Shame in Ulfeldts Plads. Just prior to this, at the King's command, the pillar had been removed, something which, as everyone knows, it had formerly been strictly held must not happen.

By the Adriatic my thoughts returned to the Danish islands and the time of Ulfeldt. The meeting with Count Waldstein and the portrait of the mother of the family hanging there translated me to my world of poetry so that I almost forgot that I was to be in the middle of Italy the following day.

In beautiful mild weather I sailed to Ancona on board the steamer the *Maria Dorothea*. We sped across the clear water with its gentle swell in sixteen hours. It was a calm, starry night. Early in the morning the coast of Italy lay before us with its lovely, blue mountains covered with shining snow. The sun was warm, and the grass and trees fresh and green to see. Yesterday evening in Trieste, now in Ancona, right in the centre of Italy, suddenly in one of the towns of the Papal States – that is the magic of which our age is capable.

Once more Italy opened before me all its picturesque grandeur. Spring had kissed all the fruit trees so that they had burst into flower. Every straw in the cornfields was filled with sunshine. Elm trees stood like caryatids with vines bound up to them, their green leaves sprouting, and above the fullness of the greenery rose the undulating, blue mountains, with their white blanket of snow. Together with Count Wenceslaus Paar from Vienna, one of the most excellent travelling companions I have ever met, and a young nobleman from Hungary, I proceeded for a few days by vetturina. Like all travellers when they come to Italy for the first time, the Hungarian expected to be attacked by robbers, and had weapons and pistols with him. "I have them double loaded," he said. "Where?" I asked as I could not see them. "I have them in my bag." This was under the seat on which I was sitting. As I was not very keen on that idea, and as I could assure him that the robbers would scarcely wait until I had got up and he had opened his bag to extract the murderous weapons, they were now taken out and fixed above us in the carriage as well as in front of us at all the inns on the way. We visited Loretto and saw the pious travellers kneeling there in the sacred house which angels are said to have carried through the air; we went through a wild, romantic countryside there in the heart of the Apennines. We saw no trace of robbers except some who were chained to a wagon and being escorted by soldiers.

At last the Campagna lay before us with its thought-provoking desolation. It was on the 31st of March 1846 I was to see Rome again. For the third time in my life I came to this great metropolis. I felt so happy and so filled with thanks and joy. How much more God gave me than He gave to so many thousands of others! And there is a blessing even in the realisation of this. When our joy is infinitely great, just as in our most profound sorrow, we have only God to cling to. I know no other word to describe my first impression than *devotion,* and as the days passed in my beloved Rome I felt what I cannot say more briefly or better than in a letter I wrote to one of my friends:

"I am putting down roots in the ruins here. I live with the petrified gods, and the roses are always in bloom and the church bells are always ringing. And yet Rome is not Rome as it was thirteen years ago when I was here for the first time. It is as though everything is modernised, even the ruins; grass and bushes have been taken up, and everything has been made tidier. The street life seems to have been pushed into the background, and I no longer hear the sound of the tambourine in the streets or see the young girls dancing their saltarellos. Even in the Campagna, enlightenment has made incursions on invisible railways. The peasants no longer believe as they used to. During the Easter festival I saw great crowds of people

341

standing in front of St. Peter's, standing just like foreign Protestants when the Pope gave them his blessing. It was contrary to all my feelings, and I felt a desire to kneel before the invisible Holy Spirit. When I was here thirteen years ago, everyone knelt, but now understanding has vanquished belief. In ten years, when railways bring the cities even closer together, Rome will be still more changed. Yet everything that happens is for the best, and people must and will always love this city. Rome is like a book of fairy tales – we constantly discover new wonders there and live in the imagination and reality."

When I went to Italy for the first time, I had not as yet learned to appreciate sculpture. The wonderful paintings in Paris drew me away from the statues. As I have already said, it was only when I came to Florence that a new world of art was revealed to me as I stood before the Venus di Medici. I can use Thorvaldsen's words and say, "The snow melted from my eyes." And now, as a result of my third visit to Rome and my repeated expeditions in the Vatican I came to love the statues far more deeply than the paintings. But where more than in Rome, and to some extent in Naples, does this art imprint itself on life so magnificently? We are quite carried away; through the work of art we learn to love nature, and the beauty of form becomes spiritual.

Among the many skilful and beautiful works I saw in the Roman exhibition and in the young artists' studios, there was a small number of sculptures that most fixed themselves in my memory. They were in the home of my fellow countryman, Jerichau. On the last occasion when I had been in Rome he was wasting away. It was a most difficult time for him; no one knew him, and he did not know himself. But now he was rising in people's estimation. I saw his group *Hercules and Hebe* and then his latest work, *The Panther Hunter*, and just during the time I was there these were ordered by a Russian prince. Dr. Stahr of Oldenburg was in Rome at that time, and it was especially he, writing in the *Allgemeine Zeitung*, who had awakened interest in Jerichau's genius. I was filled with the thought that he was now recognised, and in him I saw a new honour for our native country. I had known him as a boy. We were both born in Funen, and we met

342

in Copenhagen at Mrs. Læssøe's. No one, not even he himself, knew what was then stirring within him, and half in jest, half in earnest, he talked of his struggle with himself as he decided whether to go to America and live among the Hurons or to Rome and become an artist. He had put the paintbrush away and started modelling in clay. The bust he made of me was his last work in Copenhagen. He hoped to earn something from it, and I was to send him the money, but it was not a success. No one at that time was interested in having a work by Jerichau of course, especially when it was a bust of Andersen.

Now, as I say, his sun was rising, and he was happy, being married to the German-born Elisabeth Baumann, the warm-hearted, gifted artist whose spirited pictures were acknowledged and admired. Just at that time she was working on her great painting *Italian Women at the Well*, which was bought by Baron Hambro in London. The commission for the *Panther Hunter* enabled Jerichau to spend the summer together with his wife in Denmark. His health required it, and a few days later they were on their way.

Again I visited the jovial Küchler, and saw the lifelike pictures appear on his canvas. I spent time not only with my own fellow countrymen and Swedes, but also with the German artists who gave me a cordial welcome as semi-compatriot. Again I sat together with the people of Rome in the amusing puppet theatre and heard the children's delight; there was a ballet with jerking legs that were supposed to represent the characters.

My birthday, the second of April, was celebrated in an elegant fashion: Frau Goethe was in Rome and by chance living in the house (on the corner of Via Felice and Piazza Barberini) where I let my *Improvisatore* be born and spend his childhood. From there, she sent me a true Roman bouquet, a whole mosaic of flowers, with the inscription "From the Improvisatore's Garden".

That evening, a group of Danes, Swedes and Norwegians invited me to a lively party where my health was drunk; it was the Swedish painter, Södermark, who proposed the charming and heartfelt toast. On this occasion one of my fellow-countrymen evinced some surprise and irritation that people made so much fuss of Andersen. He could not understand it, he said. Södermark, who heard him, answered aloud that as a Swede he could understand why the Danish writer

343

was feted. I was given a couple of pretty pictures and mementos by my friends in Rome. Kolberg, the sculptor, modelled a bust of me; a few drawings were made of my face, but, as usual, without success. Daguerreotypes and photographs are the only things that can capture my true appearance.

Continually on the move, constantly seeking to make use of every hour and to see everything, I finally felt extremely oppressed by the constant sirocco. The Roman air did not suit me, and so, immediately after Easter, when I had seen the illumination of the dome and the Girandola, I hurried off to Naples by way of Terracina. Count Paar went with me, and we took rooms in Santa Lucia. The sea lay before us, and Vesuvius shone out. They were lovely evenings and moonlit nights; it was as though the sky had been lifted higher up and the stars had gone even further away. What a magnificent light effect! In the North the moon strews silver over the water; here it was gold. The revolving lantern in the lighthouse showed its burning light one moment, and the next it seemed to be quite extinguished. The torches on the fishing-boats cast their obelisk-like sheen on the water, or else the boats hid them like a black shadow beneath which the depths were illuminated. You felt you could see to the bottom where fishes and plants were moving in the water. In the street itself a thousand and one lights burned in front of the tradesmen's stalls. Then a host of children carrying candles appeared in procession to the Church of Santa Lucia. A few of the smallest ones tripped over their own feet, and lay and rolled over with their candles, and meanwhile, like a hero in the great drama of light, Vesuvius stood there glowing blood-red amidst the clouds of smoke illuminated by it.

The heat from the sun became more and more oppressive; the sirocco blew waves of dry, hot air over us. As one born and bred in the North, I thought the heat would do me good in times to come, and I knew nothing of its power. So while the Neapolitans were wise enough to stay indoors or creep along in the narrow shadows by the houses, I dashed off boldly to the Monument and the Museo Borbonico, but one day, in the middle of Largo di Castello, it seemed as though my breath suddenly left me, and as though the glowing sun was sinking into my eyes. Its rays went through my head and my back, and I fell down in a faint. When I came round I found I had

344

been taken into a café, and someone had put ice on my head. I felt paralysed in all my limbs, and from that time I only ventured out in the evening. The least exertion made me feel ill, and evenings at the home of the Prussian Ambassador, Baron Brockhausen, sitting on his large, airy terrace by the lake, or excursions by coach to Camoldoli were all I could stand. I had visited Capri and Ischia. My compatriot, Miss Fjeldsted, the ballerina, was taking the waters there, and this had been of such benefit to her that she danced a saltarello with the young girls under the orange trees in the evening, and the young people were so delighted with it that they serenaded her. However, Ischia has never appealed to me to the same extent as to other travellers, and the sun was also far too hot there. Everyone advised me to seek rest and shade in Sorrento, the home of Tasso. Together with an English family I had met in Rome, I rented apartments at Cocumella, just outside Sorrento and close by the sea, which rolled its waves into the tiny caves under our little garden. On account of the heat I was obliged to spend all day indoors, and there I wrote away on *Das Märchen meines Lebens.* In Rome, by the Bay of Naples and in the Pyrenees I wrote and finished these pictures of my life which were now written down for the first time, and which were to illustrate the German edition of my works. Quire after quire was sent by post to Copenhagen, where one of the ablest of my friends had a free hand with what I had written. After reading it he sent it to my publisher in Leipzig, and not a single page was lost on all that long journey.

The time I spent in Cocumella was very pleasant, and the view from the window and the loggia was beautiful. I could see Vesuvius and the entire bay before me; but the only walk was the long and narrow path between high walls enclosing and as good as hiding the rock gardens. In the heat from the sun you would have to be a lizard to be able to breathe well there, and you would have to find a pair of stilts to see over the walls, and so I moved to Sorrento itself where two composers, the Swede Josephson and the Dutchman Verhulst, both of whom were friends of mine, were living and spending their summer holidays.

The day on which I arrived, there was great festivity, since three young girls, the daughters of a rich merchant, were taking their vows as nuns. There were wonderfully colourful decorations in the church, and there was an orchestra. Opera buffa at that. From *The Barber of Seville* we were treated to the whole of Don Basilio's slander aria while the cannon roared outside. The garishness dominating the whole affair completely destroyed the pious mood I had brought with me, and a comical old officer who had great difficulty in kneeling did not make me feel more solemn. Only when the Mass was read by one of the girls, and her soft voice seemed to tremble, did I recover my sense of piety.

Apart from his personal charm, there was something else about Josephson that drew us closer together, and that was our common friendship with Jenny Lind. She had stood godmother to him when, as a Jew, he had been converted to Christianity, and since then she had always shown him friendship and true interest. During his travels abroad he had visited her in Berlin, going to her apartments every day. He was known as "a Swedish theologian", and from that people soon produced the title, "ein Landprediger". Rumour had it that he was engaged to the Swedish Nightingale. Who has not read and heard that story? For the man concerned it was completely incomprehensible. We often laughed at the cleverness and ingenuity of the rumour.

A few weeks passed, and the well-known Neapolitan festival for the "Madonna del Arco", which Bournonville has portrayed for us in idealised form in his ballet *Napoli*, took me back to Naples. At the same time it was my intention, now that I was feeling a little stronger, to go from there by way of Marseilles to Barcelona, and to visit the Alhambra and Seville. I had already written home for a letter of credit for those places, and I could expect it to arrive in Naples any day. I arrived there and took a room in a hotel in the centre of the town, near the Via Toledo. I had stayed there before, but that was in winter, and now I experienced Naples in all the heat of summer and with all its din. I had never imagined anything so infinitely dreadful. The sun poured its burning rays down in the narrow street and in through every door and window. Everything had to be shut, and there was not a breath of air to be felt. Every little corner and every spot in the street offering the slightest shade was full of workers chattering merrily and noisily. Carriages rumbled past, and the town criers shouted with unbearably loud voices. The noise of people in the street roared like a rough sea, and church bells rang incessantly. My neighbour – heaven knows who he was – played scales from morning to evening. It was enough to send one out of one's mind. The sirocco blew its seething hot air over us, and I was finished. At Santa Lucia, all the rooms in my old lodgings were taken, and so I had to stay where I was. Bathing in the sea afforded no refreshment, and indeed it seemed to weaken me rather than strengthen me. What did I derive from this? A fairy tale! It was here that I made up the story of *The Shadow*, but I was so indolent, so lifeless, that I failed to commit it to paper until I was at home in the North.

The glare from the sun was like a nightmare on my chest, a vampire seeking to kill me. Again I left for the countryside, but the same sunbeams followed me, and they burned there with the same strength as in the city. The air out there was certainly more elastic, but it was like the poisonous cloak of Hercules, seeming to draw all the strength and marrow out of me. I had thought myself a child of the sun, because my heart so longed for the South, but I had to admit that there was Nordic snow in my body, and that the snow was melting, and I became increasingly miserable. Most foreigners suffered the same as I during that unusually hot summer, and the Neapolitans, too, said that they had not had such a summer as this for many years. Most foreigners left, and I would have done so as well, but my letter of credit had not yet arrived. Day after day I made enquiries about it in vain. During all my travels no letters had ever been lost, and the friend in Copenhagen who was to arrange for the letter of credit was most painstaking and practical. But no letter of credit arrived, and three weeks had already passed since the time when it ought to have put in an appearance.

"There is no letter here," was the constant reply of the mighty Rothschild, to whom the letter should come first. One day, tired of my everlasting inquiries, he rather violently pulled out the drawer containing all the letters to foreigners with letters of credit in his house. "There is no letter here!" And as he rather irritably banged the drawer in again a letter fell to the floor. It was sealed with wax which on account of the heat had melted and fixed it to the back of the drawer. The letter was to me, and it contained my letter of credit. It had lain there for a whole month, and would perhaps have lain there much longer had it not been violently shaken from its perch. So now I could start on my journey!

I bought a ticket for Marseilles on the steamship *Castor*. When I went on board the people in the hotel sent the *cameriere* with me down to the harbour where I had to hire a boat to take me out to the ship, and where it was said that the boatmen extracted money from the travellers in the most despicable fashion. We agreed on about two *carlin*, but when the *cameriere* had gone and I had come some distance from land with the two fellows, they put down their oars and demanded a *scudo*, because if I would not pay, they would not touch the oars – and the steamer could sail when it wanted! – I declared that this was dishonest for we had made a bargain, but they made no answer. The younger oarsman was extremely handsome; he laughed, and it suited him splendidly, but he was not a scrap better than the other. I was in their power, and I had to promise to give them what they demanded; they wanted the money straight away, but that I definitely refused. Then, when we came to the ship I proclaimed their behaviour so everyone could hear, though I gave them the promised *scudo*, for I had given my word. That was my last memory of Naples.

The steamer was very overcrowded. The whole of the deck was taken up by carriages, and I had my bed made beneath one of them, for it was already impossible to breathe down in the cabins. Several people followed my example, and soon the deck was one long shakedown bed. – One of England's most distinguished noblemen, the Marquis of Douglas, who was married to the Princess of Baden, was on board with his lady. We came into conversation; he could hear I was Danish, but did not know who I was. We talked of Italy and all that had been written about that country, and I mentioned the Baroness de Staël-Holstein's *Corinne*. He interrupted me and said: "But there is someone from your country who has depicted Italy far better."

"We Danes do not think so," I answered. He spoke most flatteringly of *The Improvisatore* and its author. "It is a shame," I said, "that Andersen had been there for such a short time when he wrote that book."

"He had been there for many years," answered the Marquis of Douglas.

"Oh, no," I assured him, "only for nine months; I know that for certain."

"I would like to meet that man," he said.

"That can quite easily be arranged," I went on, "for he is on board this ship!" And now I told him who I was.

Meanwhile the weather became rough; the wind increased, and I had to retire to my bunk. The rain and the gale continued for days and nights, and the marquis and I did not meet again. On the second and third nights it blew a real gale, and the ship was tossed all over the place like a barrel in the open sea. The waves came at us from the side and raised their broad, foam-covered tops higher than the railings, as though they wanted to look in at us. Everything was moving and creaking, both in the ship itself and in the carriages beneath which we were lying, as though they were about to sink down and crush us. People lay moaning all around. I lay still and looked up at the scudding clouds and thought of God and those I held dear. When we finally reached Genoa most of the passengers continued their journeys by land. I would have liked to follow the general move to stay on firm ground, go to Switzerland by way of Milan, and give up Spain for this time. However, my letter of credit was made out to Marseilles and some Spanish ports. I visited the Danish consul to change a sum of money from my letter of credit, but he knew nothing of the important house in Copenhagen that had issued it. He did not know my name, and could not embark on financial transactions, and so I was forced to sail at least as far as Marseilles. The weather turned out to be extremely beautiful. The air was so refreshing, and now that I was breathing more freely the desire to see Spain returned. According to the original plan for my journey that country was to be the high point of the whole trip, and my being forced to go to Marseilles by boat I regarded as a sign that this time I *had* to see the native land of the Spanish. And the desire to go there returned.

We reached Marseilles, but a day later than planned, and so we arrived too late to go to Barcelona by the steamer, which only sailed once every ten days, and that was too long for me to wait. The journey by sea had increased my strength a little, and I thought I had sufficient endurance to make the journey over land, through the South of France, so that I would after all be able to see that as well

349

as the Pyrenees.

Before I left Marseilles I had a chance but welcome meeting with one of my Scandinavian friends, Ole Bull. He was coming from America, and he had been received in France with acclamation and the singing of serenades. We were both staying at the Hôtel des Empereurs in Marseilles. We met at the table d'hôte, and rushed over to greet each other, and we spoke of what we had seen and experienced. He told me something of which I was unaware at the time, indeed something of which I did not dream, and that was that I had many friends in America. People there had enquired about me with great interest; the English translations of my novels had been reproduced there and had been spread all over the country in cheap editions. My name had flown across the great ocean. I felt quite small at the thought, but I was glad, deeply happy. But why did I have so much better fortune than so many thousands of others? At this thought, I felt like a poor peasant lad about whose shoulders a royal cloak had been hung. But I was and remain happy at the thought. Can this be vanity, or is vanity only when I actually put my joy into words?

In the evening, when I had gone to rest, I heard music outside. It was a serenade in honour of Ole Bull. The following day he left for Algiers, and I for the Pyrenees.

The route took me through Provence. I did not see many roses, but there were plenty of pomegranate trees in blossom. And moreover, in its fresh, green aspect and in its gentle hills, the countryside had something in common with Denmark. It is stated in the guide book that the women of Arles are among the most beautiful and are descended from the Romans; and the book is right. To my surprise even the poorest girls there were lovely; they had noble figures, lovely forms and eyes which shone with spirit and expression. The entire company in the coach was taken quite by surprise and filled with delight, and the girls understood it perfectly well. They did not flee like the gazelle, but they had the same graceful movements and the same shining eyes. Yes, the human form is indeed the most beautiful of creations.

The first place I visited in Nîmes was the magnificent Roman amphitheatre. Its grandeur reminded me of what Italy can offer. I had heard virtually nothing at all of the ancient monuments in the South of France, and so I was extremely surprised. Even the "Maison Carrée" at Nîmes is of a splendour comparable to that of the Temple of Theseus in Athens; Rome possesses nothing that is so well preserved.

Nîmes is also the home of Reboul, the baker who writes those beautiful poems. Anyone who does not know him from these must know him from Lamartine's *Journey to the Orient*.

I found the house and went into the bakery. There was a man there in his shirt-sleeves busy putting bread into the oven; it was Reboul himself. A noble face, expressive of the man's character, met me. I told him my name, and he was so polite as to say that he knew it from a poem to me in the *Revue de Paris*, the one written by the French poet Martin. Then he asked me to come back about midday if I had time, when he would be able to give me a better welcome. When I returned at the appointed hour he received me in a small, almost elegant room; it was decorated with pictures, statues and books among which was not merely French literature, but also translations of the Greek classics.

A few of the pictures on the walls were gifts, he told me; they illustrated his most famous poem, *The Dying Child*. From Marmier's book *Chansons du Nord* he knew that I had treated the same theme and I told him that I had written it while I was still at school.

In the morning I had seen him as the busy baker, but now he was entirely the poet. He spoke enthusiastically about the literature of his native country, and he expressed a desire to see the North, where the natural scenery and the intellectual life were sources of special interest to him.

On leaving him, I felt great respect for this man upon whom the Muses had bestowed a gift that was by no means insignificant, and who had sufficient intelligence to remain at his honest trade in the midst of all the homage that was paid to him. He preferred to be the eccentric baker of Nîmes rather than enjoy a brief spell of homage and then disappear in Paris among the hundreds of other poets.

I went by train through Montpellier to Cette at the speed a railway train reaches in France! You fly along as though it were a race with the "wild hunt". My mind involuntarily went to an inscription on the

351

corner of the street leading to the railway station in Basel. On the very spot where the famous *Dance of Death* had once been painted on the wall there was written in large letters "Dance of Death", but just above this inscription there is another one: "To the Railway Station". These two, just on the border of France, provide food for the imagination. As the train shot along I thought of this "Dance of Death and Railway Station"; it was as though the whistle gave the signal for the dance to start! One does not have such wild fancies on the German railways or the one to Roskilde.

The islander loves the sea just as the mountain dweller loves his mountains. I know that from experience. For me, every coastal town, however small it may be, wears its own halo because of the sea. Perhaps it was the sea together with the Danish language reaching my ears from two houses in Cette that made this town seem so homely to me. I do not know, but I had the feeling of being in Denmark rather than in the South of France. When, far from our native land, we enter a house where everyone, from the master to the servants, speaks the language of our country, as was the case for me at the home of Casalis-Tutein in Cette, these sounds from home have a magic power, and like Faust's cloak they transport us home in a split second, along with the house and everything in it. The Danish consul, Jansen, was also from Copenhagen. Cette suddenly became a bit of Denmark for me.

But the summer there was not Nordic. Instead, we had the overpowering heat of Naples, and the air was quite capable of burning Faust's cloak. The heat poured down on us, and the sunbeams robbed us of all our strength. Here, too, it was years since they had known such a summer. From the countryside around came news of people who had dropped down dead from the heat. Even the nights were hot. People told me that I would not be able to endure travelling in Spain, and I myself felt the same. However, Spain *was* my goal, and I could already glimpse the Pyrenees. The blue mountains tempted me and early one morning I was in a steamer sailing across the Étang de Thau. The sun rose higher and higher; it burned down on us from above, and it burned on us from the surface of the water. Myriads of quivering jellyfish filled the water around us; it seemed that the sun's rays were evaporating the water, leaving behind nothing but a swaying mass of animal life. Neither before nor since have I ever seen anything like it. At the Languedoc Canal we all went from the steamer to a large vessel in which we were to be towed along. It seemed to be fitted out for freight more than for passengers. The deck was full of cases and trunks, and these in their turn were completely occupied by people seeking shade under their umbrellas. It was impossible to move up there, and there was no railing round this mound of trunks and human beings which three or four horses were dragging along at the end of some long ropes. It seemed to be just as tightly packed down in the cabins. People sat side by side like flies in a sugar basin. A woman who had been overcome by heat and tobacco smoke was carried down to us in the first class cabin and laid on the floor, the only spot that was empty for the moment. She needed air, but there did not seem to be any there, however many fans were waved about. There were no refreshments to be found, and it was not even possible to produce a glass of water except the yellow, lukewarm liquid which the canal had to offer. Booted feet hung down through the hatches from the deck, and it was as though they gave body to the oppressive air by shutting out the light.

Enclosed in that space, we had still to suffer the torment of listening to a man who constantly sought to say something witty and continually tried to attract our attention; the torrent of words spattered around his mouth just as the monotonous parted water constantly splashed up in front of the vessel. It was more than human nature could stand. I forced my way up among trunks, people and umbrellas and stood outside in the scorching air. And hour after hour, on both sides, behind us and in front of us, there was one and the same thing to be seen – green grass, green trees, a lock – green grass, green trees, a lock, and then the same again. It was enough to send a man out of his mind.

We were put ashore about half an hour's journey from Béziers. I felt almost as though I were going to faint, and there were no coaches here; the driver of the omnibus had not expected us so early. The way in which the sun burned down on us was simply dreadful. The little trees must have sold their shadows, I think, for there was not even an outline of them. It is said that Southern France is a bit of land from Paradise, but in the circumstances in which I saw it, it seemed to me rather that it was a bit which had been thrown up from Hell itself with all its infernal heat.

The stagecoach awaited us in Béziers. All the best seats were already occupied, and I went for the first – and I hope the last – time in the back compartment of that sort of coach. A dreadful, fat woman sat beside me; she was wearing slippers and a head-dress a yard high; however, she took this off and hung it just in front of me. Then came a merry sailor, who must have drunk the health of too many people, and then a couple of filthy farm labourers whose first manoeuvre was to take off their boots and shirts and sit there, hot and stinking of onions. And all the time clouds of dust poured in and the sun scorched and blinded us. It was impossible to stand this further than Narbonne, where, ill and suffering, I sought rest. Now some gendarmes came along and asked for my passport. And just as night was falling, fire had to break out in the nearest village – the alarm was sounded and the fire engines rushed off. It was as though all tormenting spirits had been let loose. From here right to the Pyrenees I was worn out by my passport being constantly inspected in a way I had not even experienced in Italy. As the reason for this I was given the proximity of the Spanish border, the many refugees from Spain and some murders had been committed in this region. Everything could only make the journey a torment; and my thoughts and nerves could not conceive it as anything else.

I reached Perpignan; it was as though the sun had swept everyone from the streets. It was not until evening that people appeared, but they poured out like a revolution intent on destroying the town. The crowds grew outside my window, the air resounded with loud shouts, and the noise pierced my sick body. What was it all? What did it mean? Could it be the fever that was burning thus in my head? I tottered over to the balcony, opened the door, and saw that the square was black with people. They were all looking up to where I stood, waving their hats in the air, and shouting, "Hurrah, hurrah!"

"Merciful Heaven," I thought, "this is madness. It's all something I'm imagining; there's no one there; I can't hear anyone shouting and I'm imagining it all. It's terrible!" I almost fainted, and I leaned my head over to one side. On a balcony nearby a man stood addressing the people. This was the person to whom they were shouting

354

greetings as he emerged.

"Good evening, Monsieur Arago," shouted the loudest voice, and a thousand and one others repeated it.

Then they began to play music. It was the famous Arago who was my neighbour, and the people had come to serenade him. So my fever was not playing tricks on me, and that was at least some consolation. But this tumult and these shouts were a renewed torment to me. I can remember few evenings in my life when I have felt as physically ill as I did then. The beautiful singing that followed failed to refresh me. Then Arago made a speech again. After many years away he was visiting the town in which he had been born. The people's jubilation resounded through the streets, and it pierced all my nerves. I was ill; I gave up all thought of going to Spain; I felt it impossible for me to travel further. And how was I to stand the air even here? If only I could get back to Switzerland! I trembled at the thought of the long journey, and could not see how I could possibly manage it. I was advised to go to the Pyrenees as quickly as possible and there breathe the refreshing mountain air. The spa of Vernet on the other side of Prades was recommended as being cool and good. I was given an introduction to the owner of the hotel there, and I decided to stay there for a while. There was nothing else to do. I decided to travel by night, which was the only cool time, and I reached the spa after a wearying journey that took all night and a few hours of the morning. Vernet is situated on the French side of the Pyrenees, just a little way into the mountains. The air was fresher and more bracing than anything I had breathed for months. After spending a few days there I seemed to feel well and refreshed again.

Once more my thoughts flew to Spain, which was so close to me, only a few hours' journey away. Just a little trip into the mountains, and I stood like Moses and saw before me the land I was not destined to enter. My thoughts and my hopes were that God would some winter allow me to fly down here again from the North and enter that rich and lovely land from which the sun is now holding me away with its flaming sword.

Vernet is not yet one of the best known spas, although it has the great quality that it can be visited all year round. At that time the most distinguished visitor the place had welcomed was Ibrahim

Pasha. He had been there the previous winter. His name was still like a halo round the establishment; the name of Ibrahim Pasha was on the lips of the hostess and all the waiters; his room was immediately shown to me, as though it were something extremely interesting. The two French words he could say, "merci", and "très bien" were recited regularly because of his wrong pronunciation. In all respects both great and small, Vernet gave the impression of being in a kind of state of innocence among spas. Visitors there told me immediately that it was only with respect to making out bills that the owner had placed the hotel on a level with the finest in Europe.

The life one leads there is more solitary, more cut off than at any other spa, and that can be quite an excellent thing. If, on the other hand, you require amusement, well, nothing at all is done to entertain the guests. I am talking, of course, of the time when I was there, and I do not know what might have happened in later years.

During my stay the only entertainment available to visitors was a trip into the mountains either on foot or on a donkey. However, an excursion of this kind offered such a curious and varied experience that we did not in the least miss the amusements which are usually arranged for visitors to a spa.

It is as though all kinds of different landscapes have been mixed together around Vernet: North and South, mountain vegetation and valley vegetation. From one spot there is a view across vineyards of a mountain slope that seems to present a pattern made up of samples of cornfields and green meadows with hay standing in stacks. From another there is nothing to see but the naked, metallic cliffs with strange blocks of stone jutting out, long and narrow as though they are broken statues or columns. Then the track goes beneath poplar trees in tiny meadows in which curled mint grows, such a genuine Danish scene that it might have been cut out of Zealand itself. And then before long you find yourself in the shadow of the cliff where cypresses and figs grow among the vines, that is just like a bit of Italy. But the spirit of the whole region, the countless pulses beating aloud in the Pyrenees, are the springs; the eternally running water is full of life as it babbles along. It gushes forth everywhere; it trickles through the moss and pours over the great boulders. It is full of life and darts forward with an elegance which words cannot describe.

There is an everlasting music of rushing water played by a million strings; the river nymph chatters above you, below you and around you.

High up on the cliff face, by the side of the steep precipice, lie the ruins of a Moorish castle. Clouds now hang where the balcony once hung; the path on which the donkey trudges along leads through the great hall. From this spot and from the track leading to the spa there is a view of the entire valley, which is long and narrow and looks like a river of trees winding in and out between the red, sun-baked cliffs. And in the middle of this green valley the little terraced town of Vernet rises on a mountain.

It only needs the minarets for it to look like a Bulgarian-Turkish town. A miserable church with two elongated holes as windows and a dilapidated tower nearby, forms the upper part, and beneath it come dark brown roofs and dirty grey houses with open wooden hatches instead of windows. But it is certainly picturesque. However, if you go into the town itself, where the chemist's shop is also the bookshop, the general impression is one of wretchedness. Almost all the houses are made of stone blocks, but not large blocks which have been hewn into shape; oh no, they all look as if they could have been collected from an old cobbled street, and they give the impression of having been piled up on top of each other. A couple of dark holes serve as doors and windows; swallows fly in and out, for they have built their nests under the beams in the sitting rooms.

If you personally pay a visit to any of them, at least the ones I visited, you will find transparent floors under your feet on the first storey; you have a view through worn planks down into chaotic darkness. On the walls there usually hangs a piece of fat meat with fur on one side; it was explained to me that this was used to rub shoes and boots when they were to be polished. The bedroom is garishly decorated *al fresco* with pictures of saints, angels, wreaths and crowns, as in the most primitive periods of the art of painting. The people themselves and even their children are unusually ugly; they have the faces of real dwarfs, and even a child-like expression cannot improve the ugly features – and yet no more than a few hours' journey on the other side of the mountains down in Spain beauty burgeons and shrewd brown eyes sparkle. The view of the market

357

place was the only poetical image with which Vernet presented me. Under a magnificent big tree an itinerant pedlar had spread out his wares, scarves, books, pictures, a complete bazaar with the earth itself as his counter. All the ugly young people of the town, thoroughly tanned by the sun, had congregated around these wonders. A couple of old hags peeped at them from their open hatches. A long line of visitors from the spa, ladies and gentlemen, went past riding on horses and donkeys, while two small children who were half hidden behind a pile of boards were pretending to be cockerels and kept on shouting, "Cock-a-doodle-doo".

The fortress town of Villefranche with its Louis XIV castle is a much finer market town with better houses and more facilities. It is only a few hours' journey from Vernet. The highway here passes through Olette into Spain, and so there is a certain amount of traffic. Several of the houses catch one's eye on account of their beautiful Moorish windows which are hewn in marble. The church itself is half Moorish, and the altars are similar to those in the Spanish churches. There is a figure of the Virgin Mary with the Infant Jesus made entirely of silver and gold. I visited Villefranche on one of the very first days of my stay. All the visitors from the spa were with me on this excursion, for which donkeys and horses had to be collected from the surrounding district. The hotel owner's august carriage was provided with a team of horses, and it was filled both inside and outside, just like a French canal barge. A most charming gentleman from Holstein, who was the best horseman of them all, and Alexandre Dumas' friend, the well-known painter Dauzats, led the expedition. The fortress, the casemates and the caves were all inspected, and neither did we leave out the little town of Corneilla with its interesting church. There were signs of Moorish power and art everywhere. Everything in these regions suggests Spain rather than France, and even the language is suspended somewhere between the two. Then there in the fresh mountain scenery, on the border of a country the beauty of which I was not then to behold, I finished *Das Märchen meines Lebens* for the German edition of my collected works. The English call this book, *The True Story of my Life*. This is how I finish it:

"Before I leave the Pyrenees these words which I have written will fly to Germany, these words which tell of a long period in my life. I myself shall be following, and a new and unknown period is beginning. I wonder what will happen in it. What shall I achieve? I wonder whether the really active period of my life is still to come. I do not know. But I look to the future with gratitude and am full of confidence. Throughout my life the bright and the dark days have always led to what was best for me. It is like a voyage towards a definite goal; I stand at the tiller; I have chosen my course; I have done what I can; but God commands the winds and the waves. He steers, and if the result is different from what I plan, then it is for my own good. That belief is firmly planted within my breast, and it makes me happy. When the Christmas trees are lit, when, as people say, the white bees swarm, I shall, if God be willing, be in Denmark together with those there whom I hold dear. My heart will be full of the flowers from my travels, and I shall be strengthened in body and soul, and then new works will spring on to the paper. May God bless them. I know He will. – A lucky star shines above me. Thousands must have deserved it more than I, and I myself can often not understand why I rather than countless others should be given so much joy. Let it shine. But if it sets, perhaps even now as I write these lines, it has shone, and I have received the rich share that was allotted to me. Then let it set, for that, too, will be for the best. My thanks and my love to God and to men."

Vernet, (Eastern Pyrenees) July 1846

XIII

Nine years have passed, eventful years in the history of the world, grave and great days for Denmark, sad, but also joyful days for me. They have given me all the recognition I could wish for in my native land. They have made me older and yet kept me young. They have given me calm and understanding. Now we will present the new chapters in my life.

From Vernet, where the mountain air had refreshed me, and where I thought I had gained sufficient strength for the journey home, I wanted to go to Switzerland. However, although I arranged it so that only the night was occupied travelling in the coach, spending the warm days in Perpignan and Narbonne, it was nevertheless as though I had gone from invigorating air to some element lacking the stuff of life. I was surrounded by a heavy, motionless, scorching environment. It was a torment, and before long I felt that I had been burned throughout every nerve in my body. Even the night offered no freshness, except to the flies which now found sufficient strength to dance about.

A few days' or rather a few nights' rest in Cette, where I had my mattress put out on the balcony of the house and slept beneath a starlit sky, gave me sufficient air to survive. All I know of the beauty of Montpellier is that it lay bathed in sunshine that burned me through and through. Foreign visitor though I was, I stayed in my room with tightly closed shutters and dressed as though I were about to take a bath. In the railway train, in the midst of its arrow-like flight, we received news of the fearful disaster that had occurred on the French Northern Railway. If I had been well and in good health it would have set my imagination going at any other time, but I was so affected by the sun of the South of France that, like a seasick man on a ship, I relapsed into a condition in which I was completely indifferent to what was going on. The railway ended at Nîmes, and in order to reach Avignon from there, we had to travel in a coach that was chock full and seemed to swallow all the dust it encountered.

The almond-trees were full of ripe nuts, and almonds and figs were about the only things I really enjoyed. To rest and rest all the time behind closed shutters is a bad way of travelling! The Popes' palace there looked like a fortress which had been changed into a barracks. The cathedral looks like a small wing of it. In the museum there was Vernet's bust of Thorvaldsen. Some bright spark had pencilled out the word "danois" which was written by his name. There were two paintings of Mazeppa done by Vernet, rather different from the prints; they had been "donated to the fine city of Avignon". In the evening the streets were filled with life and movement; a mountebank riding on horseback and preceded by a drum proclaimed his wares like some Dulcamare.

A large, broad vine spread its leaves across the window like a blind to catch the sunbeams.

I was very close to Vaucluse, but I lacked the strength to make that little journey. I had to be prudent and save all the strength I possessed in order to reach Switzerland, where the mountains offered cooler air. I was not destined to see Vaucluse, of which so many beautiful things have been written. I was not to behold the stream which has borne the image of Laura, the image that Petrarch's verse preserves and circulates around the world for ever.

The River Rhône flows with such speed that the steamer sailing with the current only takes one day from Lyons to Marseilles, but when it is sailing in the opposite direction against the current up to Lyons it takes no fewer than four days.

In preference to the dirty steamer I chose the fast coach which in truth travelled here with the speed of the wild horses in the ballad of Leonora. The ancient Roman theatre in Orange rose high above all the other modern buildings. The Triumphal Arch for Septimus Severus and all the rich Roman wonders which are scattered over the banks of the Rhône carried my thoughts back to Italy. I had had no idea that Southern France could boast of such a fine show of Roman remains.

The river banks presented us with ever more variety; I saw towns with lovely Gothic churches, and up on the mountains there were ancient castles standing like huge bats. There were beautiful swinging suspension bridges stretched across the rapid current against which the ships were battling their way.

At last I was in Lyon, where the Rhône swallows the Saône. There, from one of the highest-lying streets, I could see, many, many miles to the north east, a shining white cloud rising above the flat, green plain. It was Mont Blanc. There lay Switzerland! I was now so close to the place where I hoped again to be able to drink the air and lift up my body and soul in greater freedom.

But the Swiss consul refused to give me a visa until the police in Lyon had given me one, and the police there declared that my passport was not in order. While travelling, I am almost too concerned with my passport and visa, so that my anxiety to have everything in order almost borders on the comical. Yet I am always the one traveller in a thousand who is exposed to the worst passport problems. Sometimes it is because someone cannot read; sometimes a minor clerk writes the wrong number on it so that it cannot be found; sometimes an Italian frontier guard takes exception to the name Christian and thinks this is some peculiar religious sect that specifically calls itself the Christians. In Lyon I was simply told that my passport should have been sent from the frontier to Paris and furnished with a visa by the Ministry of the Interior. All that day I had to run in and out of the Préfecture de Police until I finally abandoned myself to the mercy of one of the higher ranking police officials, to whom I declared that no one before had ever demanded or even suggested that for me to go from the Pyrenees to Switzerland by way of Lyon I should send my passport to Paris, to which city I had no intention of going. I was informed it would be necessary for me to go back to Marseilles to have my passport made valid for Switzerland by the Danish consul there. I declared that I could not stand the journey and neither could I stay in Lyon, red hot as it was. I simply *had* to go to the mountains! The man to whom I had turned was polite and cultured. With my passport in his hand he questioned me on the times and places I had been in all the different towns where each visa had been stamped. He soon realised that there was no reason why I should not continue my journey, and he arranged everything in the best possible way. And the next day I could be off again. My mind was at rest, and in the evening I went in the Opera House. They were performing German operas there at that time. There was a company from Zürich,

362

and, as the saying goes, they gave value for money, performing both Flotow's *Stradella* and Weber's *Der Freischütz* on the same evening. This led to no difficulty as far as the time was concerned, since we were treated only to the music in *Der Freischütz*, the dialogue being omitted as it was assumed that the French could not understand it. However, it certainly seemed comical to see Max take his hat, nod and go off immediately after Caspar's drinking song, and then to see Caspar sing in triumph as though he had won the day purely and simply on account of that song.

I reached Switzerland. There, too, the heat was oppressive. There was less snow on the Jungfrau and even on Mont Blanc than there had been for many years, and black strips of rock were visible. But the air there was fresher, and it was cool in the evenings. I made straight for Vevey, where it was a blessing to live and breathe by the lake and be near the snow-capped mountains of Savoy. The big fires which shepherds and charcoal-burners lit on the other side of the lake shone in the evening like red stars. I visited Chillon again. Byron's name, which he himself had carved in the pillar, had been damaged since I was last there. Someone had scratched it hard to erase it. It was an Englishman who had done it, but he had been prevented from completing his task. Even if he had erased Byron's name there, it would not have been erased in the world. Two new names had been added; they were those of Victor Hugo and Robert Peel.

In Freiburg I saw the biggest and boldest suspension bridge I have yet encountered. It floats in the air, high above the valley and the river, and it sways beneath a heavy carriage. In the Middle Ages such a thing would have belonged to the world of the fairy tale, but science has raised our age into what at one time was the supernatural. Finally, we reached Bern, the place where Baggesen lived for such a long time, found a wife and was so happy. The Alps shone with the same fiery splendour as when he saw them. I spent a few days there and in Interlaken, making excursions to Lauterbrunnen and Grindelwald. The refreshing spray carried on the wind from the Staubbach as it fell and the ice-cold air in the glacier caves at Grindelwald were like Paradise after a passage through Purgatory. The brown Swiss houses on the velvet green meadows and mountain sides, the gentlest and richest scenery immediately adjoining the wildest and grandest is what is peculiar to Switzerland. The Wetterhorn, Silberhorn and the Jungfrau shone in the fiery glow of evening. It could all be so splendid and calm and good, but everywhere one was pursued by beggars yodeling and yodeling as a prelude to begging. But the time spent in those lovely mountains was refreshing and it gave me new life. I went to Basel and then on by rail through France to Strasbourg. It was only here the Rhine steamers start. The air lay heavy and warm upon the river, and the journey took all day. Finally, the ship became quite overcrowded, mostly by gymnasts who were laughing and making merry. Everyone was antagonistic towards Denmark and everything Danish, for Christian the Eighth had published the open letter. It was only here that I learned this. It was by no means pleasant for a Dane to travel in Baden. No one knew me and I made no effort to speak to anyone, but sat ill and suffering throughout the journey on the river.

By way of Frankfurt I reached my beloved Weimar, and here at the home of Beaulieu I was looked after and allowed to rest. I spent some beautiful days at the summer residence of Ettersburg, where I was invited by the Hereditary Grand Duke. In Jena itself I worked together with Professor Wolff on a German translation of several of my poems, but my health was badly undermined. I, who love the South, had to admit that I am a son of the North, whose flesh, blood and nerves are rooted in snow and cold winds. I travelled slowly homewards. In Hamburg I received the Order of the Dannebrog from King Christian the Eighth. I was told that the decision to award it to me had been taken before I left home, and so I was to have it before I reached home soil again. There I arrived two days later. In Kiel I met the Landgrave and his family together with Prince Christian, later Prince of Denmark, and his wife. A royal yacht fetched the royal party, and I was granted the comfort and convenience of travelling home on it. However, the voyage turned out to be extremely difficult, and only after a journey lasting two nights through fog and storm did I go ashore at the Customs House in Copenhagen.

I had been told that Hartmann's opera, *Little Kirsten*, for which I had written the libretto, had been produced to great acclaim during my absence. As it deserved, the music was acknowledged as being a true bouquet of Danish flowers, so remarkable and so gripping. Even

Heiberg had approved of the text. I was looking forward to seeing and hearing this little work, and it so happened that *Little Kirsten* was to be performed on the very day I arrived back home.

"Yes, you will certainly be pleased," said Hartmann. "People are very happy with both the music and the text."

I went to the theatre, and saw that people had noticed me, and when the performance was over they clapped, though at the same time there was some loud hissing.

"That has never happened before," said Hartmann. "I can't understand it."

"But I understand it perfectly," I replied. "Don't you worry about it; it was not you they meant; it was my fellow countrymen who have noticed that I have come home, and they were just wishing me welcome."

I was still physically ill. I could not recover after my summer in the South, and only the refreshing cold of the winter kept me together. I was in a nervous, weak state, while on the other hand my mind was extremely active. It was at this time that I finished my play *Ahasuerus*. H. C. Ørsted, to whom I had read everything I had written for the last few years, made an ever greater impression on me with his lively interest and his brilliant conversation. His heart beat so strongly for what was good and beautiful, and his thoughts always sought to force their way into it and find the truth it contained. He said this clearly and unequivocally, and in every poem truth was the essence of the work. One day I went to him with a Danish translation I had made of Byron's poem *Darkness*. My thoughts were then entirely filled with the great and imaginative descriptions the poet has produced here, and so I was surprised when Ørsted declared it was a complete failure as a poem, for it was false from beginning to end and each new conceit was more stupid than the last.

"The poet," he said, "might imagine the sun disappearing from the sky, but he must realise that the results will be very different from this darkness, this cold and these events. These are the imaginings of a madman."

And I felt he was right, and even at that stage I adopted into my views the truths he expresses to the poets of his age in *The Spirit in Nature*. He says that when they speak as the leading figures of their time they should take the inspiration for their images and expressions from science and not from the poetical arsenal of a past age. On the other hand, if a poet is depicting a past age, then its ideas and conceptions of the world are of course those that must be expressed by the principal characters. These opinions, which Ørsted expressed in his book and which are so true and correct, were to my surprise not understood even by a man like Bishop Mynster. Ørsted read several of the articles in his book aloud for me. Then we considered them, and with his infinite love and modesty he even listened to me when I made the objection – the only one I had to make – that the form of dialogue reminiscent of Campe's *Robinson* was now antiquated. Here, where it was not possible to portray characters, it would be no more than headings and names, and it would be just as easy to understand the whole thing without this.

"Perhaps you are right," he said gently and sensitively, "but I can't just decide to alter something now when I have seen it in this form for years. But I will think about what you have said and take it into consideration when I write more."

A vast amount of knowledge, experience and ingenuity issued from him, as well as a simple charm, something as innocent and unconscious as in a child. A unique personality with a stamp of the divine was revealed here; and to this could be added his deep religious faith. Through the glass of learning he saw God's greatness, which it is a Christian delight to recognise even with closed eyes. We often spoke of the profound blessings and truths in religion. Then we read Genesis together, and I saw the ancient myths and legends concerning the creation of the world reflected in this man who at once combined the religiosity of a child with the well-developed thoughts of a man. I always left Ørsted, grand and charming as he was, with such clarity of thought and with a mind so rich in ideas, and I must repeat that in the most trying hours when I was weighed down by melancholy and a lack of recognition, it was he who maintained my spirits and prophesied a better time to come.

One day, when I had left him and was crushed by mental anguish on account of the injustice and harshness I encountered around me, he knew no peace, old though he was, until he had visited my home late in the evening to express his sympathy and consolation once more. This moved me so deeply that I forgot all my sorrows and anguish and wept in gratitude and blessing for his infinite kindness. I regained my strength and the courage to write and to work.

In Germany I became better and better known and received many tokens of good will as a result of my *Gesammelte Werke* and the various impressions of my separate works. Those which were read most were my *Fairy Tales* and *Picture Book without Pictures*, and some writers even tried to copy the fairy tales. Many a book and work of poetry was sent to me, and something I thought especially beautiful and kindly was the dedication: "*Herzlicher Gruss deutscher Kinder dem lieben Kinderfreunde in Dänmark H. C. Andersen.*" (Kind regards from German children to H. C. Andersen, the children's friend from Denmark).

Rays of sunshine came to me from abroad, and more and more began to appear at home, too. My thoughts were fresh and my heart became young again with its memories and moods. In the great circle of life through which we journey, joy and sorrow each have their areas; sorrow often many different ones of which the world hears nothing.

There are compartments in the human heart which no one, not even those dearest to us, is allowed to look into. In a poet, deep melodies will often be heard from there and people do not know whether this is poetry or truth. Such melodies are heard, too, throughout the fairy tale of my life. They are part of me to such a slight extent that only poetry can express what perhaps moved infinitely deep within me and was the life and thought of days and nights:

I

Gently take thy rest,
As though you lay in Death's dark chest,
Memory's rose, so fair and so fine.
No longer of this world, thou art but mine,
For thee I sing, for thee my tears do flow.
The night is fair, the night is still; –
Dead! – All is dead below.

Chorus

Young man, you know our song,
"Go now to bed, and close your eyes;
Reflect yourself in dream's deep flood;
Your favourite dream's yourself and all your sighs."

The Lonely Wanderer

Yes, deep within me lies a buried treasure.
What knows the world of what is there?
What knows the world of nightly measure,
Of bitter tears beyond compare,
Those noiseless, bitter streams of tears
Which flow so heavily and deep?
– A young man thinks but of himself.
Then let him sleep.

During the course of the year several of my works had been published in England, for instance *A Poet's Bazaar*, *Fairy Tales* and *A Picture Book without Pictures*, and there they had met with the same friendly reception both on the part of the critics and the public as *The Improvisatore* had done earlier. Many were the letters sent to me by unknown friends I had won there. King Christian the Eighth had received a beautifully bound edition of my works from the well-known London publisher, Richard Bentley. One of our highly respected personages had told me that on this occasion the King expressed his delight at the recognition shown to me, but said at the same time that he was amazed at the way I was valued abroad but so often attacked and slighted at home. The King's kind feelings towards me increased even further when he read *Das Märchen meines Lebens.*

"Only now do I really understand you," he said earnestly when I entered the audience chamber to present him with my latest book. "It is so seldom I see you," he continued. "We must talk together more often."

"That depends on Your Majesty," I answered.

"Yes, yes, you are right," he replied, and then he went on to say how pleased he was at the recognition I enjoyed in Germany and especially in England. He spoke of the story of my life, and he understood it with a kind and loving heart; and before we parted he asked, "Where are you dining tomorrow?"

"In a restaurant," I answered.

"Then come and dine with me and my wife instead! We dine at four o'clock."

As I have already said, I had received a beautiful album from the Princess of Prussia containing several interesting signatures. Their Majesties saw it, and when they gave it back to me King Christian the Eighth himself had written in it the significant words:

"To gain a worthy position by dint of one's well-applied talent is better than favours and gifts."

> These lines are to remind you of the benevolent wishes
> of Christian R.

It was dated "the second of April"; the King knew it was my birthday. Queen Caroline Amalie, too, had written some appreciative words that are a source of great joy to me– no gifts could give me more joy than this treasure in spirit and word.

One day the King asked me if I ought not also to see England. I said, "Yes," and added that I was thinking of going there the following summer.

"Then you can have the money from me," said His Majesty.

I thanked him and said, "That is not necessary. I have received 800 *Rigsdaler* for the German edition of my works, and I shall use that money."

"But," the King went on with a smile, "you, represent Danish literature in England now, and so you must live well and in comfort."

"Oh, but I shall certainly be able to. And when I have used all my money I shall come home."

"You can write directly to me and tell me what you need," said the King.

"Oh no, Your Majesty, I have no need to do that now. Perhaps I shall be more in need of Your Majesty's favour on another occasion, but I must not accept it now; one must not continually pester. And I do so dislike talking about money. But if I may write to Your Majesty without asking for anything, write not as to a king, for then it will be such a formal letter, but perhaps as to someone of whom I am very fond!"

The King gave his consent, and he seemed pleased at what must have been the correct way in which I had received his kindness.

In the middle of May 1847 I went over land from Copenhagen. It was lovely spring weather, and I could see the stork flying from its nest with outstretched wings. I celebrated Whitsuntide at the old mansion of Glorup, and in Odense I saw the rifle guild festival, which had been the loveliest day of the year during my childhood. Just as in those days a new generation of boys came by, carrying the targets which had been shot through and through. The entire throng was waving green branches just like Burnham Wood approaching Macbeth's castle. There was the same merriment and the same crowd – but how differently I saw it now.

A poor, half-crazed yokel outside my window made a deep impression on me; his face had noble lines, and his eyes were shining, but there was something deranged about him, and the boys chased him and teased him. It made me think of myself, my childhood and my weak-minded grandfather, and I wondered whether, if I had stayed in Odense and been apprenticed there, time and the conditions under which I lived would not have dulled my imagination, which in those days had such power over me. And I wondered how people would have regarded me then.

I do not know, but the sight of this unfortunate halfwit whom all the boys were teasing outside my window made my heart beat wildly, and my thoughts and thanks flew up to God in gratitude for His grace and the love He showered upon me.

My journey took me through Hamburg, where I made the acquaintance of Glassbrenner, the author, and his brilliant wife, the excellent actress, Peroni-Glassbrenner. A Copenhagen newspaper has said that the merry satirist, Glassbrenner, has made a dig at me as a writer of fairy tales. I have not been able to find it, but on the other hand I have a poem from him:

An H. C. Andersen!

Verständen wir, was bunte Vögel singen,
Die Düfte, die aus Blumen zu uns dringen,
Verständen wir, was in den Gräbern lebt,
Und was das kalte Leben oft begräbt, –
Und könnten die Geheimnisse erlauschen
Aus Waldeswehn und Meeresrauschen;
Verständen wir, was holde Kinderaugen sagen:
Wir brauchten Deine Werke nicht zu übertragen.

A. Glassbrenner.

To H. C. Andersen!

Could we but understand what the bright birds sing,
The fragrances the flowers to us bring,
Could we but understand what life the graves still hold
And what our cold world oft consigns to mould –
And hearken to the secrets stored
In the forest's murmurs, in the sea's wild roar;
We would understand what's there in children's looks
And we would not need to translate your books.

A. Glassbrenner.

That does not suggest that the man has much against me.

After a visit to some dear friends in Oldenburg I continued my journey to Holland. The coach rolled along with us on a paved highway that was as smooth and clean as the floor in a dairy. Houses and towns presented us with a picture of prosperity and cleanliness. In the fortress town of Deventer it was just market day, and the streets were thronged with people in their picturesque costumes.

371

On the market square there were waffle shops, just the same as I had known in the old days in the Deer Park at home. Peals of bells rang from the bell towers, and the Dutch flag fluttered in the breeze. From Utrecht I went by rail, and within an hour I was in Amsterdam, "where they live half in water like amphibians." But it is not as bad as that, and it does not in any way remind one of Venice, the beaver city with the dead palaces. The first man I stopped in the street to ask the way answered in a way which was so easy to understand that I thought the Dutch language must be easy to follow! But he was speaking Danish. It was a French barber's assistant who had worked for Causse in Copenhagen for a time and had learned some Danish. He recognised me, and with his French accent he answered me in the best Danish he could manage.

Shady trees leaned out over the canals, and clumsy, colourful barges with husband and wife and all the family glided quietly past; the wife stood at the tiller, and Papa sat with a long pipe in his mouth. Among all the people there, I was particularly struck to see a couple of quite small boys whose clothes were divided into two colours; half the back was black and the other half red, and the same was the case with their trousers – each leg was in its own colour. Then came some little girls who were likewise clad in two colours, just as is the case with convicts at home. I asked what this signified, and was told they were from the orphanage, and that this was the way in which they were dressed there. French comedy was being performed in the theatre. Unfortunately, the National Theatre was closed during my stay, otherwise I would have been able to see a genuine Dutch tradition – people smoke during the whole of the performance, and Jan, as all waiters in Holland are always called, goes around lighting pipes and serving tea, which is drunk out of large basins. And meanwhile the play goes on. The couplets are sung and the pipes are puffed so the smoke spreads all over the auditorium and the stage. Several Dutchmen told me this, and I have no reason to believe it is an exaggeration.

The first place I went to in Amsterdam was a bookshop where I wanted to buy a volume of Dutch and Flemish poems. The man I spoke to looked at me in amazement, quickly excused himself and hurried away. I did not know what this meant and was just about to go when two men came from the adjoining room and gave me the same fixed stare; and then one of them asked me if I was not the Danish poet, Andersen. They showed me my portrait, which was hanging there in the room, and it was from this that they had recognised me. The Dutch papers had reported long ago that I was expected. A Dane by the name of Nyegaard, who had lived in Holland for many years and was there called van Nieuwenhuis, had long ago translated all my novels into Dutch. Shortly before I arrived, *Das Märchen meines Lebens* and a number of the fairy tales, *Sprookjes*, had been done into Dutch and published in Amsterdam. The publisher of *De Tijd*, the late van der Vliet, had drawn attention to my work by writing a fond and enthusiastic account of it, and my portrait had been included in the magazine.

In this way I heard and soon realised that I had many friends in Holland. H. C. Ørsted had given me a letter to Professor Vrolik in Amsterdam, and through him I was introduced to the well known Dutch poet van Lennep, the author of *De Roos van Dekama* and *Harlems Verlossing*, which are considered among the finest novels in Dutch literature. In van Lennep I found a handsome, friendly man in a comfortable, prosperous home; I was not a stranger there, but a welcome family guest. I was surrounded by pretty and friendly children, who knew my fairy tales. *De roode schoentjes* had especially made a profound impression on one of the boys, and it had occupied all his thoughts to a quite remarkable extent. He stood there, silently looking at me for a long time. He later showed me the book containing the story and also a picture in which the shoes were painted red while all the rest of the illustration was in black and white. Sara, the eldest daughter, a grown-up girl full of charm and vivacity, asked me whether the ladies in Copenhagen are beautiful, and I answered, "Yes, they are like the Dutch ladies." She wanted to hear me speak some Danish, and I had to write down for her a few of the words she liked best. At dinner van Lennep asked me if I thought I could read Dutch, and he gave me a sheet of paper on which there were written some words. It was a poem he had written for me; he read it aloud for us all, and this is how it began:

373

Den Dichter
H.C. Andersen

Onbekend, gesmaad, verstooten
Dwaalde een hulploos kieken rond
Over Funens vruchtb'ren grond,
Rijk van stroom en beek doorvloten etc.

To the writer
H. C. Andersen

Unknown, reviled, forsook,
A helpless chicken wandering round
Over Funens's fruitful ground,
Watered by many a river and brook etc.

I think it is all printed in *De Tijd*.

From Amsterdam I went to Haarlem by rail. The line runs in one place here as though it were the dyke between the open North Sea and the Haarlem Sea, and I saw the bold undertaking and the great task of pumping out an ocean. It had already sunk appreciably. The mighty organ at Haarlem, the greatest in the world, filled its 8000 metal pipes with sound under the beamed vault as I entered this mighty, inverted ship's keel. The language around me sounded strange, half German, half Dutch, and there was an inscription on several houses, "*Hier gaat man uit porren*" – they go out to rouse people – that looked almost Danish. The bells were forever ringing from the churches; the whole country looked like a great English park to me. I wrote down this first impression of Holland in a little verse in Leyden when Professor Schlegel's wife came to me with her album:

So Sunday-clad the whole land stands.
So Sunday-glad your voice, your hands.
A garden Holland, where the heart is glad.
One feels at home here, never sad.

Mrs. Schlegel understood the Danish language and knew Denmark. She had been to Copenhagen and had actually been at Oehlenschläger's one day when I had entered the room; she remembered it well. Together with her, her husband and Professor Geel I went to see the interesting sights in Leyden, among which is the entrenchment made by the Anglo-Saxons when they invaded England under Hengist and Horsa.

In the waiting-room at the railway station there were several pictures and posters on the walls. The biggest of them all was one advertising van der Vliet's *De Tijd*, and my name and portrait happened to be on it. People noticed the picture and me, and I felt quite embarrassed by it all and hurried to find a coach. I had asked for a ticket to The Hague, and on the ticket they had given me I now read "s'Gravenhage", which is the Dutch name for it. I did not know this; the train set off, and I thought I was being taken to quite a different place from where I wanted to go.

On looking out of my window in The Hague the first person I discovered down in the street was an acquaintance of mine, a friend from Rome, Verhulst, the Dutch composer, whom I was said to resemble in gait and movement if not in facial features. I nodded to him, but he did not know me, never dreaming that I should be in The Hague. An hour later, when I went out to look round the strange city, the first person I met was again Verhulst, and what a joyous meeting it was. We talked of Rome and Copenhagen, and I had to tell him of Hartmann and Gade whose music he knew. He praised Denmark, which has a Danish opera. The Dutch, I believe, have only French and Italian music. I went with him to his home on the outskirts of the city; from his windows I had a view across fertile, green fields and meadows, a typically Dutch scene. At that moment the bells rang out from the nearby church towers, and a flock of storks flew past in salute. And they are at home here; indeed, a stork is even the emblem of The Hague.

I did not know van der Vliet personally, but he had written to me on several occasions and sent me translations and reviews of my works. I entered his sitting room; he was a pleasant young man, with the air of a true child of nature. He took a warm interest in everything I had written and was surprised, almost overwhelmed, at my unexpected visit. He had expected to be told beforehand when I was coming, and had arranged his house so that I could stay there. He called his young wife, and she was just as pleased and cordial, but she spoke only Dutch. However, when we did not understand each other we nodded to each other and pressed each other's hand. There was no end to all the kindness these kind people wanted to show me. The proud father told me that their only child, still quite a little boy, was called Christian after me and the poor fiddler. The great joy which my presence seemed to give them touched me; it was a little home full of love. However, as I was only staying in The Hague for a few days, and as their home was rather a long way out of town, I chose rather to stay at the hotel, which was in the centre of the city. Both husband and wife accompanied me to my door so that we could be together a little longer. It is good to find such affection and sincerity in a foreign land. My arrival was for them like the reception of the most joyous news, and off we went, laughing and chatting, and in a merry mood. We parted, and on the steps of the hotel where I was living I found a man dressed in mourning standing before me. He addressed me by name. I knew him, but how different was this from the joyous laughter I had just left. Tears came into the man's eyes; it was Hensel, Mendelssohn-Bartholdy's brother-in-law. He had recently left Berlin, for his doctors wished him to travel abroad to take his thoughts away from the sorrow oppressing him so sorely. His wonderful, gifted wife, Mendelssohn's sister, who resembled her brother in so many ways, both in being a true musical genius and having the same features and expression, had suddenly died. I had met her and her husband at social gatherings in Berlin. She was a brilliant, lively woman with the intelligence and spirit of her brother, and like him she played with such accomplishment and expression that everyone was carried away. Just recently, when she had gone to sit in the arbor after dinner, where she had been well and full of good humour, she gave a cry and was dead. Her husband, who is famous as a portrait painter and had previously been an officer, had painted her as she looked in death. He brought the large portrait with him and had it displayed on the table in his room. It moved me, coming from joy and joyous people, to see this strong man so deeply upset and reduced to tears.

As we now know, Mendelssohn died just as suddenly the following year and followed his splendid gifted sister.

I had been in The Hague for four days. It was Sunday, and I wanted to go to the French opera, but my friends asked me to abandon the idea and join a group assembled at the Hôtel de l'Europe.

"It looks as though there is going to be a ball here this evening," I said, as we went up the stairs. "What are all these decorations for?" I asked. "Everything looks so festive."

My companion smiled and said, "It is a dinner in your honour." I went into the great hall and was amazed at the number of people congregated there. "They are some of your Dutch friends," I was told, "who are delighted to be able to spend the evening in your company."

During the short time I had been in The Hague letters had been sent all over the country to the friends of my Muse, whom van der Vliet and several others had promised to inform when I arrived. Despite the long journey a wealthy man called Kneppelhout, the author of *Opuscules de jeunesse* had even come right from the Zuyder Zee. Here I found a host of artists, literary figures, painters and actors. During dinner at a flower-decked table toasts were drunk and speeches made. I was especially moved by a toast van der Vliet drank to "Collin, the father in Copenhagen, the noble man who adopted Andersen as though he were his own son."

"Two kings," he then said, turning towards me, "King Christian the Eighth and Frederik Wilhelm of Prussia, have each given you a decoration. When these are laid on your coffin one day, may God give you the most beautiful order of all for your pious fairy-tales, the crown of honour of an immortal life."

Someone spoke of the linguistic and historical connections between Holland and Denmark. One of the painters, who had made some beautiful illustrations for my *Picture Book*, drank my health as a painter. Kneppelhout proposed a toast in French to freedom in form and imagination. Songs were sung, and humorous poems were recited, and as I still had no knowledge of Dutch drama and tragedy, Peters, the famous tragic actor from The Hague, acted the prison scene from Gravenweert's *Tasso*. I did not understand a word of it, but I sensed the true feeling with which it was rendered, and I have never seen more excellent mimicry in anyone. It was as though the actor turned pale and blushed scarlet; he seemed even to have control over the blood in his cheeks. The whole company broke out in jubilant applause. The company sang some beautiful songs and I was especially moved by the melody and the enthusiasm in the national anthem, *Wien Neerlansch bloed*. It was one of the evenings in my life when I have been most honoured. It seemed to me that the homage I had encountered culminated in Sweden and Holland. God, who knows all men's hearts, knows how humble I felt. It is a blessing to be able to weep for gratitude and joy. The next day I spent in the open air; Kneppelhout took me "in Bosch" where there was a promenade and music. We went past stretches of lovely, green meadows and down idyllic lanes with prosperous country residences and we saw *Leyden* before us. We approached it, and then drove to the village of Scheveningen which is protected from the North Sea by high sandhills and dykes. There at the table d'hôte in the hydro a small group of friends again drank to art and poetry, to Denmark and Holland. Fishing boats were anchored along the coast; music played; the sea surged. I felt so much at home here; it was a lovely evening.

The following morning, when I was to leave The Hague, my landlady brought me a pile of newspapers which already contained reports of the dinner that had been given for me. A few of my friends, of whom I had become fond there, accompanied me to the railway station. I left them with a sense of melancholy, uncertain whether we would ever meet again in this world.

Rotterdam was to my mind the first really lively Dutch town, much more so than Amsterdam. There were large numbers of big vessels in the canals. As before I saw brightly painted little Dutch barges in which the wife stood at the tiller. Even if she was not wearing slippers and spurs as in the ballad about *Young Sir Pedersen*, she did stand at the tiller, and Papa lay smoking his pipe. Everything here seemed to be hustle and bustle. One of the oldest Dutch steamers, a true snail of a ship called the Batavier was going to London the next morning, and I took a berth on it. It was heavily laden, and great baskets full of cherries were piled high above the railings. A large number of emigrants on their way to America were travelling on deck, and the children were romping about merrily. There was a German there, as portly as Falstaff, walking up and down with his thin wife, who was already on the point of being seasick and terrified of the moment we would sail out of the Maas into the great North Sea. Her greyhound was trembling as much as she was, and yet it had a coat on, tied fast with great bows. The ebb tide had set in, and eight long hours passed before we sailed out into the North Sea. Low-lying Holland seemed to sink deeper and deeper into the greyish yellow sea, and as the sun set I went to my bunk. When I came out on deck again early next morning I could just glimpse the English coast. At the mouth of the Thames, fishing boats in their thousands lay like some enormous flock of chickens, like tattered bits of paper, like a complete market or camp of tents. The Thames certainly proclaims that England rules the waves. Here, her servants fly out. Countless hosts of ships arrive every minute like relay racers, steamer after steamer. It was a runner with a ribbon of thick smoke in its hat, at the top of which glowed the red flower of fire. Cleaving the waves like swans, one great sailing ship after another glided past us. There were pleasure yachts with rich young gentlemen on board. Ship followed ship, and the further up the Thames we went, the denser the throng became. I had started to count how many steamers we might meet, but I grew tired on account of the huge number. Looking up the Thames from Gravesend it seemed as though we were going into a great smoking marsh fire, but it was only smoke from the steamships and chimneys ahead of us. There was a heavy thunderstorm, and the blue lightning flashed against a pitch-black sky. A train rushed past, its blue smoke rolling upwards, and the peal of thunder sounding like the roar of cannon.

"They know you are here, and are welcoming you," said a young Englishman to me in jest.

"Yes," I thought, "God does indeed know it."

Although I could scarcely believe it possible, the Thames became an even denser throng of steamers, boats and sailing-ships, a street that was chock-full. I could not imagine how these vast numbers could move past each other without colliding. The ebb tide soon made itself felt. The slimy, muddy bed was revealed near the banks. I thought of Quilp in Dickens' *Old Curiosity Shop* and of Marryat's portrayal of life here on the river.

At the Custom House, where we landed, I took a cab and drove off. It went on and on and would not stop in this endless city. The throng in the streets became denser and denser, carriage after carriage in two rows in each direction. There was every kind of vehicle: omnibuses filled both inside and on top, great carts that were really no more than huge packing cases only intended to display posters that were stuck on them to show the latest news; men with big signboards on a pole that they lifted high above the crowds and on which one could read of something or other that was to be seen or bought. Everyone was in motion, as though half London were streaming to one side of the city, and the other half to the other side. Where the streets intersect there are raised stone areas in the middle; people made a bee-line for them from one pavement, dodging in and out of the nearest line of traffic, and then they waited there in safety until they could see a chance of dodging through the traffic and on to the pavement on the other side. London, the city of cities. Yes, that is what I immediately felt it was, and I came to recognise this more clearly day by day. It is Paris intensified; there is the life of Naples, but not the same noise. Everything hurries and rushes past fairly quietly, omnibus after omnibus – I am told there are 4000 of them – wagons, vans, cabs, hackney-carriages and elegant coaches roll, jolt, rumble and dash along, as though there were some great event at each end of the city which they must all witness. And this tide is there all the time. Always! One day when all the people we now see there are in their graves there will be the same bustle, the same waves of omnibuses, cabs, wagons, and men wandering backwards and forwards with the sandwich boards in front and behind them, placards on poles, placards on vans telling of balloons, bushmen, Vauxhall, panoramas and Jenny Lind.

At last I reached the Hôtel de Sablonière in Leicester Square which H. C. Ørsted had recommended to me, and I was given a room where the sun shone right on to my bed as though to show me straight away that there can be sunshine in London. But it was a shade rather of reddish gold, as though it were coming through the glass of a beer bottle. Later, however, when the sun had set, the air became beautifully clear, and the stars twinkled down on streets bright with gas lights, where the crowds still surged quietly as they hurried past. I was exhausted, and I fell asleep without having seen anyone I knew. I had come to London without any letters of introduction at all. The only person I had approached at home to ask for one, an extremely distinguished man with English con-nections, a man through whom I was hoping on this single occasion to catch a glimpse of London high life, had sent me nothing.

"You do not need any letters of introduction here," said our Danish ambassador, Count Reventlow, whom I visited immediately the next morning. "You are known and introduced in England by your works. This very evening there is to be a small, select gathering at Lord Palmerston's. I will write to Lady Palmerston and tell her you are here, and then I think you will receive an invitation."

I did receive one a few hours later, and in the evening I drove there together with Count Reventlow. England's most distinguished aristocracy was present. The ladies wore the choicest gowns imaginable – there were silks with frills, glittering diamonds and exquisite bouquets. Both Lord and Lady Palmerston received me kindly, and when the Hereditary Grand Duke of Weimar, who was there with his young wife, greeted me cordially and presented me to the Duchess of Suffolk – I believe that is who it was – and she spoke enthusiastically of *The Improvisatore* – "the best book about Italy" as she was pleased to call it – I was soon surrounded by the choicest of England's ladies. They had all heard about the Danish writer and knew *The Top and the Ball*, *The Ugly Duckling* and so on. Many kind words were addressed to me. I seemed not to be a stranger at all. The Duke of Cambridge spoke to me about Christian the Eighth. Bunsen, the Prussian Ambassador, who in earlier days had been of great help to the Danes in Rome, came to me along with his lady and greeted me cordially. Many of them gave me their cards, and most of them invited me to visit them.

"This evening," said Count Reventlow, "you have made a leap into high society, in which many people need years to become accepted. But do not be too modest. You must put on a bold front here if you want to advance."

And then with a cheerful humour of his own, he continued in Danish, which no one present understood. "Tomorrow we can have

381

a look at the cards and choose the best ones. You have talked long enough with this person now; there is someone else here to whom it will be even more to your advantage to be introduced. At his house, you will find a splendid dinner table and choice company, and there are many who seek an invitation."

And so he went on. At last I was completely worn out by walking to and fro across the highly polished floor, and clambering to intellectual heights in various languages I could not speak. The heat was oppressive, and I was finally forced to tear myself away and go out into the hall to breathe and rest, or at least to lean on the banister. And I continued for three weeks in the same way as on this evening. It was at the height of the season, the time for summer gatherings such as we only know in winter. I was invited out to dinner every day; I was invited out every evening, and then to balls which lasted far into the night. Everywhere there was a throng of people in the halls and on the stairs. And since the whole of the week ahead was taken up by choice invitations, I had to go out to lunch, too. It was more than I could stand. A festive buzz and hum and rush. One single long day and night lasting almost three weeks. I can only remember odd moments and scenes from that time. Almost everywhere I met the same leading figures in a variety of gold, satin, frills and flowers. Especially roses were used to decorate the rooms beautifully; all the windows, tables, stairs and alcoves were covered with them; they were all in water in glasses, bowls and cups, but you could not see that unless you examined them closely. Their immediate appearance was one of fresh, sweet-smelling carpets. As I say, I lived in Leicester Square, at the Hôtel de Sablonière, where H. C. Ørsted had lived, and which he had recommended to me. However, Count Reventlow said that it was not fashionable enough, and here everything was arranged according to fashion. He asked me not to mention Leicester Square, saying that it would have the same effect as if a foreigner in Copenhagen were to say in fine society that he lived in Peer Madsen's Passage. I should tell people that I was living at his residence. And yet I was living close to Piccadilly, in a large square, and I had a marble statue of the Earl of Leicester standing among green trees just outside my window. Some six or eight years ago it had been fashionable to live there, but this was no longer the case. "Ritter"

Bunsen, Count Reventlow and several of the ambassadors visited me there, however, but it was not fashionable.

Everything in England is about etiquette, and even the Queen is bound by it in her own home. I was told that one day she was out in one of the lovely parks, and would perhaps have liked to stay there a little longer; but dinner was to be served at precisely eight o'clock, and so she had to be home by that time, for otherwise all England would take exception to it. In the land of freedom one can almost be stifled by etiquette; but it is only a small matter here where there are so many delightful things. Here one is in a nation which at the present time is perhaps the only really religious nation on earth; there is respect for morals and good manners. It is no use dwelling on the occasional excrescences and excesses that are always to be found in a great city.

London is the city of politeness, and the police set it an example. You only need to ask the way of a policeman in the street, and he will go with you and show you the way. You receive the politest of replies in every shop.

And as for the constantly grey atmosphere and smoke over London, the picture has been exaggerated. It is certainly to be found in some of the older and more densely populated districts, but the greater part is airy and open, just like Paris. I have seen quite a lot of beautiful sunny days in London, and many starlit nights. For a stranger in a land or a country it is in fact extremely difficult to give an accurate and true picture of it after only being there for a short time. The best way of discovering this is to read other writers' descriptions of our own country, where we understand and are familiar with most things. A tourist writes down what individual people tell him, and they all see it from their own special point of view; he himself sees it through the dazzling glass of a life of travel. He paints countryside and people as though from a railway train, and even then not so accurately in all their details.

For me London is the city of cities, not counting Rome. Rome is a bas-relief of the world by night, in which even the merriment of the Carnival is a bustling, joyful dream and Pius the Ninth only a great thought in the dream. London is a bas-relief of the world by day with its haste and bustle and the bobbin of life whirring round at lightning speed. The topic of the day here, incidentally, was Jenny Lind and nothing but Jenny Lind. In order to some extent to avoid too frequent visits, and to live in the freshest air in London she had rented a house at Old Brompton. That was all I could learn in the hotel where I was staying and where I immediately made enquiries about her. To find the place I went straight away to the Italian Opera where she was singing, and here too the policeman in the street was of help to me, taking me to the cashier at the theatre, but neither he nor any of the various porters there would or could give me any information. So I wrote a few words to Jenny Lind on one of my visiting cards; I said I had come to London and told her where I was living, and I asked her to send me her address without delay. And the next morning a joyous, heartfelt letter came to her "brother". I found my bearings on a map, saw in which district of London Old Brompton lay and took an omnibus in which the conductor gave me clear instructions as to how far I should travel with him, which road I should turn down and which house I then had to go to, to find the "Swedish Nightingale", as he called her with a smile.

A few days later, of all the thousands of omnibuses London possesses, I happened to get into just the same one. I did not recognise the conductor, but he knew me, and he asked whether I had found "Jenny Lind, the Nightingale". She lived a long way out in the outskirts of town in a delightful little house with a low hedge between it and the street. There was a crowd of people standing outside, as there almost always was, in the hope of catching sight of Jenny Lind. And today they were lucky, for when I rang the bell and she recognised me from the window she ran out to the carriage and pressed both my hands and looked at me with such sisterly eyes and such delight that she quite forgot the many people around us who were pushing forward. We had to hurry into the house, which was comfortable, charming and tasteful. A small garden opened up with a large lawn and a number of deciduous trees. And a small dog with long brown hair romped about, sprang into its mistress' lap and was patted and kissed. There were some elegantly bound books on the table, and she showed me my *True Story of My Life* which Mary Howitt had dedicated to her. There was a large sheet of paper on the table; it was a caricature of Jenny Lind in the form of a big nightingale with the face of a girl; Lumley stood strewing sovereigns on her tail to persuade her to sing. We talked of home, about the Bournonvilles and the Collins, and when I told her about the banquet the Dutch had arranged for me and how they had drunk old Collin's health, she clapped her hands and cried, "That was wonderful".

Then she promised me that I should have a ticket for the opera every time she sang, but I was not to think of paying for it – it was ridiculously expensive, she said: "Let me sing for you, and then afterwards you can sit at home and read fairy tales for me".

Only twice did my many invitations permit me to make use of the tickets she sent me. The first time I saw her was in *La Sonnambula*, which is perhaps her finest role. The virginity and purity which seemed to radiate from her gave the stage the feel of something sacred. The way in which she walks in her sleep in the last act and takes the rose from her breast, raises it in the air and involuntarily drops it was so charming, so beautiful, so strangely moving that tears came to my eyes. She received applause as enthusiastic and noisy as anything I have ever heard among the emotional Neapolitans. Flowers rained upon her; everything looked so festive. We all know how splendidly dressed one must be in the great opera house in London; all the gentlemen in the stalls and the circle wear white scarves, and the ladies sit there in their finest evening gowns, all of them with a large bouquet in their hands. The Queen and Prince Albert were there, and so were the Hereditary Grand Duke of Weimar and his wife. The Italian language sounded strange to me coming from the lips of Jenny Lind, and yet it was said that she pronounced it more correctly than the Italians themselves, and that the same was the case with German. Yet the spirit was the same as when she sang in her beautiful native language. For Jenny Lind and for this season, the composer Verdi had written a new opera called *I Masnadieri* with a libretto based on Schiller's *Die Räuber*. I heard it once, but not even Jenny Lind's acting and singing could lift this dead composition above mediocrity. Amalie's role ends with her being killed in the forest by Carl Moor, as the band of robbers is surrounded. Lablache played the part of the old Moor, and it was extremely amusing to see this gigantic, fat man come out of the tower and say that he was faint from hunger; and all the audience laughed at it, too.

It was at the same performance that I saw the famous dancer Taglioni for the first time; she danced "*le pas des déesses*". Before she appeared, my heart was really beating wildly with anticipation, just as it always does when I am waiting to see something great and magnificent. She came – she was a rather old and fairly powerfully built but quite beautiful woman; she would have been a delightful lady at some social function, but as a young goddess – "*fuimus Troes*" – I thought, and sat cold and indifferent while this elderly lady danced gracefully before me. Youth is needed, and that was something that Cerrito had. It was incomparably beautiful to see her; there was the gracefulness of a swallow in her dancing. Flight, the play of Psyche – there was none of this in Taglioni; *fuimus Troes*!

Our compatriot, Miss Grahn, was also in London and was deeply admired by all; but she did not dance while I was there as she had a bad foot. One evening during a performance of *L'Elisire d'Amore* she called me to her little box where she described the world behind the scenes for me with great vivacity and humour; she told me about everyone there. She did not seem to be one of Jenny Lind's admirers. Of course all the jubilation of the day on account of Jenny Lind was also mixed with some opposition; something that all the great and the good must experience. Her portrayal of Norma as a wounded, but noble woman, which so appealed to me and which I have already discussed, was not generally to the taste of the English who in Grisi and those who tried to follow her example had previously seen her played as a passionate Medea. The librettist of *Oberon* and several other operas, Planché, was vehemently critical; but these small difficulties disappeared in the splendour of the jubilation and admiration, and she was happy in her little home under the shady trees. One afternoon I went out to her, tired of the eternal invitations and the overwhelming adulation. "Yes," she said, "now you can see for yourself what it is to have a fuss made of you. It wearies one. And how empty it is, how infinitely empty are all the polite remarks that are addressed to one." Later, when I drove home in her carriage, people crowded round it, thinking that Jenny Lind was in it, but they only found me, an unknown, unfamiliar gentleman. Through me, old Hambro had invited her to a dinner at his country residence, but it was impossible to persuade her to accept it, not even when it was left to her to decide how many should be invited, indeed not even when it was suggested there should no one present but the old man himself and me; she refused to change her manner of life, but she was willing to let me take the worthy old man out to visit her. I did so, and the two of them got on extremely well; they even talked of money and laughed at me because I did not understand how to change my talents into gold.

A young sculptor by the name of Durham wanted to model our busts, but neither of us had much time to sit for him. However, thanks to a few words from me the young man was permitted to come for half an hour and remodel the clay bust he had already made in rough after seeing her on the stage. I gave him twice as long, and in that one hour he produced a bust which was remarkably good in consideration of the time he had had at his disposal. Together with the one of Jenny Lind it has been exhibited in Copenhagen, where they were both far too severely criticised, for there was a likeness and a spiritual understanding in both of them. And what Danish artist would have been able to produce more than this in such a short time as Durham had at his disposal? After this, years passed before I saw Jenny Lind again. As we know, she left England in an atmosphere of triumph and adulation and went to America.

Count Reventlow presented me to Lady Morgan; he had already informed me a few days previously that this old lady was expecting us, but she had put it off until a certain day because, he told me in confidence, she certainly knew me by name, but she had never read any of my books and wanted quickly to acquaint herself with *The Improvisatore*, the fairy tales and so on. She lived in a house of small colourful rooms that were full of rococo ornaments. There was a touch of French about everything, especially about the old lady, who was full of life and gaiety, spoke French, was French in all her ways and was very painted. She quoted from my book, which I knew she had read in haste, but she evinced great politeness towards me all the time. There was a hand drawing by Thorvaldsen on the wall; it was *Night and Day*, which we have in bas-relief and which he had given to her in Rome. She said that in my honour she would invite all the famous authors from London, and then I would make the acquaintance of Dickens, Bulwer, and so on. And on that same evening she introduced me to Lady Duff Gordon who had translated my fairy tale *The Little Mermaid* and who is a daughter of Mrs. Austen, the authoress. There I was to meet a large number of famous people, and so I did.

But I was received into an even larger select circle at the home of another English authoress, to whom my friend, Jerdan, the publisher of the *Literary Gazette*, introduced me; this was Lady Blessington. She lived in her mansion, Gore House, on the outskirts of London. She was a good-looking, rather corpulent lady, extremely elegantly dressed and with fingers glistening with rings. She received me warmly, as though I were an old acquaintance, pressed my hand and talked about *A Poet's Bazaar*, saying that it had a greater treasure of poetry in it than is to be found in a large number of books put together, and that she had referred to it in her latest novel. We went out on to the large balcony overlooking the garden; it was surrounded by ivy and vine; there was a large black bird from Van Diemen's Land together with two white parrots swinging out there; we stroked the black bird and persuaded it to sing for me. There were huge numbers of roses growing beneath the balcony; there was a lovely lawn and two magnificent weeping willows. A little farther away a cow was grazing for show – there was quite a rural atmosphere about it all. We went down into the garden together; she was the first English lady I really understood, but she was so careful to speak slowly, holding me tightly by the wrist and looking me in the eye as she uttered every word and then asking me whether I understood her now.

She told me of an idea she had for a book she would like me to write, for she thought it was an idea that belonged to my realm. It was about a poor man who had nothing left but hope, and a rich man who had material goods but no hope, and I was to show how unhappy he was while the poor man was happy.

The Count d'Orsay, her son-in-law, arrived, the most elegantly dressed gentleman in London, I was told, who determined England's fashion by the way he dressed. We went to his studio where there was an almost finished clay bust of Lady Blessington and also an oil painting of Jenny Lind as Norma which the Count d'Orsay had painted from memory. He struck me as a man of many talents at the same time as being extremely polite and charming. Then Lady

Blessington showed me through all her rooms; most of them contained either a bust or a portrait of Napoleon. At last we came to her workroom; there was a large number of books lying open on the table, and I noticed they were all about Anne Boleyn. We talked about poetry and art, and with great knowledge and affection she touched on my works, in which, she said, there was much of the same element that particularly appealed to her in Jenny Lind, something both fervent and natural. Then she talked of Jenny Lind's interpretation of *La Sonnambula* and the purity and virginity which were revealed in it, and there were tears in her eyes as she spoke of it. Two young girls, I think they were her daughters, brought me a bunch of the most beautiful roses. Jerdan and I were invited to spend an afternoon there, and then she said she would introduce me to Dickens and Bulwer.

When we came at the appointed hour we found the house full of festivity and magnificence. In the hall there were servants in silk stockings and with powdered hair; Lady Blessington herself was in all her splendour and finery, but with the same gentle, radiant face. She told me that Bulwer was not coming: he was living for nothing but the elections at the moment and was out collecting votes. She did not seem to be particularly fond of this writer as a person, and said that he put people off with his vanity; in addition to which he was rather deaf and difficult to converse with. Whether she was looking through a distorting glass or not, I do not know.

She spoke with quite different warmth of Charles Dickens, as did everyone else. He, too, had promised to come, and I was to meet him. I was just writing my name and a few words on the front page of *The True Story of my Life* when Dickens entered the room. He looked young and handsome and had a kind, intelligent face with a mass of beautiful hair that fell to both sides. We shook hands, looked deep into each other's eyes, spoke to each other and understood each other. We went out on to the veranda, and I was so moved and delighted to see and speak to the one living English author I loved more than any other that tears came to my eyes. Dickens realized my love and admiration. Of my fairy tales he named *The Little Mermaid*, which Lady Duff Gordon had translated for *Bentley's Magazine*, and he also knew *A Poet's Bazaar* and *The Improvisatore*.

At table I was given a seat close to Dickens; only Lady Blessington's young daughter sat between us. He drank a glass of wine with me, and so did the present Duke of Wellington, who was at that time the Marquis of Douro. At the end of the table there was a huge, full-size portrait of Napoleon, brightly illuminated by numerous lamps. The poet Milnes was present, as were the Secretary of the General Post Office, authors, journalists and noblemen; but for me Dickens was the most distinguished of them all. I met a lively group of the most distinguished men, but there were only men apart from the two daughters. No one else came to Lady Blessington's home, but these men came without reservation. Count Reventlow and several others impressed it on me that I must not tell anyone in the great salons that I visited Lady Blessington; it was not the fashion; she was in deep discredit there. The reason I heard, and I do not know whether it was right or not, was that her son-in-law, the Count d'Orsay, preferred the company of his mother-in-law to that of his wife, and that the young wife, who moreover was a step-daughter of Lady Blessington, had therefore left her husband, house and home, and gone to live with a lady friend of hers while her husband stayed behind.

Lady Blessington had made an extremely pleasing impression on me, and when a number of the more aristocratic ladies in higher circles asked me in the evenings whom I had visited, I could not refrain from naming Lady Blessington. There was always a pause, and if I then asked the reason why one could not visit her or what there was that was not quite right about her, my questions were brusquely dismissed and I was told she was not a nice person. One day I spoke of her personal charm and her character and said how moved she had been when talking about Jenny Lind's interpretation of *La Sonnambula* and all the feminine qualities she had revealed on that occasion. I had seen her shed tears at the thought.

"Play-acting," exclaimed an old lady indignantly. "Lady Blessington weeping over Jenny Lind's innocence!"

A few years later I read of the death of Lady Blessington in Paris. It was the Count d'Orsay who sat by her bedside. Among other literary ladies I must name the Quaker Mary Howitt, through whose translation of *The Improvisatore* I had been introduced and become known in England. Her husband, William Howitt is also known as an author. At that time they were publishing *Howitt's Journal* in London, and the very issue published a week before my arrival had contained a sort of eulogy of me together with the portrait that was to be seen in the windows of several bookshops. I noticed this the first day I was there and went into a little shop and bought it.

"Is it a good portrait of Andersen?" I asked the woman who sold it to me.

"Oh, it is quite striking," she said. "You will recognise him from the picture."

But *she* did not know me, even though we talked about the likeness for a long time.

Mary Howitt had recently published *The True Story of my Life*, a translation of *Das Märchen meines Lebens*, with Longman Brothers. As I say, the book was dedicated to Jenny Lind, and it has since been published in Boston. Immediately on my arrival Mary Howitt had visited me together with her daughter and invited me to visit them at Clapton, just outside London. I think it must have been about ten miles outside the city. I went by omnibus; it was full both inside and on top, and the road was never-ending. The Howitts lived comfortably; there were paintings and statues and a well-tended garden. Everyone gave me a friendly reception. A few houses away lived Freiligrath, the German poet whom I had once visited in St. Goar on the Rhine, where he sang his expressive, warm songs. The King of Prussia had given him an annual income as a poet, but he relinquished it again when Herwegh ridiculed him as a superannuated poet. After that, he wrote his songs of freedom, went to Switzerland and then to England where he supported his family by working in an office. One day in London I had met him in the crush. He knew me, but I did not know him, for he had shaved off the thick, black beard I had seen him with before.

"Are you refusing to recognise me?" he said with a laugh. "I am Freiligrath." And when I had dragged him out of the crowd and into a doorway he said jokingly, "So you won't talk to a demagogue in the middle of the crowd, friend of royalty that you are!"

It was cosy in the little drawing-room, and my portrait was hanging on the wall. Hartmann, the painter who had made the portrait at Gravensteen, entered the room at that moment. We talked about the Rhine and about poetry. But I was suffering as a result of London life and the journey out there. However, I relied on the evening's being cool, and I again went by omnibus. But before we had really left Clapton all my limbs gave way; I felt ill and weak just as I had done in Naples. I was in danger of fainting, and the omnibus filled up more and more and became ever hotter. It was constantly stopping, and soon it was full up on top, too. Booted legs hung down outside the open windows. Several times I was on the point of saying to the conductor, "Take me to a house where I can stay a while, for I cannot stand this." Sweat streamed out of all my pores. It was dreadful. And all the time we moved slowly forward; at last it seemed to me that everything was blurred around me. When, at last, I reached the Bank I got out and into a cab, and now that I was alone and there was more air I recovered and reached home, but a more terrible journey than the one from Clapton I have seldom experienced.

However, I had promised to go out there again and stay there a few days, and it was this longer stay that gave me courage to start the same journey again, and in an omnibus once more. These were intended to be a few quiet days of relaxation out there, but friends often wanted to give me more than was good for me. You must always be taken from what is near at hand to what is further away, and so on, in the afternoon of the very first day, we were off in a one-horse carriage, five persons inside and three on top. We were to visit an elderly maiden lady in her country house; the heat was awful, and the whole expedition would have provided all the material for a chapter in one of Dickens' novels.

At last we reached the home of this old lady, who no doubt had literary pretentions. There was a whole flock of children playing on the lawn in front of the house, so that it looked like a school or an institution for boarders. They danced around a large beech tree in the middle of the lawn, and they all wore garlands of ivy or beech on their heads. They were singing and jumping about. They were called over to me and told that I was Hans Christian Andersen who had written all those fairy tales, and they all crowded round me and held out their hands; then off they went again, singing and leaping about in the green grass. There were some pretty rises and clumps of trees round about casting lovely shadows. I looked longingly at them, for we had to sit in a sun-filled arbor. A deaf lady who wrote on politics arrived, and then she was followed by a host of writers whose names I did not know. I became more and more exhausted, and at last I was forced to retire and rest, lying quietly in a room all on my own throughout the afternoon; I was incapable of moving.

When the sun set and the air became a little cooler I was glad to be able to breathe again. On the way home to Clapton we could see the lights of London spread out before us; it was a magnificent illuminated scene, like a transparent plan on a gigantic scale. Several winding streets could be seen brightly outlined by the large number of gas lamps, and some stretched right out to the distant horizon; it was a phosphorescent sea with thousands of lighthouses.

The following day I was in London again.

I have seen "high life" and "poverty"; these are the two opposite poles in my memory. "Poverty", I saw personified in the form of a pale, hungry young girl in miserable, ragged clothes hiding in a corner in an omnibus. I saw "wretchedness", and yet it never uttered a word in all its misery, for that was not allowed. I remember beggars, both men and women, carrying on their breasts a large, stiff piece of paper on which were written the words, "I am dying of hunger. Have pity on me." They dare not speak, for they are not allowed to beg, and so they glide past like shadows. They stop in front of people and stare at them with an expression of hunger and melancholy on their pale, thin faces. They stand outside cafés and restaurants, choose one of the people sitting there and stare fixedly at them with such eyes, oh, such eyes as only misery can give. A woman points to her sick child and to the words which are written across her breast: "I have not eaten for two days."

I saw many of them, and yet I was told that there were only a few in my district and none at all where the rich people lived. That part of town was closed to the poor race of pariahs. Everything in London, including begging, is turned into business. It is a case of attracting attention in the best possible way, and I saw an example in which this was done in a striking manner. There, in the gutter, stood a man, in the gutter because if he had stood on the pavement or in the road he would have blocked the passage. He was dressed in clean clothes

393

and had five children with him, each child smaller than the next. They were all in mourning, and all wore a long piece of crape in their hats and caps. All of them wore clean clothes, and all of them stood in the gutter; and they all held a bundle of matches in their hands, for of course they were not allowed to beg.

Another occupation which is more respectable, and which brings in an extremely good income, is to be a road-sweeper, and there is one standing with his broom on almost every corner. He continually sweeps either the crossings from one road to the other or a part of the pavement, and anyone who feels so inclined gives him a penny. There are said to be districts where these pennies amount to a fortune in the course of a week. I think it is Bulwer who has written a little story about such a man: no one in his district knows his trade, and he is engaged and then married to a respectable young lady; every day he is away from home, but no one knows where he is, and every Saturday he comes home with a pocket full of shining silver coins. The family is anxious, fearing he is a forger, and one day they keep watch on him and discover that he is a road sweeper. I even saw an African child, a black boy wearing a turban, practising the noble art of sweeping streets.

I saw life in London. I caught a glimpse of "high life" in the rich salons, the crowds in the streets, the enthusiasm in the theatres, and something else that is part of the life of the nation, its churches. But you have to go to Italy to see churches. St. Paul's Cathedral in London looks more impressive from the outside than the inside; it is small at the side of St. Peter's, and it lacks the solemnity of Maria Maggiore and Degli Angeli in Rome. It gave me the impression of a magnificent Pantheon, with elaborate monuments of marble. There was what looked like a piece of black crape on every single statue there. This was a veil formed by the smoke that had found its way inside and given each statue a peculiar, silken covering.

On Nelson's Monument there is a young figure stretching out his hand towards one of the four inscriptions commemorating victories; he is pointing straight towards the word "Copenhagen". As a Dane, he felt as though Nelson was seeking to erase this from his triumphs.

Westminster made a far greater impression on me, both outside and inside. That is a church! What a pity it is that for the comfort of the English a smaller church has been built within the other one, and that services are held there. The first time I went in, through a side door, I found myself standing in no other place than Poets' Corner; the first monument my gaze alighted on was that of Shakespeare. I immediately forgot that his dust does not lie there; I was filled with a feeling of devotion and seriousness, and I leaned my forehead against the cold marble. Beside this there is a monument to Thomson, to the left there is one to Southey, while beneath the broad flags forming the floor lie Garrick, Sheridan and Samuel Johnson.

As everyone knows, the clergy have not allowed Byron's monument to be allotted a place there. "I missed it," I said one evening to one of England's bishops, pretending not to know the reason. "How is it that a monument by Thorvaldsen made to commemorate England's greatest poet has not been put up there?"

"It has been given an excellent position elsewhere," he answered evasively.

Among the many other monuments to kings and powerful men there was especially one I always had to stop and look at, for in one of the marble figures I saw a face which strangely resembled one I knew, and which was better than either painters or sculptors have succeeded in reproducing: I saw my own face. It really bore a strange resemblance to my own bust. One day when I was standing there a crowd of visitors happened to look at it and at me. They started and looked at me in amazement; it seemed to them that the exalted gentleman of marble was walking about the aisles of the church in flesh and blood, in my shape.

I have already said that I stayed in London just at the time when they were preparing for elections, and that this was the reason why I did not meet Bulwer. When seen for the first time, an election campaign with all its events and excesses, which we shall probably also see in our own country, is colourful and almost a popular entertainment.

Stands had been erected for speakers in several squares and streets. Amidst the throngs of people there were men walking about with voters' lists on their backs and chests so that people could read the names on them. Banners were waving, and banners were carried in procession. Scarves and great flags with inscriptions were waving from wagonloads of voters. Shouting and crying, crowds of badly dressed people went past in elegant carriages, often with elaborately dressed servants. It looked as though the gentry had fetched out the meanest of their servants, as though it were the old heathen festival in which the masters waited on their slaves. Around the platforms there is a throng of people and a buzz of voices, and sometimes rotten oranges and even carrion are thrown at the speakers.

In one of the better-class districts I saw two well-dressed young men approach the platform, but just as one of them was about to jump up on to it some bystanders sprang forward and pulled the hats down over the eyes of both of them and turned them around. And then they were pushed and jostled by the whole crowd, from one to another, right away from the platform, indeed right out of the street, so that they were not allowed to stand at all. Several miles outside London, where I made several excursions by carriage, this main preoccupation of the time was even more noticeable, dominating people's interests almost to the exclusion of everything else. I saw great processions in which the election parties came along preceded by huge banners on which were written highly effective inscriptions. Most of them were for a Mr. Hodges, whose name was especially in evidence all around. One party had dark blue and orange banners, the others had banners in light blue, and they bore inscriptions such as "Hodges for ever", "Rothschild, the friend of the poor" and so on. There was a band and all kinds of rabble in every procession. A sick old man, trembling all over his body, was taken on a wheelbarrow to cast his vote. Votes were collected on the market square; on this occasion it looked like a real market, with wooden and canvas booths in which all sorts of things were to be bought; a complete theatre had been built, and I saw them take woodland scenery across the road into the large Thespis Hall. However, something that did look decorative here and which could almost provide materials for a whole book, were the gypsy caravans that wandered, or rather drove all over the country. The entire household was contained in a cart on two wheels and drawn by a horse. It was a complete house with a roof and a chimney; the whole of it divided into two rooms of which the one at the back was a sort of parlour or kitchen with plates and pans; there in the doorway, which opened outwards as in an omnibus, the

396

wife sat spinning at her wheel; a small red curtain hung at the open windows. The husband and the son rode, but at the same time they guided the horse in front of this house on wheels.

The present Baron Hambro had rented a country house outside Edinburgh in the Bay of Stirling, and he was spending the summer there so that his sick wife could bathe in the sea. He wrote to his father and told him he must persuade me to visit him, as I had so many friends in Scotland who were looking forward to seeing me. I was nervous at the thought of the long journey, for I did not speak English sufficiently well to venture out into the country. A fresh invitation and a letter to the father telling him he should come with me made up my mind for me, and in old Hambro's company I now set off by rail from London to Edinburgh. We divided the journey into two days, and spent the night at York. It was an express train, and it rushed along without rest or pause. During the whole of the journey there was no time to leave the carriage. Previously we used to sing a song entitled "Through vale and over mountain," but here we would have to sing "Over vale and through mountain." We sped along like the wild hunt itself. The varying landscape revealed itself around us and below us, and there were parts which reminded one of Funen and Als. Occasionally we went under the ground, in endless tunnels which lasted for miles and miles and in which openings had been made in the roof for the sake of ventilation. We met a huge number of trains which flashed past us like rockets, and yet more landscapes came into view, landscapes of a more mountainous nature in which there were brick kilns with fire belching out at the top of the chimneys.

On the railway station at York a gentleman came and greeted me and presented two ladies to me; he was the present Duke of Wellington, who knew me, and who had come with his bride. We spent the night in the Black Swan at York. I saw the old city and its magnificent cathedral. I had never before seen such picturesque houses as these with their carved beams in their gable-ends and bay windows. Flocks of swallows flew above the streets, and above my head I saw my own bird, the stork.

The next day we went by rail from York to Newcastle, which was enveloped in dense smoke and steam. The viaduct and bridge outside the town were not finished, and so we all had to go in an omnibus through the town to the station on the other side. What a crowd and what confusion there was!

In England you do not receive a ticket for your luggage as happens in other countries. You have to look after it yourself, and this was a terrible bother in the various places where we had to change.

On this particular day the crowds were especially bad. There were so many people travelling, and early in the morning an express train had left which had been put on for gentlemen who were going hunting in Scotland with their dogs. All the first class carriages were occupied, and so we had to travel in the second class, which is as bad as it can possibly be, with wooden seats and wooden shutters such as other countries have in fourth class. The track was not finished over two of the deep valleys, but it was safe to travel on. The beams supporting the bridges were put on mighty columns, and the rails were fixed to these, but to the eye it looked as though all woodwork was missing, and as though we were running along the railings that lined the bridge; we could look through all the open timber-work down into the depths below where people were working on the river bed.

At last we reached the river that forms the border between England and Scotland. The land of Walter Scott and Burns lay before us. The countryside began to be mountainous, and we could see the sea; the railway runs along the coast; there were lots of boats out there. Finally we reached Edinburgh. The old town is divided from the new by a deep, narrow valley that looks like a vast dried-up moat, and down in this valley the railway runs direct from London to Glasgow. The new part of Edinburgh has straight roads and uninteresting modern buildings. One line intersects another or runs parallel to it. There is nothing more Scottish about it than the fact that it has regular squares, just like Scottish kilts. But the old part of Edinburgh is a town which is so picturesque and magnificent, so old, so murky, so distinctive. The houses, which in the main street have two or three storeys, back onto the valley dividing the old and the new parts of the city, and there they have between nine and eleven storeys. And in the evenings, when the lights have been lit by the various people living there, storey upon storey, and along with the bright gas lamps they stream over the roofs of the other houses in the elevated street, it presents a characteristic, almost festive appearance, with lights high up in the air. They can just be seen from the railway, for the train enters Edinburgh at the bottom of the town. I arrived there with old Hambro in the evening. His son was waiting for us with his carriage at the station. It was a happy and joyful meeting, and we went off at a gallop to the country house at Mount Trinity, where I was now to have my home together with the Hambros in the land of Walter Scott and the mountains of Burns. A pile of letters was like a bouquet awaiting me; everything was luxurious and cosy and with all the comfort a good English home can offer. I saw friendly and kind people who gave me a warm reception. It was a happy evening in my life.

Our house stood at the centre of a garden surrounded by low walls; the railway from Edinburgh ran close by out to the bay. The fishing village here is really quite a large town, but very much like those in Zealand. The Scottish women's dress was even more picturesque than that of the Danish women; a broad-striped skirt was always fastened up in a charming manner, revealing the parti-coloured underskirt.

The very next day I was already like one of the family. We are soon at home when we know we are cherished and welcome guests. – I found lively and attractive children there, and their old grandfather was extremely fond of them. Once more I was living in the midst of a happy family of charming and intelligent people. The daily life of the house was English in every respect. In the evening both the family and the servants joined in evening prayers; a prayer was said and a passage from the Bible was read aloud, just as I later saw it in all the families I visited. It made a good and beautiful impression on me.

Every day contained a rich variety of new experiences for me; the very first morning was taken up with visits and with looking around and becoming familiar with things. I needed physical rest and quiet, but how could I indulge in that when there were so many new things for me to absorb?

It was only a few minutes before the train was due to arrive in Edinburgh. It stopped just before entering a tunnel under the rock up which several of the streets in new Edinburgh lead; most people got out. "Are we there already?"

"No," said my companion as we set off again, "but most people don't go any further. They are afraid the tunnel is not strong enough, and that it might collapse and bring down all the street on top of it and so most people prefer to get out here. But I don't expect it will collapse while we are in it."

And we rushed into the long, black vault. It did not collapse on that occasion, but it was not pleasant. Nevertheless, I always went all the way in both directions each time I visited Edinburgh by train. The view of the old part of the city from the new is magnificent and impressive, and it offers a sight which, with its picturesque grouping, puts Edinburgh on a level with Constantinople and Stockholm. There is a long street there, which can almost be called a quay if the cutting through which the railway runs is thought of as a riverbed. From there you can see a panorama of the whole of the old part of the city with its castle and Heriot's Hospital. Where the town slopes down towards the sea there is the hill called Arthur's Seat, famous from Walter Scott's novel *The Heart of Midlothian*. The whole of the old town is like a mighty commentary on these great works which are read in countries all over the world. And so the Walter Scott Monument is situated so beautifully on a spot where from the new part of the town there is a panorama of old Edinburgh. It is in the shape of a great Gothic tower, under which there is a statue of the poet seated on a chair. His dog, Maida, lies at his feet, and in the topmost arches of the tower there are figures from his works, figures who are now known all the world over: Meg Merrilies, the Last Minstrel, and so on.

Across the chasm between the new and the old towns, right down at the bottom of which lies the railway, there is a great bridge which is on a level with the top floors of the buildings rising up from the bottom. The famous physician, Dr. Simpson, was my guide here. The main street leads along the ridge of a hill. The many side streets off it are narrow, filthy and with houses six storeys high, the oldest of which seem to be built of heavy granite boulders. They remind you of the huge buildings in the dirty towns in Italy; poverty and misery seem to peep out of the open hatches which normally serve as windows, and rags and tatters are hanging out to dry. In one of these

400

streets I was shown a dirty, gloomy building with a courtyard that looked like a stable. It had once been the sole and important hotel in Edinburgh, where kings had stayed, and where Samuel Johnson had lived for a long time.

I saw the house where Burke had lived and where the unfortunate victims had been lured inside and strangled in order to be sold as corpses. Although it was almost falling down, Knox's little house still stood in the main street, and a statue of him talking from a pulpit adorns the corner.

Past the old Edinburgh prison, which attracts attention not on account of its exterior, but because of Walter Scott's novels, you go on to Holyrood House which stands on the western outskirts of the city. There I saw a long baronial hall containing a lot of bad portraits; there were a number of uninteresting rooms to go through, and I saw where Charles the Tenth had lived. It was only when I entered Mary Stuart's bedroom that it became Holyrood House for me. The tapestry there represented *The Fall of Phaeton*, so that was what she always had before her eyes; it was almost like a forewarning of her own fall. In the small room nearby the unfortunate Rizzio had been dragged to be murdered; there are still spots of blood to be seen on the floor. There was a murky turret room on either side. Outside stood the chapel, now a lovely ruin. Here ivy, which in England and Scotland spreads with a fullness the likes of which I have seen only in Italy, covers the chapel walls, looking like a rich tapestry. Here the evergreen plant twists its way up round the windows and columns; grass and flowers grow around the gravestones.

People may well call these pictures from Edinburgh bits of travel description, but they are real parts of the story of my life. They have made such a vivid impression on my mind and my thoughts that they are only really at home there for me. They are, so to speak, the result of the days I spent there.

To this consideration of town and buildings is linked a scene that surprised me and entirely occupied my mind. A whole party of us had gone up to George Heriot's Hospital, a magnificent, castle-like building, the founder of which was a goldsmith whom we all know from Walter Scott's novel *The Fortunes of Nigel*. Visitors must come provided with written permission and in addition they must personally write their names at the porter's lodge. I wrote mine in full, Hans Christian Andersen, since it is as such I am always known in England and Scotland. The old porter read it, and then with remarkable kindness he continued to accompany Mr Hambro, who had a benevolent, jovial face and silvery hair, and asked him if he were not the Danish writer. "That is just as I imagined him to be with such a gentle face and such venerable hair."

"No," replied Mr Hambro, pointing to me: "That is the poet."

"So young!" exclaimed the old man. "I have read him, and the boys here read him. It is strange to see such a man; they are usually all old or dead before one hears about them."

I was told what he had said and went across to the old man and shook hands with him. He and a few of the boys who came along and were asked knew all about "the ugly duckling and the red shoes". It surprised and moved me to think that I was known up here and had friends among the poor boys and those about them. I had to step aside to hide my tears. God knows the thoughts that were in my heart.

"This is indeed popularity," says Boner, the English author in the foreword to *The Dream of Little Tuk, and Other Tales*, when referring to this episode.

Jerdan, the editor of *The Literary Gazette*, had given me a letter to Lord Jeffrey, the well-known editor of *The Edinburgh Review*, to whom Dickens had dedicated his *The Cricket on the Hearth*. He lived just outside Edinburgh at his country residence, a real old romantic castle, the walls of which were almost hidden by evergreen. A huge fire was roaring in the hearth in the great hall where the family soon gathered and where young and old alike surrounded me and showed their affection for me. Children and grandchildren came along, and I had to write my name in each of the various books of mine they possessed. We walked around in the great park until we came to a point from which there was a view of Edinburgh, which from there is not unlike Athens. Here too there was a Lykabettos and an Acropolis to be seen.

A few days later the whole family repaid my visit and came out to Mount Trinity. As we parted, Lord Jeffrey said, "Come back to Scotland soon so that we can meet again. I have not many years to live." Death has already summoned him; we did not meet again in this world.

I met several famous people in social life at the home of Miss Rigby, the authoress, who has visited Copenhagen and written about it, and at the home of the excellent Dr. Simpson. I made the acquaintance of a wide variety of personalities. I met the jovial critic, John Wilson, who was full of life and humour and jokingly called me brother. The most critical people had in common the desire to show good will towards me. "The Danish Walter Scott" was the name of honour with which many people graced me, unworthy though I was. Mrs. Crowe, the authoress, presented me with her novel *Susan Hopley* which has also been translated into Danish. We met at Dr. Simpson's home, and in the large circle gathered there that evening several experiments were made with inhaling ether. I thought it distasteful, especially to see ladies in this dreamy intoxication. They laughed with open, lifeless eyes; there was something unpleasant about it and I said so, recognising at the same time that it was a wonderful and blessed invention to use in painful operations, but not to play with. It was wrong to do it; it was almost like tempting God. A worthy old gentleman took my part and said the same; by asserting what I did I seemed to have won his heart.

A few days later we chanced to meet in the street. Mainly in order to have a little thing to remember Edinburgh by I had bought the entire Holy Bible in a cheap, but beautiful edition, and now he became even friendlier towards me, patted my cheek and spoke of my pious mind far more warmly than I deserved. Chance had put me in a light which he found beautiful.

A week had passed, and I wanted to see part of the Highlands. Hambro, who together with his family was going to a spa on the west coast of Scotland, suggested that I should be their guest on the journey through part of the Highlands and together with them see the places which Walter Scott has depicted in *The Lady of the Lake* and *Rob Roy.* We were not to part before reaching Dumbarton.

On the other side of the Firth of Stirling lies the little town of Kirkaldy where a mighty, ancient ruin stands on the wooded mountain side. Seagulls were flying around it and dipping their wings into the water, crying out all the time. I was told at first that it was the ruin of Ravenswood Castle, but an old man from the town came and explained that that was something people had invented to tell strangers because that name acquired a more general interest through *The Bride of Lammermoor*. But the name of Ravenswood, he said, was actually an invention on the part of the author, and the real setting of the events was to be found much further north in Scotland. The name of Ashton was also an invention since the real family was still alive and was called Stair.

The ruin itself with its murky, vaulted dungeons and its luxuriant evergreen, which covered the remains of the walls like a firm tapestry, clung tightly on to the cliff jutting out over the sea and was very picturesque and striking. The sea had receded because of the ebb tide, and the view from here to Edinburgh was magnificent and unforgettable.

We sailed up the Firth of Stirling by steamer. A modern minstrel sang Scottish ballads and accompanied himself on a violin. It sounded so melancholy, and to the sound of these notes we approached the Highlands where the cliffs lay like outposts. Mist descended over them and then lifted again; it was like a hasty event to show us Ossian's land in its proper light. The mighty Stirling Castle, high up on a rock that looks like a gigantic figure of stone that has been pushed up from the flat plains, dominates the town, the oldest streets of which are dirty and badly cobbled and look just as though they were from the olden days. It is said that the Scots like to tell their country's history; and indeed, here in the street where Darnley's house stands, a shoemaker wearing his apron came out straight away and gave information and explanations concerning Darnley and Mary Stuart, about times past and the feats of the Scots. There is an absolutely wonderful view from the Castle out across the historically famous plains where the battle was fought between Edward the Second and Robert Bruce. We drove across to the mound where King Edward planted his standard. Succeeding generations have chipped away so many bits and pieces of the stones among which it stood that iron railings have been put round the rest of them to prevent the destruction continuing.

There is a humble smithy close by; it was there James the Fourth sought shelter, sent for a priest and made his confession, and when the priest heard that he was the King he plunged a knife into his heart. The smith's wife showed us her little parlour and said that it was there in the corner where her bed now stood that the murder had taken place.

The whole region looked rather Danish, though it was poorer, and it looked as though the season was colder than it really was. The limes were blooming there, while at home they were still in bud.

Travel is expensive in England and Scotland, but you receive value for money. Everything is excellent; guests are looked after, and even the smallest village inn is comfòrtable. That at least is how I found it.

Callander is not much more than a hamlet, but there I felt almost as though I were staying at the castle of some count; there were soft carpets on the stairs and in the passages; the fire was blazing merrily, and we were glad of that although the sun was shining outside and all the Scots were going about with bare knees, which in fact is also how they dress in winter. They wrapped themselves in their colourful plaids; even the poor boys had one, even if it was only a rag. Outside my window a river wound round an old mound that looked like one of our burial mounds; there was a humpback bridge covered with the most luxuriant evergreen, and nearby the cliffs rose into the air and the mountain country revealed itself to us. We left early in the morning so as to be in time for the steamer across Loch Katrine. The road became wilder and wilder. We came to the heather and found it was in bloom. We passed a few lonely stone-built houses. Loch Katrine, long and narrow with deep and dark water, lay between brownish green mountain slopes; heather and scrub covered the shores, and as far as I could see I had the impression that if the Jutland heath is a motionless, calm sea, then this region is the heath in a tempest! The waves of mountains are dead, but they are all green, covered with grass and scrub. On our left in the lake lay a small, wooded island; it was Ellen's Isle, from which *The Lady of the Lake* had steered her boat, the island which Walter Scott has made known to us and interesting for us through his poem.

At the furthermost end of the lake, where we went ashore, there was a poor inn, a sort of improvised lodging for the night, large and certainly roomy, with bed beside bed: there must have been about fifty of them. But the roof was low; there were reed mats on the floor, and the windows were tiny, just like in a turf cottage. That is what our night's lodgings looked like, the place where travellers from Loch Lomond, Rob Roy's land, could find shelter until the following morning when the steamer sailed over Loch Katrine.

We did not stay there long. All the passengers continued their journey, most of them on foot, but some on horseback. Hambro had procured a little carriage for his wife and myself, since we were both too weak to manage the tiring journey across the heath on foot. There was no proper road here, only a track. We drove where the carriage could best make progress, over hills and through valleys, over lumps of earth and stones that were marked in a way suggesting a future road. The coachman walked beside the horse. One moment we were reeling and jolting downhill at a wild speed, the next we were slowly being dragged uphill; it was a journey like no other. There was no house to be seen, and we met not a soul. All around us there were silent, gloomy mountains shrouded in mist; monotonous and always the same. The one and only living creature we saw for miles was a lonely shepherd who was bitterly cold and wrapped in his grey plaid. Silence reigned over all the landscape.

Ben Lomond, the highest mountain peak, finally broke through the mist, and soon we could see Loch Lomond below us. Although there was a sort of road leading down, the descent was so steep that it was extremely dangerous to take the carriage down. So it had to be left behind, and on foot we approached the well-supplied inn where a lot of people were waiting for the steamer to arrive. The first person I met on board was a fellow-countryman, C. Puggaard, who has given such an excellent account of the geology of Møn. On board we were all wrapped in our plaids. Through rain and drizzle, mist and wind the steamer went right up to the most northerly point of the lake which ends where a small river flows into it. Some passengers left and others joined us. We were in the area forming the setting for the whole of *Rob Roy*:

> *Land of brown heath and shaggy wood,*
> *Land of the mountain and the flood.*

as it is put in *The Last Minstrel*. Then we sailed back down the lake with Rob Roy's Cave on the right hand. Huge rocks had fallen into the lake. Here a boat brought a whole party out to us. Among them was a young lady who gave me a fixed and penetrating look. Soon afterwards one of the gentlemen stepped across to me and said that there was a young lady who believed she recognised me from my portrait and would like to know if I were not the Danish poet Hans Christian Andersen. I said I was, and the young lady rushed across to me, filled with heartfelt delight, and with a show of confidence as though we were old acquaintances she pressed my hand and said in a natural and beautiful way how glad she was to see me. I asked her for one of the many mountain flowers she had with her from Rob Roy's mountain, and she chose the best and the prettiest for me. Her father and all her family gathered around me and asked me to go with them and be their guest, but I neither could nor would leave my companions. Hambro enjoyed the homage that was paid to me. Before long, the attention of all the passengers was turned on me, and it was surprising how large the circle of my friends became. It makes you strangely glad to be given a good reception when you are so far from home and as it were to belong to so many kind and friendly people.

We went ashore at Balloch, drove along past Smollett's monument in the town of his birth, and towards evening we were in Dumbarton, a real Scottish town close to the Clyde. That night there was a gale with prolonged and enormously powerful gusts of wind. It was as though we could hear the roar of the sea all the time, everything creaked, the windows rattled and a sick cat miaowed all night long. Towards morning the wind dropped, and it was as quiet as the grave after such a night. It was a Sunday, and that means something in Scotland. Everything comes to a standstill, and not even the trains are allowed to run. The only one still running is the one from London to Edinburgh, much to the annoyance of the strictly religious Scots. All houses are shut, and people sit at home, either reading the Bible or getting themselves drunk or so I have generally been told.

It was alien to my nature to sit indoors a whole day in that way and see nothing at all of the town, and I suggested going for a walk. However, I was told that it just would not do; people would be annoyed. Nevertheless, towards evening we all went a walk out of the town, but there was silence everywhere, and folk peeped out of their windows and looked at us, so we soon turned back again. A young Frenchman I talked to assured me that together with two Englishmen he had recently been out with a fishing rod on a Sunday afternoon. An old gentleman had passed by and in the strongest and angriest terms reproached them for their "ungodliness", enjoying themselves on a Sunday instead of sitting at home reading the Bible, adding that the least they could do was to refrain from annoying and disturbing other people. Such piety on Sundays cannot be genuine in all people. Where it is genuine I will respect it, but as an inherited habit it becomes a mask and only results in hypocrisy.

Together with Hambro I went into a little bookshop to buy some books and a map.

"Do you have a portrait of the Danish poet Hans Christian Andersen?" asked Hambro in fun.

"Yes," the man replied, and added, "He is supposed to be in Scotland himself."

"Would you recognise him?"

The man looked at Hambro, fetched my portrait, stared at him and said, "Why it must be you."

That shows how much the portrait resembled me. I was not permitted to remain unknown, and when the good man in Dumbarton heard that I was the author he forgot everything else and asked if he might fetch his wife and children in to see me and talk to me. They came and seemed happy to meet me, and I had to shake hands with them all. I felt and understood that I really was known up there in Scotland, or at least that my name was.

"No one at home will believe this," I said to Hambro. "It's more than I deserve."

I became moved and shed tears as I always did when I was surprised by something unexpected, something undeserved, people saw in me as a writer. It all far surpassed the most daring dreams and hopes of my youth. I myself often felt that it was only a dream, a vain dream, which I shall not even be able to tell my friends when I awaken.

In Dumbarton I said good-bye to Hambro. His wife and children were going to a spa near the sea; I was going by steamer up the Clyde to Glasgow. The parting made me deeply sad for throughout all my time in Scotland I had lived in the company of these charming people. Hambro himself had been like a fond and painstaking brother to me; everything he thought would please me was done for me. It was as though he discovered all my wishes; and his excellent wife was full of spirit and feeling and was filled with a deep and sympathetic understanding. The children were so trusting and full of life.

I have not seen any of them since then. The mother I shall only see again in God's Heaven, for she has left her loved ones behind on earth and gone there. My thoughts fly to her in gratitude. It is a comfort and a consolation to have good friends on earth and in Heaven.

Before leaving Dumbarton I was somewhat undecided as to whether to return to London and then go back home, or whether to extend my stay in Scotland and go still further north, right up to Loch Laggan. Queen Victoria and Prince Albert were staying there, and I had been told in a letter that they would be graciously pleased to receive me.

At the end of my stay in London, when I had been extremely ill and was suffering from the strain of social life, I had received a gracious invitation to visit the Queen and the Prince on the Isle of Wight. I was so sick and weak that I simply felt incapable of making the journey down there and of presenting myself. And flattered as I was at the unusual kindness, I was distressed at not being well and strong enough to accept it. I discussed the matter with the Danish Ambassador, Count Reventlow, and since he knew how ill and weak I felt, he said it would be best if I told them so quite plainly in a letter. And he said that I should add that as I was going to the mountains of Scotland to rest there and breathe more freely and as the Queen happened to be going to Scotland at the same time, I should ask her gracious permission to present myself to her if I happened to be in the same part of the country. From one of the gentlemen at court I received a private letter telling me that Her Majesty and His Royal Highness were gracious and kind enough to say that if I went to Loch Laggan Her Majesty would receive me there.

My stay in Scotland was not such a rest as I had expected, and after a stay of three weeks I was not much stronger than when I went there. In addition to that I was told by people whom I considered to be well informed that there was no decent inn within miles of the spot and that I would have to appear with my own servant. In short, I would have to appear rather better off than my purse allowed. I felt that I could not write to King Christian the Eighth, who had been gracious enough to offer to support me on my journey, since I had told him that I must decline his kindness. It would moreover be weeks before I received a reply. What a torment it was for me! So I wrote another letter explaining that my health had not improved and that I therefore thought it best for me to return home, which I did immediately, having at the same time to refuse the various invitations I had received from some of Scotland's rich and noble gentlemen to visit their homes.

I was also unable to visit Abbotsford, to which place I had a letter of introduction. Walter Scott's son-in-law, Lockhart, whose guest I had been in London, had given me such a warm and delighted reception, and his daughter, her grandfather's favourite, had told me all about her dear grandfather. Together with her I had seen weapons and other remembrances which had belonged to the great writer, including the wonderful likeness in which he is sitting with Maida, his dog, looking at me as though he were alive. Miss Lockhart gave me some words written by him, the man who had once been known as the "Great Unknown". I had to give up all thoughts of Abbotsford as well as Loch Laggan and, depressed on account of this, I took the train home, first from Glasgow to Edinburgh.

However, I must tell of one event that in itself was quite small, but which for me was a new indication of my lucky star in things both great and small. During my last stay in Naples I had bought a simple palm walking stick; it had accompanied me on a few journeys, among others this one to Scotland. When I was travelling with Hambro's family across the heath between Loch Katrine and Loch Lomond, one of the sons had it to play with, and when we caught sight of Ben Lomond he lifted it in the air and shouted, "Now, palm-tree, can you see the highest mountain in Scotland? Can you see the great lake?" and so on. And I promised that when it went to Naples with me again the stick should tell its friends there all about the land of mists where the spirits of Ossian lived and about the land where the red flower of the thistle was held in esteem since it was given a place in the coat of arms of the people and the nation. The steamer came before we expected it, and we had to hurry aboard.

"Where is my stick?" I asked.

It had been left behind in the inn. When, after having been with us up to the most northerly point of the lake, the boat came back and Puggaard went ashore I asked him to take the stick to Denmark with him. I arrived in Edinburgh, and that morning, as I was standing on the station waiting to leave for London, the train from Scotland arrived a few moments before our train was due to leave. The guard got out and came towards me; he seemed to know me and he gave me my walking stick, saying with a little smile, "It has travelled quite well alone." A small label had been attached to it with the inscription, "The Danish Poet, Hans Christian Andersen," and it had been handled with such organisation and care that it had been passed from hand to hand, first with the steamer on Loch Lomond, then with the omnibus driver, then by steamer again, and then by the train, all with the help of its little address card. It was put into my hands just as the signal sounded to fly away from Scotland. I still have to tell the story of my stick's adventures; I hope I may do it one day just as well as it managed to travel all alone.

I went south through Newcastle and York.

I met the English author, Hook, and his wife in the train. They knew me and told me that there had been reports of me and my visit to the Queen in all the Scottish newspapers!

And I had not been anywhere near where she was staying. But the newspapers knew all about it, and later I saw a paper which reported that I had read some of my fairy tales aloud. Yet there was not a word of truth in it. At one of the stations on the way I bought the latest number of *Punch*. I was mentioned in it. It was an attack, a brief comment that I, a foreigner, a writer from abroad, had been given the honour of an invitation from the Queen, something that had never been given to an English author. This, together with the various reports of a visit which had never taken place, worried me. As far as the satirical paper *Punch* was concerned, my companions said, "It's a sign that people are popular when they are mentioned in that paper; many an Englishman would give a fortune to achieve it."

But I would have preferred to have been spared. Downcast and depressed by this remark and by having attracted public attention to myself in this way I was quite ill when I reached London. Count Reventlow promised to speak of me to the noble and exalted Queen and Prince Albert in the best possible terms.

I stayed in London for a few days. I had still not seen anything there except "high life" and some of the outstanding men and women in the country. On the other hand, I had not made the acquaintance of art galleries, museums and so on, and I had not even had time to visit "The Tunnel". I decided to go and see this early one morning. I had been advised to go on one of the numerous small steamers which sail up and down the Thames in London, but just as I was about to leave I felt so ill and miserable that I gave up all thought of the long journey to the tunnel. And by doing so, perhaps I saved my life, for on the very same day and at the very same hour as I would have gone on board one of these small ships, one of them, "The Cricket", blew up with 100 people on board. News of the accident spread over London straight away, and although it was by no means certain that I would have been on that ship, the possibility, indeed the probability, was so obvious that I experienced a solemn feeling of gratitude and thanked God for the sickness which had more and more really overwhelmed me just before the decisive moment when I should have gone on board.

London was now deserted by fine society. The opera season had finished and most of my acquaintances had gone to various spas or to the Continent. I longed for Denmark and for those whom I loved there, but before I left England I was invited to spend a few more days in the country at Sevenoaks, at the home of Richard Bentley, my publisher. This small town, close to the famous Knole Park, is only a short distance from the railway leading to the Channel. So it was a convenient and welcome visit for me on my way home.

I had been to Sevenoaks before, and it is quite a small town. This time I went by rail to Tunbridge where I was met by Bentley's carriage. I was surrounded by a Danish scene; the meadows were so green and there were many pretty knolls on which a few old trees were scattered. There was something park-like about the whole

412

landscape with trimmed hedges or perhaps iron railings usually forming the boundaries.

There were splendid, solid, comfortable rooms, roses and evergreen in the garden, and close by was the well-known Knole Park, where the old mansion belongs to the Earl of Amherst. An ancestor of one of the previous owners was a poet, and in honour of him one of the rooms there is graced with the name of "The Poet's Room". At the end of the room, there is a life-size portrait of the noble old poet, and portraits of all the other famous poets decorate the other walls as company for the one who reigns there.

In one of the houses nearby there was a little shop, exactly like the old curiosity shop which Dickens has portrayed in *Master Humphrey's Clock*. The day here in the company of so many kind people passed like a day of celebration. I felt at home in the genuine, old, excellent English family life where all the comfort and cosiness which riches and charm can create were to be found. Of the many poems I had to write in albums here one, I wrote to Bentley himself gives adequate expression to my thoughts and my mood.

> With longing filled, which yet was mixed with fear
> I went to Shakespeare's land, my youth's desire,
> The woods and fields were as in Denmark here,
> And in a trice a home I did acquire.
>
> And though the language does not suit my tongue
> My eyes beheld the kinship with the North;
> This England gave me sunshine all day long,
> And Aaron's staff of daily life sprang forth.

However much I needed rest and peace after the great exertions my stay in England and Scotland had cost me, these days were yet for me the richest days of sunshine in my life, the overflowing cup of honour and recognition. Although weary and exhausted by it, I quite naturally felt pangs of melancholy on leaving so many people who had only wished to give me joy and pleasure. And among those many people whom I loved and was not to see again, at least not for a long time, was Charles Dickens. Since we had met at Lady Blessington's

413

he had called on me without finding me at home, and we did not meet again in London. I had received a few letters from him there, and he personally even left for me the beautiful illustrated edition of his collected works, at the front of each volume doing me the honour of writing, "Hans Christian Andersen, from his friend and admirer Charles Dickens". I heard that he was at some spa somewhere on the Channel coast together with his wife and children, but no one knew where.

I was to sail from Ramsgate to Ostend on my way home. In the hope that a letter with Dickens' address would find him I wrote to him telling him the day and the time of my arrival at Ramsgate. I asked him to send his address to the hotel where I was going to stay; saying that if he was not too far away I would pay him a visit so as to spend some more time with him. There was a letter from Dickens awaiting me at the Royal Oak: he was about five miles away, at Broadstairs, and he and his wife would expect me to dinner. I took a carriage and drove off to the little seaside town. Dickens was renting the whole of a house that was narrow and small, but also neat and charming, and he and his wife gave me a hearty welcome. It was so splendid to be with them that for a long time I did not notice what a beautiful view there was from the dining-room where we were sitting. The windows faced the Channel, and the open sea rolled in just below them. The tide went out while we were eating, and the water receded extremely quickly. The great sandbank there, on which lie the bones of many a sailor, could be seen in all its splendour, and the lighthouse was lit. We talked of Denmark and Danish literature and about Germany and its language, which Dickens wanted to learn. An Italian organ-grinder happened to come and play outside while we were eating. Dickens spoke in Italian to the man whose face beamed with delight at hearing his native language.

After dinner the children came in. "The house is full of them," said Dickens. There were no fewer than five of them; the sixth was not at home. All the children kissed me, and the smallest of them kissed his own outstretched hand and then gave it me.

At coffee a young lady came to visit. Dickens told me she was one of my admirers, and he had promised her she should be invited if ever I came. The evening flew past. Mrs. Dickens seemed to be

414

about the same age as her husband, a little corpulent and with such a profoundly kind face that one immediately had confidence in her. She was full of enthusiasm for Jenny Lind and would so much like to have her signature, but this was exceedingly difficult to procure, she said. I had with me the little letter in which Jenny Lind wished me welcome in London and told me where she was living, and this I gave to Mrs. Dickens. We parted late in the evening, and Dickens promised me he would write to me in Denmark.

But we were to meet once more before I left. Dickens surprised me by going to Ramsgate the following morning and he was standing on the jetty when I arrived to go on board. "I had to come and say a final farewell to you," he said and went on board with me; and there he stayed until the ship's bell gave the signal for departure.

We shook each other's hand, and with his sincere, wise eyes he looked at me in such a friendly way, and as the ship sailed he was standing as far out as he could go, by the lighthouse. He waved his hat. Dickens was the last person to send me a greeting from the coast of my dear England.

I went ashore at Ostend, and the first people I met were the King of Belgium and his wife. They were the first people I greeted on the Continent, and they returned my salute in a friendly fashion. Apart from them I did not know a single person, but I knew who they were. The same day I went by rail to Ghent. There in the early morning, while I was waiting for the train to Cologne, several of the passengers who were to travel on that train came along and introduced themselves to me; they said they knew me from my portrait. An English family approached and one of the ladies came across to me; she was an authoress, she said, and had been in my company several times in London, but then everyone was gathered around me, wanting to speak to me. She had asked Reventlow to introduce her to me, but he had answered, "You can see that it is completely impossible."

I laughed and said that had really been the case. I really had been the fashion for a short time, but that I was now entirely at her disposal. She was natural and friendly and she wondered at the lucky star that made me so famous.

"How little it is," I said, "and I wonder for how long!"

"But it has certainly given me pleasure, although it is worrying to be raised to such heights when it is not certain I have the strength to keep myself up there."

I was so grateful, so filled with the thoughts of the honours and good fortune that had come my way. Throughout Germany, where people had read of the honour that had been done me in England, I was shown much friendliness and esteem. In Hamburg I met some men and women compatriots.

"Good heavens, Andersen, are you here!" was the reception I was given. "Oh, you should see what fun *Corsaren* has made of your stay in England. There is a drawing of you with a laurel wreath and bags of money. Oh Lord, it's so funny!"

I arrived in Copenhagen. A few hours later I was standing by my own window and looking out when two well dressed gentlemen went past. They saw me, stopped and laughed, and one of them pointed up and said loud enough for me to hear every word,

"Look, there's that orangutan of ours that's so famous abroad."

It was brutal – it was malicious – it reached my heart – I cannot forget it.

I also met sympathetic friends. There were many who were delighted with the honours which had been bestowed on me both in efficient Holland and mighty England, and through me on the Danish nation. One of our young authors amicably offered me his hand and said frankly and charmingly, "I have not really read you properly before, but now I will. People have said bad things about you and spoken disparagingly of you, but you are something, you must be something, more than they are prepared to accept here at home. People are not received and accepted in England as you have been if they are not good. I will frankly confess to you that I have quite altered my opinion of you."

Rather different was what one of my dearest friends told me and showed me in print.

He had sent one of our leading magazine editors a few English newspapers containing reports of all the honour that had been shown me in London, in addition to which he spoke extremely highly of *The True Story of my Life*. However, the man had not been willing to include in his paper what had been said of me, for, he said, "People would only think they were making a fool of Andersen over there". He found it unbelievable, and he knew the same would be the case for the majority of my fellow countrymen.

It was stated in one paper that I had received money for this journey from the state, and it pointed out that I went abroad every year.

I told King Christian the Eighth what they said.

"You have done what few would have done," he said. "You refused my well-intentioned offer. People are unjust to you here in Denmark. They do not know you."

The first little book I wrote after my arrival home, a small volume of *Fairy Tales*, I sent to England. They were published about Christmas time as *A Christmas Greeting to My English Friends* with the following dedication:

Charles Dickens:

"I am once more in my quiet little room in Denmark, but every day my thoughts are in dear England where a few months ago my friends changed reality into a beautiful fairy tale for me.

While I was busy with a larger work, five little stories sprang forth, just as flowers spring forth in the woods. I feel a wish and a desire to send the first flowers which have bloomed in my garden of poetry to England as a Christmas greeting, and I dedicate them to you, of whom I have already become fond through your works, you, my dear, noble Charles Dickens, who for ever have become a part of my heart now we have met. You were the last person to shake hands with me on the English coast, you were the last person to shout goodbye to me, and so it is quite natural that my first greeting from Denmark should be to you, and I send it with as sincere feeling as a devoted heart can do."

Hans Christian Andersen
Copenhagen, 6th December 1847

The little book was given an extremely good reception and it was reviewed in a way which was most flattering to me, but the first letter

417

from Dickens himself, expressing his thanks and greetings, warmed my heart and soul like a real beam of sunshine.

It reveals all his lovable nature; it whispers of kindness to me and that makes me a rich man. I have already shown all my most prized treasures, so why not show this one, too! Dickens will not misunderstand me.

To Hans Christian Andersen

A thousand thanks, my dear Andersen, for your kind and dearly-prized remembrance of me in your Christmas book. I am very fond of it and feel deeply honoured by it, and I cannot tell you how much I esteem so generous a mark of recollection from a man of such genius as you possess.

Your book made my Christmas fireside happier. We were all charmed with it. The little boy, the old man, the pewter soldier, are my particular favourites. I have read that story over and over again with the most unspeakable delight.

I was in Edinburgh a few weeks ago, where I saw some of your friends who talked much about you. Come over to England again soon! But whatever you do, don't leave off writing, for we cannot afford to lose any of your thoughts. They are too purely and simply beautiful to be kept in your heart.

We have long since come back from that sea-shore where I said adieu to you, and we are in our own house again. Mrs. Dickens says I am to give you her love. So says her sister. So say all my children. And as we are all in the same mind, I beg you to receive mine into the bargain as the love of your true and admiring friend,

Charles Dickens

At Christmas time that year my poem *Ahasuerus* appeared in Danish and German. Years before this, when the idea of writing such a work had occupied my thoughts, Oehlenschläger had already spoken to me of it. "What is this I hear?" he said. "I am told you are writing a drama embracing the whole world and its history. I don't understand it." I explained to him the idea I have already discussed. "But in what form can you manage all that?" he asked.

"I alternate between all forms, lyric, epic, dramatic, sometimes in verse, sometimes in prose."

"But that cannot be done," exclaimed the great poet eagerly. "I, too, know what it is to write works of poetry. There is something called form and limits, and one has to respect them. Green in one place and charcoal in another. What do you say to that?"

"I could certainly give you an answer," I replied good-naturedly, although a mischievous imp was urging me on and I had to obey. "I could certainly give an answer, but you will be angry if I say what I think."

"Good heavens, I shan't be annoyed with you," he said.

"Very well, but it is really only to show that I have an answer; I will keep to what you said, that one has to confine greenery and charcoal within their own limits. That is to say, keeping to the metaphor, that we have to take the charcoal alone. We could also continue and take sulphur alone and saltpetre alone, but then someone might appear who will mix them all together and then he has discovered gunpowder."

"Andersen, what terrible things you do say, discovered gunpowder indeed. You are a good soul, but what everyone says about you is right: you are too vain."

"But is that not part of our trade," I was prompted to say by the boisterous imp dominating my mood.

"Trade! Trade!" repeated the lovable and magnificent poet, who simply did not understand me on this point.

Now, when *Ahasuerus* appeared, he read it, and as I expressed a wish to know whether he had changed his former opinion, he wrote me a well meaning and frank letter. He told me quite openly how little this work appealed to him, and since his words will be of interest at all times, and since other people must have had the same opinion of my work, I will not conceal his judgement.

My dear Andersen,
I have always acknowledged and valued your delightful talent for telling fairy tales simply and wittily and in an original manner, as well as your ability to depict the life you

419

see around you in novels and travel descriptions. I have also taken delight in your talent in the field of drama, for instance in *The Mulatto*, although the materials were given to you and had already been arranged in literary form, and although its beauties were chiefly lyrical. But even when, a few years ago, you read a part of your *Ahasuerus* for me, I said quite frankly that the scope and the tone of the work did not please me.

Nevertheless, it seemed to be an unpleasant surprise to you last time we discussed it when I repeated what I had said, adding, however, that I had as yet read only a small part of the book. I have now read the whole of it with great attention, and I cannot alter my opinion.

The book makes an unpleasant and disorderly impression on me; you must forgive me for saying it so bluntly. For you demand to know my opinion, and I have to give it if I do not wish to beguile you with a series of polite phrases meaning nothing at all.

If I have any understanding of dramatic composition, then Ahasuerus is not the stuff of a drama. Goethe presumably also gave it up for the same reason. The fantastic baroque myth would probably need treating in a humorous manner like a fairy tale. He would have to be a shoemaker; a shoemaker who would not remain at his last and who was too arrogant to believe what he could not understand. To make him into an abstract concept for speculative poetry is not to make him into a subject for true poetry, least of all suitable for a drama. One of the necessities of a drama is a compressed and well-arranged action expressed and revealed in characters. That is not the case in your work. Throughout the whole of it Ahasuerus appears as a diffident, contemplative observer. The other characters act just as little, and the whole work consists of aphorisms, fragments, sometimes stories, all of which are loosely connected.

It seems to me there is rather too much pretentiousness and too little achievement in this poem. It encompasses neither more nor less than the history of the whole world, from the birth of Christ to the present day.

420

For anyone who has made a thorough and honest study of history with its great events and magnificent characters it cannot be particularly exhilarating to be given these lyrical aphorisms, coming as they often do from pixies, swallows, nightingales, mermaids and so forth. Admittedly there are sometimes beautiful lyrical or descriptive passages, for example, those on the gladiators, the Huns and the savages; but that is not sufficient. So much for form and material; but from the point of view of poetical inspiration the true depth and loftiness which belong to the great and sublime are also missing.

The whole work is like a dream; your natural tendency to write fairy tales also reveals itself here, for all the pictures appear as fairy-tale-like dream pictures. The spirit of history does not appear in all its different forms. Our thoughts are given too little to occupy them; the images are not new or sufficiently original, and there is nothing to move our hearts. On the contrary, there is something outrageous about the way in which Barrabas achieves honour and glory after his crime, for without seeing his actions or developments in his character, we are merely told first that he murders an old woman, and later that there is joy in Heaven at his conversion.

That is my opinion. I may be wrong, but I speak honestly and according to my conviction, and I cannot alter it for the sake of politeness or flattery.

Forgive me, then, if, through no fault of my own, I have grieved you, and be assured moreover that in other respects I recognise and respect in you an able and original poet.

Your most devoted,

A. Oehlenschläger

23rd December 1847

There are many things in this letter about my work that are true and correct, but I consider and place my writing differently from the great and noble poet. I have not called *Ahasuerus* a *dramatic* poem, and it is not to be considered as such. It does not and cannot contain dramatic complexities, and neither does it contain the colourful character-drawing of a drama. *Ahasuerus* is a poem which in varying form is intended to show and illustrate the idea of Man's rejecting God and yet progressing towards perfection and recognition. I sought to show this succinctly, clearly and sufficiently, and I believed I could achieve this by means of the varying forms. The mountain peaks of history have served as the background to it all.

It is not to be compared with a drama by Scribe or an epic poem by Milton. It should be examined in the light of my poetical nature to see whether the idea has been made clear through the form I have chosen. The aphoristic details are like pieces of a mosaic which together form a whole picture.

We can say of any building, that we can only see stone upon stone; each one can be taken separately, but that is not how we must view it; we must look at the totality achieved through their juxtaposition.

However, in recent years several voices have been raised which are more in agreement with the hopes which I had and still partly have in this work, which must always mark a significant transition in my life as a poet.

The first person, and I might almost say the only person, to whom this work made any immediate or great appeal, was Ludvig Müller, the historian. He considered *Ahasuerus* and my *Fairy Tales* to be the two of my books that ensured me a place of importance in Danish literature.

A similar token of recognition reached me from abroad. The *Bildersaal der Weltliteratur* contains a valuable selection of lyrical and dramatic poetry from all countries from ancient times right to the present day – from the drama of India, the Psalms of the Hebrews, the popular poets of Arabia to the troubadours and the poets of our own time. Included among the works of Danish authors appearing in the section called Scandinavia are a few scenes from *Ahasuerus* as well as others from *Earl Hakon, King René's Daughter* and *Tiber.*

Here in Denmark, just as I am writing these pages, that is to say eight years after the work first appeared, it seems to me that *Ahasuerus* is given a more important place than before in the kind and thorough review of my *Collected Works* in the periodical *Dansk Maanedsskrift.* It is recognised as what I myself consider it to be, a sign of my future development as a poet.

XIV

The year 1848 arrived, a strange year, a volcanic year, in which the great waves of time also swept with murderous force across my native land.

King Christian the Eighth lay sick already in the very first days of January. The last time I saw him was one evening when I had received a note inviting me to come to tea in the evening and bring something with me to read to His Majesty. Apart from the King himself, I found the Queen, a lady-in-waiting and a courtier. The King greeted me tenderly and kindly, but he had remained lying on the sofa. I read a couple of chapters from my novel *The Two Baronesses*, which I had still not completed at that time, and in addition I read two or three fairy tales. After this the King seemed to be brighter, and he laughed and talked in a lively, cheerful fashion. Later, when I left, the King nodded happily and kindly from his couch, and the last words I heard him say were, "We'll meet again soon."

But we did not. He became very ill. I felt anxious and feared that I should lose him, and every day I went to Amalienborg to inquire about him. It soon became clear that he was not going to recover. Deeply distressed, I took this news to Oehlenschläger, who strange to say did not yet know that the King's life was in danger. He saw my distress, and burst into tears. He was so deeply devoted to the King. The next morning, on the steps of Amalienborg I met Oehlenschläger supporting himself on Christiani; they were just coming from the antechamber. Oehlenschläger was pale; he did not say a word, but pressed my hand as he went by, and there were tears in his eyes. All hope for the King had been virtually abandoned.

I was out there several times on the twentieth of January; in the evening I stood in the snow on the square and looked up at the windows behind which my King lay dying. At a quarter past ten he passed away.

In sorrow and from the bottom of my heart I wrote some stanzas on him. The line:

423

was used against me out of hatred. People supposed it to be a reference to myself. All Copenhagen was astir. The new order of things was established. On the 28th of January the Constitution was proclaimed.

Christian the Eighth lay in state. I went to pay my last respects, but I was so painfully moved that I became ill and had to be taken into one of the adjoining rooms.

On the 25th of February the body of the King was taken to Roskilde; I sat at home and heard the bells toll.

Great movements spread out all over Europe. Revolution broke out in Paris, and Louis Philippe and his family left France. Like mighty seas, revolt swept through the cities of Germany; at home we still only read about it. Denmark alone was the home of peace! Here people could still breathe freely and think about art, the theatre and beauty.

But the peace only lasted a short while, and the great reverberations soon reached us. A revolt broke out in Holstein. The news struck us like a flash of lightning, and everything was in commotion.

An incredibly large crowd of people gathered in the great hall of the Casino, and the next morning a deputation went to Frederik the Seventh. I was standing in the palace yard and saw the great throng. The King's reply and the dismissal of the Ministry were soon known all over the city.

I witnessed widely differing impressions of the events in various circles. Throughout the day and evening, great throngs of people paraded through the streets singing patriotic songs. There were no excesses, but there was something unpleasant in meeting these almost alien hordes and these faces that were completely unfamiliar to me. It was as though an entirely new generation had emerged. So a number of friends of law and order joined the crowds of people and prevented them from going too far. I myself was made a member of the committee responsible for order and was given the task of helping to stop things from getting out of hand. All that was needed when the mob called the name of some place where they might have run wild was for a single person to shout, "Forward!", and then the whole crowd of them went off in that direction!

The public sang in the theatre, and the orchestra was forced to play patriotic songs.

It was announced everywhere that the town was to be illuminated, and strangely enough, the people who were the least kindly disposed to this new ministry put candles in their windows so as not to have their window panes smashed.

A deputation from Holstein came to Copenhagen. There was a great sense of bitterness towards them, but in his proclamation the King said, "We entrust the safety of the delegates from Schleswig-Holstein to the honour of our Danish people".

The students upheld it, going around in the crowd and calming them down as best they could. Soldiers were stationed in the streets through which the deputation had to pass on their way to the steamer. The people waited there for them. However, they were taken from the palace to the canal behind it and from there to the Custom House, and so they got on board without being noticed.

Preparations for war were made on both land and sea. Everyone helped as much as they could. One of our capable officials came to my home and said that it would be a good thing if I pleaded our cause through the press in England where I was known and read. I wrote straight away to Mr. Jerdan, the editor of *The Literary Gazette*, in which my letter, giving, as it does, a true picture of the atmosphere and situation at home, was immediately published.

Copenhagen, 13th April 1848

Dear Friend,

It is only a few weeks since I wrote to you, and during that time such a series of events has taken place that it is as though years had passed. Politics have never been my business; a poet has a different mission, but now that movements are sweeping across countries so that it is impossible to be anywhere on earth without feeling them in our fingertips, something must be said about them. You know what the situation in Denmark is at the moment. War has come upon us. But it is a war that is being waged by all the enthusiastic Danish people, a war in which aristocrats and peasants, filled with their just cause,

425

voluntarily join the ranks. It is of this enthusiasm I must tell you, this patriotic feeling which fills and uplifts the entire Danish nation.

The false light in which the leading members of the Schleswig-Holstein party for years have portrayed us to the honest and clever German people through the press, the manner in which the Prince of Noer has taken Rendsburg, saying that the Danish King was not free and that he was acting in His Majesty's interests, has filled the Danish people with indignation, and they have risen as one man; all the petty differences of daily life are disappearing and giving place to noble characteristics. Everything is in motion, but with order and unity. Contributions of money are streaming in from all estates and all classes, and even the poor artisan's assistants and servant girls are giving their mite. It was learned that there was a shortage of horses, and within a few days so many were sent from the towns and from the country districts that the Minister of War has announced that no more are needed. In all houses the women are picking lint; in the top classes in the schools the boys are at work making cartridges; most of those capable of carrying arms are practising the use of them. Young counts and barons volunteer as privates in the soldiers' ranks, and the fact that all are equal in their love of their country and their desire to defend it strengthens the bravery and enthusiasm of the soldiers, as you can well imagine.

Among the volunteers is the son of the Viceroy of Norway, a young man who belongs to the most distinguished of families. He was here on a visit during the winter, and, filled with enthusiasm for our honest cause, he wanted to take part in the battle, but as a foreign citizen he could not be accepted. So he immediately bought a Danish farm, registered as a Danish citizen, put on a military uniform and marched off with one of the battalions as a common soldier; he had decided to share the fate of his comrades and to live on his black bread and his threepence a day. And Danish men of all classes had done the same as he; both the lord of the manor and the student, rich and poor are marching together and they take

426

part in the singing and excitement as though it were a festival. Our King himself has gone to the headquarters of the Danish army, upright in his intention and his will to fight for his good cause. His Life Guards are with him; some of them are from Holstein, and on their departure from Copenhagen these men were excused from marching against their countrymen, but every one of them asked leave to march along with the others, and it was granted them.

Heaven is with us up to the present, and we hope, in the future too. The army is advancing quickly and victoriously; the island of Als has already been taken, as have the towns of Flensburg and Schleswig; we stand on the border of Holstein and have taken more than a thousand prisoners; most of them have been transferred to Copenhagen, and they are extremely angry about the Prince of Noer, who, despite his promise to sacrifice his life and blood along with them, deserted them in the first battle; he left them as the Danes advanced on Flensburg with shots and fixed bayonets.

The storms of change are passing over many countries in our time, but there is One who is over them all and does not change; that is God, and He is just. He is on the side of Denmark who only demands her right, and that must be acknowledged and shall be acknowledged. Truth is the conquering power both in people and nations.

"Rights to all nationalities and advancement for those who are good and able." That must be the solution in Europe, and so I look to the future with hope. The Germans are an honest people who love the truth; they will realise what the situation up here is, and their bitterness will pass and must be transformed into friendship and esteem. May that time soon come. May God make His Face to shine on all lands!

Hans Christian Andersen

This letter was one of the small number from Denmark that were published in several foreign newspapers.

I suffered more mental anguish than most people on account of this unhappy war which had come upon us. I felt as never before how firmly planted I had become in the soil of my native country, and how Danish my heart was. I could have put myself in the line of battle and would gladly have given my life to contribute to victory and peace. But at the same time vivid recollections went through my mind of all the kindness I had received in Germany, the great recognition people there had shown for my talents and the countless people there whom I had to love and to whom I had to be grateful. I suffered infinitely. And when, as often happened, some deeply agitated person seemed to realise this and made some angry and bitter remark about me, it was often more than I could bear. I will not give examples of this; it is best that all bitter words from that time should disappear, and that the wounds between closely related people should be healed. Here, too, it was H. C. Ørsted who raised my spirits and talked about the better days when I would be recognised, days which have now arrived.

There was unity; there was love. Several of my young friends took part as volunteers, among them Valdemar Drewsen and Baron Henrik Stampe. Ørsted was deeply moved by the course of events, and he wrote three poems in one of our daily papers, *Battle, Victory* and *Peace*.

Deeply we feel that the enemy still is our brother,
Linked as he's been to us over the years.
Yet it is he who brought strife to this land, to his mother,
And now 'tis a question of victory or tears.

That was the basic tone.

To don the red jacket had previously been an act of despair, for then the common soldier was only a poor wretch. But now the red jacket had come to honour and glory. Ladies in silks and ribbons walked about arm in arm with the red-coated soldiers. One of the first men from the higher classes whom I saw going about in this way was Løvenskjold, the son of the Viceroy of Norway. And then there was the young Count Adam Knuth, who had only recently been confirmed. He lost a leg through a sharp-nosed bullet. Løvenskjold fell, and so did Lundbye, the painter, whose death was due to an accident. An eye-witness told me about it. Lundbye stood leaning sadly on his rifle. Some peasants went past the spot where the other rifles were stacked in front of him, and they chanced to knock them over. A shot was heard, and Lundbye was seen to fall to the ground. He had been shot up through the jaw; his mouth had been torn apart and a piece of flesh and part of his beard shot away. He gave a few weak sighs, was wrapped in a flag and laid in the ground.

The young men's enthusiasm moved me to tears, and one day when I heard a story told at the expense of young gentlemen who had previously always worn kid gloves and were now digging trenches with red, blistered hands, I rose up and exclaimed from the bottom of my heart, "I could kiss those hands for them!"

Hosts of young men marched off almost every day. I accompanied a young friend on the way, and when I came home I wrote the song *I cannot stay, for I know no rest*, and it was soon sung by all, for it expressed their own thoughts.

As the song has it, "The Easter bells rang out".

That unhappy Easter Day in Schleswig dawned. The enemy forces split ours; an oppressive sadness lay over the country; but we had not lost courage, and our strength gathered again. People came closer together, as was seen in things both great and small.

The Prussians entered Jutland, and our troops retreated to Als. In the middle of May I went to Funen and found Glorup filled with our troops, whose headquarters were in Odense. At Glorup there were forty soldiers as well as several high-ranking officers. General Hedemann held manoeuvres outside the mansion.

All volunteers among the common soldiers were treated as officers by the old Count and were given seats at his table every day.

Most of the officers had taken part in the campaign over in Schleswig, and they gave vivid accounts of their experiences there. Their quarters for the night had sometimes been the open street in a little village where they slept up against the houses, in wind and rain, and with only their packs under their heads. Or there might have been a number of them crowded into small rooms where their couches consisted of tall settles with brass fittings that pressed right into their flesh. But sleep, they did, tired and overstrained as they were. A young doctor told of marching with the soldiers over the bare stretches of heath; he used a church as a hospital. The candles from the altar were lit, but it remained more or less dark. Far away he heard signal shots being fired: the enemy was coming. I sensed all this exciting scene in the night as clearly as though I had experienced it myself.

The Prussians had forced their way up into Jutland, and they demanded a forced contribution of four millions; and soon afterwards there came news of another battle.

All our thoughts and hopes turned towards the Swedes who were coming to our aid. They were to land in Nyborg, and everything there was ready for a festive reception.

The mansion of Glorup took in sixteen Swedish officers with their orderlies and in addition twenty musicians and subalterns. Among the Swedes there were four men whom the Duke of Augustenburg had had to supply, or rather whom his estates in Sweden had had to send to fight against their own master.

Everyone gave the Swedes a rapturous welcome. Typical and pleasing was the genuine eagerness displayed by Miss Ibsen, the old housekeeper at Glorup. The large number of men whom the mansion there was to find accommodation for gave her plenty to think about. "We must make a big bed for them out in the barn," she was told.

"Are they to lie in the straw!" she said. "No, indeed; they shall have beds. If they are coming here to help us they shall also have beds."

And she had wood sawn and knocked together, and out of planks and doors she very quickly had beds made for them in between ten and twelve rooms. Eiderdowns were also found; they were certainly of coarse quality, but her "barracks", as she called it, shone with white linen. Later, in the Leipzig periodical *Nordischer Telegraf*, I wrote a description of the Swedish soldiers' stay in Funen as I saw it from Glorup, and as a concentrated picture it deserves a place here:

The Swedes in Funen in 1848

I must tell you a little of the Swedes in Funen. Their stay here is among the brightest and most beautiful pictures from this summer. I saw the festive reception they were given in the villages, the waving flags and the happy faces; for miles around in the country clusters of peasants gathered by the roadsides, old and young alike, and asked expectantly, "Are the Swedes coming now?" And they were greeted with food and drink, flowers and handshakes. They were kind men and well-disciplined soldiers. Their morning and evening prayers and their Sunday services were most moving. It all took place in the open, according to the old military tradition from the days of Gustavus Adolphus.

Divine service on Sundays was in the old manor house where one of the commanders-in-chief together with the officers and the entire band was quartered. With the band playing, the troops marched into the large, square courtyard and took up positions with the officers in front; they began to sing hymns, accompanied by the band. Then the chaplain stepped forward on the broad steps, the railings of which were covered with a large cloth. I can clearly remember the last Sunday there: during the service, which had begun in dull, windy weather, the chaplain talked of the Angel of Peace descending in the shape of God's gentle, refreshing sunshine, and just as he said this the sun happened to break through and shine on the bright helmets and pious faces. But most solemn of all were the morning and evening services. The companies were stationed on the open highway; a subaltern read a short prayer and then they all joined in a hymn without the accompaniment of music. When the hymn was ended a lusty shout of "God Save the King" was heard from all along the ranks. I saw many of our old peasants standing behind the ditches and fences with their heads bared and their hands folded, silently taking part in the service.

After their daily exercises the Swedish soldiers were to be seen faithfully helping with this year's rich corn harvest in the fields belonging to the farm on which they were staying. They were busy and full of life. At the mansion, where the regimental band was quartered, they played music every afternoon until sunset; the long avenue of lime trees in the park filled with people from all the surrounding area; it was a daily festival. In the evenings the Swedish violins were to be heard in the servants' hall, and there was dancing to the delight of everyone. The peasants from Funen and the soldiers from Sweden soon understood each other's language. It was a delight to see how each of them revealed their kind hearts, and how everyone willingly gave as far as his resources allowed.

"But did the Swedish army not go out and fight?" some people will perhaps ask. Are all the fine impressions of the moment only to be gained from sword blows? The esteem, friendship and understanding which has been felt in later years especially by the younger people of the university towns has now, as a result of the Swedes' sojourn in Funen spread to thousands of ordinary people. What did the peasant from Funen and the peasant from Sweden know of the close relationship there is between them? Memories of the old days when the two countries were enemies still lived, but now they have been dispersed. Now the neighbouring peoples have come much closer to each other. The good seeds of understanding have been sown, and good understanding is a plant of peace and it alone bears blessings. In the farms, in the parsonages and in the mansions many an eye was dimmed with tears when the time came to part.

On the jetty in Nyborg, where the Swedish and Danish flags were both waving as our friends embarked, many a visit to each other in the coming years of peace was planned. The Danes will not forget the Swedes; we have felt and heard their heartbeats. Many a small Swedish town, which can scarcely be wealthy, collected money, "the widow's sacred mite", for their Danish brothers. When the news of the Danish defeat in Schleswig spread over the country, there was a congregation in a church far up in Sweden where the priest prayed for the King and their native land, and then an old peasant stood up and said, "Father, will you not pray for the Danes, too?" That is one of those small features that bring out the divine quality within us.

The nations of the North understand, value and love each other; may this spirit of unity and love enfold all realms on earth!

I spent the greater part of the summer at Glorup. I was there both in the spring and the autumn, and so I witnessed both the arrival and the subsequent departure of the Swedes. I myself did not visit the scene of battle, but stayed at Glorup where people arrived from the fighting every day, some who had gone there out of curiosity and others who were visiting their loved ones. Like some fine perfume, news of beautiful events in the battle area reached us and filled my thoughts.

I heard of an old grandmother who was standing with her grandchildren by the roadside when our troops came along; she had strewn sand and flowers for them and together with the little ones she shouted, "God bless the Danes".

I heard of a trick of nature: it was said that in a peasant's garden in Schleswig there grew red poppies marked with a white cross, a perfect example of the Danish flag. One of my friends visited Als and then he went over to Dybbøl where all the houses were cracked and holed by cannonballs and caseshot, and yet on one of the houses there was still the symbol of peace, a stork's nest with a whole family of storks. All the fierce shooting, fire and smoke had not driven the parents away from their young, which were not yet able to fly.

In the late summer the postman brought me a letter from abroad. It was from someone I did not know, and the contents moved me deeply and at the same time showed me how quickly events were rumoured abroad. The letter was from a high-ranking official, the subject of a foreign monarch. He wrote that, although he had never seen me and had not the slightest acquaintance with me, he believed, on account of my writings and especially *Das Märchen meines Lebens*, that he could have confidence in me. Then he told me that early one morning the news had reached the town where he lived that the Danes had made an attack on Kiel and had set it on fire. All the young men in the town were incensed at this, and in the heat of the moment his youngest son had marched off along with some other young men to help their beleaguered countrymen. In the Battle of Bau the young man had been taken prisoner and transferred to Copenhagen on board the ship of the line, the *Dronning Maria;* after a fairly long stay there he had been one among several who were permitted to leave the ship. However, after going ashore there were some who had been guilty of excesses, so that after that no one was allowed his freedom unless he could produce a citizen of Copenhagen to guarantee his good conduct. The writer did not know a single person in Copenhagen. I was the person he knew through my writings and in whom he placed confidence and hope, and so he wished to ask me to stand surety for his son who was a truly good and noble man. He requested me, too, to find him lodgings with some Copenhagen family that "did not hate the Germans too much".

I was moved by this trust, and I immediately wrote on the matter to one of my most influential friends in Copenhagen, enclosing the German letter, so that he might be able to see the whole matter just as it had been presented to me. I then asked whether, on my responsibility, he could do what was requested and be of any service to the young man. I knew that every hour's delay meant an hour's imprisonment, and so I immediately dispatched a messenger on horseback with my package to the nearest market town. With the next post I received the reply that there was no need to do anything at all, since all prisoners had been released and sent by steamer to Kiel. I was delighted on behalf of the concerned father, delighted because I had straight away done what my heart had prompted me to do. But I did not answer the letter; there was no need to do so. The man has never learned of my sympathy, and only now in the blessed days of peace am I sending him a greeting, as I have often thought I ought to do, and I may add that I was deeply moved by his letter and acted as many of my fellow countrymen would probably have acted if they, too, had been honoured with the same trust.

I left Glorup late in the autumn. The approach of winter had brought a pause in the military operations, and for a time the apparent quiet turned my thoughts and activities rather to the occupation to which I was accustomed. In the course of the summer at Glorup I had finished my novel *The Two Baronesses*, in which the freshness and truth in my descriptions of the island scenery must have benefited from my stay.

I dedicated the English edition to my English publisher, the well-known and highly esteemed Richard Bentley.

The book appeared, and in view of the time and the circumstances it was given a good reception. In one of our newspapers the novel and the events of the day were certainly confused. It argued it was not fitting that, in her delight at the liking for London expressed by her favourite, the squire, the old baroness should drink to England. It was felt that it was a little too early to let her do that since England had still not done anything for us Danes.

Heiberg read this book, wrote a few kind words to me and invited me to visit him together with some of his other friends, and there he proposed a charming toast to me, "for the novel which we leave as

434

refreshed as after a walk in the woods in spring". It was the first truly heartfelt friendly gesture I had received from this poet for many years. It was good to hear it, and "bitter memories were forgotten and the new and good ones were kept within my heart."

The centenary of the Royal Theatre was to be celebrated on the 18th December. Heiberg and Collin agreed to ask me to write the prologue for the festival. Bournonville was to write a ballet for the same occasion, and he produced *Old Memories*. As though in a magic lantern, we were shown all the most vivid scenes in the ballets on the repertoire. My plan for the prelude had won the applause of the management since they quite approved of my idea, completely based as it was on the situation at that moment. I knew the mood in which people went to the theatre and knew precisely how unimportant it was for them now as their thoughts were with the soldiers fighting the war. So I had to make sure that my work went with them, and then from there bring back their thoughts to the Danish theatre. I was convinced that our strength today did not lie in the sword, but in intellectual achievements, and I wrote what is known as *The Bulwark of Art*, under which title it is now to be found in my collected works.

On the evening of the centenary it was enthusiastically received, and it was put on again for those who possessed season tickets and used as an attraction for the whole week. As I say, on the actual centenary evening it was received with great applause – people were moved by it – but now came the newspapers, and one of them especially reproached me because there were constant, nauseating references to Denmark and the Danish flag in the prologue. This paper said that we should let others praise us and not praise ourselves, for then it sounded rather like the boasting of Holberg's *Jacob von Thybo* and so on.

Another newspaper gave such a review of the play that I did not know whether the reviewer had written it out of simplicity or vindictiveness. At the fourth performance it was already the old story. People no longer clapped, and it is on this performance that the review is based in the periodical *Nord og Syd*, the editor of which disliked my work. However, it had the intended effect on the evening itself, and I still consider the idea and the form to be well chosen and the only right thing to do in those days and with the people feeling as they did at that time.

435

The Wedding by Lake Como was staged in January, and now Gläser, the composer, to whom the public had long been indifferent, indeed unjust, was highly praised and his music received with loud applause. The newspaper reviews were warm and full of acknowledgement for him. His music and Bournonville's production were especially praised. I, on the other hand, received no mention. But Gläser spoke warmly and sincerely of the honour I had helped him to gain.

Christmas, Fredrika Bremer had made her first visit to Copenhagen during the Christmas period. I was her only personal acquaintance there, and otherwise the only person with whom she had any contact was the present Bishop Martensen, with whom she had corresponded. So I had the pleasure of receiving her, helping her and taking her about in Copenhagen, something which was both easy and pleasant with a woman of her importance. She stayed throughout the winter and far into the summer, at which time she visited Ingemann in Sorø. She also paid a visit to Svendborg and went to see the cliffs of Møn. Her heart became firmly fixed in the Danish cause, as is seen in the little book that represents the visible fruits of her stay here. It is called *Life in the North*, and has been published in Swedish, English, German and Danish. Her entire heart and all her thoughts were for the Danes:

> Bravery and humanity,
> Heroism and nobility
> Are now as aye
> The Danish cry.

She wrote this little verse in Copenhagen, and it expressed the warmth with which her profound spirit embraced the Danes.

However, her little book did not receive the recognition, not to mention the thanks, which she rightly deserved here. We always criticize, especially when we see that the heart is engaged. People censured it and dwelt on the slightly exaggerated description of the throngs of people in Østergade, throngs to which we were accustomed but she was not, never having visited London or the large cities in America. As I say, her little book, which revealed such a warm heart for Denmark, did not receive the recognition due to it, although its pages radiate the sympathy and the tears I so often saw in her eyes as a result of her deep awareness of the fate of the Danish people and nation. She was here during those difficult but intense days.

One evening in April the news arrived that on Maundy Thursday the ship of the line *Christian den Ottende* had been blown up with all the crew on board. A cry of anguish went up, great and terrible. It was a sorrow for the entire nation.

I felt as though I were standing on a sinking wreck.

A single life saved from the ship was like a victory, a great treasure gained. I met my friend Captain Christian Wulff in the street. His eyes were shining and he pressed my hand.

"Do you know whom I have brought home?" he asked.

"Lieutenant Ulrich! He was not blown up. He's safe; he escaped and reached our outposts, and I have brought him home!"

I did not know Lieutenant Ulrich at all, but I burst into tears of joy. "Where is he? I must see him."

"He went to the First Lord of the Admiralty and then he was going to see his mother. She thinks he's dead."

I went to the nearest grocer's shop and found a directory and discovered where Ulrich's mother lived. However, when I arrived there I was suddenly afraid that she still knew nothing at all about it, and so I asked the maid who opened the door, "Are they sad or happy in this house?"

The maid's face lit up: "They are happy, for their son has come home as though he has fallen from the sky."

And then I went straight into their drawing room where the whole family sat dressed in mourning. They had taken to wearing it that very day, and the son they thought to be dead was safe and happy among them. I fell on his neck; I could do nothing else. I had to weep, and they felt with me and understood that I had not come as a stranger. When I told Miss Bremer this story, to which she later referred in her book, she was just as moved as I had been. Her heart is as tender as it is noble and warm.

I was ill, suffering both mentally and physically. I needed different surroundings. Miss Bremer spoke of her beautiful native land, where I also had friends. I decided to go either to Dalecarlia or perhaps to Haparanda for midsummer's day. Miss Bremer's *Midsummer Journey* made this idea attractive to me. She was tireless in writing to her many friends all over Sweden, for such are necessary in that country. There are not always inns to stay at, and it is often necessary to seek a night's lodging in the parsonage or manor house. Before I left she arranged a farewell party for me in the Swedish manner, which we, in our reflective Copenhagen, neither know nor like. We put on fancy dresses and there were recitations. There were many guests, among them H. C. Ørsted, Martensen and Hartmann. I received a beautiful silver cup with the inscription "A keepsake from Fredrika Bremer".

A little poem accompanied it:

> The swallows you join as they fly off north,
> You, Danish swallow, rich in song;
> You journey to winter and frozen earth
> To sing of summer all day long.
>
> And thousands of voices on Sweden's shore
> Shall bid you welcome over there.
> To this dear country give greetings and more,
> And give my firm friends there goodness and cheer.
>
> Drink, noble bard, out of friendship's deep bowl;
> It is yours everywhere and henceforth;
> But nowhere is Andersen's glorious skoal
> drunk as warmly as here in the North.

F. B.

On Ascension Day I travelled on to Hälsingborg. It was lovely spring weather; the young birch trees filled the air with such a refreshing scent and the sun was warm. The whole journey was like a poem, and that is how it sounds in the pictures and moods I describe in *Pictures of Sweden*.

Gothenburg was like a half English or Dutch town with gas lamps. It was magnificent and, I thought, more advanced than the other Swedish towns. Only the theatre had not moved with the times, and the original play they were presenting was dreadful. It would probably even be more appropriate to call it coarse. I was told that the leading role was played by the author himself. What infuriated me was that

438

the entire action was about someone who was still alive, a learned old scholar who for fun was called Arab on account of his knowledge of the Oriental languages. In the play we see that he would like to marry. The whole thing was based on anecdotes from the man's life. The play itself consisted solely of unconnected scenes without any action or individuality, but the central figure was still alive, living, I was told, in the Stockholm workhouse. The actor portrayed his personality and gave a true picture of him to the accompaniment of enthusiastic applause. I left after the second act; it infuriates me to ridicule someone when the only thing gained is to make fun.

I believe the town is indebted to a businessman by the name of Wijk for its harbour and its magnificent bathhouse with its marble baths. I found in him an extremely charming host and within a few hours in his splendid, comfortable home I made the acquaintance of the leading figures in Gothenburg. Of the ladies among these I must name the brilliant authoress Miss Bolander.

Once more I saw the mighty Trollhättan waterfall, and I have since sought to paint it in words. The impression it produces is always new and great, but a new impression accompanying it is just as much alive in my memory. This was a meeting that occurred outside Venersborg, where the steamer went alongside for the sake of the passengers. There on the jetty stood a little boy piper whom I had seen with the Swedish troops in Funen the year before. He gave me a delighted wave like an old friend, and he was quite surprised to see me in his own country. While he had been billetted with the Swedish soldiers at Glorup, they were to go out on manoeuvres one day. The boy had a slight pain in his stomach and the good housekeeper refused to allow him to go with them: the child needed a diet of gruel, she said. The officer maintained there was nothing wrong with him. "I am his mother here," she said. "The child is ill, and he is not coming out to play the pipes today." The boy asked about the housekeeper and the old Count, but for him it was the housekeeper who ruled the roost.

I arrived in Stockholm and immediately changed clothes in order to visit our ambassador from whom I hoped to receive some news of the war that was completely filling my thoughts. On the way there I was unfortunate enough to meet Dr. Leo, a German who spoke Danish; I knew him from Copenhagen where I had received him kindly and introduced him to Miss Bremer who was visiting us.

Later, in his *Charactere aus meiner skandinavischen Mappe*, published as a serial in the periodical *Novellen-Zeitung*, he speaks about us in anything but flattering terms. He produces a sort of caricature of me from our meeting in the street in Stockholm where, he says, I appeared in my finest attire immediately after leaving the steamer. He says I walked along the promenade in white kid gloves *in order to be seen* and so that my arrival might be in the papers the following day. He did me an injustice in this, and he upset me, but I will also remember that he has made beautiful translations of several of my books, and he has spoken well and kindly of me at other times and in other places. I offer him my hand again and without a "kid glove" on it.

Lindblad, whose beautiful melodies Jenny Lind has introduced to the world, was one of the first people I met. He resembles her as a brother resembles a sister; they have both the same expression of melancholy, but he has more powerful features. I would still like to write the libretto for an opera, as he asked me to do, so that through his melodies it might be carried on the wings of the folk song.

In the Theatre the Italian Society in Stockholm were performing the opera *Queen Christine*, which its Italian conductor, Foroni, had composed to a libretto by Casanova, the singer. It seemed to me to be full of splendid harmonies rather than actual melodies. The act containing the conspirators was the most effective; there was no lack of beautiful *décor* and good costumes, and an attempt had been made to make Christine and Oxenstjerna look like the real historical figures. The strangest thing about it all was in Christine's Swedish capital city to see Christine herself appear as a figure in an opera on the stage.

I had been introduced into the Literary Association by Mr. Bagge, the publisher, and at a celebration there I was given a seat beside the poet, Beskow. Dr. Leo was also present, and the president grasped the opportunity to propose the health of "our two distinguished foreign guests, Mr. Andersen of Copenhagen, the author of *The Improvisatore* and *Fairy Tales Told for Children* and Dr. Leo of Leipzig, the editor of the *Nordischer Telegraf*". Later in the evening, Mr. Bagge proposed a charming and sincere toast to me and my native country, and he asked me to tell my compatriots of the Swedish people's enthusiasm and sympathy for us. I answered in the words of one of my songs:

Sharp as a sword the Sound once lay
Betwixt the neighbouring sands;
A branch of roses appeared one day
To link these warring lands;
The roses each breathed poesy,
Rejected warring swagger.
Who could pursue this wizardry?
Why, Tegner and Oehlenschläger.

And then I added that several new poets had appeared both in Sweden and Denmark, and through them the two peoples had learned to understand each other better and better. They felt the beating of each other's hearts, and we have recently come to appreciate the beating of the Swedish heart, just as I appreciated it at that moment. Tears came to my eyes, and those around me broke out in cheers.

Beskow presented me to King Oscar. The King received me so cordially that it was as though we had already spoken to each other several times, and yet this was the first time we had met. I thanked His Majesty for the Order of the North Star with which he had honoured me on an earlier occasion. We talked of the similarities between Stockholm and Constantinople and between Lake Roxen and Loch Lomond, and then of the discipline and the devoutness of the Swedish soldiers, and the King said he had read what I had written about the Swedish soldiers during their stay in Funen. He spoke of his warm sympathy for the Danish people and of his friendship for our King. We talked about the war. I said it was an essential part of our nation's character that when it felt it had right on its side, it insisted on it and forgot that it was so small. I understood the noble King's entire charming disposition.

I said that the good things the Danes saw him do for them would earn him the gratitude of the entire nation. We talked about the Hereditary Grand Duke of Weimar, of whom he, too, was very fond. Then His Majesty asked me if I would soon be back from Uppsala, which I was now going to visit, as he would like to invite me to dinner. "My wife, the Queen," he said, "also knows your works and would personally like to make your acquaintance."

On my return I dined at the Palace. The Queen, who in looks much resembles her mother, the Duchess of Leuchtenberg, whom I had met in Rome, gave me a kind reception and said that she had long known me from my works and from *Das Märchen meines Lebens*. I was seated at table beside Beskow, just opposite the Queen. In particular, Prince Gustav carried on a bright and lively conversation with me. After dinner I read *The Flax*, *The Ugly Duckling*, *A Mother* and *The Collar*. While I was reading *A Mother* I saw tears in the eyes of the noble royal couple. They spoke warmly and with so much sympathy and interest. How charming they both were, so delightfully natural! As I left, the Queen gave me her hand which I pressed to my lips. She and the King honoured me by giving me another invitation and listening to me read once more. A feeling of mutual sympathy, if I may use such an expression here, drew me especially to the charming young Prince Gustav. His big, blue, soulful eyes had an expression of sincerity which made a great impression on me, and his unusual talent for music interested me. There was something so approachable and faithful about his personality, and we discovered that we had in common our warm affection for the Duke of Weimar. We spoke of him, of the war and of music and poetry.

On my next visit to the palace, Beskow and I were invited to go to the Queen's chambers an hour before dinner. Princess Eugenie, the Crown Prince and Princes Gustav and Oscar were present, and the King soon joined us. Poetry called him away from his duties, he said. I read *The Fir Tree*, T*he Darning Needle*, *The Little Match Girl*, and, on request, *The Flax*. The King listened attentively. "The profound poetry in these small works," as he put it, appealed greatly to him, and he said that he had read the fairy tales, *The Fir Tree* among others, while travelling in Norway. All three princes shook hands with me, and the King invited me to come on his birthday, the fourth of July, when Beskow would be my cicerone.

The people of Stockholm wanted to give me some public mark of honour. I knew how envious people at home would be and how much this would give evil tongues to gossip about. It spoiled my good mood, and I was terribly nervous at the prospect of being the central figure that evening. I felt like a criminal and trembled at the thought of the many toasts and the long evening.

The brilliant and famous Mrs. Carlén was among the guests, as was the less famous but excellent authoress known under the pseudonym of "Vilhelmina". Mrs. Strandberg, the actress, and several ladies took part in the festive evening that had been arranged. Mrs. Carlén invited me to go a walk and she took my arm. However, we were not to go into the garden as I wanted because I could see there were not many spectators there. We had to follow a specific route, for, I was told, the public also wanted to see Mr. Andersen. It had been arranged, and was well meant but rather embarrassing. I had a mental picture of a woodcut of it all at home in the periodical *Corsaren*. Oehlenschläger, whom people were accustomed to looking up to with a sense of awe, had been caricatured surrounded by Swedish ladies during his triumphant visit to Stockholm. In the avenue before me I saw a large group of children coming towards us and carrying a huge bunch of flowers. They strewed flowers in front of me and gathered around me while the crowds of people about me were very dense: people took off their hats in respect. And what was I thinking? "People will mock me in Copenhagen for this; I shall never hear the end of it." I was completely out of spirits but had to look pleased in front of all the good, kind people. I made a joke of it all, kissed one of the children and chatted with another. At supper Pastor Mellin, the poet, proposed my health after talking about my works; then some verses, written for the occasion by "Vilhelmina" the authoress, were recited and followed by a beautiful poem by Mr. Carlén:

> It happen'd while they were parading
> That many a soldier sent
> A glance at a famous stranger
> Who there on the pavement went.
> But close with wide opened eyes
> – When the stranger was moving away –
> Was left at his mother's side
> A boy only two feet in height
>
> Oh mother, my dearest and kindest
> But can it really be true?
> That it's he over there who has written
> The tales that you've read through and through.

443

The soldier of tin so steadfast,
Karo, and the old farmer's cow
And the girl with the doll in the tree
And the bird singing sweet in the bough.

Oh, ask him to come home this evening
To sit in our grandmother's bower
And let us have pudding and pancakes
And whatever is in your power.
And I will put on my jacket
To make myself smart, you'll agree.
Imagine him reading a story
For me and for little Marie!

From nature, great bard, have you taken
The laurels that go with your art.
By storm they can never be shaken
For they're all rooted deep in your heart.
Children you've made of us even
In the midst of the turmoil of life.
Oh thank you, and e'er may your heaven
With pleasure for children be rife.

I replied that I would consider all the honours which had been showered on me as a sort of advance payment, and that I hoped that God would give me strength to repay them through a work expressing my love of Sweden. And I have tried to keep my promise. Jolin, the actor who has also written a number of comedies, recited a story in dialect from Dalecarlia; Strandberg, Walin and Günther, all of them singers from the Royal Theatre, sang Swedish songs; the orchestra played, beginning with the Danish National Anthem. At eleven o'clock in the evening I drove home. I was happy in my heart because of all the friendly people. I was happy to retire for the night.

I was soon on my way to Dalecarlia. In Uppsala one of Fredrika Bremer's letters introduced me to the poet Fahlcrantz, the brother of the famous landscape painter, who himself has something of a reputation thanks to his works *Ansgar* and *Noah's Ark*. I met his friend, the poet

Böttiger, who is married to Tegnér's daughter, Disa, two happy people whose home was filled with the sunshine and poetry of domesticity.

My room in the hotel adjoined a large hall where the students were celebrating the sixth of June. When they learned that I was their neighbour, a deputation came to me and asked me if I would not go and hear them sing. They were full of merriment and gaiety, and they sang beautifully. I immediately looked for one to whom, judging by their faces, I could attach myself. I liked the look of a tall, pale man, and I soon discovered I had made the right choice. He sang so beautifully and pronounced his words so distinctly. He was the most gifted of them all, and later I learned he was Wennerberg, the poet and the composer of *Gluntarna*. Later I heard him and Beronius sing these modern songs written in the style of Bellman. That was at the home of the county sheriff, where I met Uppsala's leading men and women and was given a most cordial welcome. There, for the first time, I met Atterbom, the poet who wrote *The Flowers*, the man who sang of *The Isle of Bliss*. Marmier says there is a sort of freemasonry among poets; they know and understand each other. I realised how true this is in the company of this delightful old poet.

> Much as the chariot of time may thunder,
> the joy of the fairy tale never refute.
> 'Tis delightful to love, to admire and to wonder;
> and from me that's a triple tribute.
>
> Atterbom

You need your own carriage when travelling in Sweden. I would have been forced to buy one if the sheriff had not been kind enough to offer to lend me his for the whole of my long journey. Professor Schröder supplied me with a whip and small coins for the tolls, and Fahlcrantz planned my route for me. Now began a journey unlike any other I have made in my travels, a journey not very different from travelling in parts of America where there are as yet no railways. Compared with what I was used to it was like travelling a hundred years ago.

When I reached Leksand where the great, broad Lake Siljan was radiant before me, people were binding garlands on maypoles in preparation for Midsummer Eve. Great willow trees leaned out over the swiftly flowing river, the Dal River, on which wild swans were swimming. Beyond Mora and towards the Norwegian border the mountains faded into blue. Everything – all the life and movement, the picturesque costumes, the warmth of the summer – was so different from what I had imagined up here in the quiet, cold North. And what life there was now in the midsummer festival. Countless boats came along brim full of gaily dressed people on their way to church, old and young and even small babies. It was a picture so full of life and colour that words can give but a poor impression of it. Professor Marstrand, on whom my description of the festival and the oral account I later gave him made a great impression, went up there two years on the run to experience the midsummer festival, and he captured the scene on canvas in both spirit and colour.

It was still possible for a traveller to find an inn at Leksand, but no further north than that. So in Rättvik I had to follow local custom and go and seek lodgings for the night in the parsonage. But even before he heard my name, the parson made me welcome, and after that it was just like a party. And the next day, when I went with him to the nearby bathhouse, a whole flock of children were standing near the jetty waving their bonnets, for they knew the man who had written the fairy tales. "Andersen is up here in Dalecarlia," was the news one of these little ones jubilantly came home and told yesterday. At that moment I thought of my poor little friends in Heriot's Hospital in Edinburgh. I thought of the young people in Scotland now that I was standing in this circle of merry children up in Dalecarlia, and my heart became humble and soft, and full of gratitude to God. I prayed that He would forgive the sighs and sorrows with which I might come to Him in difficult times and in moments of hurt and bitterness.

It is the memories of former times, the sunshine which legend and history cast over a part of the country that often give it a power and importance exceeding its picturesque beauty. Up here it is the loyalty of the people of Dalecarlia, the flight and all the deeds of Gustav Vasa that fix themselves in our minds. The setting for that romantic time in his life is almost unchanged in all its grandeur and loneliness. In the series of pictures I have painted in *Pictures of Sweden* I have as best I could described the impression it all made on me. The endless, spreading stretches of forest with their solitary stacks of charcoal and their deep, sparkling lakes where the linnea blooms on the rocks and where the wild swans build their nests were all fresh and almost foreign for me. I felt as though I had been transported hundreds of years back in time. I visited Falun with its copper mines and all its beautiful surroundings, and a little event there remains fixed in my memory; it was one of those events that can be called coincidence, but which many put on a higher plane. In my pictures from Sweden I have given this event the title *What the Straws Said*. This is not something I have invented; it is something I have experienced.

A number of young girls were sitting in the sheriff's garden at Falun. For fun they took four blades of grass in their hands and tied their ends together. When they manage to make a complete ring of the four blades, popular belief has it that whatever they were thinking of while they fastened them together comes true. None of them could do it, and so they wanted me to try.

"But I don't believe in it," I assured them.

However, I took four blades and promised that if I were lucky I would make my wish. I fastened the ends, opened my hand, and the straws stayed together. Involuntarily, the blood rushed to my cheeks; I was filled with superstition, and contrary to all my rational thoughts I believed in it because I wanted to. "And what did you wish?" they asked me, and I told them: "That Denmark may win a great victory and soon achieve an honourable peace."

"God grant it may," they all exclaimed.

And that day the prophecy of the straw was – by coincidence – fulfilled: news soon reached Sweden of the Battle of Fredericia.

I returned to Uppsala by way of Gävle. I went through Dannemora and saw the cavernous mines there from above. I had previously visited Rammelsberg in the Harz, Baumann's Cave, the salt mines at Hallein and the catacombs beneath Rome and Malta. None of these places gave me pleasure; they were unpleasant, oppressive, horrible nightmares. I prefer not to go beneath the ground until my dead body is laid to rest there.

At Old Uppsala I got out to look at the now thoroughly excavated barrows bearing the names of Odin, Thor and Freyr. When I was there thirteen years earlier they had been closed for hundreds of years. The old woman who had the key to the entrance to the barrow, and whose

447

late aunt had filled the horn with mead for me on that occasion, was delighted to hear my name. Now, she said, she would light up the barrow for me, just as she did for the distinguished gentlemen from Stockholm who visited the place. While she set about this, I went up to the top of the barrow alone, and offered prayers and thanksgiving to God for all the goodness I had received in the time that had passed since I was last here, finishing with the words, "Thy will be done with me." It is thus I unconsciously have my divine service, sometimes in the beauty of the woods, sometimes on the graves of antiquity and sometimes in the quiet of my small room. When I came down again wax candles had been set up in the passageway, and I saw the old urn containing what she said were the bones of Odin, that is to say the bones of his offspring, the Ynglinga Family. Round about lay the ashes of burned animals.

After visiting my friends in Uppsala again I reached Stockholm where I was received like a member of the family by old Mrs. Bremer. At that time Agathe, the brilliant, but seriously ailing sister of Fredrika Bremer was still alive. It was she to whom all the letters from America were written, but she was dead when Fredrika arrived home. It was comfortable, luxurious and good in the old mother's house where on several occasions I met members of the family, which is one of the best in this good land of Sweden. So it was quite interesting to see the difference between reality and all the stories told in Denmark and abroad about this writer's family and conditions. When she first made her appearance it was said that she was a governess to some noble family or other, and then it was said that she was the free and independent owner of the estate of Årsta.

It is not only to be near the able and splendid figures who are still alive that I feel a need when in a strange town, but I must also visit the graves of the beloved dead and either give them a flower or take one from their graves. In Uppsala I had visited Geijer's grave; his monument had still not been erected and the grave was overgrown with grass and nettles. In Stockholm I visited the grave holding the bodies of Nicander and Stagnelius. I went out to Solna near Stockholm, where in the little churchyard lie Berzelius, Choræus, Ingelman and Crusell, while Wallin lies in the larger cemetery.

My real abode in Stockholm was the home of Baron Beskow,

the poet, whom Carl Johan raised to the nobility. He is one of those endearing personalities from whom a gentle light seems to radiate over life and the world. He is sincere and talented, as is confirmed by both his drawings and his music. Even the voice of this elderly man is gentle and clear when he sings. His importance as a poet is well known, and through Oehlenschläger's translations his tragedies have also become known in Germany. He is honoured and loved both by his king and the people, and in addition he is an unusually cultured person and a fond and loyal friend:

> Loving you are, so gentle and kind
> Honest and truthful, ever refined,
> Modest and rich in poetry's gold
> With words such as these I your picture enfold.

The last day of my stay in Stockholm was King Oscar's birthday, and I was honoured with an invitation to the reception held to mark the occasion. When I took leave of them, the King and Queen and all the princes were so gentle and cordial. I was deeply moved, just as when we leave those whom we hold dear.

On page 85 in the fourth volume of his memoirs, Oehlenschläger refers to Count Saltza, and the reader becomes inquisitive to know just who this man was, but we are not told. Oehlenschläger says the following about him:

"An acquaintance of Bishop Münter paid me a visit once during those years. He was a tall, stately Swedish gentleman who gave his name as he entered, though I did not hear what it was. As I now refrained from asking him to repeat what he was called I hoped to hear it again in the course of our conversation or to be able to deduce who he was. He said he had come to ask me what I thought of the subject for a vaudeville he intended to write. He told me what it was. It was quite a charming idea, and I approved of it, thinking, 'So he writes vaudevilles.'

Then he went on to talk about Münter as an old friend of his.

'For I must tell you,' he went on, 'I have also studied theology and have translated the Revelation of St. John.'

449

'A vaudeville-writer who is also a theologian,' I thought.

'Münter is also a freemason,' he continued, 'and he has learned all his freemasonry from me, for I am the Grand Master.'

I continued secretly adding together: 'A writer of vaudevilles, a theologian, the Grand Master.'

Then he began to talk about King Carl Johan whom he praised highly and said, 'I know him well. I have drunk many a good glass of wine together with him.'

I said, 'A writer of vaudevilles, theologian, Grand Master and intimate friend of Carl Johan.'

He continued, 'Here in Denmark people do not go about wearing their decorations. I am going to church tomorrow, and I shall wear mine.'

'You are of course at liberty to do that,' I answered, and he went on, 'I have them all.'

I said, 'Vaudeville-writer, theologian, Grand Master, the intimate friend of Carl Johan and Knight of the Order of Seraphim.'

At last the stranger began to talk about his son whom he had encouraged to remember that his ancestor had been one of the first to mount the walls when Jerusalem was conquered. Now I realised that it must be the Count von Saltza. And so he was."

So much for Oehlenschläger.

In the antechamber, while I was waiting for an audience with King Oscar, Beskow had presented me to old Count Saltza who, immediately very kindly and with typical Swedish hospitality, invited me on my way back to Denmark to visit him on his estate of Mem if he was at home. This I would be able to discover as soon as the steamer came alongside. Otherwise I should visit him at his estate at Säby near Linköping which was further on my journey and not far from the canal. I took them to be just the ordinary friendly words one hears so often and did not think of taking advantage of the invitation.

However, on my journey home, as we were leaving Roxen early in the morning and were about to go up through the thirteen locks by Wreta Church, the royal graves in which I have written about in *A Picture-Book without Pictures*, Josephson the composer came aboard.

As I have already related, I had shared lodgings with him in Sorrento and on Capri, and I had most recently met him in Uppsala. He was Count Saltza's guest at Säby, and since they had worked out which steamer I would be travelling on he had been sent to the lock here with a carriage to fetch me. It showed a kindly disposition in the old man, so I quickly gathered my clothes together and drove in pouring rain to Säby, a mansion built in the Italian style, in which the old Count Saltza lived together with his charming and intelligent daughter, the Dowager Baroness Fock.

"There is some spiritual relationship between us two," said the old man. "I felt it as soon as I saw you. We were not strangers to each other."

He gave me such a warm welcome, and this old man, who possessed so many fine qualities, soon became dear to me for his intellect and charm. He told of his acquaintance with kings and princes; he had corresponded with Goethe and Jung Stilling. He told me that his forefathers had been Norwegian peasants and fishermen, who went to Venice and saved Christian prisoners and were created Princes of Saltza by Charlemagne. The little fishing village, which was once situated where St. Petersburg now stands, had belonged to his great-grandfather, and I have heard that once when the Emperor of Russia was in Stockholm, Saltza is supposed to have said to him as a sort of joke, "The Imperial City is actually built on land belonging to my forefathers." To which the Emperor is said to have answered in jest, "Very well then, come and take it from us."

There is a legend that the Empress Catherine the First was Swedish, and this is born out by what Saltza relates and has recorded. He tells of a connection between the story of her childhood and the life of his great-grandfather. The notes he has made on this subject are of great interest. This is what he told me:

One day his father was reading a short history of Russia, but he soon put the book down and said that what it had to say about the Empress Catherine was not right. He knew better, and he told him the following story:

My great-grandfather was General Hans Abraham Kruse, the commander of the Green Dragoons. When he was their Lieutenant Colonel and living at the Lieutenant Colonel's residence at Braten, his servant Jean Rabe happened to say he would like to marry Mrs. Kruse's chambermaid, Catherine Almpaph.

Mrs. Kruse, who had been born Annike Sinclair, arranged a splendid wedding for them, and the bridal bed was adorned with gold braid which Mrs. Kruse had worn on her crimson coat as a lady-in-waiting to the wife of Charles the Tenth.

After this it became a saying in the family that 'it is as fine as Jean Rabe's marriage bed'.

Jean became field sergeant in the Elfsborg Regiment, but he died young, as did his wife, leaving behind a single daughter, Catherine.

The child was taken to General Kruse's old wife at Hökälla where she remained for two years. Then Countess Tiesenhausen, Mrs. Kruse's cousin, came on a visit. She thought Catherine, who was now eight years old, a pretty and clever child, and she adopted her. They spent the winter together in Stockholm and in spring they went to Pomerania where the Countess was to receive a large inheritance. However, when they came to Rügen, there was a ship guarding the place, and they were forbidden to land as there was an outbreak of plague. So they returned to Stockholm and spent the following winter there, staying at what is known as the Ankarcron House in Regeringsgatan.

An aunt of the Countess died at Tallinn, and so the Countess went there in May, despite the fact that the Russians at that time were occasionally attacking and causing chaos in Estonia. This was actually the Countess' native land, so she also spoke German and had German servants. Catherine naturally also had to learn this language.

The journey went well, and after three days' stay there Catherine was sent off on an errand out of town. When she returned she discovered some writing on the door of the house saying that no one was to enter as it was infected by the plague. Catherine cried out; the porter answered from inside that the Countess and nine other people were already dead, and that he himself was shut up there. Weeping bitterly Catherine ran up the street, where she met Pastor Glück, the parson from Majam, who had come to the town in search of a nursemaid for his little son who was to be weaned. The priest saw the despair in this sturdy, rosy-cheeked girl and asked her what had happened.

When he heard her story and learned that she had not been inside the house he engaged her as a nursemaid, and, isolated as she now was, she accepted the position, although she had previously been used to better things. They soon became very fond of her in the parsonage, and finally the parson's wife could not manage without her. Count Saltza's great-grandfather used to stay at the parsonage when he was out hunting in that area.

After the Battle of Narva the Russians under Charles the Twelfth laid waste to Estonia. They were led by Anesen Lapuchin, who burned down Majam Church, took all the servants from the Saltza's estate and dispatched all the faithful vassals to Siberia. While the parsonage was in flames Lapuchin saw Catherine for the first time, and he kept her as his prize.

Menshikov had been made a prince and was the Tsar's favourite. On visiting Lapuchin and seeing Catherine, who waited on them, he declared that she was beautiful. The next day she was sent to him as his bondswoman. He was not particularly interested in women and saw in her nothing more than a pretty servant.

One day she was on her knees scrubbing his floor when the Emperor entered the room, but, since Menshikov was not at home he turned to go again. Then, on the table, he saw the plate of sweetmeats that was always placed ready for him when he came. He took some of them. Catherine did not know him and continued to scrub the floor. He looked at her and with his hand he stroked the hair covering her forehead to one side.

"You are a beautiful girl," he said.

She blushed. He patted her cheek, gave her a kiss and went away. Catherine indignantly told Menshikov about the unknown officer who had come and eaten some of the sweetmeats and taken the liberty of kissing her. When she described him Menshikov realised that it had been the Emperor, and he made use of the opportunity. Orders had just been given to the effect that servants were to wear clothes of a different cut from before, and so Catherine was dressed in one of the new women's garments. It was very splendid and suited her well. The bonnet was similar to that of the Dutch peasants. She was ordered to give the Emperor a plate of sweetmeats made of boiled fruits together with a servile, ingratiating letter expressing the wish that the Emperor would neither scorn the sweetmeats nor her who brought them. History tells us how she then became the Emperor's wife.

During her reign, the great-grandfather returned from imprisonment in Siberia, where he had spent sixteen years. A great banquet had just been arranged in the imperial gardens in Moscow; he was invited, and came in the company of the old Prince Gagarin who had been Saltza's faithful friend in captivity. Old Gagarin disliked Menshikov intensely, and when Menshikov entered and failed to return his greeting, he said to him, "Did you not see I saluted you?" Menshikov did not answer him but smiled scornfully and was scolded roundly by the old man. Menshikov called to his followers, overwhelmed the old man and stamped on him. Saltza, who made to defend his friend, was also attacked. Catherine saw it from the dais on which she was standing; she recognised the voice of her old friend and called to Menshikov, "If you touch a hair of Saltza's head, your own will be exhibited above the Kremlin tomorrow." And the struggle ended.

After that Saltza became President of the Department of Commerce and he always enjoyed the favour of the Empress. He still has descendents living in Russia.

Old Saltza is supposed to be able to see spirits. Carl Johan, for whom it had been prophesied by Lenormand that he would

454

become King, showed him friendship and confidence, and strangely enough it is told that the death of the King occurred on the date Saltza had prophesied. There in the great hall at Säby, where Saltza and I were now sitting, Carl Johan and Queen Eugenie had often dined. There were paintings on the walls of Saltza's gallant forefathers; the chairs and other furniture were in the rococo style, and the great room was heated by means of two fireplaces. There I sat with the admirable old gentleman. We talked about spirits, and with great earnestness and conviction he told me how his great-grandfather had revealed himself to him one night and asked him whether he would like to go with him and see God's Heaven, adding, "But first you must experience what it is to die."

"He touched me," said the worthy old gentleman, "and I fell down as though in a faint."

"Is dying no more than that?"

"No," said great-grandfather, "and then I was standing in the forecourt of God's Heaven. It was the most beautiful garden."

The description which Saltza gave of this was just as of something on earth, and I found nothing new in it. There he met his brother and sister. When she died, his sister had only been a small child, and so he did not know her before she told him who she was.

"It was good you came," she said, "for today is the Feast of the Holy Name, and I am to go from the children's heaven into God's great Heaven."

"But," I objected, "why does a child not go straight into God's great Heaven? That is what the Bible says."

"That might be so, but now I have seen it," he said.

Meanwhile, what he said about God was very beautiful.

"There I stood in Heaven, and there came a brightness that was more than I could stand. I threw myself to the ground, and there was a sound of music, such as I have never heard before. And I felt so full of joy, so unspeakably uplifted!"

"What is it?" I asked.

"That was God going by," answered my great-grandfather.

455

The old man told me all this with such earnestness and conviction that it made a strange impression on me. "Up there I learned of everything that is to happen," he said. "I know what the result of everything will be. I was only fifteen years old then."

During my stay at Säby, the old Count's name day, Frederik's Day, was celebrated, and it was extremely interesting to see the way it kept up in Sweden.

In one of the rooms downstairs an arch of oak leaves had been made, and above his name a beautiful oak crown decorated with roses instead of jewels had been fixed. While we were sitting at coffee, shots were heard out on the lake. A servant entered and announced in a loud voice, almost as though he had learned the words by heart: "A ship is anchored outside. It is called *The North Star* and is carrying travellers from afar."

But at the same time he could not refrain from smiling and showing that it was all play-acting. The travellers from afar were shown in. Shots were fired from the ship, and the steward, his wife and two daughters entered. It was they who had arrived from the estate on the other side of the lake. At dinner several stewards were present as well as a large number of the estate officials. Later, families from the surrounding estates came to offer their congratulations. Outside, the schoolboys and girls from the estate marched up and stood in rows, all with a little green sprig in their hands. They were led by their schoolmaster. He made a speech in verse to the old Count, who went out to them and was received with a resounding "Hurrah!" I saw that the schoolmaster was presented with some money, and the children were given food and coffee, after which they were permitted to dance in the great hall while a peasant played the violin. The Baroness mixed with them in a friendly fashion, showed the peasants all the rooms and halls in the mansion and gave them plenty to eat and drink. It was festive and delightful. Then the post happened to arrive with letters and newspapers.

"News from Denmark; a victory at Fredericia," someone shouted in delight. They were the first complete reports of it there had been in print. Everyone was interested; I grasped the list of the dead and wounded.

In honour of the Danish victory old Saltza let the champagne pop. His daughter had hastily made a Danish flag, and it was raised. The old man had earlier talked about the hatred that had existed in former times between Danes and Swedes. He had saved three bullets, one of which had wounded his father, one his grandfather and one killed his great-grandfather. Now, at a time of fraternal feelings between the two nations, he raised his glass and drank to old Denmark. And he talked of Danish glory and the Danish victory in such a sincere and beautiful manner that tears welled up in my eyes.

There was an elderly German governess present in the company. I think she came from Brunswick. She had lived in Sweden for several years and now, when she heard what Saltza had to say against the Germans in his speech, she burst into tears and said innocently to me, "I cannot help it." And when I had expressed my thanks for Saltza's toast, the first thing I did was to offer the German lady my hand and say, "Good days will come again, and Danes and Germans will stretch out their hands to each other, just as we do now, and they will drink the blessed toast of Peace."

And we chinked glasses.

It was good to be there, and I felt at home; and the countryside with its forest, cliffs and lake was beautiful. I left the kindly home and the singular old count with feelings of melancholy, and as a farewell greeting I wrote in his album:

> A heart beats strong behind those silver stars,
> And in your castle walls a poet's harp is sounding;
> Blessed is he to whom God grants many years,
> When they are years like yours, in memories abounding.

The enthusiasm I found here for Denmark and the Danes was echoed throughout the country, and as a Dane I clearly heard it expressed.

In Linköping I stopped at the home of Professor Aman, and in the garden there I was surprised to see that a number of young men had gathered to give me a festive reception. Ridderstad, the poet, had written three beautiful songs; the first was to the melody of the Danish national anthem, and then there was a Greeting to Denmark:

457

O wondrous land!
With gentle groves and isles,
With sunlit shores and smiles.
O wondrous land!

O battling land!
Our Scandia's southern bound,
Brave is your struggle profound.
O battling land!

Victorious land!
With valour you wielded you sword
With honour you all kept your word.
Victorious land!

Brother land!
Loyally we stretch out our hands;
Uniting in strength our two lands.
Brother land!

O wondrous land!
The shield maids applaud you;
And freedom will laud you;
O wondrous land!

And, as they sang, a most glorious rainbow was suddenly seen shining in the heavens like a sign of peace. I was strangely moved. Then there was a song in honour of the Danish flag; and between each of the songs a heartfelt speech was made on Sweden's love for Denmark and joy at our victory. Among the toasts drunk at the banquet there was one for the fallen at Fredericia. I was moved to tears, and felt "so Danish at heart". Swedish and Danish flags flew side by side, and when I left for Berg, where I was to take the steamer the following morning, Ridderstad and a host of my friends sent me on my way with songs and greetings:

With lyre in your arms
And with poetry abounding;

With lyre in your breast,
In a heart that is pounding,
So rich in your song,
You wander from land unto land.

Sing out, heaven and earth!
Sing songs for those living !
Sing songs for those dying !
Like the swan 'neath its sky
In song you must live
And in song you must die.

I wanted to stay a few days at Motala. The entire expanse of countryside near there can truly be called the garden of the Göta Canal. There is a lovely mixture of Danish and Swedish scenery, rich deciduous forests around the lakes, cliffs and rushing streams. In the little inn close to the factory a young bachelor by the name of Nygren gave up his comfortable room to me and went to lodge at a friend's house so that I might have a comfortable stay. Yet it was the first time we two had met. He was the late C. D. Nygren, a poetical nature, a friend of Fredrika Bremer and an admirer of my works. Outside my window the Motala flowed by between the deciduous trees and the fir trees so swiftly, so glassy and green and clear that I could see every stone and every fish in its depths. The opposite bank of the canal contains the grave of Platen, and every steamer salutes it with a cannon shot. In these surroundings I received a sincere, cheerful, heavenly letter from Dickens who had acquired and read *The Two Baronesses*. It was a day of rejoicing for me, and my table was decorated with some very beautiful roses that had been brought for me.

From Motala I made an excursion to old Vadstena where the magnificent castle is now no more than a loft in which to store corn, and where the great convent is a lunatic asylum. Just before leaving Motala I stayed in the little hostelry down by the jetty. I was due to leave before daybreak, and so I went to bed early and immediately fell asleep. But I was awakened by the lovely sound of many voices singing. I got up; it sounded beautiful. I opened the door and asked the maid whether it was some important guests they were serenading.

459

"It is for you, sir," she said.

"For me!" I exclaimed in amazement, completely unable to understand it.

They were still singing: our national anthem. The singing was for me; I will not say for the poet, but for Andersen the *Dane*. It was love of the Danes which here, too, was blossoming for me. The factory workers at Motala had heard that I had come back from Vadstena and that I was to continue my journey the next morning. The good folk had gone down there to give me a token of their esteem and their sincere interest. Now I went out to them and shook hands with those standing nearest to me. I was profoundly moved and grateful. Of course, I did not sleep that night after that.

Wherever I went, every day was like a festival. Everywhere the interest in Denmark sounded so sincere and so faithful. Danes have no idea of what it was like. I met friends and was shown hospitality even in tiny Mariestad. I was everywhere invited to stay with families in their homes as their guest. I was offered carriages and horses. In short I was shown every possible attention.

At Kinnekulle I spent several days with the elderly Count Hamilton and his family, partly at Hönsäter and partly at Blomberg where one of his sons, who is married to Geijer's daughter, has his home. There is a remarkable similarity between his wife and Jenny Lind, and she has even something of the same ring in her voice. She sang all her father's songs beautifully. Little Anna, the only child in the house, who was usually shy with strangers, came to me quite happily; we seemed to know each other straight away.

In Venersborg, too, I found a circle of friends who took me out into the beautiful countryside, and my stay at Trollhättan was extended by several days. There, in the woods by the locks I found a wonderful home at the house of Lieutenant Colonel Warberg and his wife. I was looked after so tenderly and kindly, as well as I always am looked after by people abroad.

From Gothenburg I went on an excursion to the island of Marstrand where Fredrika Bremer was on a visit to her sister Agathe, who was taking the waters there. The archipelagos there form excellent harbours with deep water. There were wild roses in flower on cliffs that were warmed by the sun. The Italian Opera Troupe from Stockholm gave a concert there one morning. I found all the life of a Southern spa. Fredrika Bremer was going to America. She went with me to Gothenburg. A group of people soon gathered around us on the ship and sang Danish and Swedish songs. Our national anthem seemed to be the Swedes' favourite song, and it was sung again on this occasion. It was like a farewell to me.

A few days later I was in Denmark.

Pictures of Sweden, which must be my most carefully composed book, gives the mental result of this journey, and I believe that in it my most striking characteristics are revealed more than in any other single work of mine: my nature descriptions, the fairy-tale element, humour and the lyrical quality of the prose. The Swedish paper Bore was the first to comment on it: "The customary tourist impressions and reflections are not to be found in this book. The entire work is a prose poem divided into a number of independent tableaux which together form a whole. It is written in that naive, child-like, ingenuous style and with that ready eye for nature and ordinary life that have made many of Andersen's poems and stories so beloved here in Sweden. Pictures from real life are woven together with historical memories and figures of the imagination in a delightful and natural manner, and the whole work is a true, poetical fairy tale of travel, a picture of midsummer in the far North."

Also here in Denmark, where critics in recent years had not only adopted a more seemly tone when discussing my works, but had shown an interest in them and a true appreciation of them, this book was spoken of with praise and generosity. They especially emphasised the section called 'A Story':

"It is a beautiful work, filled with the spirit of poetry and a pure love of mankind, whereby it is endowed with the power to uplift the reader. It does one good to read this section. It is told, too, with lofty calm, apart from the first page written in the well-known fairy-tale style which is quite out of place here."

And perhaps the reviewer is right in this respect.

There is special praise for *The California of Poetry*:

"In striking pictures it paints science and superstition for us, the two extremes which it rightly designates as the basis of the two tendencies in literature, sickly romanticism and lucid, lively humanistic writings.

461

Our author speaks out energetically against Romanticism and proudly rejects all its colourful rags which only conceal and disfigure the naked beauty of Classicism. In this section, as in the work as a whole, Andersen shows himself to be fired with a healthy and beautiful pride and delight in the human spirit, a quiet, refreshing satisfaction with all the good and beautiful things in life, and in general a mild and humane view of life."

In England, where my book *Pictures of Sweden* appeared at the same time as the Danish original, I met the same good will, the same expressions of praise as, I think I may say, had almost always been the case until I met criticism from the one person from whom I least expected an attack to come. It was from the person who introduced my works to England and gave me such a friendly reception there: Mary Howitt. It surprised me; it was so unexpected and so inconceivable. I have earlier referred to our meeting in London and recalled how friends who were interested in me arranged for the approval my works won in the great land of England also to be of financial benefit to me.

The gifted and highly respected publisher, Richard Bentley, continued to be my publisher, and I was to send him a manuscript in *English* from Copenhagen. This was done, and so Mary Howitt did not translate *The Two Baronesses* or *Pictures of Sweden*, but I did not expect her to be angry with me on that account and condemn me in the strongest terms as is the case in the work which she published together with William Howitt, *The Literature and Romance of Northern Europe*. All *Danish* authors, both great and small, were dealt with in a friendly and charming manner, but not I, who had once been her favourite. After giving a favourable mention to the books by me which she has translated, she writes:

> But Andersen's subsequent productions have been failures; those published in England have dropped nearly dead from the press; and the reason for this is very obvious. Andersen is a singular mixture of simplicity and worldliness. The child-like heart which animates his best compositions appears to your astonished vision in real life, in the shape of a *petit maitre* sighing after the notice of princes. The poet is lost to you in the egoist; and once perceiving this, you have the key

to the charm of one or two romances and the flatness of the rest; for he always paints himself – his own mind, history and feelings. This delights in a first story, less in the second, and not at all in the third; for it is but *crambe repetita*.

Perhaps much of Andersen's fame in this country arose from the very fact of the almost total ignorance here of the host of really great and original writers which Denmark possessed; Andersen stood forward as a wonder from a country of whose literary affluence the British public was little cognizant, while in reality he was but an average sample of a numerous and giant race.

How differently the same gifted lady conceived and spoke of me only a few years before when I visited London. Then, in the widely read *Howitt's Journal* she wrote:

At this moment, when Hans Christian Andersen is in our land, we do not think we could offer our readers a more welcome gift than an excellent portrait and a description of the life of this exceptional man. Whether we regard him as a man who in his own character reveals true nobility of sentiment and moral worth, or as a brilliant man whose works alone have raised him from utter poverty and insignificance to be an honoured guest of kings and queens, Hans Christian Andersen is one of the most remarkable and interesting men of his time.

Like most men of great and original gifts he belongs to the people; and in his works, which are based on the life of the ordinary men and women, he describes what he himself has seen and suffered. Yet poverty and adversity have never embittered his heart; on the contrary, everything he has written is extremely lively and rich in the most gentle sympathy and love for his fellow men. Human life with all its trials, privations and tears is something sacred to him; he acquaints us with the depths of the human heart not to portray hidden and repulsive passions or crimes, but to show us how lovable it is in its naturalness and truth, how moving in its weakness and its wants, how much it must be loved and pitied, shown patience and opposed. In short, this great writer, with all the burning zeal of a poetical nature and with his great ability to portray passionate minds, is to the greatest extent imbued with a Christian spirit.

How can I compare these two judgements written down at different times by a lady possessed of intelligence and, I believe, one whose heart beats warmly for me and my Muse. When Miss Bremer returned from America, having travelled through London, I asked her about Mary Howitt, whom I knew she had visited.

"Dear Mary Howitt," she said, "she spoke so well of you, spoke with tears in her eyes and said, 'He won't have anything to do with me'."

How is one to understand such kindly spoken words when she has written so harshly about me? They must have been the result of momentary bad humour; that is something we can all have. She might also have changed her opinion of me, just as she already has done once. There is no anger in my heart, and through these pages I stretch out my hand across the sea to her in reconciliation.

Meanwhile the novel *The Two Baronesses* was given an enthusiastic reception, and the same was the case in Sweden. Indeed the very same year as Mary Howitt's severe criticism was written, this book received the honour of being made accessible to a wider section of the population due to its inclusion in The Popular Library along with *The Story of My Life*. These books are generally known under the title of "Shilling Editions", and they are sold in their thousands.

The translation in this case is excellent, and in a postscript Kenneth Mackenzie, the translator, expresses himself with such warmth and acknowledgment that Mary Howitt's sharp words are drowned. The criticism in *The Athenaeum* of my latest book to be published in England, *A Poet's Day Dreams* as they call my stories, indicates the same warm interest and favour.

The New Year 1850 opened with a great sorrow for me, a sorrow, too, for Denmark and the realm of art. The first letter I wrote that year to Weimar tells of it:

Oehlenschläger died on the 20th of January, the same day as

King Christian the Eighth died, indeed almost at the same hour. Late in the evening I twice went past the palace to visit Oehlenschläger, for I knew from the doctors that death was approaching him; and it was strange for me to look up and see the dark windows in the palace at Amalienborg and to think that two years ago I walked about there full of concern for my beloved King and that I was once more experiencing the same feelings for a king, a king among poets.

His death was without suffering; he had his children around him and asked them to read a scene from his *Socrates* to him, the scene where Socrates speaks of immortality and the certainty of an eternal life. He was so calm, and he prayed that his death struggle might not be a hard one; then he laid his head back and was gone.

I saw his corpse; jaundice had given it the appearance of a statue of bronze; there was nothing to show that this was merely a dead man; his forehead was beautiful and his expression so noble. On the 26th of January he was accompanied to his grave by the people; the people in the real meaning of the word, for there were officials, students, sailors, soldiers, all classes who of their own accord took it in turn to carry his coffin on the long road out to Frederiksberg where he was born and where he wished to be laid to rest.

The actual funeral ceremony was in Copenhagen Cathedral. Two poets were asked by the funeral committee to write the cantata; one of them was old Grundtvig, and I was the other. The Bishop of Zealand spoke. As a memorial performance at the Theatre it was decided to perform his tragedy *Earl Hakon* and the scene from *Socrates* that was read for Oehlenschläger in the hour of his death.

During recent years Oehlenschläger had, to my delight, become so gentle and cordial towards me, and he warmly expressed his recognition of me. One day when I was upset because of the way the newspapers were mocking me, he gave me a small North Star. I had just received this order from the King of Sweden on the day when Christian the Eighth was buried.

"I have worn this," said Oehlenschläger. "I will give it to you in memory of me. You are a true poet. That is what I say, so let the others talk as they like."

And he presented me with the Order of the North Star, which I still have and keep. There had been a banquet for Oehlenschläger on the 14th of November 1849 in the Shooting Range; now his funeral feast was to follow only such a short time later. We know that the poet had requested that his tragedy *Socrates* might be performed on this occasion, but this was not done. I do not understand that in the hour of his death the great poet could think of this little occasion in honour of him; I would have preferred him to say the same as Lamartine's "dying poet", who in reply to someone who mentions the great memory of him here on earth says, "Does the swan in its flight to eternity ask whether the shadow of its wings is still floating on the lowly lawn?"

At the memorial performance the Royal Theatre was filled with people, all of whom were in mourning. The boxes at the front were hung with crape, and Oehlenschläger's seat in the stalls was made to stand out with black ribbons and a laurel wreath.

"How charming of Heiberg," said a lady. "Oehlenschläger would himself be touched by it if he could see it."

And I could do no other than reply, "Yes, it would delight him to see that he had a seat after all."

When Heiberg had been appointed director of the Theatre all the free seats for poets, composers, former directors and various officials were reduced to the end seats in the few rows we have in the front stalls, and moreover all singers, actors and ballet-dancers were admitted to them. If they all came there was only room for a third of them even if some of them stood up. As long as he lived Oehlenschläger went to the theatre every evening, but now if he failed to arrive early, or if one of those sitting there was not considerate enough to give him his seat, he had to stand.

On a few occasions he had found me also standing there and wryly commented, "I don't know how I dare come here."

But on that evening he had a seat. It was the very seat he had always had under the previous directors, just as Thorvaldsen had also had one. Heiberg can be excused because he had been ordered by the Parliament to reduce the number of free seats, but I am still of the opinion that there ought to have been a seat for a man like Oehlenschläger, the leading Danish dramatist.

So during the memorial performance a tinge of bitterness passed through my heart, and it was not the first time I had felt this in the Royal Theatre.

I will now turn my attention to something one of our authors has spoken of:

"Only the Casino"

For the past two years the people of Copenhagen had had a popular theatre. One might almost say it had sprung up without our realising it. No one thought about it, or at least no one thought it would be a success.

Several people, including Mr. Overskou, had thought, spoken and written of such a theatre, but it had remained on paper. We had at that time a talented young man who, without being in possession of any funds himself, was endowed with the remarkable ability to procure financial means when it was a question of carrying out an idea. He was a true genius at his task, and it was he who managed to give the people of Copenhagen a *Tivoli* which in layout and design can stand comparison with any other place of amusement of its kind; indeed it can surpass most of them. He also gave us the *Casino*, which provided the common people with music and plays at a modest price, and it also gave the city itself a large and tasteful setting for its most popular concerts and masquerades. In short it was a building for real entertainments. This man was Georg Carstensen. Most recently, his name and skills have received high praise in America as he is the man who together with Charles Gildemeister built a Crystal Palace which is remarkable for its architecture and its usefulness. Carstensen was a man of rare affability, and that, I believe, was his greatest fault. People often mocked and laughed at him and called him "maître de plaisir", and yet his work was of lasting value; it has been and remains a source of benefit and great pleasure.

When the *Casino* was built, the actual theatre in it was not considered to be its most important feature. It was only little by little, under the leadership of the energetic actor, Lange, that it increased in

467

public favour as well as developing its own strengths. At one time the shares in the *Casino* were so low that it was said that a single one was sold for a glass of punch, but it was not long before it all took a decided turn for the better.

The repertoire was very limited; no Danish author with any reputation at all had shown any desire to write or submit a work for this theatre. Mr. Lange asked me for a contribution, and my attempt was given a reception far beyond all expectations. In *The Arabian Nights* I had read a fairy tale, *Prince Zeyn Alasnam and the King of the Spirits*, a story which was especially suited to be the libretto for an opera. However, much as the idea interested me, I abandoned it as fairy-tale opera was so little understood and valued here in Denmark even if it was provided with the most delightful music. I had a good example of this in *The Raven*.

On reading Gozzi I found the above theme dealt with as a fairy-tale comedy. However, in *Der Diamant des Geisterkönigs* Raimund had treated it even better and in a manner more suitable for the stage. As everyone knows, I had on a previous occasion tried my hand at writing fairy-tale comedies for the Royal Theatre in *The Flower of Fortune.* It had certainly been shelved after the seventh performance, but it had won considerable applause, and I was personally convinced that the talent which the whole world recognised in me as a writer of fairy tales must also be able to flower in this field. So I based my *More than Pearls and Gold* on Raimund's play, and I think I may say that this play made the Casino Theatre.

People of all classes came to see it, rich and poor alike; there were seats for 2,500 people in the Casino, and all tickets were sold out for an unbroken series of performances. It was a huge delight to me, and I gained a great deal of recognition from it. My agreed fee was 100 *Rigsdaler*. It will be remembered that at that time no theatre in the country except the Royal Theatre paid an author for his work, so this really meant something, and an additional hundred *Rigsdaler* were sent to me when the play continued to fill the house. After this other young authors followed my example: Hostrup, Overskou, Erik Bøgh, Recke and Chievitz all produced excellent plays. The cast became better year after year; the demands of the public continually increased, and they were always exceeded. The praiseworthy efforts that were to be seen here have naturally been overlooked by some people.

"Only the Casino," is what people said, but when talented people say this irrespective of the fact that they never go there, or when, for instance, the author of *A Hundred Years* speaks scornfully of Casino plays in his work, then it is unjust.

I had written a new work for this theatre, a fairy-tale comedy called *The Sandman*. In one of my fairy tales I had already tried to bring this Nordic dream-god to life and give him shape and character, and now I wanted to show him in living form on the stage and allow him to demonstrate the truth that health, good humour and peace of mind are worth more than money.

I planned my work and wrote it out. Mr. Lange showed the greatest care, indeed one might call it affection, in the manner in which he produced this play. He did this in as worthy a fashion as possible on the small, cramped stage in the Casino, although the play really required a large stage. It was a pleasure for me to work with the actors there. They were interested in the play and showed respect for the author. They were not the almighty guardian spirits of poetry, like those I had met in the "real" theatre. *Ole Lukøje* was performed in the Casino, and the theatre was full to overflowing.

The evening for the performance arrived, and within a few hours I experienced the changing sea of public opinion. People normally need weeks for this, but as I say, I experienced both storm and calm in the course of a single evening. People did not understand my work: they laughed and shouted during the first act and at the end of the second act they poured scorn on the whole thing. Some people left at the beginning of the third act, and up in the club they said, "It's a lot of nonsense. They are in China now. Heaven knows where his imagination will take them next."

But at the beginning of the third act all was quiet for a while. Until now, people had talked to each other and drowned out the play, but now they began to listen. They became quieter and quieter, and suddenly they understood the idea, and a wave of enthusiastic applause filled the house. By the time the curtain fell everyone had been gripped by the play; they clapped and expressed their approval. During the expressions of displeasure, scorn and mockery that had come before this I had not felt any distress. It was the first time in my life I had been clearly aware of the injustice I was suffering. I felt insulted by the scornful crowd. I was hurt, and the applause that now burst upon my ears sounded empty to me and meant nothing at all. As I left, several people came up to me and expressed their thanks, but I could not accept them: "I have been mocked and scorned, and I must forget that first."

The play ran for many evenings to a full house and before enthusiastic audiences. I was given that recognition by the people themselves, the common people as the poorer ones are called. I received thanks greater than any newspaper critic or dialectically interesting researcher in the different social strata could have given me. One evening at the end of the play a poor artisan stood there with tears in his eyes, and as we went out of the door together he gripped my hand and said, "Thank you, Mr. Andersen; that was a most wonderful comedy." Those words meant more to me than the warmest of reviews.

And there is one more episode I must describe. At the home of a civil service family I was in the habit of visiting, the lady of the house told me one morning that she had been surprised at the unusually happy look on the face of their stable-hand when she spoke to him.

"Has something specially good happened to Hans, since he is looking so pleased today?" she asked one of the maids and was told that one of the tickets they had been given the day before had almost not been used, but then someone had given it to Hans, the stable-boy. This Hans was known to everyone as a yokel who went around in a constant daze.

"He has changed completely." said the girl. "When he came home from *Ole Lukøje* last night he was so pleased with everything he had heard and seen."

"I always thought that distinguished people and people with money were so happy, but now I can see that the rest of us are just as fortunate. That's what I learned out there; it was all just like a sermon, except that we saw it all, and it was lovely."

No man's judgement has delighted and flattered me more than the opinion of that poor, uneducated labourer.

An elderly and extremely intelligent lady who only rarely went to the theatre saw a performance of *Ole Lukøje* and wrote so honestly and approvingly of the way in which Christian's part was performed:

470

What filled me with enthusiasm and what I shall never forget was the inspired way in which Schmidt acted. No, it is a shame to say acted, for it was nature itself, the most charming, delightful nature imaginable. Aged grandmother though I am, I wept with joy at his inexpressibly sweet, child-like love. Give him an old grandmother's kind regards, and tell him that I followed every word he uttered and every movement he made with a beating and wondrously happy heart. I was his grandmother and he my grandchild. If only he was never to grow a day older than he is now, for that part cannot be played, or rather undertaken by an older person.

The play was given a series of performances, and there was a good audience each time. However, it was soon rumoured that, together with a young man of letters, another of the authors who had recently written most of the plays for the Casino had produced a parody on my fairy-tale comedy. This, it was said, was to be performed in the provincial theatres, or at least in Mr. Boucherie's marionette theatre. It hurt me to think that while I recognised this author's talents, and gave them all my endorsement, he could so completely close his eyes to the poetical qualities in my work and, I understood, would even represent me on stage in person and make fun of me. I expected anything that could hurt and insult me, for I had experienced it so often, and I suffered terribly as a result. It was in this cowed and depressed mood and before I had read the parody, that I was staying at Glorup. There I received a letter from H. C. Ørsted showing his view of me as a poet. It reveals our affection for each other, and as a contribution to the matter it will surely not be out of place to include it here since the letter itself is of interest and significance on account of the person who wrote it:

Copenhagen, 18th July 1850

Dear Friend,

The depression of which you write to Mathilde is something from which you ought to tear yourself away if you have not already done so before this letter reaches you. You have enriched literature with so many excellent works that no one but yourself can accuse you of having achieved too little. I scarcely believe that even your opponents dare hold such an opinion any longer. But even if an occasional opponent should be unkind to you, you can comfort yourself with the thought that almost all men of distinction have been subjected to attacks of that kind.

I have often seen English journalists treat the most excellent men in their own country with scorn. Among other things, I remember reading once that the great statesman Pitt had been called a nincompoop. Pope in the last century and Byron in this could both complain of bitter attacks.

In Germany neither Goethe nor Schiller fared better. Different though they were, and although they felt antagonistic to each other for a long time, Oehlenschläger and Baggesen had one thing in common, and that was the fact that they were both bitterly attacked. If we seek examples outside the ranks of the poets I can mention my brother and Bishop Mynster, both of whom have been subjected to harsh criticism.

Take as little notice as possible of attacks on you. One thing will always be certain: you have produced some excellent works, which both at home and abroad will ensure your name's undying fame.

You write that you have planned *The Sandman* with deep thought and reflection, just as has been the case with your other fairy-tale works. This I do not doubt. As far as most things in your works are concerned, I can explain them to my own satisfaction as much as it is ever possible with a fairy tale. With one exception the same is true of *The Sandman*. The mental vision which you present to us seems to me to be clear enough. However, it remains a practical difficulty for me, if I may call it that, to see such a huge vision, in which so many people move and suffer, portrayed in such a way that the very figures who at one moment are part of a dream should, the next moment, be real characters. Perhaps my opinion is wrong, but even if it were correct, *The Sandman* would not cease to be a work full of inspiration and art. I will go still further and suppose that it did not merit this praise but ranked far below your other works. Even then it ought not to grieve you for long, although it might irritate you a little, for no one can deny that Goethe,

Oehlenschläger, Baggesen and many, many other famous poets have published works ranking far below their masterpieces.

I hope that, as before, you will not defend yourself against your attackers. I will even advise you not to take revenge in some way or another, not even by means of some well-placed side swipe. On the other hand I believe that it might be a good thing if you sooner or later wrote a treatise on the aesthetical value of the fairy-tale element in poetry. In such a treatise you could counteract many a misunderstanding. It would be best if you used the works of other writers to illustrate your arguments; but of course you would not need to exclude your own. However, it should naturally not contain any trace of polemic. Finally I must say that I would definitely not advise you to embark upon such a work if it would prevent you to any significant extent from writing any of your own works of literature. Indeed, I would then on the contrary advise you against it.

Yours ever,
H. C. Ørsted.

That summer, at Glorup and in the beautiful mansion of Corselitze on the island of Falster, I finished what is perhaps my most thoroughly planned work, *Pictures of Sweden*. It was the last of my books to be heard by H. C. Ørsted, and he approved highly of it. The two sections in it that I have called, *Science and Belief* and *The California of Poetry*, both of which were the results of his brilliant and convincing conversations and of my conception of *The Spirit in Nature*, gave us the stuff for many a conversation.

"You have often been accused of not having sufficient learning," he said one day in his gentle, jovial manner, "but perhaps you will be one of the poets who achieve most for learning."

A similar note was later struck in a Postscript to the English edition in Routledge's Popular Library. It must not be thought that I intended to work for science as such. No, as a poet I intended to take my inspiration from veins that science had not yet investigated to any extent, and it is from such a place that I took my fairy tale *The Drop of Water*. This Ørsted also mentions in his book *The Spirit in Nature*, stressing the scientific discoveries which have already found a place in the world of poetry.

He understood and was delighted by the fervour and respect I showed in my interest in all the more recent discoveries, all these mighty, material vehicles of the spirit.

"And yet," he said one day in jest, "you have sinned against science and forgotten what you owe to it. You have not even mentioned it with a single word in your lovely poem, *Denmark, My Native Land*. So now I have tried to make up for it."

And he gave me a verse which he had written and put between the third and fourth verses of my poem; this is how it runs:

> See, thoughts were born in Danish minds
> And through the world spread out their finds.
> They searched throughout the heavenly tracts
> And in the earth found secret facts.
> Beloved Danish strand,
> where eyes do freely roam
> inspired by thoughts of home,
> Denmark, my native land.

One day when I went through *Science and Belief* and *The California of Poetry* for him, he pressed my hand gently and said that now I had made up for it again.

While I was at Glorup that summer he sent me the second part of *The Spirit in Nature*, about which he wrote, "I dare not hope that it will make the same favourable impression on you as I had the pleasure of hearing the first part had done, for the main object of this book is to illustrate the earlier one. Yet it is not completely devoid of new ideas, and I myself can assure you that the tone and my way of thinking are unchanged."

I was completely taken with the book, and I expressed my thanks and my delight in a long letter of which the following is an extract:

"You did not think that this book would make the same impression on me as the first part. I cannot separate them from each other; for me they form one rich stream of thought. And something that makes me especially glad is the fact that I only

474

seem to see my own thoughts in it, thoughts which I have not previously been able to express to myself. It is my belief and my conviction put before me in clear language. I cannot understand Bishop Mynster. It seems to me that he must surely be able to see and understand what is as clear as daylight to me. I have read *The Relationship between Science and Various Important Aspects of Religion* not only to myself but aloud to a number of other people. Especially this section is suitable to read aloud and I wish I could pass it on to everyone. In the pious populace in general I value their ability to believe blindly. Yet I find it a far greater blessing in faith also to *know.* Our Lord has no objection to being viewed through the understanding which He Himself gave us. I will not go to God blindfolded. I will have my eyes open. I will see and know, and even if I do not gain any other objective than the man who only believes, my thoughts are at least enriched. I am delighted with your book, and I am delighted with myself because I can read it so easily that it seems almost to be the result of my own thoughts. On reading it I seem to be able to say, 'Yes, that is what I would have said, too.'

The truth it contains has entered into me and become a part of me. Meanwhile I have as yet only read half the book. I was torn away from it by the news of the war, and since then I have had thought for nothing but events there. However, I could no longer postpone writing and thanking you from the bottom of my heart.

For a whole week I have not been able to do anything. I am so deeply moved. I forget the victory won by our brave soldiers and think instead of all the young men who have sacrificed their lives; for I knew several of the fallen. You know that Colonel Læssøe was a friend of mine. I had known him from the time when he was a young cadet, and I always felt he would go far. His understanding was infinitely clear, and his will firm, and to that one can add that he was knowledgeable and highly cultured. I was very fond of him. Although he was younger than I, he often went further than I in his bold and daring thinking, and he mocked me in fun when he found unhealthy traits in

475

my imagination. On our way back to town after visiting his mother we have often had an eager discussion about the present day, the world and the future, and now he is gone. I gather that his poor old mother is completely heartbroken; I cannot conceive how she can bear her sorrow. He fell on the same day as Schleppegrell and Trepka, in a small town near Isted.

I am told that the first of our soldiers to reach the town were given food and drink by the inhabitants. So those who came after them were made to feel safe, and when they reached the town centre doors and gates were thrown open and the insurgents and inhabitants, both men and women, rushed out carrying arms and shot our men down. The determination of our soldiers is without parallel: they advanced through a deep marsh in the face of enemy fire, springing from mound to mound, and although they were falling like flies, their comrades followed them and drove the enemy from their safe position. If only this battle might be the last, but we do not know what might still lie ahead and whether the dear lives of all those men might have been sacrificed in vain.

Oh God, let truth become truth; let peace shine upon the countries once more. Sorrow visits most families during these days; these are bitter, serious times. I feel a sort of desire to go over and see the richness of the life there, but I combat this desire, for I know that I shall be too deeply affected by the sight of all the suffering I shall encounter there. If only I could do something, if only I could refresh and encourage some of those who are suffering; but I cannot.

My very best filial wishes to you,
Yours affectionately,
H. C. Andersen.

When the news of the Battle of Isted reached us I could not rejoice in the victory, for I was so affected and moved by Læssøe's death. I wrote to his mother in the middle of the night. I did not know what strength God had given her to bear this heavy loss.

Colonel Læssøe

> In battle you fell for Denmark's fame;
> Your fiery heart stopped though it won our acclaim.
> Your spirit was clear as the brightest day;
> With a cry of 'Advance' it rose o'er the affray
> And saw both the triumph and grief come our way.
>
> Weep, o sad mother, afflicted with grief
> But young as he was, and however brief,
> His life we'll remember for aye."

After the battle and the victory came peace, and I heard of this with a heart full of joy.

The return of the soldiers gave us days of festivity. They shone into my life, and there they will always remain in memory and beauty.

I wrote a song for the Swedish and Norwegian volunteers, and they received the Danes with it by the iron gate on Frederiksberg Allé. The inscription: "His promise he has kept, our valiant Danish soldier," adorned the West Gate as a greeting to them. All the guilds gathered with their banners and emblems which we had previously only been accustomed to seeing in the theatre in the drama *Hans Sachs*. It inspired many an insignificant man to realise the importance his class had in the town and to discover that he had his own banner. Music was heard. The fountains played on Gammeltorv, something which otherwise only occurred on the King's birthday.

Danish, Norwegian and Swedish banners waved from all the houses, and many of the inscriptions on them were ingenious and beautiful. One of them ran "Victory, Peace, Reconciliation". Everything was so festive; we felt "so Danish at heart".

When the first soldiers came, tears streamed down my cheeks.

> Here they are coming, the ramparts resound.
> How fine and how splendid they look,
> These brave and magnificent soldiers.
>
> With flowers on their hats they come and on guns

477

And looking like spring on the march.
Approach them and talk to them all,
For these are the men whom we bless today.
They struggled and suffered and held on as few,
And they know how we hold them in awe.
The tender, sweet lips of our noblest young miss
Could today, at this hour, give a kiss
To these men all so splendid and brave.

The riding school had been fitted out as a great hall of victory with waving banners and garlands.

The officers' table was laid beneath three palm trees decorated with golden fruits. The common soldiers sat at long tables, and students and other young men acted as waiters. Music, singing and speeches mingled in festive succession; bouquets and garlands rained down. It was a delight to be there; it was a joy for me to talk to the fine, upright fellows who were not aware they were heroes.

I asked one of them, a man from Angeln in Schleswig, if they were comfortable in the barracks, and his reply was: "It's like being in Paradise. The first night it was so comfortable that we couldn't sleep. We lay on mattresses and were given blankets. Over there we didn't take our clothes off for three months, and in barracks the worst thing was the horrible smoke from the wet firewood. It's lovely to be here, and these Copenhageners are nice people." He praised Flensburg as a real Danish town. "On hot days people drove right down to Schleswig from there with wine and water for us. It was a blessing."

The soldiers were a modest crowd, all of them, especially the infantry. They all pointed to the bravest of their comrades, and any wreath which happened to fall in the throng was put on the shoulders of the man they found most deserving of it. In the riding school, where sixteen hundred men – both infantry and hussars – were entertained and where many speeches were made, one of the officers said to a common soldier, "You ought to stand up and make a speech, too. You speak so well."

"It would be out of place here," he answered.

"No, it would be nice if an ordinary soldier spoke."

"Well, then, it must be a hussar," said the soldier with great modesty.

There was an abundance of lively words spoken in the inspiration of the moment, and they were just as eagerly received as spoken. The occasional figure stood up and then was unable to find words to express his feelings. I remember for instance a speech made by a respected member of Parliament. "You are from Jutland, and I am from Jutland; we suffered a lot, and you suffered a lot. And here we are now. Some of you are from this town and some of you are from that town. And I'm from that one."

Mr. Lange, the manager of the Casino, had supplied a large number of tickets for each performance so that many of the soldiers could go there free of charge. It was an unspeakable joy for me to be of some service to them, to obtain tickets for them, talk to them and explain things to them. I heard and saw many remarkable things on that occasion. Most of these men had never been in a theatre before and had no idea what it was like.

The foyer and the corridors were gaily decorated with flags and greenery. During an interval, I came across two soldiers standing outside.

"Well, are you enjoying it?" I asked.

"Oh, it's all so lovely."

"But what about the play?"

"Is there still more?" they both asked.

They had remained out in the corridors, looking at the gas lamps and the flags and watching their comrades and other people going up and down the steps.

During these festive days another private occasion was celebrated: one might call it a family festival. On account of the changing times, Collin had retired from his duties as privy councillor two years before this. His jubilee occurred on the 18th of February 1851. It was celebrated quietly by the family.

Triumphal leaves our soldiers now display;
And Denmark echoes proud to victory's thrill.
And fair and fitting must it be today
To celebrate our army's skill.
For good you fought and for the true
May blessings for this land ensue.

At the very same time as the soldiers' came home to celebrations and while song and joyful salutes echoed around us, there were also difficult days when we looked back and remembered: Mrs. Emma Hartmann and H. C. Ørsted both died that same week.

The sense of humour and joie de vivre which were part of this remarkably gifted woman were revealed in the form of a natural grace which knew no negative features or shadows. Everything about her was a harmony of beauteous qualities imparted to her by genius. She was one of the people who drew me into the orbit of their spirit, their humour and their heart, and so she was reflected in me like sunlight in a plant. It is impossible to describe the vast amount of joy and fun and zeal that emanated from her.

The words which Boye, the poet and cleric, spoke by her coffin are so true; "Her heart was a divine temple filled with abundant love, and she took all that love and spread it generously around her, not only to her own but to the many outside her family, to the poor, the sick and the sorrowing; she gave all she had to give."

And that was all given and dispensed with a kind word and a joke. Yes, those words spoken by her grave are true, that: "Happy thoughts and joyous feelings dwelt within, and she was so willing to let them all escape like birds on the wing with song and gaiety, so that every day was like a gentle spring day in the house for those who were gathered around her."

Yes, they sang as they liked, and so everyone was happy. It was as though words became ennobled when they came from her lips. Like a child, she could say anything, and you felt that it was being proffered in a flawless vessel. Many a jest and many an amusing idea came from her lips, but she thought it both amusing and terrible that such everyday chatter as she could generate could be written down on paper or even declaimed on the stage. Instances of this were words spoken by the King of the Spirits in *More than Pearls and Gold* and Grethe's lines in the same play about the stork and having "storkish" thoughts. How could such be offered to a public that was so apt to criticise? She certainly went to see both that play and *Ole Lukøje*, but she had her own reasons for doing so.

One day her two eldest sons came home from school far away in

Christianshavn through a driving snowstorm. A third son, who was quite a small boy then, had got lost on the way, and there she sat filled with fear and anxiety. I arrived at that moment and promised to go and find the lost child. She knew I was not well and that I was not keen on going all the way to Christianshavn; but how could I think of doing anything except help her? She was moved by this, and I have been told that when I had gone she walked up and down the floor in a mixture of anxiety and gratitude and then exclaimed, "It was matchless of him. So I shall go and see his *More than Pearls and Gold*. And if he brings my sweet little boy home I will go and see *Ole Lukøje*, too."

"Yes, that's what I have promised," she said when I returned. "I'll go and see it, even if it is dreadful."

And she saw it, and she laughed and as a result was more amusing than either of the plays. She was extremely musical, and several of her compositions are known, though none of them bear her name. With all her brilliant soul she understood Hartmann, foreseeing the recognition and importance he was bound to have abroad as well as in Denmark. Here she became profoundly earnest; her thoughts radiated clarity, and yet this was the woman whom most people only saw laughing and full of fun.

One of our last discussions concerned Ørsted's *The Spirit in Nature* and especially about the immortality of the soul. "It's a thought vast enough to give us vertigo. It is almost too much for us here on earth," she exclaimed. "But I will believe it; I must believe it." And her eyes shone. And a moment later she had a joke on her lips again. They were humorous words about us miserable human beings who could imagine "going all the way up to God".

It was a morning of sorrow. Hartmann threw his arms about my neck and said with tears in his eyes, "She is dead."

"Now sorrow sat where during her life the mother had sat surrounded by flowers, where as the good fairy she had nodded kindly to her husband, her children and her friends, where she had spread gladness about her like sunshine in the home, and where she was the centre and the heart of it all."

At the very time of her mother's death the youngest of the children, a little girl called Maria, suddenly fell ill. I have preserved some of her features in one of my fairy-tales, *The Old House*. It was this little girl who, as a child of two, always had to dance when she heard music or singing, and when she came into the room on a Sunday while her brothers and sisters were singing hymns she would start dancing. But her sense for music would not allow her not to do what was correct, and so she automatically stood throughout each hymn, first on one leg and then on the other, involuntarily dancing to its rhythm.

In the hour of her mother's death this little head bowed down; it was almost as though the mother had prayed to Our Lord, "Let me take one of the children with me: the smallest, for she cannot do without me." And God heard her prayer. The same evening as her mother's coffin was borne to the church the little girl died, and a few days later she was laid to rest close by her mother from whose coffin one of the wreaths, still fresh and green, stretched out its arms to welcome the little girl.

On her bier the little child seemed to have become a grown person. I have never seen a more beautiful picture of an angel, and her innocence still rings in my ears in words which are almost too child-like for this world. One evening when she was only a few years old and was to have a bath, I asked her in fun, "May I come with you?"

"No," she replied, "because I am so little; but you may when I grow up."

Death does not erase the mark of beauty in a person's face; indeed it often intensifies it. Only the decomposition of the body is ugly. Never did I see anyone so beautiful and so noble in death as this mother. A sublime calm was spread over her features, a blessed earnestness, as though she were standing before her God. She was the most beautiful person I have seen in death.

The air around her was filled with the perfume of flowers.

> All flowers she loved, and may these flowers
> Like a carpet adorn her bier.
> Music she loved, so may music's powers
> Our farewell convey through our tears.

So we sang by her coffin, and over it rang out the true words: "Never did she hurt anyone with her judgement when she judged this world

482

and its conduct. Never did she lessen the honour and praise due to the upright, and never did she allow slander to sully an honest name with impunity. Never did she weigh her words from fear of their effect, and not always did she ponder beforehand whether some of her words might be misunderstood by people less candid than she."

In the Garrison Cemetery, near the houses in the street alongside, just inside the iron railings there is a grave. It is always better kept than the other graves. There are more flowers on it, and it is carefully tended and in it lies the dust of Emma Hartmann and little Maria.

Four days later, I lost H. C. Ørsted. It was almost too much for me to bear. I lost so infinitely much in those two; first Emma Hartmann who, when I was bowed down and distressed, had raised my spirits with her humour and merriment, her jest and gaiety, the woman in whom I could find more sunshine than in any other; and now Ørsted whom I had known and come to love through almost all the years I had been in Copenhagen. He was one of those most interested and understanding throughout the varying fortunes of my life. During his final days I went to and fro between the Hartmanns and Ørsteds. There I was for the last time to meet the friend who had given me the greatest spiritual support in my struggle and in the trials of my spirit. But as yet I did not think of this possibility. Ørsted was so young in spirit; he spoke of the time he was looking forward to staying in the Pheasant House in Frederiksberg Park. The year before it had seen his jubilee late in the autumn, and for as long as he lived the city had given him and his family the summer residence in which Oehlenschläger had been the last to live.

"We'll go out there when the trees are in bud and there's a bit of sunshine," he said. But during the very first days of March he fell ill, though he himself retained his good spirits. Mrs. Hartmann died on the sixth of March. Deeply distressed I went to visit Ørsted, and there I learned that he was dangerously ill. He had an inflammation in one lung.

"He's going to die from this."

This sad thought filled my mind while he himself believed he was getting better.

"I'll get up on Sunday," he said.

But on the Sunday he was standing before his God.

When I arrived he was in his death agony. His wife and children were standing by his bedside. I sat in the room outside and wept. I was near breaking down.

There was a sense of peace about the home, the quiet peace of a Christian soul.

The funeral took place on the eighteenth of March. I suffered physically. It was a struggle and a great effort for me to walk the short distance from the University to the Church. The slow ceremony dragged on for a whole two hours. It was Dean Tryde who officiated, not Bishop Mynster. The bishop had not been asked to, said people apologetically. But should it be necessary to ask a friend to speak over his friend? I felt the urge to weep, but I could not; it felt as though my heart were going to break.

Mrs. Ørsted and their youngest daughter Mathilde sat in the house of mourning. They heard the bells tolling ceaselessly during all those heavy hours of the funeral ceremony. The sounds of the trombones did their hearts good. Later in the day I visited them. We talked of the peculiar coincidence that Hartmann's Funeral March should have been played, the march he wrote for Thorvaldsen's funeral. When we last heard it Ørsted was with us, and Hartmann had played it.

It was at Miss Bremer's home, the evening before her departure for Sweden, when she had given a small party. Little Maria Hartmann, who had been laid to rest this very morning, had on that occasion been dressed as an angel and had the task of presenting me with a wreath and a silver beaker. Hartmann played a few pieces for us. Miss Bremer got up and asked him to play his Funeral March, but as its music sounded from the strings of the piano she was strangely moved, as though it presaged something, as though it were an omen to me. And she took my hand and asked me not to see anything mournful in it: "It means going forward to greater things," she said.

Now it was being played for Ørsted, the man for whom I originally thought the dinner was being arranged on that occasion. Now the Funeral March was being played for him, and over his coffin it resounded:

Forward to greater things

So full of truth he was, so ever kind,
Though child at heart, a philosophic mind.
For he, he knew already here
The secrets God on death makes clear.
A rock in Denmark, seen from far afield.
We knew what wisdom in it was concealed.
How kind he was, so simple and so straight,
And yet so great. His name will never die,
For by his lightning thought a light was lit
To tell where countless treasures lie,
A son of Denmark, too, of humble birth
And yet a king, a regal soul on earth.
Gone is his life; he was so fair, so good.
His name with which we ne'er shall part.
In us who knew him well, he put down root,
Part of the world has vanished with his heart.

XV

Peace reigned over the lands. The spring sun shone and I felt the urge to travel and the need to refresh myself, and so I hurried away from the city out to the bright green woods, to dear friends by Præstø Bay, to Christinelund. The young people living there wanted the stork to build a nest on their house, and they had put a wheel on the gable as a base for it, but no stork came.

"Just wait till I arrive," I wrote, "then the stork will come."

And so it did, just as I had said. Early in the morning on the very day they were expecting me to arrive later, two storks came, a male and a female, and when I drove into the courtyard they were busy at work building their nest. That year I saw the stork in flight, and an old superstition maintains that that means we ourselves are going to fly away and travel. However, my flight was only a short one that summer. The towers of Prague were the most southerly thing I saw. My chapter of travel that year was no more than a few pages, but as you can see, the vignette on the first page is of the flying storks building their nest on the roof in the shelter of the beech wood which had recently sprung into leaf.

At Christinelund, spring had in fact printed its own vignette, an apple bough in flower growing in a ditch; it was spring itself in its loveliest form. At the sight of it I got the idea for the little story *There is a Difference*.

Most of my works are rooted in something outside myself, as is the case here. Everyone who looks with a poet's eye at life and the countryside around will see and sense such revelations of beauty as could be called "the poetry of chance".

Let me give a couple of examples: on the very day on which King Christian the Eighth died we all know a wild swan flew into the spire of Roskilde Cathedral and crushed its breast; Oehlenschläger preserved the memory of this strange occurrence in his poem in memory of the King. When fresh wreaths were to be laid on Oehlenschläger's grave and the withered ones taken away it was discovered that a song bird had built its nest in one of them. One mild Christmas when I was at Bregentved Manor there was one morning a thin covering of snow on the stones by the obelisk in the garden; without thinking of it I wrote the following words with my stick in the snow:

> Immortality is rather like snow;
> Tomorrow it's no longer on show.

I went away. A thaw came, and some days later the frost returned. I went to the same spot again, and found all the snow melted except for a tiny patch, and in that patch stood the one word "Immortality". I was deeply affected by this coincidence, and I was filled with the thought, "God, my God, I have never doubted."

The place where I actually spent the summer that year was my beloved Glorup, the home of my friend, the noble old Count Gebhard Moltke-Hvitfeldt. This was the last year we two met there; God called him home the following spring. But it was as though my stay there that summer put the crown on all those delightful days I had spent there. He gave a feast for the soldiers from his estate who had taken part in the war. I have already spoken of the old man's patriotic feelings and the lively interest he took in the events of his day. I have spoken of the time spent by the Danish and Swedish troops at Glorup. Now the bells of victory had rung out, and now the soldiers there were to have a really happy day and night. The arrangements for the event were left to me. My thoughts were entirely devoted to this event; it was a success and it gave me great pleasure.

On either side of a large pond in the garden there was a long avenue of lime trees. In one of these avenues I had a tent erected that was a hundred feet long, thirty-two feet broad and twenty feet high. The floor was made of hewn planks, and there was room to dance there. The trees forming the avenue served as columns, and the trunks were wrapped in shiny pieces of red damask that had once been wallpaper, but which now lay in a corner where they had been discarded. The capitals were made up of parti-coloured shields and large bunches of flowers. A large canvas served as the roof, but below it hung an assortment of garlands and shields bearing the Danish flag arrayed in all directions from the centre. The great room was lit by

487

twelve chandeliers in the Danish colours. The red background formed by the walls was adorned with the King's device in flowers, and the names of all the generals were written on colourful painted shields. Between the two entrances there was a large orchestra beneath a fan of Danish flags; raised boxes were placed around the sides, and at the far end of the room, between some flowering forget-me-nots, there were two vases containing torches and wrapped in crape; two small, black shields bore the names of the first and the last officer to fall, Hegermann-Lindencrone and Dalgas. Two others bore the inscription *To the Common Soldier*. Higher up, among the shields naming the places where victories had been won there was a mighty shield adorned with the verse:

> To the Common Soldier.
> For all you suffered for our land,
> In battle, on guard and in blast,
> In many an eye the tears now stand;
> God bless you for aye standing fast.

Above it all hung a wreath of copper beech with a golden crown and golden laurel branches. The whole arrangement had a remarkably powerful effect on the people it was intended for.

"That's fit for the King to see," said one peasant.

"That's cost over a thousand *Daler*," said another.

"You can just as well say a million," said his wife.

"It's like Paradise," said a palsied old man who had been carried to the feast. "All those lovely things and all that music; and what a lot of things to eat."

Never have I received as much unanimous recognition and praise for any work of poetry as I did here for my architectural talent; but it was something that could not fail to be easy for me as I had seen so many splendid festive arrangements of that sort invented by Bournonville and previously by Carstensen.

The festivities took place on the seventh of July in fine weather. The soldiers marched up at one o'clock and received a speech of welcome in the courtyard from the local parson. *The Valiant Soldier* was played, and the procession moved across to the dance hall, where the tables were laid with an abundance of good things. Cannon shots were heard from the little islet where the flag was flying; the orchestra played, and joy and delight shone in everyone's eyes. The old Count proposed the health of the King, after which I read some verses to the common soldier. This was followed by my song. Among the many hearty toasts that were drunk, a soldier proposed one for the man who had built the lovely hall, and another said in all innocence that I must have earned a nice penny from it.

It was towards evening before the girls came. Each man had been left to invite one himself, and then the dancing started in the brilliantly lit dance hall. The avenue alongside the pond was illuminated; a small three-masted ship decorated with coloured lanterns lay out on the water; I myself had made most of the cut-outs for the lanterns and lamps.

"I shall have another celebration like it again next year," said His Excellency. "It's lovely to be able to give pleasure to so many people, and they are such fine folk, such stalwarts."

But this was the last celebration he made. God summoned him home the following spring. Yet that year, too, there was a celebration; it was his children's silver wedding, and the peasants from the estate, all of them, were invited.

Meanwhile the soldiers' festivities marked the climax of the days I spent there that summer, and all my eager help had its reward in itself, for I received the joy of knowing that those hours stand as a radiant page in my fairy-tale life.

The war years lay between my last stay in Germany and the present. I had not yet visited the scene of war, for it was contrary to my feelings to visit it out of curiosity alone while others were engaged in more serious things. Now peace had been concluded; now we could meet and gather again in friendship. Yet my thoughts were occupied with the bloody events and the places where men had fought and suffered. That was where I had to go first.

One of my young friends accompanied me on the journey. We met at Svendborg and soon the steamer took us to Als, where trenches and earthen huts were still to be seen. As we sailed up the Flensburg Fjord every brickworks and every jutting promontory told of the war. In Flensburg itself it was especially the graves of the fallen we wished to visit. The cemetery stands high above the town and the fjord, and there was especially one grave I sought and found there: that of Frederik Læssøe. He lies between Schleppegrell and Trepka. While there I plucked one green leaf for his mother and one for myself and thought of his short, active life and the feelings of friendship he had for me.

Soon we approached the actual scene of the battle. New houses were being built to replace those that had been burned down, but all around the bare earth still showed how the rain of bullets had so to speak scraped away the turf. My soul was filled with serious, sad thoughts. I thought of Læssøe and his last moments, and I thought of the many others who had breathed their last here. To me it was holy ground I was passing over.

The town of Schleswig was still under martial law. Helgesen was the commanding officer. I had never seen him before, and he was to be the first man I met when I entered the hotel owned by Mrs. Esselbach. His powerful figure immediately attracted my attention, and his features also reminded me a little of a portrait I had seen of him. This must be the hero of Frederiksstad, so I went up to him and asked if he were not the commanding officer. He said that he was, and when I mentioned my name he immediately generously offered to put himself at my disposal. One of his officers took me to the Dannevirke fortifications and gave me an accomplished and lively explanation of them. Queen Thyra's mighty earthworks seemed to have risen again. I saw bear traps there, great holes with spikes at the bottom. A whole shanty town still stood there, and the officers' houses in it even had glass windows. Soldiers had their guard-room in one of them now.

I spent the evening in Helgesen's company. He was friendly, open and frank, and his manner reminded me of Thorvaldsen. He mentioned one of my fairy tales which had given him much amusement, and quite typically it was *The Steadfast Tin Soldier*.

There were Danish soldiers on guard at the Kronværket fortifications outside Rendsburg. I nodded to them, and the honest, straightforward fellows understood there were Danes in the carriage, and they smiled and nodded in return. But I found the journey through the town of Rendsburg itself unpleasant; it was as though I was travelling through a pit of death in this place where the revolt had originated. All the evil memories came to mind. The town itself has always looked dull and oppressive to me, and now it was a painful, unpleasant sensation to visit it as a Dane. In the train I found a seat beside an old gentleman who took me for an Austrian. He praised the Austrians, whom he called my countrymen, and then went on to speak ill of the Danes. I said that I was a Dane, and with that our conversation came to an end. I thought I saw baleful eyes about me, and I did not breathe more freely until all Holstein, including Hamburg, lay behind me.

In the coach after mine on the Hanoverian railway I heard a Danish song and the voices of Danish girls; they threw a bunch of flowers in to me – again, my bouquet was only in words.

> As we speed along
> Fair sounds the song
> Sweet voices cast their spell
> Make hearts and bosoms swell.

My thoughts were occupied with Denmark and the Danish cause, and Danish sounds filled the air about me beyond the Elbe. Never before had I had such a sense of being Danish as I entered German territory.

In Leipzig and Dresden I saw my first acquaintances and friends. They were unchanged, cordial and wonderful. The time we spent together was happy and intense. It did our hearts good to feel that the heavy days of bloodshed were past. Almost everyone readily acknowledged the strength and unity of the Danish people and the strength this gave them, and a few even said, "The Danes were in the right." That there were also people who had the opposite view is indeed true, but these people said nothing. I had no cause to complain. I saw and sensed friendly faces and a kindly atmosphere. Indeed, the "poetry of chance", if I may use that expression again, even gave us a taste of its art in honour of Denmark. I must tell of that little event.

It was seven years since I had last visited the beautiful estate of Maxen a few miles from Dresden, the home of the hospitable von Serre family of whom I have already spoken with gratitude. Then, the evening before I left, I went for a walk with Frau von Serre and found a tiny larch tree that was so small that I could have put it in my pocket. It had been thrown away, and it lay on the roadway; I picked it up and saw it was broken. "Poor little tree," I said. "It mustn't die." And I looked around on the rocky ground for a crack containing sufficient soil for me to plant the tree. "They say I have a fortunate touch," I said, "so perhaps it will grow." Only right on the edge of the rocky slope could I find a little soil in a crack in the rock, and there I planted the tree. Then I went off and forgot all about it.

"Your tree in Maxen is growing excellently," Dahl, the painter, told me in Copenhagen some years later on arriving from Dresden. And now in Maxen I heard all about the "Danish poet's tree", as it was called, words it had borne as an inscription for several years.

The tree had taken root. Branches had sprung from it and it had grown to be a big tree, for it had been tended and looked after. Frau von Serre had had soil put around it and later she had had part of the rock blasted away. A path had recently been made close by it, and in front of the tree stood the inscription, "The Danish Poet's Tree." During the war against Denmark it had not suffered any damage; people said it would die of its own accord, for nothing would be able to come of it. A huge birch tree grew nearby. Its great branches stretched out over the larch tree and that alone would be enough to stop it and kill it.

But one day during the war there was a heavy storm; the lightning struck the birch tree and knocked it down from the cliff, and "the Danish poet's tree" was left standing free and unscathed.

I arrived at Maxen and saw my lush tree and the splintered stump of the birch nearby. A new tablet stood there resplendent with the inscription. It was Major von Serre's birthday, and all the intelligentsia of Dresden were gathered there. The workers from the estate's marble quarries and lime kilns came with songs and flowers.

Every time I go on my travels I have the peculiar fortune of experiencing something remarkable and interesting, and this was the case, too, on the train between Leipzig and Dresden. There was an old lady sitting in the same compartment as I. She had a large basket of food on her knee, and by her side was a twelve-year-old boy called Henry. The boy was tired after travelling both night and day and he was looking longingly for the towers of Dresden. Opposite to me I had a lively young lady who talked vivaciously about art, literature and music, about all of which she seemed to be well informed. She had been in England for several years. They all came from Breda. While the train was stopped and I had got out together with two other passengers, we tried to guess who she could be. At first I thought she must be an actress, while another was of the opinion that she must be a governess in some very distinguished English family.

During the journey the old lady quietly nudged me and said, "She is a remarkable person."

"Who is she?" I asked quickly.

"Demoiselle…" she stopped suddenly, for the young lady, who had been leaning out of the carriage, turned and spoke to us again. My curiosity was really roused. "Antoinette" shouted her brother to her. "I can see Dresden, Antoinette."

When we got out of the carriage I whispered to the old woman, "Who is the young lady?"

And as we parted she whispered secretively to me, "Demoiselle Bourbon".

In Dresden I asked who Antoinette Bourbon was, and I was told that this was the name of the daughter of the famous Geneva watchmaker who claimed to be the son of the unfortunate Dauphin, Louis the Sixteenth, and Marie Antoinette. His children had lived for some time in England and were now resident in Breda, though they sometimes went incognito to Dresden. An elderly French lady who was convinced that they really were the children of the Dauphin lived with them and for them. That is what I was told, and it corresponded to what I had seen on my journey. And it is right enough that Antoinette's face was regal and spirited. She could quite well pass for the Dauphin's daughter, or at least the daughter of a man who had the features of the Bourbons.

Weimar was deserted. I knew that all my friends were scattered around the country, so I postponed an extension of my journey and a visit there until the following year.

During the autumn here in Denmark, I received the title of Professor on the sixth of October 1851.

Spring arrived, and as soon as the woods burst into leaf I too burst my bonds and went to continue my journey where I had interrupted it on the last occasion, and that was in my beloved Weimar. And my

493

friends there were faithful to me and gave me a splendid welcome. The reception I received was sincere as always, right from the house of the Grand Duke to the many friends and acquaintances who lived in different parts of the town. Meanwhile, since we had last seen each other Beaulieu de Marconnay had been made Lord Marshal and director of the theatre. He was married and had a happy home where, as in former times, I was received like a friend, I might almost say as a brother. There were already a couple of lovely children playing in the drawing room, and they stretched their little hands out to me; and their mother herself was like the guardian angel of a house blessed with perfect happiness.

Something else that gave me a fresh bunch of memories during this visit to Weimar was my friendship with Liszt who, as everyone knows, has been appointed conductor there and has had a great influence on the musical life of the theatre as a whole. The task he has set himself is to promote important dramatic compositions which otherwise would have difficulty in being produced on a German stage.

Thus Weimar has given a performance of Berlioz' *Benvenuto Cellini* in which the leading character is of a certain interest to the people of Weimar on account of Goethe's *Benvenuto*.

Meanwhile it is the music of Wagner that especially appeals to Liszt, and he devotes all his energy to making it known and appreciated, partly by producing it and partly by writing about it. He has published a whole book in French on the two works *Tannhäuser* and *Lohengrin*. The first of these operas is already of some significance for Weimar by virtue of its very theme, as it is related to the cycle of Thuringian legends. The setting is at and near Wartburg.

Wagner is said to be the most important composer of our time, but that is something which, with my plain, natural feelings I cannot accept. It seems to me that all his music is composed through his intellect. In *Tannhäuser* I cannot but admire the incomparably well declaimed recitative, for instance when Tannhäuser returns from Rome and tells of his pilgrimage. It is wonderful! I recognise the grandeur and the descriptive element in the music's poetry, but for me it lacks music's true flower – melody. Wagner himself has written the texts for his operas, and as a poet in this sphere he ranks high.

There is variety, there are dramatic situations. The first time I heard the music itself it was like a mighty ocean of harmonies engulfing me. It gripped me both mentally and physically.

When, late in the evening, Liszt came to me in my box after the performance of *Lohengrin* and was himself full of life and enthusiasm, I sat there tired and worn out.

"What do you say now?" he asked, and I answered, "I am half dead."

Lohengrin seems to me to be a wondrous tree soughing in the wind but bearing neither blossom nor fruit. I hope I will not be misunderstood, and my judgement of music is moreover of little significance, but in this art as in poetry I demand three elements, understanding, imagination and feeling, and the third of these is revealed in the melody.

In Wagner I see a modern intellectual composer who is great on account of his understanding and will. He is a mighty innovator, rejecting all old valueless qualities, but I feel he lacks that divine element which was granted to Mozart and Beethoven. A large and able group of people share Liszt's view, and in some places most people think as they do. I believe Wagner enjoys this kind of recognition in Leipzig, but that was not always the case. One evening in the Gewandthaus several years ago, when I was present, the overture to *Tannhäuser* was performed after a number of works by various composers, all of which were loudly applauded. It was the first time I had heard it, and the first time I had heard the name of Wagner. The descriptive quality of this great tone poem filled me with excitement and I applauded enthusiastically. But I was as good as the only one to do so. People all round looked at me and told me to hush, but I remained faithful to my impression of the music and applauded again and shouted "Bravo". But inwardly I felt embarrassed, and the blood rose to my cheeks. Now, on the other hand, everyone there applauded Wagner's *Tannhäuser*. I told Liszt what had happened that evening, and both he and all his musical associates rewarded me with a "Bravo" because I had had the right feeling.

From Weimar I continued my journey to Nuremberg. There is an electro-magnetic wire along the railway! My heart is as Danish as anyone's. It beats more strongly on seeing an honour done to my country. And that is what I felt in this railway train. There was a father with his son in the same carriage as I, and he pointed out the electro-magnetic wire to him. "That is something that a Dane called Ørsted has invented," he said. I was glad to belong to the nation that had given birth him.

Nuremberg lay before us. In one of my stories, *Under the Willow Tree*, I have depicted this magnificent old city, while the journey through Switzerland and the Alps provided me with the background to this work. I had not visited Munich since 1840, and then, as I have written in *A Poet's Bazaar*, it was "like a rose-bush from which new shoots spring forth every year; but every shoot is a street and every leaf a mansion, a church or a monument". Now the rose bush had grown into a great tree in full bloom; one flower was called the Basilica and another was the Bavaria column, and that is how I had to express myself again when King Ludwig asked me about my impression of Munich. "Denmark has lost a great artist and I a friend," he said when we spoke of Thorvaldsen.

To my mind, Munich is the most interesting city in Germany, and it is especially King Ludwig who has brought this about thanks to his sense of art and his vast energy. The theatre, too, is prospering. It possesses one of the ablest directors in Germany, Dr. Dingelstedt, the poet. Every year he visits the most important German theatres to inform himself on the talents developing there. He goes to Paris, knows the repertoires and discovers the interests of both the public and the theatres.

The Royal Theatre in Munich will soon be offering a model repertoire. Here, too, there is an interest in the actual *mise-en-scène* such as is completely unknown at home where, for instance, the side scenes for *The Daughter of the Regiment*, which is set in the Tyrol, contain palms and cacti, while in one act of *Norma* the heroine is seen living in Socrates' Greek parlour and in the next in Robinson Crusoe's hut of palm trees. The wings can well show sunshine streaming in, while in the background we have an open balcony with a view of a dark blue, starry sky!

Everything is done without any thought or attention to detail, and there is no end to it.

"But who notices that sort of thing, and who worries about it?"

people say. "No newspapers complain about it!"

The repertoire in Munich is full of variety, and there is an obvious desire to be aware of the most important productions of the day in the different countries. The director writes to the best known authors in those countries.

A letter I received from him expressing praise for me started a correspondence between us; he wanted to know something of the theatre repertoire in Denmark, especially with reference to original plays. And in the same letter he talks of the present King of Bavaria's knowledge of my works and his gracious interest in me.

So Dingelstedt was the first person I visited immediately on arriving in Munich. He straight away made one of the best boxes in the theatre available to me, and during the whole of my stay it was at the disposal of myself and my travelling companion. He informed King Max of my arrival, and the following day I was invited to dinner at the hunting lodge of Starnberg where His Majesty was in residence. Privy Councillor von Dönniges came to fetch me. We travelled by a fast train, arriving just before dinner at the small castle which is beautifully situated by a lake with a view of the Alps beyond.

King Max is a youthful and extremely charming person; he gave me a most gracious and friendly reception, and he told me that my works, especially *The Improvisatore*, *A Poet's Bazaar*, *The Little Mermaid* and *The Garden of Paradise*, had made a deep impression on him. He spoke of other Danish authors and knew the works of Oehlenschläger and H. C. Ørsted. He appreciated the robust intellectual life seen in both the arts and science in my native land. From von Dönniges, who had been to Norway and Zealand, he had heard of the magnificence of the Sound and of our beautiful beech woods. And he knew of the treasures of which we possess more than anyone else in the Nordic Museum.

At dinner the King did me the honour of proposing a toast to my Muse, and when we rose from table he invited me to go sailing with him. The weather was dull, but the clouds were moving quickly. There was a large closed boat on the lake; oarsmen in colourful dress saluted with their oars, and soon we were gliding swiftly across the water.

On board I read the fairy-tale *The Ugly Duckling*, and during a lively discussion about poetry and nature we came to an island where a beautiful villa was being built on the orders of the King. Nearby, a great mound had been excavated. It was thought to be a burial mound like those at home in Scandinavia. They had found bones there together with a flint knife. The King's attendants held back a little, and the King invited me to sit on a bench with him close to the lake.

He spoke of my works and of everything that God had given me. He talked about how remarkable a man's career can be in this world and of the consolation there was in having faith in God. Near where we were sitting there was a large elderberry in bloom, and that gave me an opportunity to discuss the Danish dryad in such a tree, as is seen in my fairy tale *The Elder-Mother*. I talked of my latest work, which was a dramatic treatment of that same figure, and when we went past the tree I asked permission to pluck one of its leaves as a remembrance of this time. The King himself plucked one and gave it to me. Now it is together with all my other dear remembrances, and it tells me of the evening I spent there.

"If only the sun would come out!" said the King. "Then you would see how radiant the mountains can become."

"I am always fortunate," I exclaimed. "It's almost certain to shine." And at that moment the sun really did come out, and the Alps shone a beautiful pink. Later, while we were sailing home, I read the stories *A Mother*, *The Flax* and *The Darning Needle*.

It was a lovely evening, and the surface of the water was perfectly still; the mountains became an intense blue, and the whole scene glowed, so that it was all like a fairy tale.

I reached Munich about midnight. The *Allgemeine Zeitung* has given a charming account of this visit under the title of *König Max und der dänische Dichter*.

From Munich I went to Switzerland, to Lake Como and then on to Milan. This city was still under martial law, and my passport was nowhere to be found in the police station when I was due to leave. They sent for me, and such an occurrence was sufficient to spoil all the enjoyment I derived from my journey. An open letter from the Austrian Ambassador in Copenhagen recommending me to the civil and military authorities was now of great use to me. The police were extremely polite to me, but my passport was not to be found.

Then they took out all those they had received, and I found mine; it had been arranged rightly enough according to its number, but the gendarmes had written it down wrongly and it did not correspond to the number they had written on the receipt. Everything was in order again, but, as usual, I had more trouble with my passport than anyone else, and that is the one thing I keep an eye on while travelling, even to a farcical extent.

I travelled back through the St. Gotthard and past the Lake of Lucerne, and I spent some days in those lovely surroundings. At Schaffhausen I said farewell to Switzerland and went on through the romantic Black Forest, the home of Auerbach's *Dorfgeschichte*. Bluish smoke was rising from black charcoal stacks. Delightful people went past. The mountain road called "die Hölle" was a real bit of the Alps.

I witnessed a moving scene on a railway station between Freiburg and Heidelberg. A large party of people, both old and young, who were about to emigrate to America got into the carriages. Their friends and relatives were taking leave of them. What a scene of despair this was. They wept aloud and wailed. I saw one old woman hold tight to one of the carriages, and she had to be torn off it. The train moved out, and she threw herself to the ground. We sped away from all those lamentations and cheers. The scenery changed continually for those who were going away, but for those who were left behind there was nothing but the sense of loss and sorrow and all those things that reminded them of those who had gone away.

I visited the ruins of Heidelberg Castle one fresh, warm summer's day. Cherry trees and elderberries were growing in the rooms and halls of the ruin. Birds were singing above us, and suddenly a voice called out my name. It was Kestner, the Hannoverian Ambassador from Rome, the son of Werther's Lotte. He was on a visit to Germany. This was our last meeting; he died the following year.

I was in Copenhagen again at the end of July. Her Majesty the Dowager Queen Caroline Amalie honoured me by giving me a gracious invitation to Sorgenfri. I stayed there for several days, living in the room that had belonged to the late Privy Councillor Adler. Many memories, from my childhood and right up to these brighter and better days passed through my mind, and my soul turned in gratitude towards God in all His goodness.

I now became better acquainted with the countryside round about, a part of Denmark of which I had only had a fleeting knowledge before. Still more I learned to value the pious, deeply kind personality of the noble Queen who had known so much suffering.

I had written the fairy-tale comedy *Mother Elder* for the Casino. Both the manager and all the actors had considerable expectations of this work. The first performance was received with great applause. There was certainly some hissing mingled with it, but that is what happened with every new work at that time. The newspaper *Dagbladet* gave a friendly and appreciative review of it, but *Berlingske Tidende* and *Flyveposten*, which normally were very tempered in their judgements of me as they also were of others, were scathing in their criticism of this work and failed to find any coherence whatsoever in it. I replied by reciting the contents of it, which form quite a well-thought-out little story. On the other hand I met appreciation from most of our poets. Heiberg and Ingemann both wrote charming letters to me expressing their approval. C. J. Boye made some very warm and heartfelt comments on it, and I believe that *Mother Elder* was the only play he ever went to see in the Casino. However, the newspaper critics as a whole exercised their power and cooled people's interest. On this occasion I came to the conclusion that most of my countrymen fail to appreciate the fanciful. They refuse to ascend to the heights, preferring to stay down on earth and live honestly on uninteresting dramatic dishes straight from the cookery-book. However, Lange continued to produce the play, and little by little the situation improved until at last *Mother Elder* was received with undivided applause. At one of the performances I happened to be sitting near a fine old country-dweller. During the very first scene of the play (where the spirits of the elements appear) he turned to me, although he did not know me, and said, "It's damned hard to work out what's going on in all this."

"Yes, it is a little difficult," I said, "but it's easier to follow later on. There's going to be a scene in a barber's shop where people are being shaved, and there's quite a lot about love."

"Oh, there is, is there!"

By the time the play was over, he had found it very attractive indeed, or else he had realised that I was the author, for now he turned to me and assured me, "It was a wonderful play, and very easy to understand. It's just the beginning that's a bit difficult until you get into it."

In February 1853 *The Nix* was performed in the Royal Theatre. Professor Gläser had poured a wealth of melodies into this work, a truly Nordic sound, as was generally recognised.

At Whitsuntide I left Copenhagen and went out to Ingemann's in those fresh woodland surroundings, a home to which my heart continued to take me every summer, just as it had done in my schooldays in Slagelse. Everything there, including people's hearts, was unchanged. However far away it flies, the wild swan always returns to its old familiar place by the lake in the woods, and I share the wild swan's nature.

Ingemann must surely be our most popular writer, and his novels are still alive and widely read although the critics immediately tried to gnaw the life out of them. They have made themselves loved by high and low in the Nordic countries. The Danish peasant reads them and through them comes to love his native land and its historical associations. A profound harmony resonates from each of these works, even from the lesser ones. As an example of this we might think of *The Mute Girl*. It is here as though the tree of poetry rustled in the great movements of the moment, which we have all felt and which our grandchildren will hear from the lips of the old. In addition Ingemann has a sense of humour and the eternally young heart of a poet. It is a great happiness to know such a personality as he, and an even greater happiness to know that one has a tried and faithful friend in him.

In the parlour there with all its pictures, with the shade from the lime trees outside and with the blue lake shining and glittering, everything is still almost the same as it was when I went out there one lovely summer's day as a pupil from Slagelse School. It all became a many-coloured garland of poetry for me now. Here were the memories of everything I saw, experienced and won during the long period that had elapsed since then and which forms the greater part of the fairy tale of my life.

Spring started so beautifully that year, greeting me with green woods and the song of the nightingale, and yet this was soon nothing but empty splendour, for heavy, anxious days lay ahead. Cholera broke out in Copenhagen. I was no longer in Zealand, but I heard of all the horrors and deaths caused by this illness. The first news of a death which pained me personally was that of the poet C.J. Boye. In recent years he had been so charming to me and so full of appreciation, and I had become deeply attached to him.

One of the days which gave me the greatest pain and torment during that bitter time was one that should have been filled with joy and merriment. I was at Glorup, where Count Moltke-Hvitfeldt was celebrating his silver wedding. I was the only guest from outside the family, and it was ages since it had been arranged that I should be there. All the peasants from the estate were guests. I believe there were over sixteen hundred of them in all. Everything was sparkling with festivity. There was dancing and merrymaking. There was music, and flags were flying and rockets shooting up into the air. And in the midst of all this merriment I received a letter telling me that two of my friends had been snatched away. The angel of death was going from house to house. Now, on my last evening, it stopped at my home of homes, the Collins.

"Today we have all moved out," they wrote to me. "God alone knows what will happen within the next twenty-four hours."

It was as though I had received the news that all those who were dear to my heart were to be snatched away from me. I lay weeping in my room while the air outside was filled with merry dance music and jubilation. Rockets lit up the entire scene; it was more than I could bear. Every day there came fresh sad tidings. Cholera broke out in Svendborg, too, and my doctor and my friends all advised me to stay out in the country. More than one hospitable home was open to me in Jutland.

I now spent a large part of the summer at the home of Michael Drewsen at Silkeborg. I have given a picture of this beautiful spot with all its memories and legends, which reminds one of the wonders of the Black Forest and the splendid isolation of the Scottish heath:

Where once read monks by reed-ringed lake,
Behind the heather on moorland track,
An active life its start must take,
Great millwheels turn, are never slack
A tiny town already grows;
Towards the stream the alders lean;
The eagle lives with Denmark's crows
And countless barrows decked in green.

Surrounded by that lovely scenery and in a hospitable home I went about in deep sorrow. My heart was profoundly distressed. I was in a state of nervous anxiety, a torment of uncertainty. When the post-horn sounded I ran out to fetch letters and newspapers, and I was on the verge of collapse for the few moments I had to wait. I was oppressed, tormented and sick at heart, and so as soon as the epidemic in Copenhagen grew less intense and people believed that I could safely return I hurried off to those beloved people whom I had feared I should never see again.

In the spring, just before the epidemic broke out, my excellent publisher, Reitzel, had died. We had become attached to each other with true mutual liking which had later turned into a firm friendship, and this had lasted throughout all my activities as a writer. His last decision had been to produce a cheap edition of my collected works. A *Gesammt-Ausgabe* had already been published in Germany seven years before this, accompanied by *Das Märchen meines Lebens*, which was only a sketch but was received with sympathy and interest abroad. The *Magazin für die Literatur des Auslandes* gives a review of it which is full of appreciation:

"Almost the only works of this kind of which literature can boast are Goethe's *Poetry and Truth*, Rousseau's *Confessions* and Jung-Stilling's *Life*, but in future Andersen's most recent work, *Das Märchen meines Lebens* will undoubtedly be counted amongst them."

My autobiography is compared with those of the two last-mentioned authors and receives warm appreciation. I have heard the same thing from England and America, where it has been introduced

503

in translations by Mary Howitt and Dr. Spillan. Now, while I was still young and fresh in spirit I was to be given the happiness of publishing my collected works in Denmark, too. This was a wish of considerable importance to me as it gave me the opportunity to arrange and reject a few branches which bore far too few leaves. And then my autobiography would put the whole of it in the right light. I would not publish the earlier sketch, but fresh and more complete memoirs of what I had experienced and achieved! It was to be a kind of portrayal of all the important people with whom my journey through life had brought me into contact, and my impressions of the age in which I lived and the things by which I was surrounded. Written as though for a coming generation, this must surely have some historical interest, while a simple portrayal of all that God let me suffer and overcome would give strength to many a talent in its struggle for recognition.

I started on the work in the autumn of 1853. Just at that time, in October, it was twenty-five years since I had taken my final school examination, and during the last few years it had become the custom to celebrate our silver jubilees, if I may call them by that name. The most interesting thing about the whole celebration was our first meeting in the hall and our seeing so many people we had not met for such a long time. Some had become fat and unrecognizable, others old and grey, but at that moment the spirit of youth shone from all our eyes. This meeting was the real high spot for me. At dinner speeches were made and several songs were sung; one of them which I had written gave excellent expression to my feelings, and, as it turned out, to those of the others. Here it is:

> Again we gather now around a table.
> The last time was for our great exam,
> And each was so keen to show himself able
> And show off his skill with iamb and pentam.
> Today, only those who so wish need to speak
> And give us a word or a song;
> We all can take our choice or we can stay silent.
> For now we are gathered for fun;
> Set books aside, but keep the coffee ready…

Now and then we would meet in the street,
At least those who lived fairly near.
But those whose homes for country air compete
'twas rare they came to the town for their cheer
So then we were summoned to come here today.
You've heard it all, the news was sent by letter
And here we'll drink champagne hip-hip-hurray,
In spite of all those years, life's suddenly much better.

The spirit of the age caught up with all,
We grew more deeply rooted in our way.
Where once we only longed to leave our stall
Now, through the new the old did fray.
But one thing never frayed, I'm very sure,
The bonds that bind us from the distant past.
This evening, as we think of times of yore,
We celebrate the bonds that ever last.

Then Professor Clausen proposed a charming and witty toast to Paludan-Müller and me, the two poets from those who took their examination that year who had gained an honourable place in our literature.

A few days later I received the following printed circular:

"Among the students from 1828 who remained longest at the celebration on the 22nd of October the wish was expressed for a common undertaking whereby we might preserve the memory of the year which binds us together. After some consideration we decided to base our plan on the idea of the 'four great and twelve lesser poets' of that year and found a scholarship under the name of the Andersen-Paludan-Müller Scholarship, which in the course of time and when it has reached suitable proportions with the help of annual contributions should be employed to give support to some Danish poet who has no public employment."

To what extent and in what form this will be realised lies in the future, but the thought fills me with joy, for it shows recognition and appreciation by a group of Danes who passed their final school examinations in one and the same year.

Travel is like an invigorating bath both for my spirit and my body. The following year I went away for a few weeks to enjoy the freshness of spring in Vienna, Trieste and Venice. I have only preserved three or four impressions from this time.

The cherry trees were in bloom at the dear Saxon home at Maxen. The lime-kilns were steaming and Königstein, Lilienstein and all those miniature mountains rose in the air and beckoned to me. Once more it was as though it was but a long winter's night – with nightmares about cholera – since I last stood there. I felt as though I were seeing the same blossoms, the same clouds and shadows, the same hospitable home and the dear friends who lived there.

On the wings of steam I sped through mountains and valleys. I caught a glimpse of the tower of St. Stephen's Cathedral in the Imperial City, and there, after many years, I was again to meet Jenny Lind-Goldschmidt. Her husband, whom I met for the first time here, gave me a friendly welcome, and a strapping little son looked at me with his big eyes. I heard her sing again; there was the same spirit and the same wealth of tone.

Taubert's little song "*Ich muss nun einmal singen, ich weiss nicht warum*" might have been conceived on her lips. It was like a joyous bird. The nightingale cannot sing thus, nor can the thrush; a childlike heart is needed, the thoughts of a soul. It must be sung by Jenny Goldschmidt. It is her dramatic presentation, the dramatic truth, that is her strength and greatness, and it is only in the concert hall, in the arias and songs she sings there that she lets us hear this but she has left the stage. This is a sin against the spirit. It is renouncing her mission, the mission that God gave her.

Distressed and yet happy and strangely thoughtful, I sped towards Illyria, the land where Shakespeare has set so many of his immortal scenes, the land where Viola finds her happiness.

It is a surprisingly beautiful sight, I discovered, suddenly to look down at sunset from the high cliffs on to the gleaming, red Adriatic. In this light Trieste seemed even darker than it was. The gas lamps had just been lit and the streets shone in fiery outline. From our carriage there was a view as though from a balloon slowly sinking to earth. The glistening sea and the brilliantly lit streets are things which, although I only saw them for a few moments, I shall remember for years.

From Trieste it takes six hours by steamer to Venice.

"A mournful wreck on the water," was the impression it made on me in 1833 when I was there for the first time. Now that I was there again, seasick after the swell of the Adriatic, it seemed to me not that I escaped ashore but only that I escaped from a small vessel into a larger one. The only good thing about it, I thought, was that the silent town had been joined to the living mainland by the molo carrying the railway.

Seen by moonlight, Venice is a lovely sight, a strange dream which is worth knowing; the noiseless gondolas glide like Charon's barges between lofty palaces reflected in the water. But by day it is ugly. The water in the canals is dirty, and cabbage stalks, lettuce leaves and all kinds of things float in it. Water rats swim out from the cracks in the houses, and the sun burns down hot between the walls.

Full of joy I sped by steam train from that watery grave, out across the endless dyke that is surrounded by mouldy green stretches of water and sandbanks. On the mainland the vines hung in festive garlands and the black cypresses pointed up to the blue sky. Verona was my destination that day. There, in the warm sunshine, some hundreds of people were sitting on the steps of the amphitheatre. They did not take up much space; they were watching a play being performed on a stage that had been put up in the centre in there. It had painted scenery and reflected the Italian sunshine. The orchestra was playing dance music, and there was something of a travesty about it all, something so wretchedly modern about this scene played out on the remains of ancient Rome.

During my first visit to Venice I was stung on my hand by a scorpion and now in Verona, which thanks to the railway had become a neighbouring town, I was to suffer the same fate. I was stung both on my neck and my cheek; it burned and swelled up, and I suffered a great deal. It was in this condition I saw Lake Garda and the romantic Riva with its fertile valley of vines; but pain and fever made me go on. We travelled by night in the most radiant moonlight; the road was wild and romantic, one of the most beautiful I have seen. It was a natural scene such as not even the imagination of a Salvator Rosa could create on canvas. It has left the same impression on me as a beautiful dream in a night of pain.

A little after midnight we reached Triente, which provided us with all the discomforts Italy can offer to travellers. We had to wait at the city gate while a gendarme came slowly along and demanded our passports, which we had to surrender to an unknown hand in the middle of the dark night against a promise that they would be returned early the following morning; but we received no ticket for them, no receipt, no guarantee of any sort from an Austrian territory that was very strict about passports. Then we struggled along broad but pitch-dark streets to a palatial but completely dead hotel. There, after we had knocked and made a din for a long time, a sleepy, half-dressed cameriere came and led us up some cold, broad staircases, along endless corridors and murky passages to a huge, lofty old hall with two beds ready made, both of which were intended for a whole family with their children. There was a sleepy lamp standing on the marble table and the doors could not be closed, so we could look through them into other great halls with beds also for complete families. There were blind doors in the walls, secret stairs and red wine spilt on the floor looking just like real bloodstains. Those were my surroundings and that is the place where I spent my last night in Italy. My stings burned, my blood burned and it was impossible to think of sleep and rest. Morning arrived at last; the bells rang on our veturino's horse and we sped away from Triente and its naked mulberry bushes, the leaves of which had been plucked off and taken to market. By way of the Brenner Pass and Innsbruck we reached Munich.

There I found friends, attention and help. The King's physician, the charming old Privy Councillor Gietl tended me in a most friendly and sympathetic manner, and after a rather painful fortnight I was in a condition to accept the King's invitation to the castle of Hohenschwangau where King Max and his Queen were spending the summer.

A fairy tale could be written about the Alpine rose elf flying

508

through the halls of Hohenschwangau with all their paintings, and there seeing something that was more beautiful than his own flower.

The castle of Hohenschwangau is situated between the Alps and the River Lech. It stands on a marble cliff in an open, fertile valley between two clear, dark green lakes, one of which is on rather higher ground than the other. The castle of Schwanstein used to stand there. Guelfs, Hohenstaufens and Scheyerns had once been its masters, and their deeds still live there in the pictures that are painted on the castle walls. As Crown Prince, King Max had the castle restored and made into the magnificent residence it now is.

None of the castles on the Rhine is as lovely as Hohenschwangau, and none of them has surroundings such as these, the broad valley and the snow-capped Alps. The high, vaulted gateway is magnificent as it rises there with two statues of knights bearing the coats of arms of Bavaria and Schwangau, a lozenge and a swan. In the courtyard, where a jet of water gushes from a wall adorned with an al fresco painting of the Madonna, three mighty limes afford shade. And in the garden, in a profusion of flowers among which the loveliest of roses bloom amidst all the greenery, you fancy you are standing again by the lion fountain in the Alhambra. Even at this height the icy, fresh rush of water throws its fountain forty feet into the air. Over the entrance to the castle the living words of poetry greet those about to go in:

> *Willkommen, Wandrer, holde Frauen,*
> *Die Sorge gebt dahin,*
> *Lasst eure Seele sich vertrau'n*
> *Des Dichtungs heiteren Sinn.*

> Welcome, wanderer, fair women,
> Put away your cares,
> Let your souls put their trust
> In poetry's serene spirit.

An armoury in which old suits of mail, helmets and lances looked like the figures of living knights was the first place we entered. After that came a series of richly decorated halls where even the stained

509

glass in the windows tells legends and stories, and where every wall is like a complete book in itself telling of vanished times and people.

"Hohenschwangau is the most beautiful Alpine rose I saw here in the mountains; may it always remain the flower of good fortune."

These are the words I wrote in German in an album there; they are kept in my heart, and there they will remain.

There I spent a few lovely, happy days. King Max received me, if I may say so, as a cherished guest, and the noble and intelligent King was extremely kind and gracious to me. Everything there was good and exalted. His Majesty himself presented me to the Queen, who was born a Princess of Prussia. She was of rare beauty and female charm. After dinner on the first day the King took me for a quite enchanting little ride in an open carriage. We drove several miles, right into the Austrian Tyrol, and this time I was spared the questions about my passport which were always a torment to me; we were not stopped. The countryside presented a continual variety of lovely, picturesque scenes. The country people stood by the roadside and saluted their King, and the carriages we encountered stopped while His Majesty drove past. This drive through the high, sunlit mountains lasted a couple of hours, and throughout that time the King talked to me with great interest about *Das Märchen meines Lebens*, which he had recently read. He asked me about several of the Danish people I name in it and said how beautiful and good everything was for me now and what a feeling of joy I must have after overcoming so much and finally winning through to achieve recognition.

I said that my life often really did seem to be a fairy tale to me, so rich and remarkably full of variety. I had known what it was to be poor and lonely as well as sitting in luxurious halls. I knew what it was to be mocked as well as honoured. Even this very moment, as I sped along by the side of a king in the sunlit Alps, was a fairy-tale chapter in my life.

We talked about the most recent literature in Scandinavia. I mentioned *Salomon de Caus*, *Robert Fulton* and *Tycho Brahe* and showed how the poetry of our time portrayed men of foresight and drive. Intelligence, feeling and piety were all apparent in the way in which the noble King spoke; this was and will always remain of the hours there never to be forgotten.

510

In the evening I read for the dear Royal Couple. I read *Beneath the Willow Tree* and *It is Quite True*. Together with von Dönniges I climbed one of the nearby mountains, and I saw the lovely and impressive scenery. Time passed far too quickly.

The Queen graciously allowed me to write a few lines in her album. It was resplendent with the names of kings and emperors, and among them was one from the realm of science, Professor Liebig, a charming and attractive personality of whom I had become fond since making his acquaintance in Munich.

Deeply moved and grateful to the beloved Royal Couple, I left Hohenschwangau where I was told I would be welcome again. I took a huge bouquet of Alpine roses and forget-me-nots along with me in the carriage which took me to Füssen.

From Munich I continued my journey home by way of Weimar.

Carl Alexander had assumed the administration; he was staying at that time at his castle of Wilhelmsthal near Eisenach. I went there and spent some sublimely happy days with that noble prince in the infinitely beautiful countryside right at the heart of the Thuringian forest.

Old Wartburg, on which the present Grand Duke has over a number of years spent large sums of money from his own fortune in order to rebuild it exactly as it used to be, was now virtually finished with magnificent pictures on the walls illustrating the legends and stories connected with the castle. The Hall of the Minstrels was already restored to its former greatness with rows of columns. And what a splendid view there was of mountains and forests, the real scenery of the age of the Minnesingers: the Venusberg where Tannhäuser disappeared, the three "Gleichen" and even the loneliness of the forest which Walther von der Vogelweide and Heinrich von Ofterdingen knew so well. Both legend and history still have their setting quite unchanged.

The widow of the Duke of Orleans (together with her two sons, the Duke of Paris and the Duke of Nemours) lives in the little castle down in the town of Eisenach. All manner of people told me how well loved she and her children were by everyone there and how much good she did, as far as her strength would permit her, and how kind and interested she showed herself to be. She was a true blessing for

511

the little town. In the street I met the young princes together with their teachers; they were poorly dressed but looked intelligent and kind.

The Grand Duke of Weimar himself presented me to the Duchess.

I could clearly see all she had experienced and suffered, all the varying events in her life, and tears came involuntarily to my eyes before I had really begun to speak to her. She saw it and kindly held out her hand to me. And I looked at the picture of her late husband which hung on the wall and portrayed him in the freshness of youth just as I had seen him at the ball in the Hôtel de Ville at Paris. When I spoke of that time, tears came also in her eyes. She talked about him and about her children, and she told me kindly that they knew my fairy tales. There was something sincere about her, something fervent and sad, some bold feminine quality just as I had expected of Hélène of Orleans. She was dressed ready to travel, for she was to go some distance by train. "Will you dine with me tomorrow?" she asked. I had to answer that I was due to leave that very day. "But in a year's time I will come again."

"A year," she repeated. "What a lot of things can happen in a year; so much can happen in a few hours."

And tears shone in her eyes and she looked serious.

She stretched out her hand to me in a kindly fashion when I took leave of her, and I was strangely moved as I left this noble princess to whom fate had been unkind but whose heart is regal and warm and strong in her faith in God.

I was soon in Denmark and hard at work, not only on the publication of my *Works* but also arranging Mosenthal's "people's play" *Der Sonnenwendthof*, which I had seen at the Burgtheater during my stay in Vienna. I found it very attractive, and I drew Heiberg's attention to it. He was not interested, but Mr. Lange was, and he asked me to arrange for him to produce it in the Casino. And through the director of the Burgtheater I received the play from Mosenthal and was given "a free hand" with it. Since it was in the same vein as Auerbach's *Dorfgeschichten* I gave it the title of *A Village Story*, a title which was plain enough for all of us to understand. As everyone knows, it was heartily applauded when it was produced, and it has been repeatedly performed since. Apart from the songs which I had added, and which were necessary if it was to be performed in the Casino I had arranged the last act so that in the Alpine cottage Anna takes a burning brand and in the light from it recognises Mathias just as she saw him when the smithy at Ilsang burned down.

With the help of his Danish friends in Vienna Mosenthal read my translation, and he immediately wrote to me a letter full of thanks and appreciation, and as for the few alterations I had made he added, "The songs inserted into it are excellently chosen, and the effect in the last scene, when the burning brand is swung round, is so vivid that we are considering adopting it in the performance here."

As I have already said, my *Fairy Tales*, which were about to appear in a rather large edition illustrated by Vilhelm Pedersen, were so to speak completed, and the new ones that followed and which might still be written I was now given an opportunity to call *Historier*, "stories", the word in our language which I personally consider to be most suitable for my *Fairy Tales* as a whole when their scope and special nature are taken into account. Everyday language puts both simple tales and the boldest and most imaginative depictions into this category. Nursery tales, fables and narratives are by children and peasants and in the popular language all referred to by the brief designation of "stories".

A few small volumes appeared in English and German, and they were extremely well received. An English edition called *A Poet's Day Dreams* was published by Richard Bentley. The review in *The Athenæum* in 1853 shows that Mary Howitt's altered opinion of me failed to have any effect on the favourable verdict accorded to it by the English critics. It says:

"By the form and fashion of this little book (dedicated to Mr. Dickens), it appears to be meant for a Christmas and New Year's gift. But it will be welcome in any month of flowers or harvests as at the canonical time 'when icicles hang by the wall;' since it may be read and remembered by poets and by the children of poets long after this busy year and its busy people shall have been gathered to their fathers. Our antipathy to sentimentality (as the word is commonly understood) needs not to be again expressed. For what is false and sickly, be it ever so graceful, ever so alluring, we have neither eye, ear nor heart; but for sentiment, as something less deep than passionate emotion, less high than enthusiastic faith, less wild than the meteoric extravagances of Genius, we have a liking apart and peculiar, and those who have not, relish Imagination only by halves. For quaintness, humour and tenderness M. Andersen's little tales are unique. Let those who desire warrant for our assertion read *Good-for-Nothing*, *Grief of Heart*, *Under the Willow Tree* and *It is very True* in this volume. Let any who accuse these of being small try to produce anything which shall be so complete, so delicate and so suggestive. They are on the most tiny scale, it is true, and mostly concern tiny things and trite affections, but they are, nevertheless, real works of Art, and such as deserve a warm welcome from all who love Art and its works."

At this present time, just as I am about to complete my fiftieth year and, as my *Collected Works* are being published, the periodical *Dansk Maanedsskrift* has published a review of it by Mr. Grimur Thomsen. The depth and warmth which this author showed already at an early stage in his book on Lord Byron are also manifested here in this shorter work in which are revealed his knowledge of the works he discusses and his affection for them. It seems almost that Heaven wished me to end this chapter of my life by seeing the fulfilment of H. C. Ørsted's words to me in those difficult days when no one appreciated me. My native land has given me the cherished bouquet of recognition and encouragement.

In his review, Mr. Grimur Thomsen has, with a few words about my fairy tales, succeeded in touching the string which strikes the right note from this, the most profound of my poetical works. It is scarcely a coincidence that the examples he gives of the essence and meaning of my works as a whole are taken from my *Stories*, that is to say my most recent works. "The fairy tale makes a merry judgement of appearance and reality, of the outer shell and the kernel inside. A dual current runs through them. There is an upper current of irony which plays and jokes with great and small, which plays shuttlecock with both high and low; and then there is the deep undercurrent of serious thought which with justice and truth puts 'everything in its right place'. This is true humour, Christian humour."

This clearly expressed what I have desired and striven to achieve.

The story of my life right up to the present moment is thus laid before me so eventful, so beautiful and so full of comfort. There came good even out of evil and joy out of pain. It is a poem more full of profound thoughts than I could possibly have written. I feel that I am a child of good fortune. So many of the noblest and best men and women of my day have dealt kindly and openly with me, and it is but seldom that my confidence in mankind has been disappointed. Even the heavy days of bitterness contain the germs of blessings. All the injustice I thought I suffered and every hand that clumsily interfered in my development brought good results after all.

As we progress towards God, all pain and bitterness are dispersed, and what is beautiful is left behind. We see it like a rainbow against dark clouds. May men be mild in their judgement of me as I am in my judgement of them. I am sure they will be. The story of a life has something of the sacred quality of a confession for all noble and good men. I have told the story of my life here openly and full of confidence as though I were sitting among cherished friends.

Hans Christian Andersen
Copenhagen, the Second of April 1855